ng-book

The Complete Book on AngularJS

Ari Lerner

ng-book

The Complete Book on AngularJS

Ari Lerner

This book is for sale at https://www.ng-book.com

This version was published on 2013-12-28

ISBN 978-0-9913446-0-4

Tweet This Book!

Please help Ari Lerner by spreading the word about this book on Twitter!

The suggested tweet for this book is:

I just bought #ngbook, the Complete Book on AngularJS! I'm ready to build advanced, modern webapps!

The suggested hashtag for this book is #ngbook.

Find out what other people are saying about the book by clicking on this link to search for this hashtag on Twitter:

https://twitter.com/search?q=#ngbook

Contents

Dedication

I dedicate this book to my parents, Lisa and Nelson Lerner for without their support and encouragement none of this would have been possible.

Special thanks

To the lovely Q for the constant motivation and incredibly talented editing and my cofounder and friend, Nate Murray.

Introduction

Foreword

I've become somewhat numb to all of the JavaScript libraries and frameworks being released on a seemingly daily basis. While the ability to choose from a variety of libraries and frameworks is a good thing, including too many scripts in an application can be a bad thing for maintenance – at least in my opinion. I've always been concerned about the dependencies that are created as more and more scripts are added into an application and often longed for a single script (or two) that could provide the core functionality I wanted.

When I first heard about AngularJS it caught my attention immediately because it appeared to offer a single framework that could be used to build a variety of dynamic, client-centric applications. After researching it more, my initial impressions were confirmed, and I was hooked. AngularJS includes a robust set of features and offers a way to break up code into modules, which is good for reuse, maintenance, and testability. It provides key features, such as support for DOM manipulation, animations, templating, two-way data binding, routing, history, Ajax, testing, and much more.

While having a core framework to build on is great, it can also be intimidating and challenging to learn. As I dove into AngularJS I became overwhelmed with different topics and quickly became a little frustrated and wondered if it was the framework for me. What was a service, and how was it different from a factory? How did scope fit into the overall picture? What was a directive, and why would I use one? Putting the pieces together and seeing the big picture was the initial hurdle that I had to get over. It definitely would've been nice to have a concise resource to consult that flattened out the learning curve.

Fortunately, you have an excellent resource at your disposal in *ng-book: The Complete Book on AngularJS* that will help make you productive right away. Ari Lerner has taken the knowledge and expertise that he's gained and laid it out in a way that is easy to follow and understand. If you're looking to learn more about data binding, how "live" templates work, the process for testing AngularJS applications, the role of services and factories, how scope and controllers fit together, and much more, then you're in the right place. AngularJS is an extremely powerful and fun framework to work with, and the examples shown throughout this book will help you get up to speed quickly on the framework. Best of luck with your AngularJS development projects!

Dan Wahlin Wahlin Consulting http://weblogs.asp.net/dwahlin[1] http://twitter.com/DanWahlin[2]

---

[1] http://weblogs.asp.net/dwahlin
[2] http://twitter.com/DanWahlin

Acknowledgments

First, I want to thank everyone who has encouraged me along the way to write this book. Anyone who says authoring a book is easy has not written one him- or herself.

I want to personally thank Q Kuhns for her tireless grammatical editing and support, Erik Trom for his patience and attention to detail, and Nate Murray for his neverending optimism and clarity of thought.

Big thanks go out to the entire Hack Reactor[3] staff and the summer class of 2013 for giving me the space to explore how to teach AngularJS in a formal setting.

I also want to thank my 30x500 alumni, Sean Iams, Michael Fairchild, Bradly Green, Misko Hevery, and the AirPair team.

Lastly, I would very much like to thank all of the help with our public pre-release of the book. We've received fantastic help and support from the community. We would like to send special thanks to:

- Philip Westwell
- Saurabh Agrawal
- Dougal MacPherson

About the Author

Ari Lerner is the co-founder of fullstack.io[4], based in San Francisco, CA. He worked at AT&T's innovation center in Palo Alto, CA, for five years, building large-scale cloud infrastructure and helping architect the bleeding-edge developer center, including designing publicly facing APIs and developer toolsets.

He and his team were featured in the AT&T annual report for 2012 for their work in modernizing the company workflow and internal processes.

He left his job at AT&T to pursue building fullstack.io, a full-stack software development product and services company that specializes in the entire stack, from hardware to the browser.

He lives in San Francisco with his lovely girlfriend and adorable dog.

About This Book

ng-book: The Complete Book on AngularJS is packed with the solutions you need to be an AngularJS[5] ninja. AngularJS is an advanced front-end framework released by the team at Google[6]. It enables you to build a rich front-end experience, quickly and easily.

---

[3]http://www.hackreactor.com
[4]http://fullstack.io
[5]http://angularjs.org
[6]http://google.com

ng-book: The Complete Guide to AngularJS gives you the cutting-edge tools you need to get up and running on AngularJS and creating impressive web experiences in no time. It addresses challenges and provides real-world techniques that you can use immediately in your web applications.

In this book, we will cover topics that enable you to build professional web apps that perform perfectly. These topics include:

- Interacting with a RESTful web service
- Building custom reusable components
- Testing
- Asynchronous programming
- Building services
- Providing advanced visualizations
- And much more

The goal of this book is not only to give you a deep understanding of how AngularJS works, but also to give you professional snippets of code so that you can build and modify your own applications.

With these tools and tests, you can dive into making your own dynamic web applications with AngularJS while being confident that your applications will be scalable.

Audience

We have written this book for those who have never used AngularJS to build a web application and are curious about how to get started with an awesome JavaScript framework. We assume that you have a working knowledge of HTML and CSS and a familiarity with basic JavaScript (and possibly other JavaScript frameworks).

Organization of This Book

This book covers the basics of getting started and aims to get you comfortable with writing dynamic web applications with AngularJS right away.

Then we'll take a look at how AngularJS works and what sets it apart from other popular JavaScript web frameworks. We'll dive deeply into detail about the underpinnings of the flow of an AngularJS application.

Finally, we'll take all of our knowledge and build a relatively large application.

Additional Resources

We'll refer to the official documentation on the AngularJS[7] website. The official AngularJS documentation is a great resource, and we'll be using it quite often.

We suggest that you take a look at the AngularJS API documentation, as it gives you direct access to the recommended methods of writing AngularJS applications. Of course, it also gives you the most up-to-date documentation available.

Conventions Used in This Book

Throughout this book, you will see the following typographical conventions that indicate different types of information:

In-line code references will look like: `<h1>Hello</h1>`.

A block of code looks like so:

```
var App = angular.module('App', []);

function FirstController($scope) {
  $scope.data = "Hello";
}
```

Any command at the command line will look like:

```
$ ls -la
```

Any command in the developer console in Chrome (the browser with which we will primarily be developing) will look like:

```
> var obj = {message: "hello"};
```

Important words will be shown in **bold**.

Tips and tricks will be shown as:

Tip

Tip: This is a tip message

---

[7]http://angularjs.org

Warnings and gotchas are shown with the warning sign, like so:

This is a warning

This is a warning message

We identify errors like so:

Error

This is an error message

Important callout information is noted as:

Info

Info box

Discussion topics are presented as:

Discussion

This is a discussion box

Development Environment

In order to write any applications using AngularJS, we first need to have a comfortable development environment. Throughout this book, we'll be spending most of our time in two places: our text editor and our browser.

We'll refer to the text editor as your editor throughout the book, while we'll refer to the browser as the browser. To use this book, we highly recommend you download the Google Chrome browser, as it provides a great development environment using the developer tools.

We'll only need to install a few libraries to get going. To run our tests, we'll need the Karma library and nodejs. It's also a good idea to have git installed, although this is not a strict requirement.

This book won't cover how to install NodeJS. Visit nodejs.org[8] for more information.

While most of our work will be done in the browser, parts of this book will focus on building RESTful APIs to service our front end with data endpoints.

---

[8]http://nodejs.org

The Basics of AngularJS

The goal of this chapter is to get you comfortable with the terminology and the technology and to give you an understanding of how AngularJS works. We'll start putting the pieces together to enable you to build an AngularJS application, even if you've never written one before.

How Web Pages Get to Your Browser

Let's think of the Internet as a post office. When you want to send a letter to your friend, you first write your message on a piece of paper. Then you write your friend's address on an envelope and place the letter inside of it.

When you drop the letter off at the post office, the mail sorter looks at the postal code and address and tries to find where your friend lives. If she lives in a giant apartment complex, the postal service might deliver the mail to your friend's front desk and let the building's employees sort it out by apartments.

The Internet works in a similar way. Instead of a bunch of houses and apartments connected by streets, it is a bunch of computers connected by routers and wire. Every computer has a unique address that tells the network how to reach it.

Similar to the apartment building analogy above, where we have many apartments that share the same address, several computers can exist on the same network or router (as when you connect to WiFi at a Starbucks). In this case, your computer shares the same IP address as the other computers. Your computer can be reached individually, however, by its "internal IP address" (like the *apartment number* in our analogy), about which the router is aware (as the apartment building employees in our analogy are aware of your friend's apartment number).

> IP stands for Internet Protocol. An IP address is a numerical identifier assigned to each device participating in a network. Computers, printers, and even cell phones have IP addresses.
>
> There are two main types of IP addresses: *ipv4* and *ipv6* addresses. The most common addresses today are ipv4 addresses. These look like **192.168.0.199**. *Ipv6* addresses look like **2001:0db8:0000:0000:0000:ff00:0042:8329**.

When you open your web browser on your computer and type in `http://google.com`, your web browser "asks" the internet (more precisely, it "asks" a DNS server) where `google.com`'s address is. If the DNS server knows the IP address you're looking for, it responds with the address. If not, it passes the request along to other DNS servers until the IP address is found and served to your computer. You can see the DNS server response by typing this code into a terminal:

```
$ dig google.com
```

> If you are on a Mac, you can open the terminal program called Terminal, usually located in your /Applications/Utilities. If you are using Windows, you can find your terminal by going to the Start Button and typing cmd in the Run option.

Once the DNS server responds with the IP address of the computer you're trying to reach (i.e., once it finds google.com), it also sends a message to the computer located at that IP address asking for the web page you're requesting.

> Every path of a web page is written with its own HTML (with a few exceptions). For example, when your browser requests http://google.com[9], it receives different HTML than if it were to request http://google.com/images[10].

Now that your computer has the IP address it needs to get http://google.com, it asks the Google server for the HTML it needs to display the page.

Once the remote server sends back that HTML, your web browser *renders* it (i.e., the browser works to make the HTML look the way google.com is designed to look).

What Is a Browser?

Before we jump straight into our coverage of Angular, it's important to know what your browser is doing when it renders a web page.

There are many different web browsers; the most common browsers today include Chrome, Safari, Mozilla Firefox, and Internet Explorer. At their core, they all basically do the same thing: fetch web pages and display them to the user.

Your browser gets the HTML text of the page, parses it into a structure that is internally meaningful to the browser, lays out the content of the page, and styles the content before displaying it to you. All of this work happens behind the scenes.

Our goal as web developers is to build the structure and content of our web page so that the browser will make it look great for our users.

With Angular, we're not only building the structure, but we're constructing the interaction between the user and our app as a web application.

---

[9]http://google.com
[10]http://google.com/images

What Is AngularJS

The official AngularJS introduction describes AngularJS as a:

> client-side technology, written entirely in JavaScript. It works with the long-established technologies of the web (HTML, CSS, and JavaScript) to make the development of web apps easier and faster than ever before.

It is a framework that is primarily used to build single-page web applications. AngularJS makes it easy to build interactive, modern web applications by increasing the level of abstraction between the developer and common web app development tasks.

> The AngularJS team describes it as a "structural framework for dynamic web apps."

AngularJS makes it incredibly easy to build web applications; it also makes it easy to build complex applications. AngularJS takes care of advanced features that users have become accustomed to in modern web applications, such as:

- Separation of application logic, data models, and views
- Ajax services
- Dependency injection
- Browser history (makes bookmarking and back/forward buttons work like normal web apps)
- Testing
- And more

How Is It different?

In other JavaScript frameworks, we are forced to extend from custom JavaScript objects and manipulate the DOM from the outside in. For instance, using jQuery[11], to add a button in the DOM, we'll have to *know* where we're putting the element and insert it in the appropriate place:

```
var btn = $("<button>Hi</button>");
btn.on('click', function(evt) { console.log("Clicked button") });
$("#checkoutHolder").append(btn);
```

[11]http://jquery.com/

Although this process is not complex, it requires the developer to have knowledge of the entire DOM and force our complex logic inside JavaScript code to manipulate a foreign DOM.

AngularJS, on the other hand, augments HTML to give it `native` Model-View-Controller (MVC) capabilities. This choice, as it turns out, makes building impressive and expressive client-side applications quick and enjoyable.

It enables you, the developer, to encapsulate a portion of your entire page as one application, rather than forcing the entire page to be an AngularJS application. This distinction is particularly beneficial if your workflow already includes another framework or if you want to make a portion of the page dynamic while the rest operates as a static page or is controlled by another JavaScript framework.

Additionally, the AngularJS team has made it a point to keep the library small when compressed, such that it does not impose heavy penalties for using it (the compressed, minified version weighs in under 9KB at the time of this writing). This feature makes AngularJS particularly good for prototyping new features.

License

The AngularJS source code is made freely available on Github[12] under the MIT license. That means you can contribute to the source and help make AngularJS even better.

In order to contribute, the Angular team has made the process relatively straightforward. Any major changes should be discussed on the Angular mailing list[13], thus making the potential change available for modification, allowing other developers to join in the discussion, and preventing code/work duplication.

More information on contributing can be found at contribution[14] section of the Angular website.

---

[12]http://github.com

[13]https://groups.google.com/forum/?hl=en#!forum/angular

[14]http://docs.angularjs.org/misc/contribute

Data Binding and Your First AngularJS Web Application

Hello World

The quintessential place to start writing an AngularJS app is with a *hello world* application. To write our *hello world* application, we'll start with the simplest, most basic HTML we can possibly write.

We'll take a more in-depth look into AngularJS as we dive into the framework. For now, let's build our *hello world* application.

```
<!DOCTYPE html>
<html ng-app>
<head>
  <title>Simple app</title>
  <script
    src="https://ajax.googleapis.com/ajax/libs/angularjs/1.2.6/angular.js">
    </script>
</head>
<body>
  <input ng-model="name" type="text" placeholder="Your name">
  <h1>Hello {{ name }}</h1>
</body>
</html>
```

Figure 1

Although this demo isn't incredibly interesting or exciting, it does show one of the most basic and impressive features of AngularJS: *data binding*.

Note that in this chapter, we're not using **best practices** for writing controllers yet, as we're introducing the first core concept. This is the only place in this book where we suggest to use the code snippets as a learning tool, not as a suggestion for production usage.

Introducing Data Binding in AngularJS

In classic web frameworks, such as Rails, the controller combines data from models and mashes them together with templates to deliver a view to the user. This combination produces a single-way view. Without building any custom JavaScript components, the view will only reflect the data the model exposes at the time of the view rendering. At the time of this writing, there are several JavaScript frameworks that promise automatic data binding of the view and the model.

AngularJS takes a different approach. Instead of merging data into a template and replacing a DOM element, AngularJS creates *live* templates as a view. Individual components of the views are dynamically interpolated live. This feature is arguably one of the most important in *AngularJS* and allows us to write the *hello world* app we just wrote in only 10 lines of code without a single line of JavaScript.

This feature works by simply including angular.js in our HTML and explicitly setting the ng-app attribute on an element in the DOM. The ng-app attribute declares that everything inside of it belongs to this Angular app; that's how we can nest an Angular app inside of a web app. The only components that will be affected by Angular are the DOM elements that we declare inside of the one with the ng-app attribute.

Views are interpolated when the view is evaluated with one or more variable substitutions; the result is that the variables in our string are replaced with values.

For instance, if there is a variable named name and it is equal to "Ari", string interpolation on a view of "Hello {{ name }}" will return "Hello Ari".

Automatic data binding gives us the ability to consider the view to be a projection of the model state. Any time the model is changed in the client-side model, the view reflects these changes without writing any custom code. It just *works*.

In the *Model View Controller* (or *MVC*) view of the world, the controller doesn't have to worry about being in the mix of rendering the view. This fact virtually eliminates the concern of separating view and controller logic, and it has the corollary effect of making testing simple and enjoyable.

MVC is a software architecture pattern that separates representation from user interaction. Generally, the *model* consists of application data and functions that interact with it, while the *view* presents this data to the user; the *controller* mediates between the two.

 This separation presentation[15] makes a clear division between objects in our web app so that the view doesn't need to *know* how to save an object – it just needs to know how to display it. Meanwhile, the model doesn't need to interact with the view – it just needs to contain the data and methods to manipulate the view. The controller is where we'll place the logic to bind the two together.

Without getting into the source (available at AngularJS.org[16]), Angular simply remembers the value that the model contains at any given time (in our example from *hello world*, the value of name).

When Angular thinks that the value could change, it will call $digest() on the value to check whether the value is "dirty." Hence, when the Angular runtime is running, it will look for potential changes on the value.

This process is dirty checking. Dirty checking is a relatively *efficient* approach to checking for changes on a model. Every time there could be a potential change, Angular will do a dirty check inside its event loop (discussed in depth in the *under the hood* chapter) to ensure everything is consistent.

When using frameworks like KnockoutJS, which attaches a function (known as a change listener) to the change event, the process is significantly more complex and relatively more inefficient. Dealing with change coalescence, dependency tracking, and the multitude of event firing is complex and often causes problems in performance.

 Although there are more efficient ways to do it, dirty checking always works in every browser and is predictable. Additionally, a lot of software that needs speed and efficiency uses the dirty checking approach.

AngularJS removes the need to build complex and novel features in JavaScript in order to build fake automatic synchronization in views.

Simple Data Binding

To review the code we just wrote, what we did was bind the "name" attribute to the input field using the ng-model directive on the containing model object ($scope).

All that means is that whatever value is placed in the input field will be reflected in the model object.

---

[15]http://martinfowler.com/eaaDev/uiArchs.html

[16]http://angularjs.org

The *model object* that we are referring to is the $scope object. The $scope object is simply a JavaScript object whose properties are all available to the view and with which the controller can interact. Don't worry if this concept doesn't make sense quite yet: It'll make sense with a few examples.

Bi-directional in this context means that if the view changes the value, the model *observes* the change through dirty checking, and if the model changes the value, the view update with the change.

To set up this binding, we used the ng-model function on the input, like so:

```
<input ng-model="person.name" type="text" placeholder="Your name">
<h1>Hello {{ person.name }}</h1>
```

Now that we have a binding set up (yes, it's *that* easy), we can see how the view changes the model. When the value in the *input* field changes, the person.name will be updated and the view will reflect the change.

Now we can see that we're setting up a bi-directional binding purely in the view. To illustrate the bi-directional binding from the other way (back end to front end), we'll have to dive into Controllers, which we'll cover shortly.

Just as ng-app declares that all elements inside of the DOM element upon which it is declared belong to the Angular app, declaring the ng-controller attribute on a DOM element says that all of the elements inside of it belong to the controller.

To declare our above example inside of a controller, we'll change the HTML to look like:

```
<div ng-controller='MyController'>
  <input ng-model="name" type="text" placeholder="Your name">
  <h1>Hello {{ name }}</h1>
</div>
```

In this example, we'll create a clock that will tick every second (as clocks usually do) and change the data on the clock variable:

```
function MyController($scope) {
  var updateClock = function() {
    $scope.clock = new Date();
  };
  setInterval(function() {
    $scope.$apply(updateClock);
  }, 1000);
  updateClock();
};
```

 The controller function takes one parameter, the $scope of the DOM element. This $scope object is available on the element and the controller (as we can see), and it will be the bridge by which we'll communicate from the controller to the view.

In this example, as the timer fires, it will call the updateClock function, which will set the new $scope.clock variable to the current time.

We can show the clock variable that's attached on the $scope in the view simply by surrounding it in {{ }}:

```
<div ng-controller="MyController">
  <h5>{{ clock }}</h5>
</div>
```

At this point, our sample web app looks like:

```
<!doctype html>
<html ng-app>
  <head>
    <script src="https://ajax.googleapis.com/ajax/libs
      /angularjs/1.2.0-rc.2/angular.js"></script>
  </script>
  </head>
  <body>
    <div ng-controller="MyController">
      <h1>Hello {{ clock }}!</h1>
    </div>
    <script type="text/javascript">
      function MyController($scope) {
        $scope.clock = new Date();
        var updateClock = function() {
```

```
      $scope.clock = new Date();
    };
    setInterval(function() {
      $scope.$apply(updateClock);
    }, 1000);
    updateClock();
  };
</script>
</body>
</html>
```

See it live here[17].

Although the code as it is written above works in a single file, it will become tough to collaborate on the web app with other people or separate out the functionality of the different components. Instead of containing all of our code in the index.html file, it's usually a good idea to include JavaScript in a separate file.

The above code will change to:

```
<!doctype html>
<html ng-app>
  <head>
    <script src="https://ajax.googleapis.com/ajax/libs/
      angularjs/1.2.0-rc.2/angular.js">
    </script>
  </head>
  <body>
    <div ng-controller="MyController">
      <h1>Hello {{ clock }}!</h1>
    </div>
    <script type="text/javascript" src="js/app.js"></script>
  </body>
</html>
```

We will place the JavaScript from above in the js/app.js file instead of embedding it directly into the HTML.

---

[17]http://jsbin.com/uHiVOZo/1/edit?html,output

```
// In app.js
function MyController($scope) {
  $scope.clock = new Date();
  var updateClock = function() {
    $scope.clock = new Date();
  };
  setInterval(function() {
    $scope.$apply(updateClock);
  }, 1000);
  updateClock();
};
```

Best Data Binding Practices

Due to the nature of JavaScript itself and how it passes by value vs. reference, it's considered a *best-practice* in Angular to bind references in the views by an attribute on an object, rather than the raw object itself.

If we were to apply best practices to the clock example above, we'd change the usage of the clock in our view to:

```
<!doctype html>
<html ng-app>
  <head>
    <script src="https://ajax.googleapis.com/ajax/
      libs/angularjs/1.2.6/angular.js"></script>
  </head>
  <body>
    <div ng-controller="MyController">
      <h1>Hello {{ clock.now }}!</h1>
    </div>
    <script type="text/javascript" src="js/app.js"></script>
  </body>
</html>
```

In this case, rather than updating the $scope.clock every second, we can update the clock.now property. With this optimization, we can then change our back end to reflect the change with:

```
// In app.js
function MyController($scope) {
  $scope.clock = {
    now: new Date()
  };
  var updateClock = function() {
    $scope.clock.now = new Date()
  };
  setInterval(function() {
    $scope.$apply(updateClock);
  }, 1000);
  updateClock();
};
```

 It's a good idea to try to place all of our bindings in the view in this manner.

Modules

In JavaScript, placing functional code in the global namespace is rarely a good idea. It can cause collisions that are tough to debug and cost us precious development time.

When looking at data binding in the previous chapter, we wrote our controllers in the global namespace by defining a single function:

```
function MyController($scope) {
  var updateClock = function() {
    $scope.clock = new Date();
  };
  setInterval(function() {
    $scope.$apply(updateClock);
  }, 1000);
  updateClock();
};
```

In this chapter, we'll talk about how to write efficient, production-ready controllers by encapsulating our functionality in a single core unit called a *module*.

In Angular, a module is the *main* way to define an AngularJS app. The module of an app is where we'll contain all of our application code. An app can contain several modules, each one containing code that pertains to specific functionality.

Using modules gives us a lot of advantages, such as:

- Keeping our global namespace clean
- Making tests easier to write and keeping them clean so as to more easily target isolated functionality
- Making it easy to share code between applications
- Allowing our app to load different parts of the code in any order

The Angular module API allows us to declare a module using the `angular.module()` API method. When declaring a module, we need to pass two parameters to the method. The first is the name of the module we are creating. The second is the list of dependencies, otherwise known as injectables.

```
angular.module('myApp', []);
```

This method is called the *setter* method for the Angular module; it's how we define our
module.

We can always reference our module by using the same method with only one parameter. For
instance, we can reference the myApp module like so:

```
// this method fetches the app
angular.module('myApp')
```

 This method is known as the *getter* method, whereby we can get the Angular module for
later reference.

From here, we can create our applications on top of the `angular.module('myApp')` variable.

When writing large applications, we'll create several different modules to contain our logic. Creating
a module for each piece of functionality gives us the advantage of isolation in which to write and
test large features. For more information on writing isolated modules per feature, check out the
architecture chapter.

Properties

Angular modules have properties that we can use to inspect the module.

name (string)

The name property on the modules gives us the name of the module as a string.

requires (array of strings)

The `requires` property contains a list of modules (as strings) that the `injector` loads *before* the
module itself is loaded.

Scopes

Scopes are a **core** fundamental of any Angular app. They are used all over the framework, so it's important to know them and how they work.

The scopes of the application refer to the application model. Scopes are the execution context for expressions. The $scope object is where we define the business functinality of the application, the methods in our controllers, and properties in the views.

Scopes serve as the glue between the controller and the view. Just before our app renders the view to the user, the view template links to the scope, and the app sets up the DOM to notify Angular for property changes. This feature makes it easy to account for promises, such as an XHR call, to be fulfilled. See the promises chapter for more details.

Scopes are the source of truth for the application state. Because of this *live binding*, we can rely on the $scope to update immediately when the view modifies it, and we can rely on the view to update when the $scope changes.

$scopes in AngularJS are arranged in a hierarchical structure that mimics the DOM and thus are nestable: We can reference properties on parent $scopes.

> If you are familiar with JavaScript, then this hierarchical concept shouldn't be foreign. When we create a new execution context in JavaScript, we create a new function that effectively creates a new "local" context. The Angular concept of $scopes is similar in that as we create a new scope for child DOM elements, we are creating a new *execution context* for the DOM to live in.

Scopes provide the ability to watch for model changes. They give the developer the ability to propagate model changes throughout the application by using the apply mechanism available on the scope. We define and execute expressions in the context of a scope; it is also from here that we can propagate events to other controllers and parts of the application.

It is ideal to contain the application logic in a controller and the working data on the scope of the controller.

The $scope View of the World

When Angular starts to run and generate the view, it will create a binding from the root ng-app element to the $rootScope. This $rootScope is the eventual parent of all $scope objects.

The $rootScope object is the closest object we have to the *global* context in an Angular app. It's a bad idea to attach too much logic to this *global* context, in the same way that it's not a good idea to dirty the JavaScript global scope.

This $scope object is a plain old JavaScript object. We can add and change properties on the $scope object however we see fit.

This $scope object is the *data model* in Angular. Unlike traditional data models, which are the gatekeepers of data and are responsible for handling and manipulating the data, the $scope object is simply a connection between the view and the HTML. It's the *glue* between the view and the controller.

All properties found on the $scope object are *automatically* accessible to the view.

For instance, let's say we have the HTML:

```
<div ng-app="myApp">
  <h1>Hello {{ name }}</h1>
</div>
```

We can expect the {{ name }} variable to be a property of the containing $scope:

```
angular.module('myApp', [])
  .run(function($rootScope) {
    $rootScope.name = "World";
});
```

Hello World

Simple $rootScope binding

It's Just HTML

Our app renders our HTML and delivers it to the browser for presentation. This HTML contains all standard HTML elements, both Angular-specific and non-Angular-specific. The elements that do **not** contain Angular-specific declarations are left unmodified.

```
<h2>Hello world</h2>
<h3>Hello {{ name }}</h3>
```

In the previous example, Angular won't touch the `<h2>` element, while it will update the `<h3>` with any scope modifications.

Through Angular, we can use different types of markup in a template. These types include the following:

- Directives: the attributes or elements that augment the existing DOM element into a reusable DOM component
- Value bindings: the template syntax {{ }} binds expressions to the view
- Filters: formatting functions that are available in the view
- Form controls: user input validation controls

What Can Scopes Do?

Scopes have the following basic functions:

- They provide `observers` to watch for model changes
- They provide the ability to propagate model changes through the application as well as outside the system to other components
- They can be nested such that they can isolate functionality and model properties
- They provide an execution environment in which expressions are evaluated

The majority of the work we'll do in developing our Angular app is building out the functionality of a scope.

> Scopes are objects that contain functionality and data to use when rendering the view.
> It is the single source of truth for all views. You can think of scopes as `view models`.

In the previous example, we set a variable name on the `$rootScope` and reference it in a view, like so:

```
angular.module('myApp', [])
  .run(function($rootScope) {
    $rootScope.name = "World";
});
```

And our view can now reference this `name` property to show to the user:

```
<div ng-app="myApp">
  <h1>Hello {{ name }}</h1>
</div>
```

Instead of placing variables on the $rootScope, we can explicitly create a child $scope object using a controller. We can attach a controller object to a DOM element using the ng-controller directive on a DOM element, like so:

```
<div ng-app="myApp">
  <div ng-controller="MyController">
    <h1>Hello {{ name }}</h1>
  </div>
</div>
```

Now, instead of attaching the name variable on the $rootScope, we can create a controller that will manage our variable:

```
angular.module("myApp", [])
.controller('MyController',
function($scope) {
  $scope.name = "Ari";
});
```

The ng-controller directive creates a new $scope object for the DOM element and nests it in the containing $rootScope.

$scope Lifecycle

When the browser receives a JavaScript callback that executes *inside* of the Angular execution context (for more information on the Angular execution context, check out the digest loop chapter), the $scope will be made aware of the model mutation.

 If the callback executes outside of the Angular context, we can force the $scope to have knowledge of the change using the $apply method.

After the scope expression is evaluated and the $digest loop runs, the $scope's watch expressions will run dirty checking (see the digest loop for more details on dirty checking).

 We'll dive deep into expressions in the Expressions chapter. The scope's expression is whatever we set the scope variable. When we set the scope name above, we're setting it to an expression: $scope.name = "Ari", even if it's just a string.

Creation

When we create a controller or directive, Angular creates a new scope with the $injector and passes this new scope for the controller or directive at runtime.

Linking

When the $scope is linked to the view, all directives that create $scopes will register their watches on the parent scope. These watches watch for and propagate model changes from the view to the directive.

Updating

During the $digest cycle, which executes on the $rootScope, all of the children scopes will perform dirty digest checking. All of the watching expressions are checked for any changes, and the scope calls the listener callback when they are changed.

Destruction

When a $scope is no longer needed, the child scope creator will need to call scope.$destroy() to clean up the child scope.

Note that when a scope is destroyed, the $destroy event will be broadcasted.

Directives and Scopes

Directives, which are used all throughout our Angular apps, generally do not create their own $scopes, but there are cases when they do. For instance, the ng-controller and ng-repeat directives create their own child scopes and attach them to the DOM element.

But before we get too far, let's take a look at what controllers are and how we can use them in our applications.

Controllers

Controllers in AngularJS exist to augment the view of an AngularJS application. As we saw in our Hello world example application, we did not use a controller, but only an implicit controller.

The controller in AngularJS is a function that adds additional functionality to the scope of the view. We use it to set up an initial state and to add custom behavior to the scope object.

When we create a new controller on a page, Angular passes it a new $scope. This new $scope is where we can set up the initial state of the scope on our controller. Since Angular takes care of handling the controller for us, we only need to write the constructor function.

Setting up an initial controller looks like this:

```
function FirstController($scope) {
  $scope.message = "hello";
}
```

 It is considered a *best-practice* to name our controllers as [Name]Controller, rather than [Name]Ctrl.

As we can see, Angular will call the controller method when it creates the scope.

The observant reader will notice we created this function in the global scope. Doing so is usually poor form, as we don't want to dirty the global namespace. To create it more properly, we'll create a module and then create the controller atop our module, like so:

```
var app = angular.module('app', []);
app.controller('FirstController', function($scope) {
  $scope.message = "hello";
});
```

To create custom actions we can call in our views, we can simply create functions on the scope of the controller. Luckily for us, AngularJS allows our views to call functions on the $scope, just as if we were calling data.

To bind buttons or links (or any DOM element, really), we'll use another built-in directive, ng-click. The ng-click directive binds the mouseup browser click event to the method handler, which calls the method specified on the DOM element (i.e., when the browser fires a click event on the DOM element, the method is called). Similar to our previous example, the binding looks like:

```
<div ng-controller="FirstController">
  <h4>The simplest adding machine ever</h4>
  <button ng-click="add(1)" class="button">Add</button>
  <a ng-click="subtract(1)" class="button alert">Subtract</a>
  <h4>Current count: {{ counter }}</h4>
</div>
```

Both the button and the link are bound to an action on the containing $scope, so when they are pressed (clicked), Angular calls the method. Note that when we tell Angular what method to call, we're putting it in a string *with* the parentheses (add(1)).

Now, let's create an action on our FirstController.

```
app.controller('FirstController', function($scope) {
  $scope.counter = 0;
  $scope.add = function(amount) { $scope.counter += amount; };
  $scope.subtract = function(amount) { $scope.counter -= amount; };
});
```

Setting our FirstController in this manner allows us to call add or subtract functions (as we've seen above) that are defined on the FirstController scope or a containing parent $scope.

Using controllers allows us to contain the logic of a single view in a single container. It's good practice to keep slim controllers. One way that we as AngularJS developers can do so is by using the dependency injection feature of AngularJS to access services.

One major distinction between AngularJS and other JavaScript frameworks is that the controller is not the appropriate place to do any DOM manipulation or formatting, data manipulation, or state maintenance beyond holding the model data. It is simply the glue between the view and the $scope model.

AngularJS also makes it possible to set any types on the $scope, including objects and show the object's properties in the view.

For example, we will simply create a person object on the controller MyController that has a single attribute of name:

```
app.controller('MyController', function($scope) {
  $scope.person = {
    name: "Ari Lerner"
  };
});
```

We can access this person object in any child element of the div where ng-controller='MyController' is written *because* it is on the $scope.

For instance, now we can simply reference person or person.name in our view.

```html
<div ng-app="myApp">
  <div ng-controller="MyController">
    <h1>{{ person }}</h1>
    and their name:
    <h2>{{ person.name }}</h2>
  </div>
</div>
```

{"name":"Ari Lerner}

and their name:

Ari Lerner

Controller object

As we can see, the $scope object is how we pass along information from the model to the view. It is also how we set up watch events, interact with other parts of the application, and create application-specific logic.

Angular uses scopes to isolate the functionality of the view, controllers, and directives (we'll cover these later in the book), which makes it very easy to write tests for a specific piece of functionality.

Controller Hierarchy (Scopes Within Scopes)

Every part of an AngularJS application has a parent scope (as we've seen, at the ng-app level, this scope is called the $rootScope), regardless of the context within which it is rendered.

 There is one exception: A scope created inside of a directive is called the *isolate* scope.

With the exception of isolate scopes, all scopes are created with prototypal inheritance, meaning that they have access to their parent scopes. If we are familiar with object-oriented programming, this behavior should look familiar.

By default, for any property that AngularJS cannot find on a local scope, AngularJS will crawl up to the containing (parent) scope and look for the property or method there. If AngularJS can't find the property there, it will walk to that scope's parent and so on and so forth until it reaches the

$rootScope. If it doesn't find it on the $rootScope, then it moves on and is unable to update the view.

To see this behavior in action, let's create a ParentController that contains the user object and a ChildController that wants to reference that object:

```
app.controller('ParentController', function($scope) {
  $scope.person = {greeted: false};
});

app.controller('ChildController', function($scope) {
  $scope.sayHello = function() {
    $scope.person.name = "Ari Lerner";
    $scope.person.greeted = true;
  }
});
```

If we bind the ChildController under the ParentController in our view, then the *parent* of the ChildController's $scope object will be the ParentController's $scope object. Due to the prototypal behavior, we can then reference data on the ParentController's containing $scope on the child scope.

For instance, we can reference the person object that is defined on the ParentController inside the DOM element of the ChildController.

```
<div ng-controller="ParentController">
  <div ng-controller="ChildController">
    <a ng-click="sayHello()">Say hello</a>
  </div>
  {{ person }}
</div>
```

Say hello
{"greeted":true,"name":"Ari Lerner"}

Nested controllers

This nested structure of controllers closely resembles the nested structure of the DOM itself.

As we can see, once we press the button, we can reference the ParentController's $scope.person value inside the ChildController just as though person was defined in the ChildController's $scope object.

It is a best practice to keep our controllers as slim as possible. It's bad practice to allow any DOM interaction or data manipulation inside the controller.

For instance, this example of a thick controller contains a lot of logic for controlling the view, and it manipulates the DOM:

Thick controller

```
angular.module('MyController', function($scope) {
    $scope.shouldShowLogin = true;
    $scope.showLogin = function() {
     $scope.shouldShowLogin = !$scope.shouldShowLogin;
    }
    $scope.clickButton = function() {
     $("#btn span").html("Clicked");
    }
    $scope.onLogin = function(user) {
     $http({
       method: 'POST',
       url: '/login',
       data: {
         user: user
       }
     }).success(function(data) {
       // user
     })
    }
})
```

A better designed app would allow directives and services to handle the dirty logic. We can transform our controller using directives and services into a much thinner, more manageable one:

Thin controller

```
angular.module('MyController', function($scope, UserSrv) {
  // The content can be controlled by
  // directives
  $scope.onLogin = function(user) {
    UserSrv.runLogin(user);
  }
})
```

Expressions

Expressions are used all over AngularJS apps, so it's important we get a solid understanding of what expressions are and how AngularJS uses and evaluates them.

We've seen examples of Angular expressions already. The {{ }} notation for showing a variable attached to a $scope is actually an expression: {{ expression }}. When setting up a $watch, we use an expression (or a function) that Angular will evaluate.

Expressions are roughly similar to the result of an eval(javascript). Angular processes them; therefore, they have these important, distinct properties:

- All expressions are executed in the context of the scope and have access to local $scope variables.
- An expression doesn't throw errors if it results in a *TypeError* or a *ReferenceError*.
- They do not allow for any control flow functions (conditionals; e.g., if/else).
- They can accept a filter and/or filter chains.

Expressions all operate on the containing scope within which they are called. This fact enables us to call variables bound to the containing scope inside of an expression, which, in turn, enables us to loop over variables (we'll see this looping in action with ng-repeat), call a function, or use variables for math expressions from the scope.

Parsing an Angular Expression

Although your Angular app will run parse for you automatically when running the $digest loop, sometimes it's useful to parse an Angular expression manually.

Angular evaluates expressions by an internal service (called the $parse service) that has knowledge of the current scope. This setup gives us access to the raw JavaScript data and functions that are defined on our $scope.

To manually parse an expression, we can inject the $parse service into a controller and call the service to do the parsing for us. For instance, if we have an input box in our page that's bound to the expr variable, like so:

```
<div ng-controller="MyController">
  <input ng-model="expr"
         type="text"
         placeholder="Enter an expression" />
  <h2>{{ parsedValue }}</h2>
</div>
```

In MyController, we can then set a $watch and parse the expression expr.

```
angular.module("myApp", [])
.controller('MyController',
function($scope, $parse) {
  $scope.$watch('expr', function(newVal, oldVal, scope) {
    if (newVal !== oldVal) {
      // Let's set up our parseFun with the expression
      var parseFun = $parse(newVal);
      // Get the value of the parsed expression
      $scope.parsedValue = parseFun(scope);
    }
  });
});
```

 See it live here[18].

Interpolating a String

Although it's uncommon to need to manually interpolate a string template in Angular, we do have
the ability to manually run the template compilation. Interpolation allows us to *live* update a string
of text based upon conditions of a scope, for instance.

To run an interpolation on a string template, we need to inject the $interpolate service in our
object. In this example, we'll inject it into a controller:

---

[18]http://jsbin.com/UWuLALOf/1/edit?html,js,output

```
angular.module('myApp', [])
  .controller('MyController',
    function($scope, $interpolate) {
        // We have access to both the $scope
        // and the $interpolate services
});
```

The $interpolate service takes up to three parameters, with only one required function.

- text (string) - The text with markup to interpolate.
- mustHaveExpression (boolean) - If we set parameter to true, then the text will return null if there is no expression.
- trustedContext (string) - Angular sends the result of the interpolation context through the $sce.getTrusted() method, which provides strict contextual escaping.

 See $sce for more details about the last parameter.

The $interpolate service returns an interpolation function that takes a context object against which the expressions are evaluated.

With these parameters set up, we can now run an interpolation inside the controller. For instance, let's say we want to show *live editing* of the body of text in an email. We can run an interpolation when the text changes to show the given output.

```
<div ng-controller="MyController">
  <input ng-model="to"
         type="email"
         placeholder="Recipient" />
  <textarea ng-model="emailBody"></textarea>
  <pre>{{ previewText }}</pre>
</div>
```

In our controller, we set up a $watch to monitor changes on the email body and interpolate the emailBody into our previewText property.

```
angular.module('myApp', [])
  .controller('MyController',
    function($scope, $interpolate) {
      // Set up a watch
      $scope.$watch('emailBody', function(body) {
        if (body) {
          var template = $interpolate(body);
          $scope.previewText =
            template({to: $scope.to});
        }
      });
});
```

  See this in action here[19].

Now, inside of our `{{ previewText }}` body, we can use `{{ to }}` as a variable in the text and allow it to be *live-updated* along with the rest of the text.

  If it's desirable to use different beginning and ending symbols in our text, we can modify them by configuring the `$interpolateProvider`.

To modify the beginning string, we can set the starting symbol with the `startSymbol()` method. The `startSymbol()` takes a single argument:

- value (string) - the value to set the starting symbol

To modify the ending symbol, we can use the `endSymbol()` function. This function takes a single argument, as well:

- value (string) - the value to set the end symbol

To modify the starting symbol, we can create a new module and inject the `$interpolateProvider` into the `config()` function.

We'll also create a service, which we will cover in depth in the services chapter.

---

[19]http://jsbin.com/oDeFuCAW/1/edit?html,js,output

```
angular.module('emailParser', [])
  .config(['$interpolateProvider',
    function($interpolateProvider) {
      $interpolateProvider.startSymbol('__');
      $interpolateProvider.endSymbol('__');
}])
.factory('EmailParser', ['$interpolate',
  function($interpolate) {
    // a service to handle parsing
    return {
      parse: function(text, context) {
        var template = $interpolate(text);
        return template(context);
      }
    }
}]);
```

Now that we have created this module, we can inject it into our app and run the email parser on the text in our email body:

```
angular.module('myApp', ['emailParser'])
  .controller('MyController',
    ['$scope', 'EmailParser',
      function($scope, EmailParser) {
        // Set up a watch
        $scope.$watch('emailBody', function(body) {
          if (body) {
            $scope.previewText =
              EmailParser.parse(body, {
                to: $scope.to
              });
          }
        });
}]);
```

Now, instead of requiring the text to use the default syntax with the {{ }} symbols, we can define our symbols to use __ instead.

As we're setting the symbols to __ on either side, we'll need to change the HTML to use this syntax instead of {{ }}:

```
<div id="emailEditor">
  <input ng-model="to"
         type="email"
         placeholder="Recipient" />
  <textarea ng-model="emailBody"></textarea>
</div>
<div id="emailPreview">
  <pre>__ previewText __</pre>
</div>
```

Interpolation

 See it in action here[20].

---

[20]http://jsbin.com/ivuJEXI/1/edit

Filters

In AngularJS, a filter provides a way to format the data we display to the user. Angular gives us several built-in filters as well as an easy way to create our own.

We invoke filters in our HTML with the | (pipe) character inside the template binding characters {{ }}. For instance, let's say we want to capitalize our string. We can either change all the characters in a string to be capitalized, or we can use a filter.

```
{{ name | uppercase }}
```

We can also use filters from within JavaScript by using the $filter service. For instance, to use the lowercase JavaScript filter:

```
app.controller('DemoController', ['$scope', '$filter',
  function($scope, $filter) {

    $scope.name = $filter('lowercase')('Ari');
}]);
```

To pass an argument to a filter in the HTML form, we pass it with a colon after the filter name (for multiple arguments, we can simply append a colon after each argument). For example, the number filter allows us to limit the number of decimal places a number can show. To pass the argument 2, we'll append :2 to the number filter:

```
<!-- Displays: 123.46 -->
{{ 123.456789 | number:2 }}
```

We can use multiple filters at the same time by using two or more pipes. We'll see such an example in a minute when we build a custom filter. Before we get to that, however, let's look at the built-in filters that come out of the box with AngularJS.

currency

The currency filter formats a number as currency. In other words, 123 as currency looks like: {{ 123 | currency }}.

Currency gives us the option of displaying a currency symbol or identifier. The default currency option is that of the current locale; however, we can pass in a currency to display.

date

The date filter allows us to format a date based upon a requested format style. The date formatter provides us several built-in options. If no date format is passed, then it defaults to showing `mediumDate` (as you can see below).

Here are the built-in localizable formats:

```
{{ today | date:'medium' }}      <!-- Aug 09, 2013 12:09:02 PM -->
{{ today | date:'short' }}       <!-- 8/9/13 12:09 PM -->
{{ today | date:'fullDate' }}    <!-- Thursday, August 09, 2013 -->
{{ today | date:'longDate' }}    <!-- August 09, 2013 -->
{{ today | date:'mediumDate' }}  <!-- Aug 09, 2013 -->
{{ today | date:'shortDate' }}   <!-- 8/9/13 -->
{{ today | date:'mediumTime' }}  <!-- 12:09:02 PM -->
{{ today | date:'shortTime' }}   <!-- 12:09 PM -->
```

The date formatter also enables us to customize your date format to our own liking. We can combine and chain together these format options to create one single date format, as well:

Year Formatting

```
Four-digit year: {{ today | date:'yyyy' }} <!-- 2013 -->
Two-digit padded year: {{ today | date:'yy' }} <!-- 13 -->
One-digit year: {{ today | date:'y' }} <!-- 2013 -->
```

Month Formatting

```
Month in year: {{ today | date:'MMMM' }} <!-- August -->
Short month in year: {{ today | date:'MMM' }} <!-- Aug -->
Padded month in year: {{ today | date:'MM' }} <!-- 08 -->
Month in year: {{ today | date:'M' }} <!-- 8 -->
```

Day Formatting

```
Padded day in month: {{ today | date:'dd' }} <!-- 09 -->
Day in month: {{ today | date:'d' }} <!-- 9 -->
Day in week: {{ today | date:'EEEE' }} <!-- Thursday -->
Short day in week: {{ today | date:'EEE' }} <!-- Thu -->
```

Hour Formatting

```
Padded hour in day: {{ today | date:'HH' }} <!-- 00 -->
Hour in day: {{ today | date:'H' }} <!-- 0 -->
Padded hour in am/pm: {{ today | date:'hh' }} <!-- 12 -->
Hour in am/pm: {{ today | date:'h' }} <!-- 12 -->
```

Minute Formatting

```
Padded minute in hour: {{ today | date:'mm' }} <!-- 09 -->
Minute in hour: {{ today | date:'m' }} <!-- 9 -->
```

Second Formatting

```
Padded second in minute: {{ today | date:'ss' }} <!-- 02 -->
Second in minute: {{ today | date:'s' }} <!-- 2 -->
Padded millisecond in second: {{ today | date:'.sss' }} <!-- .995 -->
```

String Formatting

```
am/pm character: {{ today | date:'a' }} <!-- AM -->
4-digit representation of time zone offset: {{ today | date:'Z' }} <!-- -0700 -->
```

Some examples of custom date formatting:

```
{{ today | date:'MMM d, y' }} <!-- Aug 09, 2013 -->
{{ today | date:'EEEE, d, M' }} <!-- Thursday, 9, 8 -->
{{ today | date:'hh:mm:ss.sss' }} <!-- 12:09:02.995 -->
```

filter

The `filter` filter selects a subset of items from an array of items and returns a new array. This filter is generally used as a way to *filter* out items for display. For instance, when using client-side searching, we can filter out items from an array immediately.

The filter method takes a string, object, or function that it will run to select or reject array elements.

If the first parameter passed in is a:

string

It will accept all elements that match against the string. If we want all the elements that do **not** match the string, we can prepend a ! to the string.

object

It will compare objects that have a property name that matches, as with the simple substring match if only a string is passed in. If we want to match against *all* properties, we can use the $ as the key.

function

It will run the function over each element of the array, and the results that return as non-falsy will appear in the new array.

For instance, selecting all of the words that have the letter e in them, we could run our filter like so:

```
{{ ['Ari', 'Lerner', 'Likes', 'To', 'Eat', 'Pizza'] | filter:'e' }}
<!-- ["Lerner","Likes","Eat"] -->
```

If we want to filter on objects, we can use the the object filter notation as we discussed above. For instance, if we have an array of people objects with a list of their favorite foods, we could filter them like so:

```
{{ [{
    'name': 'Ari',
    'City': 'San Francisco',
    'favorite food': 'Pizza'
    }, {
    'name': 'Nate',
    'City': 'San Francisco',
    'favorite food': 'indian food'
    }] | filter:{'favorite food': 'Pizza'} }}
<!-- [{"name":"Ari","City":"San Francisco","favorite food":"Pizza"}] -->
```

We can also filter based on a function that we define (in this example, on the containing $scope object):

```
{{ ['Ari', 'likes', 'to', 'travel'] | filter:isCapitalized }}
<!-- ["Ari"] -->
```

The isCapitalized function, which returns true if the first character is a capital letter and false if it is not, is defined as:

```
$scope.isCapitalized =
  function(str) { return str[0] == str[0].toUpperCase(); }
```

We can also pass a second parameter into the filter method that will be used to determine if the expected value and the actual value should be considered a match.

If the second parameter passed in is:

true

It runs a strict comparison of the two using `angular.equals(expected, actual)`.

false

It looks for a case-insensitive substring match.

function

It runs the function and accepts an element if the result of the function is truthy.

json

The `json` filter will take a JSON, or JavaScript object, and turn it into a string. This transformation is very useful for debugging purposes:

```
{{ {'name': 'Ari', 'City': 'San Francisco'} | json }}
<!--
{
  "name": "Ari",
  "City": "San Francisco"
}
-->
```

limitTo

The `limitTo` filter creates a new array or string that contains only the specified number of elements, either taken from the beginning or end, depending on whether the value is positive or negative.

If the limit exceeds the value of the string, then the entire array or string will be returned.

For instance, we can take the first three letters of a string:

```
{{ San Francisco is very cloudy | limitTo:3 }}
<!-- San -->
```

Or we can take the last 6 characters of a string:

```
{{ San Francisco is very cloudy | limitTo:-6 }}
<!-- cloudy -->
```

We can do the same with an array. Here we'll return only the first element of the array:

```
{{ ['a', 'b', 'c', 'd', 'e', 'f'] | limitTo:1 }}
<!-- ["a"] -->
```

lowercase

The lowercase filter simply lowercases the entire string.

```
{{ "San Francisco is very cloudy" | lowercase }}
<!-- san francisco is very cloudy -->
```

number

The number filter formats a number as text. It can take a second parameter (optional) that will format the number to the specified number of decimal places (rounded).

If a non-numeric character is given, it will return an empty string.

```
{{ 123456789 | number }}
<!-- 1,234,567,890 -->
{{ 1.234567 | number:2 }}
<!-- 1.23 -->
```

orderBy

The orderBy filter orders the specific array using an expression.

The orderBy function can take two parameters: The first one is required, while the second is optional.

The first parameter is the predicate used to determine the order of the sorted array.

If the first parameter passed in is a(n):

function

It will use the function as the `getter` function for the object.

string

It will parse the string and use the result as the key by which to order the elements of the array. We can pass either a + or a - to force the sort in ascending or descending order.

array

It will use the elements as predicates in the sort expression. It will use the first predicate for every element that is **not** strictly equal to the expression result.

The second parameter controls the sort order of the array (either reversed or not).

For instance, let's sort an array of objects by their name. Say we have an array of people, we can order the array of objects with the `name` value:

```
{{ [{
    'name': 'Ari',
    'status': 'awake'
    }, {
    'name': 'Q',
    'status': 'sleeping'
    }, {
    'name': 'Nate',
    'status': 'awake'
    }] | orderBy: 'name' }}
<!--
  [
  {"name":"Ari","status":"awake"},
  {"name":"Nate","status":"awake"},
  {"name":"Q","status":"sleeping"}
  ]
-->
```

We can also reverse-sort the object. For instance, reverse-sorting the previous object, we simply add the second parameter as `true`:

```
{{ [{
    'name': 'Ari',
    'status': 'awake'
    }, {
    'name': 'Q',
    'status': 'sleeping'
    }, {
    'name': 'Nate',
    'status': 'awake'
    }] | orderBy:'name':true }}
<!--
  [
  {"name":"Q","status":"sleeping"},
  {"name":"Nate","status":"awake"},
  {"name":"Ari","status":"awake"}
  ]
-->
```

uppercase

The uppercase filter simply uppercases the entire string:

```
{{ "San Francisco is very cloudy" | uppercase }}
<!-- SAN FRANCISCO IS VERY CLOUDY -->
```

Making Our Own Filter

As we saw above, it's really easy to create our own custom filter. To create a filter, we put it under its own module. Let's create one together: a filter that capitalizes the first character of a string.

First, we need to create it in a module that we'll require in our app (this step is good practice):

```
angular.module('myApp.filters', [])
.filter('capitalize', function() {
  return function(input) {}
});
```

Filters are just functions to which we pass input. In the function above, we simply take the input as the string on which we are calling the filter. We can do some error checking inside the function:

```
angular.module('myApp.filters', [])
.filter('capitalize', function() {
  return function(input) {
    // input will be the string we pass in
    if (input)
      return input[0].toUpperCase() +
        input.slice(1);
  }
});
```

Now, if we want to capitalize the first letter of a sentence, we can first lowercase the entire string and then capitalize the first letter with our filter:

```
<!-- Ginger loves dog treats -->
{{ 'ginger loves dog treats' | lowercase | capitalize }}
```

Form Validation

When taking input from our users, it's important to show visual feedback on their input. In the context of human relationships, form validation is just as much about giving feedback as well as getting the "right" input.

Not only does it provide positive feedback for our user, it will also semi-protect our web app from bad or invalid input. We can only protect our back end as much as is possible with our web front end.

Out of the box, AngularJS supports form validation with a mix of the HTML5 form validation inputs as well as with its own validation directives.

There are many form validation directives available in AngularJS. We'll talk about a few of the core validations, then we'll get into how to build your own validations.

```
<form name="form" novalidate>
  <label name="email">Your email</label>
  <input type="email" name="email" ng-model="email" placeholder="Email Address" />
</form>
```

AngularJS makes it pretty easy for us to handle client-side form validations without adding a lot of extra effort. Although we can't depend on client-side validations to keep our web application secure, they do provide instant feedback of the state of the form.

To use form validations, we first must ensure that the form has a name associated with it, like in the above example.

All input fields can validate against some basic validations, like minimum length, maximum length, etc. These are all available on the new HTML5 attributes of a form.

It is usually a great idea to use the `novalidate` flag on the form element, as it prevents the browser from natively validating the form.

Let's look at all the validation options we have that we can place on an `input` field:

Required

To validate that a form input has been filled out, we simply add the HTML5 tag, `required`, to the input field:

```
<input type="text" required />
```

Minimum Length

To validate that a form input input is at least a certain {number} of characters, we add the AngularJS directive `ng-minlength="{number}"` to the input field:

```
<input type="text" ng-minlength=5 />
```

Maximum Length

To validate that a form input is equal to or less than a number of characters, we can add the AngularJS directive `ng-maxlength="{number}"`:

```
<input type="text" ng-maxlength=20 />
```

Matches a Pattern

To ensure that an input matches a regex, we can use `ng-pattern="/PATTERN/"`:

```
<input type="text" ng-pattern="/a-zA-Z/" />
```

Email

To validate an email address in an input field, we simply set the `input` type to `email`, like so:

```
<input type="email" name="email" ng-model="user.email" />
```

Number

To validate an input field has a number, we set the `input` type to `number`:

```
<input type="number" name="age" ng-model="user.age" />
```

URL

To validate that an input represents a URL, set the `input` type to `url`:

```
<input type="url" name="homepage" ng-model="user.facebook_url" />
```

Custom Validations

AngularJS makes it very easy to add our own validations, as well, by using directives. For instance, let's say that we want to validate that our username is available in the database. To do so, we'll implement a directive that fires an Ajax request whenever the form changes.

```
angular.module('validationExample', [])
.directive('ensureUnique', function($http) {
  return {
    require: 'ngModel',
    link: function(scope, ele, attrs, c) {
      scope.$watch(attrs.ngModel, function() {
        $http({
          method: 'POST',
          url: '/api/check/' + attrs.ensureUnique,
          data: {'field': attrs.ensureUnique}
        }).success(function(data,status,headers,cfg) {
          c.$setValidity('unique', data.isUnique);
        }).error(function(data,status,headers,cfg) {
          c.$setValidity('unique', false);
        });
      });
    }
  }
});
```

Control Variables in Forms

AngularJS makes properties available on the containing $scope object available to us as a result of setting a form inside the DOM. These properties enable us to react to the form in *real time* (just like everything else in AngularJS). The properties that are available to us are:

(Note that these properties are made available to us in the format:)

```
formName.inputFieldName.property
```

Unmodified Form

This property is a boolean that tells us whether the user has modified the form. It is `true` if the user hasn't touched the form, and `false` if they have:

```
formName.inputFieldName.$pristine;
```

Modified Form

This property is a boolean that tells us if and only if the user has actually modified the form. It is set regardless of validations on the form:

```
formName.inputFieldName.$dirty
```

Valid Form

This property is a boolean that tells us whether or not the form is valid. If the form is currently *valid*, then the following will be true:

```
formName.inputFieldName.$valid
```

Invalid Form

This property is a boolean that tells us whether or not the form is invalid. If the form is currently *invalid*, then the following will be true:

```
formName.inputFieldName.$invalid
```

The last two properties are particularly useful for showing or hiding DOM elements. They are also very useful when setting a class on a particular form.

Errors

This property is another useful one that AngularJS makes available to us: the $error object. This object contains all of the validations on a particular form and a record of whether they are valid or invalid. To get access to this property, use the following syntax:

```
formName.inputfieldName.$error
```

If a validation *fails*, then this property will be true; if it is false, then the value has passed the input field.

A Little Style Never Hurts

When AngularJS is handling a form, it adds specific classes to the form based upon the current state of the form (i.e. if it's currently valid, unchanged, etc.). These classes are named similarly to the properties that we can check, as well.

These classes are:

```
.ng-pristine {}
.ng-dirty {}
.ng-valid {}
.ng-invalid {}
```

They correspond to their counterpart on the particular input field.

When a field is invalid, the .ng-invalid class will be applied to the field. This particular site sets the CSS class as:

```
input.ng-invalid {
  border: 1px solid red;
}
input.ng-valid {
  border: 1px solid green;
}
```

$parsers

When our user interacts with the controller and the $setViewValue() method has been called on the ngModelController, the array of $parsers functions are called as a pipeline. The first $parser is called and passes its value to the next, and so on and so forth.

These functions have the opportunity to convert the value and change the validity state of the control by using the $setValidity() functions.

Using the $parsers array is one way we can create a custom validation. For instance, let's say we want to confirm a value is between two numbers. We'll push a new function on the $parsers array that is called in the validation chain.

The value that we return from this $parser function is the value that will be passed down the chain to the next parser. We return undefined if we don't want the model to update.

```
angular.module('myApp')
.directive('oneToTen', function() {
  return {
    require: '?ngModel',
    link: function(scope, ele, attrs, ngModel) {
      if (!ngModel) return;
      ngModel.$parsers.unshift(
        function(viewValue) {
          var i = parseInt(viewValue);

          if (i >= 0 && i < 10) {
            ngModel.$setValidity('oneToTen', true);
            return viewValue;
          } else {
            ngModel.$setValidity('oneToTen', false);
            return undefined;
          }
        });
    }
  };
});
```

$formatters

When the bound ngModel value has changed and has been run through the $parsers array, then the value will be passed through to the $formatters pipeline. These functions have the opportunity to modify and format the value, as well as change the validity state of the control similar to the $parsers array.

We use these functions primarily to handle visual changes in the view, rather than purely for validation purposes. For instance, let's say we want to call a formatter on a value. Using the $formatters array, we can set a filter to run on the value:

```
angular.module('myApp')
.directive('oneToTen', function() {
  return {
    require: '?ngModel',
    link: function(scope, ele, attrs, ngModel) {
      if (!ngModel) return;

      ngModel.$formatters.unshift(function(v) {
        return $filter('number')(v);
      });
```

```
      }
    };
  });
```

Putting It All Together

Let's build a signup form. This signup form will include person's name, his or her email, and a desired username.

Let's start by looking at what the form will look like when it's done:

Signup form

Play with it[21]

Let's start by defining the form:

```
<form name="signup_form" novalidate ng-submit="signupForm()">
  <fieldset>
    <legend>Signup</legend>

    <button type="submit" class="button radius">Submit</button>
  </fieldset>
</form>
```

This form's name is `signup_form`, and we are going to call `signupForm()` when the form is submitted.

Now, let's add the name of the user:

---

[21]http://jsbin.com/ePomUnI/5/edit

```
<div class="row">
  <div class="large-12 columns">
    <label>Your name</label>
    <input type="text"
        placeholder="Name"
        name="name"
        ng-model="signup.name"
        ng-minlength=3
        ng-maxlength=20 required />
  </div>
</div>
```

We'll discuss styling in a future chapter, but we'll include styles in this chapter as an introduction. We're using the Foundation[22] framework in this chapter for CSS layouts.

We've added a form that has an input field called name that is bound (by ng-model) to the object signup.name on the $scope object.

 Don't forget to add a name to the input field. Adding a name to the input is important: That is how we'll reference the form input when showing validation messages to the user.

We've also set up a few validations. These validations say we have to have a minlength of three or more characters in our name. We also impose a maximum limit of 20 characters (meaning the input will be invalid at 21 characters and higher). Lastly, we've required that the name be filled out for the form to be valid.

Let's use the properties to show and/or hide a list of errors if the form is invalid. We'll use the $dirty attribute to make sure the errors don't show up if the user hasn't touched the field:

```
<div class="row">
  <div class="large-12 columns">
    <label>Your name</label>
    <input type="text"
            placeholder="Name"
            name="name"
            ng-model="signup.name"
            ng-minlength=3
            ng-maxlength=20 required />
    <div class="error"
        ng-show="signup_form.name.$dirty && signup_form.name.$invalid">
      <small class="error"
```

---

[22]http://foundation.zurb.com

```
      ng-show="signup_form.name.$error.required">
          Your name is required.
    </small>
    <small class="error"
          ng-show="signup_form.name.$error.minlength">
          Your name is required to be at least 3 characters
    </small>
    <small class="error"
          ng-show="signup_form.name.$error.maxlength">
          Your name cannot be longer than 20 characters
    </small>
  </div>
  </div>
</div>
```

Breaking this down, we're only going to show our errors if the form is invalid and changed, just as before. This time, we'll look through each of the valiations and only show a particular DOM element if the particular validation property is invalid.

Let's look at the next set of validations, the email validation:

```
<div class="row">
  <div class="large-12 columns">
    <label>Your email</label>
    <input type="email"
      placeholder="Email"
      name="email"
      ng-model="signup.email"
      ng-minlength=3 ng-maxlength=20 required />
    <div class="error"
        ng-show="signup_form.email.$dirty && signup_form.email.$invalid">
      <small class="error"
          ng-show="signup_form.email.$error.required">
          Your email is required.
      </small>
      <small class="error"
          ng-show="signup_form.email.$error.minlength">
           Your email is required to be at least 3 characters
      </small>
      <small class="error"
          ng-show="signup_form.email.$error.email">
          That is not a valid email. Please input a valid email.
      </small>
```

```
      <small class="error"
             ng-show="signup_form.email.$error.maxlength">
             Your email cannot be longer than 20 characters
      </small>
    </div>
  </div>
</div>
```

This time (with the entire form included), we're looking at the email field. Note that we set the type of the input field to *email* and added a validation error on $error.email. This validation is based off the AngularJS email validation (and the HTML5 attribute).

Finally, let's look at our last input field, the username:

```
<div class="large-12 columns">
  <label>Username</label>
    <input   type="text"
             placeholder="Desired username"
             name="username"
             ng-model="signup.username"
             ng-minlength=3
             ng-maxlength=20
             ensure-unique="username" required />
  <div class="error"
       ng-show="signup_form.username.$dirty && signup_form.username.$invalid">
    <small class="error"
           ng-show="signup_form.username.$error.required">
           Please input a username
    </small>
    <small class="error"
           ng-show="signup_form.username.$error.minlength">
           Your username is required to be at least 3 characters
    </small>
    <small class="error"
           ng-show="signup_form.username.$error.maxlength">
           Your username cannot be longer than 20 characters
    </small>
    <small class="error"
           ng-show="signup_form.username.$error.unique">
           That username is taken, please try another
    </small>
  </div>
</div>
```

In our last field, we're using all the same validations as previously except that we've added a custom validation. This custom validation is defined using an AngularJS directive:

```
app.directive('ensureUnique', function($http) {
  return {
    require: 'ngModel',
    link: function(scope, ele, attrs, c) {
      scope.$watch(attrs.ngModel, function(n) {
        if (!n) return;
        $http({
          method: 'POST',
          url: '/api/check/'+attrs.ensureUnique,
          data: {'field': attrs.ensureUnique}
        }).success(function(data) {
          c.$setValidity('unique', data.isUnique);
        }).error(function(data) {
          c.$setValidity('unique', false);
        });
      });
    }
  }
});
```

When the form input is valid, this will make a *POST* request check to the server at /api/check/username to check if the username is available. Now, obviously since we're only talking about front-end code here, we don't have a back end to test this on, although it could easily be written.

Lastly, putting our button together, we can use the Angular directive ng-disabled to disable and re-enable the button depending on the validity of the form:

```
<button type="submit"
  ng-disabled="signup_form.$invalid"
  class="button radius">Submit</button>
```

Play with the example so far[23]

As we said above, the form itself will have $invalid and valid attributes given to us for free.

Although live validation is great, it can be abrasive to the user when they see errors pop up while they are typing, long before they have put in a *valid* value. You can be *nicer* to your users if you show the validations either only after they have submitted the form *or* after they have moved off of the input. Let's look at both ways to do that.

---

[23]http://jsbin.com/ePomUnI/5/edit

Show Validations after Submit

To show validations only after the user has attempted to submit the form, you can capture a 'submitted' value on the scope and check for that scope to show the error.

For instance, let's take a look at the first example and only show the errors when our user has submitted the form. On the ng-show directive on the form input, we can add a check to see if the form has been submitted (which we will implement shortly):

```html
<form name="signup_form" novalidate
    ng-submit="signupForm()"
    ng-controller="signupController">
  <fieldset>
    <legend>Signup</legend>
    <div class="row">
      <div class="large-12 columns">
        <label>Your name</label>
        <input type="text"
            placeholder="Name"
            name="name"
            ng-model="signup.name"
            ng-minlength=3
            ng-maxlength=20 required />
      <div class="error"
            ng-show="signup_form.name.$dirty && signup_form.name.$invalid &&
            signup_form.submitted">
        <small class="error"
         ng-show="signup_form.name.$error.required">
            Your name is required.
        </small>
        <small class="error"
         ng-show="signup_form.name.$error.minlength">
            Your name is required to be at
            least 3 characters
        </small>
        <small class="error"
         ng-show="signup_form.name.$error.maxlength">
            Your name cannot be longer than
            20 characters
        </small>
      </div>
      </div>
    </div>
```

```
    <button type="submit" >Submit</button>
  </fieldset>
</form>
```

Now, the error div will only show up if the `signup_form.submitted` variable has been set to true. We can implement this behavior in the `signupForm` action, like so:

```
    app.controller('signupController',
  function($scope) {
```

$scope.submitted = false; $scope.signupForm = function() { if ($scope.signup_form.$valid) { // Submit as normal } else { $scope.signup_form.submitted = true; } }

```
    });
```

If our users try to submit the form while there is an invalid element, we can now catch it and show them the appropriate errors.

Try it out[24]

Show Validations Only after Blur

If we want to retain the *real-time* nature of the error input, we can show our users the errors after they have blurred off of the input form (i.e., when they are no longer in a given field). To do so, we like to add a small directive that will attach a new variable to the form.

The directive we like to use is the `ngFocus` directive, and it looks like:

```
app.directive('ngFocus', [function() {
  var FOCUS_CLASS = "ng-focused";
  return {
    restrict: 'A',
    require: 'ngModel',
    link: function(scope, element, attrs, ctrl) {
      ctrl.$focused = false;
      element.bind('focus', function(evt) {
        element.addClass(FOCUS_CLASS);
        scope.$apply(function() {
          ctrl.$focused = true;
        });
      }).bind('blur', function(evt) {
```

---

[24]http://jsbin.com/ePomUnI/6/edit

```
        element.removeClass(FOCUS_CLASS);
        scope.$apply(function() {
          ctrl.$focused = false;
        });
      });
    }
  }
}]);
```

To implement the ngFocus directive, we can simply attach this directive to the input element, like so:

```
<input ng-class="{
  error: signup_form.name.$dirty &&
  signup_form.name.$invalid}"
  type="text"
  placeholder="Name"
  name="name"
  ng-model="signup.name"
  ng-minlength=3
  ng-maxlength=20 required ng-focus />
```

The ngFocus directive simply attaches an action to the blur and focus events on the form input, adds a class (ng-focused), and sets the form input field, $focused, as true. Then we can show our individual error messages depending on whether or not the form is focused. For instance:

```
<div class="error"
  ng-show="signup_form.name.$dirty &&
    signup_form.name.$invalid &&
    !signup_form.name.$focused">
```

Play with the full example[25]

It's possible to check to see if the input field is empty, as well, by using the $isEmpty() method on the ngModel controller. The method will return true if the input is empty and false if it's not.

---

[25]http://jsbin.com/ePomUnI/7/edit

Introduction to Directives

As web developers, we're all familiar with HTML. Let's take a moment to review and synchronize our terminology around this most fundamental of web technologies.

HTML Document

An HTML document is a plain text document that contains structure and may be styled through CSS or manipulated with JavaScript.

HTML Node

An HTML node is an element or chunk of text nested inside another element. All elements are also nodes; however, a text node is not an element.

HTML Element

An element comprises an opening tag and a closing tag.

HTML Tag

An HTML tag is responsible for marking the beginning and end of an element. A tag itself is declared using angle brackets.

An opening tag contains a name that becomes the name of the element. It can also contain attributes, which decorate the element.

Attributes

To provide additional information about an element, HTML elements can contain attributes. These attributes are always set in the opening tag. We can set them in a key-value pair, like `key="value"`, or as only a key.

Let's take a look at the `<a>` hyperlink tag, which is used to create a link from one page to another:

Some tags, like the hyperlink tag, have special attributes that act much like arguments to the tag. For example, the `href` attribute of a link tag enables the behavior of the link tag and also turns the text node in between the opening and closing tags blue by default on all browsers.

```
<a href="http://google.com">
  Click me to go to Google</a>
```

The `<a>` tag defines a link between another page on our site or off our site, depending on the contents of the `href` attribute, which defines the link's destination.

It is noticeably different from the following HTML element, the button:

```
<button href="http://google.com"
  type="submit">Click me</button>
```

The link tag is, by default, underlined and blue, while the button, by default, looks like a clickable button in our browser.

The link tag knows that, when provided an `href` attribute that points to `http://google.com`, it should change the URL in the address bar and load Google's home page when a user clicks on the link.

The button tag, on the other hand, is completely oblivious when provided an `href` attribute and does not perform the same behavior (the attribute is ignored).

Thus, changing the URL in the address bar and bringing you to a new page is part of a link's pre-programmed behavior, but not part of a button's pre-programmed behavior.

Finally, both tags perform the same behavior when provided a title attribute: They provide a tooltip to the user upon hover.

```
<a href="http://google.com"
  title="click me">
    Click me to go to Google
</a>
<button type="submit"
      title="click me">Click me</button>
```

In summary, the web browser renders our HTML elements' style and behavior; this capability is one of the fundamental strengths of the web.

Each vendor, whether it be Google or Microsoft, tries to adhere to the same HTML spec, therefore making programming for the web consistent across devices and operating systems.

> Past versions of Internet Explorer have not complied with the common HTML spec, so we need to perform some tricks to get older versions of IE to work. See the Internet Explorer chapter for more details.

Recently, new HTML tags have begun to emerge. These are a part of the HTML5 spec. For example, the video tag, which specifies a video, movie clip, or streaming video:

```
<video href="/goofy-video.mp4"></video>
```

These new HTML5 tags work on on newer browsers and are generally *not* supported by Internet Explorer version 8 and lower.

Directives: Custom HTML Elements and Attributes

Given what we know about HTML elements, directives are Angular's method of creating new HTML elements that have their own custom functionality. For instance, we can create our own custom element that implements the video tag and works across all browsers:

```
<my-better-video my-href="/goofy-video.mp4">
Can even take text</my-better-video>
```

Notice that our custom element has custom open and closing tags, my-better-video, and a custom attribute, my-href.

To make our tag more usable, we could just override the browser-provided video tag, which means we could instead use:

```
<video my-href="/goofy-video.mp">
  Can still take children nodes
</video>
```

As we can see, directives can be combined with other directives and attributes; this combination is called composition.

To effectively understand how to compose a system from smaller parts, we must first understand the primitive pieces. Facilitating that understanding will be the underlying goal of the next few chapters. Let's get started.

Bootstrapped HTML

When the browser loads our HTML page along with Angular, we only need one snippet of code to boot our Angular application (we learned about it in the introductory chapter).

In our HTML we need to mark up the root of our app using the *built in* directive ng-app. This directive is meant to be used as an attribute; thus, we could stick it anywhere, but let's choose the opening <html> tag, which is normative:

 A built-in directive is one that ships out of the box with Angular. All built-in directives are prefixed with the ng namespace. In order to avoid namespace collisions, do not prefix the name of your own directives with ng.

```
<html ng-app="myApp">
  <!-- $rootScope of our application -->
</html>
```

Inside of our `<html>` element, we can now use any of the built-in or custom directives we want. Furthermore, all of the directives we use within this root element will have access to $rootScope as a result of the prototypical inheritance in our JavaScript code *if the method of the directive has access to scope.* Access to scope, in this case, means that scope has been linked to the DOM, which is done late in the directive lifecycle.

Because the life cycle of a directive is sufficiently complex, it warrants its own section. In that section, we'll also discuss which methods within a directive have access to scope and how scope is shared between one directive and the next. See the directives explained chapter for more information.

Our First Directive

The quickest way to get our feet wet is to just dive right in. Let's go ahead and create a very basic custom directive. Consider the following HTML element, which we'll define in a moment:

```
<my-directive></my-directive>
```

Provided we've created an HTML document and included Angular as well as the ng-app directive in the DOM to mark the root of our app, when Angular *compiles* our HTML, it will *invoke* this directive.

 We'll learn more about the *compile* stage of the directive lifecycle in understanding compile.

Invoking a directive means to run the associated JavaScript that sits behind our directive, which we define using a directive definition.

The myDirective directive definition looks like:

```
angular.module('myApp', [])
.directive('myDirective', function() {
  return {
    restrict: 'E',
    template: '<a href="http://google.com">
    Click me to go to Google</a>'
  }
});
```

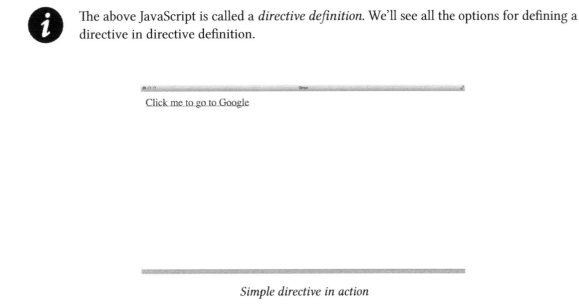

The above JavaScript is called a *directive definition*. We'll see all the options for defining a directive in directive definition.

Simple directive in action

With the .directive() method, provided by the Angular module API, we can register new directives by providing a name as a string and function. The name of the directive should always be pascalCased, and the function we provide should return an object.

Camel casing words is the practice of writing compound words or phrases without spaces such that each word, usually with the exception of the first word, begins with a capital letter, and the phrase becomes a single word. For instance: bumpy roads in camel case notation would be bumpyRoads.

In our case, we declare the directive in HTML using my-directive, the directive definition **must** be myDirective.

The object that we return from the .directive() method comprises methods and properties that we use to define and configure our directive.

In an attempt to master the simplest directive possible, we've only defined our directive with two options: restrict and template.

In directives explained, we'll cover all of the available methods and properties we can use when defining our own directives, but for the moment, let's check out the input HTML as compared to the output HTML by using Google Chrome and its developer tools.

First, open up your HTML document using Chrome. You'll see a blue link that says "Click here". Take a look at the source code by going to View > Developer > View Source. You should see the following picture:

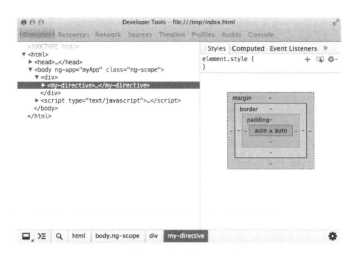

Chrome Developer tool

Notice it's no different from the source code you entered into your text editor; however, notice also that there is no link tag output to the screen yet. Clearly there's supposed to be a link that says "Click here". What's going on?

To investigate, right click on the link, and in the drop-down menu provided by Chrome, left click on `Inspect Element`:

Inspecting element

Doing so will open up the Chrome developer tools and provide you with the generated source, which Angular provides to Chrome after the page is loaded and after Angular has invoked our directive's definition. Let's take a look:

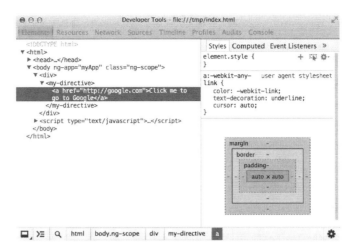

Unwrapping the directive

By default, Angular nests the HTML provided by our template string inside of our custom HTML tag, `<my-directive>`, in the generated source code.

Let's add one more option to our directive definition: We can remove our custom element (`<my-directive>`) from the generated DOM completely and output only the link we're providing to the template option. To do so, set the `replace` option to `true`:

```
angular.module('myApp', [])
.directive('myDirective', function() {
  return {
    restrict: 'E',
    replace: true,
    template: '<a href="http://google.com">Click me to go to Google</a>'
  }
})
```

Look at the generated source again. We can see that we no longer have the original call to the directive, but only the source that we set as the `template`. This *replace* method replaces the custom element instead of wrapping it in our directive call.

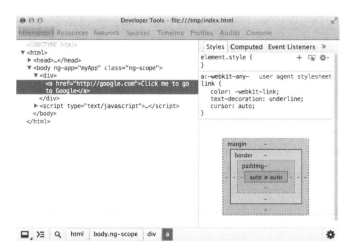

Replacing existing element

From now on, we'll refer to these custom elements we've created (using the `.directive()` method) as directives, because, in fact, we do not need to make a new custom element to *declare* our directive.

 Declaring a directive is the act of placing a function within our HTML as an element, attribute, class, or comment.

The following are valid formats for declaring the directive we built above:

```
<my-directive></my-directive>
<div my-directive></div>
<div class="my-directive"></div>
<!-- directive: my-directive -->
```

In order to allow for Angular to invoke our directive, we'll need to change the `restrict` option inside our directive definition. This option tells Angular which declaration format(s) to look for when compiling our HTML. We can specify one or many formats.

For example, in the directive we're building, we can specify that we want our directive to be invoked if it is an element (E), an attribute (A), a class (C), or a comment (M):

```
angular.module('myApp', [])
.directive('myDirective', function() {
  return {
    restrict: 'EAC',
    replace: true,
    template: '<a href="http://google.com">
    Click me to go to Google</a>'
  };
});
```

Regardless of how many ways we *can* declare a directive, we'll stick to using an attribute (the way that is compliant across the most browsers):

```
<div my-directive></div>
```

And to be more explicit about our intentions with this directive, we'll set the restrict option to the letter A (for attribute):

```
restrict: 'A'
```

When following this convention, however, we need to be aware of each browser's built-in styles and make a decision about whether to wrap or replace our directive's template.

A Note on Internet Explorer

If you've got a copy of Internet Explorer handy, try opening this live example on jsbin[26]. You'll notice that despite declaring your directive twice, only one link is showing up.

Technically, we can fix that by declaring new tags in the head of our document (see Angular with IE), but doing so can cause us headaches in the future if we neglect to be consistent.

Thus, a good rule of thumb to follow is to always declare our directive as an attribute (as we've done). It'll save us some hassle later.

A noteworthy exception is when extending built-in HTML tags. For example, Angular overrides `<a>`, `<form>`, and `<input>`. Such cases don't cause browser compatibility issues because these tags already have browser support.

Expressions

Given that a directive can (and usually should) be invoked as an attribute, we're inclined to ask about the value passed to that attribute:

---

[26]http://jsbin.com/IJAzUJE/1/edit

```
<h1 ng-init="greeting = 'Hello World'">
  The greeting is: {{ greeting }}
</h1>
```

Live Example[27]

Notice that we've passed the *expression* greeting = 'Hello World' to the built-in directive ng-init. Inside the expression, we've set a property named greeting to the value Hello World. Then we're evaluating the expression greeting inside brackets: {{ greeting }}.

In both cases, we're evaluating a normal JavaScript expression on the current *scope*. Depending upon where the expression is placed, it can be the $rootScope, instantiated when Angular *invokes* ng-app during application boot or a child object such as a controller.

Declaring Our Directive with an Expression

Given that we now know that we can declare a directive with or without an expression, let's revisit the valid ways of declaring an expression:

```
<my-directive="someExpression">
</my-directive>
<div my-directive="someExpression">
</div>
<div class="my-directive:someExpression">
</div>
<!-- directive: my-directive someExpression -->
```

A reasonable question at this point is within which environment the expression given to a directive runs. We'll find our answer by familiarizing ourselves a bit with the elusive, but extremely important, concept of *current scope*, provided by the controller hierarchy of the surrounding DOM.

Current Scope Introduction

Let's quickly familiarize ourselves with scope as provided by the DOM via the built-in directive ng-controller. This directive exists for the purpose of creating a new child scope in the DOM:

---

[27]http://jsbin.com/IdUYexO/2/edit

```
<p>We can access: {{ rootProperty }}</p>
<div ng-controller="ParentController">
  <p>We can access: {{ rootProperty }}
  and {{ parentProperty }}</p>
  <div ng-controller="ChildController">
    <p>
      We can access:
      {{ rootProperty }} and
      {{ parentProperty }} and
      {{ childProperty }}
    </p>
    <p>{{ fullSentenceFromChild }}</p>
  </div>
</div>
```

```
angular.module('myApp', [])
.run(function($rootScope) {
  // use .run to access $rootScope
  $rootScope.rootProperty = 'root scope';
})
.controller('ParentController', function($scope) {
  // use .controller to access properties inside `ng-controller`
  // in the DOM omit $scope, it is inferred based on the current controller
  $scope.parentProperty = 'parent scope';
})
.controller('ChildController', function($scope) {
  $scope.childProperty = 'child scope';
  // just like in the DOM, we can access any of the properties in the
  // prototype chain directly from the current $scope
  $scope.fullSentenceFromChild
    = 'Same $scope: We can access: ' +
    $scope.rootProperty + ' and ' +
    $scope.parentProperty + ' and ' +
    $scope.childProperty
});
```

Live example, with colored scopes for learning purposes[28]

More detailed information on ng-controller itself is available in the ng-controller section of the built in directives chapter.

---

[28]http://jsbin.com/URuyoG/1/edit

Be aware that there are other built-in directives, like ng-include and ng-view, that also create a new child scope, meaning they behave similar to `ng-controller` when invoked. We can even create a new child scope when building a custom directive of our own.

Passing Data into a Directive

Let's recall our directive definition:

```
angular.module('myApp', [])
.directive('myDirective', function() {
  return {
    restrict: 'A',
    replace: true,
    template: '<a href="http://google.com">Click me to go to Google</a>'
  }
})
```

Notice that in our template we are hard coding the URL and the text of our link:

```
template: '<a href="http://google.com">
  Click me to go to Google
</a>'
```

With Angular, we aren't limited to hard coding strings in the template of our directive.

We can provide a nicer experience for others using our directive if we specify the URL and link text without messing with the internal guts of the directive. Our goal here is to pay attention to the public interface of our directive, just as we would in any programming language. In essence, we'd like to turn the above template string into one that takes two variables: one for the URL and one for the link's text:

```
template: '<a
  href="{{myUrl}}">{{myLinkText}}</a>'
```

Looking at our main HTML document, we can declare our directive with attributes that will become the properties myUrl and mylinkText, set on the inner scope of our directive:

```
<div my-directive
    my-url="http://google.com"
    my-link-text="Click me to go to Google">
</div>
```

Reload the page and notice that the div where we declared our directive has been replaced by its template; however, the link's `href` is empty, and there's no text inside the brackets.

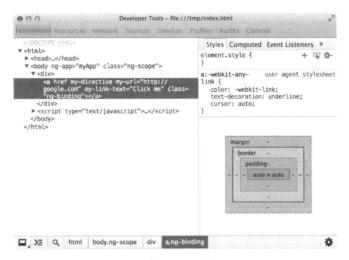

Updating template

To set properties on the inner scope of our directive, we have a few options. The simplest option is to simply use the existing scope currently provided by the controller (`ng-controller`) inside of which we're nested.

While simple, however, sharing state leaves us vulnerable. If that controller is removed or if a property with the name `myUrl` is later defined on its scope, we'll be forced to change our code, which is costly and frustrating.

To overcome this common issue, Angular provides the ability to create a new child scope or create an *isolate scope*.

> In contrast to inherited scope (child scope), discussed earlier (in current scope introduction), an **isolate scope** is **completely** separate from the current scope of the DOM. In order to set properties on this fresh object, we'll need explicitly pass in data via attributes, similar to the way we pass arguments into a method in JavaScript or Ruby.

When we set the `scope` of our directive to a clean object with its own properties,

```
scope: {
  someProperty: "needs to be set"
}
```

We're creating what is referred to as an *isolate scope*. Essentially, that means the directive gets its own $scope object, which we can only use inside other methods of the directive or inside the directive's template string:

```
template: '<div>\
  we have access to {{ someProperty }}\
  </div>',
controller: function($scope) {
  // a directive can have its own controller,
  // in which case we can do
  //=> ERROR!!!
  $scope.someProperty === "needs to be set"
}
```

ERROR?

Up until now we've omitted one minor detail. Inside the scope object, we can't actually set someProperty like we've done above.

```
scope: {
  // this won't work
  someProperty: "needs to be set"
}
```

Instead, the value is set in the DOM, via an attribute, which we mentioned acts similarly to how passing an argument to a function works:

```
<div my-directive
  some-property="someProperty with @ binding">
</div>
```

Now, inside of our fresh scope object, we set the value of someProperty to the binding strategy, @. This binding strategy tells Angular to copy the value provided by the attribute some-property in the DOM to the value of someProperty on our fresh scope object:

```
scope: {
  someProperty: '@'
}
```

Note that, by default, someProperty maps to the DOM attribute some-property. If we wanted to explicitly specify the name of the attribute we wanted to bind to, we could do so:

```
scope: {
  someProperty: '@someAttr'
}
```

In this case, the HTML attribute would be named some-attr instead of some-property:

```
<div my-directive
    some-attr="someProperty with @ binding">
</div>
```

Now, when we try to access someProperty inside our directive, for example in the directive's template or controller (as we did above), we'll receive the value copied from the DOM attribute:

```
template: '<div>\
  we have access to {{ someProperty }}\
  </div>',
controller: function($scope) {
  // a directive can have its own controller,
  // in which case we can fetch the
  // $scope.someProperty to be
  // "someProperty with @ binding"
}
```

Back to our main example: to copy data from the DOM into the isolate scope of our directive, we use attributes:

```
<div my-directive
    my-url="http://google.com"
    my-link-text="Click me to go to Google"></div>
```

```
angular.module('myApp', [])
.directive('myDirective', function() {
  return {
    restrict: 'A',
    replace: true,
    scope: {
      myUrl: '@',        // binding strategy
      myLinkText: '@' // binding strategy
    },
    template: '<a href="{{myUrl}}">' +
      '{{myLinkText}}</a>'
  }
})
```

 Live Example[29]

The default convention (used above) is for the attribute name and the property name to be the same (except that the property name is camel-cased).

As the name of the property on our scope is oftentimes private, it is possible (although unusual) to specify the name of the attribute we want to link our internal property to:

```
scope: {
  myUrl: '@someAttr',
  myLinkText: '@'
}
```

The above isolate scope code says:

Set the value of our directive's private $scope.myUrl property to the value provided by the attribute some-attr. That value may be hard coded or it may be the result of evaluating an {{ expression }} within the current scope, e.g., some-attr="{{ expression }}"

In our HTML, we would use some-attr instead of my-url:

---

[29]http://jsbin.com/eloKoDI/1/edit

```
<div my-directive
    some-attr="http://google.com"
    my-link-text="Click me to go to Google">
</div>
```

Furthermore, we could evaluate an expression within the scope of the DOM and pass the result to our directive, where it would eventually be set as the value of our bound property:

```
<div my-directive
  some-attr="{{ 'http://' + 'google.com' }}">
</div>
```

Taking this example one step further, let's see what happens if we create a text field and bind the input value to a property on the $scope of our isolate directive:

 Note the use of the built-in directive ng-model on the input tag. Using the ng-model directive binds the input text to the myUrl attribute on the $scope object.

```
<input type="text" ng-model="myUrl" />
<div my-directive
    some-attr="{{ myUrl }}"
    my-link-text="Click me to go to Google">
    </div>
```

This code just works; however, but if we move our text field *inside* the scope of our directive and try to make a binding in the other direction, it doesn't work:

```
<div my-directive some-attr="{{ myUrl }}"
 my-link-text="Click me to go to Google">
 </div>
```

And here:

```
template: '<div>\
  <input type="text" ng-model="myUrl" />\
  <a href="{{myUrl}}">{{myLinkText}}</a>\
  </div>'
```

Observing the `href` within the Chrome developer tools suggests that we're not binding our internal `$scope` property `myUrl` to the external attribute `some-attr` in the opposite direction. The value was copied onto our isolate scope via an attribute value, so shouldn't it also **set** that same attribute's value?

Chrome Developer tool

This behavior occurs because the built-in directive, `ng-model`, is set up with a two-way binding between its **own** isolate scope and the scope of the DOM (provided by a controller).

Let's imitate that setup in an attempt to make our example work. Our goal is to understand two-way bindings and the behavior of `ng-model` in the process.

Two-way bindings are perhaps the most important feature in Angular that we can't get with, say, jQuery out of the box. To understand the magic, however, we need to implement it ourselves. Luckily, we're only a few keystrokes away. Let's finish our example by creating a two-way data binding between our isolate `$scope` and the isolate `$scope` inside `ng-model`. We do that by binding our internal `$scope.myUrl` property with a property named `theirUrl` on the `$scope` of the current controller (or `$rootScope`) using scope lookup in the DOM.

In the process, let's also add an additional text field so that each side of the binding has its own text field. Having two fields will make it easy to see how scope is being linked via prototypal inheritance in the DOM:

```
<label>Their URL field:</label>
<input type="text" ng-model="theirUrl">
<div my-directive
    some-attr="theirUrl"
    my-link-text="Click me to go to Google"></div>
```

```
angular.module('myApp', [])
.directive('myDirective', function() {
  return {
    restrict: 'A',
    replace: true,
    scope: {
      myUrl: '=someAttr', // MODIFIED
      myLinkText: '@'
    },
    template: '\
    <div>\
      <label>My Url Field:</label>\
      <input type="text"\
        ng-model="myUrl" />\
      <a href="{{myUrl}}">{{myLinkText}}</a>\
    </div>\
    '

  }
})
```

Live Example[30]

In the Chrome developer tools, inspect the value of the href while typing into either text field. Awesome:

Chrome Developer tool

The only change we really made besides adding our original text field back to the main HTML document is the use of the = binding strategy instead of @. (See binding strategies explained).

In summary, this example explains the magic of one of the fundamental selling points of Angular, two-way data binding.

When working with built-in directives, it's useful to know what's going on so you can take into account their behavior when connecting them with your own directives.

In the next chapter, we'll take a closer look at more of the built-in directives that Angular provides so that we're familiar with how to use them and why they exist.

Once we've been introduced to those built-in directives, we'll be ready to dive into all the advanced options available when building a directive in directives explained.

---

[30]http://jsbin.com/IteNita/1/edit

Finally, we'll build our own advanced directive and then learn how to think about architecture in our application, a subject where custom and built-in directives play important roles.

Built-In Directives

Angular provides a suite of built-in directives. Some directives override built-in HTML elements, such the the `<form>` and `<a>` tags. When we use tags in our HTML, it may not be immediately obvious that we are, in fact, using a directive.

For example, the `<form>` tag is augmented with a great deal of functionality under the hood, such as validation behavior that we normally don't get with a standard HTML form.

Other built-in directives are clearly visible via their `ng-` namespace prefix. For example, `ng-href`, which we'll cover below, prevents a link from becoming active until the expression provided to `ng-href="someExpression"` has been evaluated and returns a value.

Lastly, some built-in directives do not have an HTML counterpart, such as the `ng-controller` directive, which can be used as an attribute on any tag, but is most often found on an element that has many children that should share the same scope.

Note that all directives prefixed with the `ng` namespace are part of the built-in library of directives that ship with Angular. For this reason, never prefix directives you make with this namespace.

Basic ng Attribute Directives

Our first set of directives has similarly named standard HTML tags and is easy to remember because we simply add the `ng` prefix to each:

- `ng-href`
- `ng-src`
- `ng-disabled`
- `ng-checked`
- `ng-readonly`
- `ng-selected`
- `ng-class`
- `ng-style`

Boolean Attributes

The following Angular directives help make working with HTML boolean attributes easier.

As defined by the HTML specification[31], a boolean attribute is an attribute that represents a true/false value. When the attribute is present, then the attribute's value is assumed to be true (regardless of its actual value). If absent, the attribute is assumed to be false.

When working with dynamic data via data bindings in Angular, we cannot simply set the value of the attribute to true or false, because by definition of the spec, the attribute is false if it *is not present*. Thus Angular provides an ng-prefixed version of these attributes that will evaluate the expression provided to insert or remove the corresponding boolean attribute on the decorated element.

ng-disabled

Use ng-disabled to bind the disabled attribute to form input fields:

- <input> (text, checkbox, radio, number, url, email, submit)
- <textarea>
- <select>
- <button>

When writing normal HTML input fields, the presence of the disabled attribute on an input field makes the field disabled. To bind the presence (or not) of this attribute, use ng-disabled.

For example, let's disable the following button until the user enters text into the text field:

```
<input type="text" ng-model="someProperty" placeholder="Type to Enable">
<button ng-model="button" ng-disabled="!someProperty">A Button</button>
```

In the next example, we'll disable the text field for five seconds until the isDisabled property becomes true inside the $timeout:

```
<textarea ng-disabled="isDisabled">Wait 5 seconds</textarea>
```

```
angular.module('myApp', [])
.run(function($rootScope, $timeout) {
  $rootScope.isDisabled = true;
  $timeout(function() {
    $rootScope.isDisabled = false;
  }, 5000);
});
```

Both Live Examples[32]

---

[31]http://www.w3.org/html/wg/drafts/html/master/infrastructure.html#boolean-attribute

[32]http://jsbin.com/iHiYltu/1/edit

ng-readonly

Similar to the other boolean attributes, the HTML spec only looks at the presence of the attribute `readonly`, not its value.

To allow Angular to bind to an expression that returns a truthy or falsy value and, in turn, output (or not) the `readonly` attribute, use `ng-readonly`:

```
Type here to make sibling readonly:
<input type="text" ng-model="someProperty"><br/>
<input type="text"
  ng-readonly="someProperty"
  value="Some text here"/>
```

Live Example[33]

ng-checked

The standard `checked` HTML attribute is a boolean attribute, and as such, is not required to take a value. In order for Angular to bind the presence of the `checked` attribute to the value of an expression, use `ng-checked`.

In the following example, we set the value of `someProperty` to `true` using the `ng-init` directive. Binding the value of `someProperty` to `ng-checked` then tells Angular to output the standard HTML `checked` attribute, which will check the box by default.

```
<label>someProperty = {{someProperty}}</label>
<input type="checkbox"
       ng-checked="someProperty"
       ng-init="someProperty = true"
       ng-model="someProperty">
```

In this example, we do the opposite:

```
<label>anotherProperty = {{anotherProperty}}</label>
<input type="checkbox"
       ng-checked="anotherProperty"
       ng-init="anotherProperty = false"
       ng-model="anotherProperty">
```

Note that we also used `ng-model` to bind the value of `someProperty` and `anotherProperty` inside their respective label tags, for the sake of demonstration.

Live Example[34]

---

[33]http://jsbin.com/etIviKI/1/edit
[34]http://jsbin.com/IXOLIRA/1/edit

ng-selected

Use ng-selected to bind the presence (or not) of the selected attribute to the option tag:

```
<label>Select Two Fish:</label>
<input type="checkbox"
       ng-model="isTwoFish"><br/>
<select>
  <option>One Fish</option>
  <option ng-selected="isTwoFish">Two Fish</option>
</select>
```

Live Example[35]

Boolean-like Attributes

While not technically HTML, boolean attributes like the ng-href and ng-src act in a similar manner and are therefore defined alongside the ng boolean attributes within the Angular source code and presented here.

Both ng-href and ng-src are so likely to help improve refactoring and prevent errors when changing code later in a project that it is recommended to use them in place of href and src, respectively.

ng-href

When dynamically creating a URL from a property on the current scope, always use ng-href instead of href.

The issue here is that the user is able to click a link built with href before interpolation takes place, which would bring them to the wrong page (often a 404).

On the other hand, by using ng-href, Angular waits for the interpolation to take place (in our example, after two seconds), and then activates the link's behavior:

```
<!-- Always use ng-href when href includes an {{ expression }} -->
<a ng-href="{{myHref}}">I'm feeling lucky, when I load</a>

<!-- href may not load before user clicks -->
<a href="{{myHref}}">I'm feeling 404</a>
```

Delay the interpolation of the string value for two seconds to see this behavior in action:

---

[35]http://jsbin.com/oQazOQE/2/edit

```
angular.module('myApp', [])
.run(function($rootScope, $timeout) {
  $timeout(function() {
    $rootScope.myHref = 'http://google.com';
  }, 2000);
});
```

Live Example[36]

ng-src

Angular will tell the browser to NOT fetch the image via the given URL until all expressions provided to ng-src have been interpolated:

```
<h1>Wrong Way</h1>
<img src="{{imgSrc}}" />

<h1>Right way</h1>
<img ng-src="{{imgSrc}}" />
```

```
angular.module('myApp', [])
.run(function($rootScope, $timeout) {
  $timeout(function() {
    $rootScope.imgSrc = 'https://www.google.com/images/srpr/logo11w.png';
  }, 2000);
});
```

Live Example[37]

When viewing the live example, check out the network panel within the Chrome developer tools. Notice that one request is red, indicating that there was an error. This error occurs when we use src instead of ng-src under 'Wrong Way'.

Directives with Child Scope

The following directives create a child scope that prototypically inherits from its parent. This inheritance provides a layer of separation meant for storing methods and model objects that work together to achieve a common goal.

---

[36]http://jsbin.com/IgInopi/1/edit

[37]http://jsbin.com/eguclqU/1/edit

ng-app and ng-controller are special directives, in that they modify the scope of directives nested inside of them.

ng-app creates the $rootScope of an Angular application, while ng-controller creates a child scope that prototypically inherits from either $rootScope or another ng-controller's $scope.

ng-app

Placing ng-app on any DOM element marks that element as the beginning of the $rootScope.

$rootScope is the beginning of the scope chain, and all directives nested under the ng-app in your HTML inherit from it.

In your JavaScript code you can access the $rootScope via the run method:

```
<html ng-app="myApp">
  <body>
    {{ someProperty }}
    <button ng-click="someAction()"></button>
  </body>
</html>
```

```
angular.module('myApp', [])
.run(function($rootScope) {
  $rootScope.someProperty = 'hello computer';
  $rootScope.someAction = function() {
    $rootScope.someProperty = 'hello human';
  };
});
```

Live Example[38]

While useful for the purpose of demonstration, using $rootScope on a regular basis is like using global scope – don't do it.

We can only use ng-app once per document. If we want to place multiple apps in a page, we'll need to manually bootstrap our applications. We will talk more about manually bootstrapping apps in the under the hood chapter.

ng-controller

Instead of defining *actions* and *models* on $rootScope, use ng-controller, which is a built-in directive whose purpose is to provide a child scopes for the directives that are nested inside. We'll use this directive to place a controller on a DOM element.

ng-controller takes a single argument:

---

[38]http://jsbin.com/ICOzeFI/2/edit

expression (required expression)

The expression is an Angular expression

A child $scope is simply a JavaScript object that prototypically inherits methods and properties from its parent $scope(s), including the application's $rootScope.

Directives that are nested within an ng-controller have access to this new child $scope, but be mindful that the scoping rules for each directive do apply.

Recall that the $scope object within a controller should be responsible for the *actions* and *models* shared by directives in the DOM.

An action refers to a traditional JavaScript method on the $scope object.

A model refers to a traditional JavaScript object {} where transient state should be stored. Persistent state should be bound to a service, which is then responsible for dealing with persisting that model.

It's important to **not** to set a **value** object (string, boolean, or number) directly on the $scope of a controller for a number of technological and architectural reasons. Data in the DOM should **always** use a . (dot). Following this rule will keep you out of unexpected trouble.

Controllers should be as simple as possible. Although we can use the controller to prototype our functionality, it's a good idea to refactor the logic out using services and directives. See application architecture for more information.

Using a controller, we can modify our previous example by placing our data and action on a child scope:

```
<div ng-controller="SomeController">
  {{ someModel.someProperty }}
  <button ng-click="someAction()">Communicate</button>
</div>
```

```
angular.module('myApp', [])
.controller('SomeController', function($scope) {
  // create a model
  $scope.someModel = {
    // with a property
    someProperty: 'hello computer'
  }
  // set actions on $scope itself
  $scope.someAction = function() {
    $scope.someModel.someProperty = 'hello human';
  };
});
```

Live Example[39]

In this iteration of our example, notice two differences from the previous:

First, we're using a child scope of $rootScope, which provides a clean object with which we can work. Using this scope means that actions and models used on the scope will not be available everywhere in the app; they'll only be available to directives within this scope or child scopes.

Secondly, notice that we're explicit about our data model, which, as we mentioned, is extremely important. To see why it is important, let's look at another iteration of this example that nests a second controller inside of our existing controller and doesn't set properties on a model object:

```
<div ng-controller="SomeController">
  {{ someBareValue }}
  <button ng-click="someAction()">Communicate to child</button>
  <div ng-controller="ChildController">
    {{ someBareValue }}
    <button ng-click="childAction()">Communicate to parent</button>
  </div>
</div>
```

---

[39]http://jsbin.com/OYikipe/1/edit

```
angular.module('myApp', [])
.controller('SomeController', function($scope) {
  // anti-pattern, bare value
  $scope.someBareValue = 'hello computer';
  // set actions on $scope itself, this is okay
  $scope.someAction = function() {
    // sets {{ someBareValue }} inside SomeController and ChildController
    $scope.someBareValue = 'hello human, from parent';
  };
})
.controller('ChildController', function($scope) {
  $scope.childAction = function() {
    // sets {{ someBareValue }} inside ChildController
    $scope.someBareValue = 'hello human, from child';
  };
});
```

Live Example[40]

Because of the way prototypal inheritance works with value objects in JavaScript, changing someBareValue via an action in the parent *does* change it in the child, but not vice versa.

To see this problem in action, try clicking on the child button **first** and then the parent button. Doing so makes it clear that the child controller has *copy*, not a *reference* to someBareValue.

 JavaScript objects are either copy by value or copy by reference. String, Number, and Boolean are copy by value. Array, Object, and Function are copy by reference.

Had we set our string as a property on a model object, it would have been shared via reference, which means changing the property on the child will change it on the parent. The following example shows the correct way:

```
<div ng-controller="SomeController">
  {{ someModel.someValue }}
  <button ng-click="someAction()">Communicate to child</button>
  <div ng-controller="ChildController">
    {{ someModel.someValue }}
    <button ng-click="childAction()">Communicate to parent</button>
  </div>
</div>
```

---

[40]http://jsbin.com/UbIRIHa/1/

```
angular.module('myApp', [])
.controller('SomeController', function($scope) {
  // best practice, always use a model
  $scope.someModel = {
    someValue: 'hello computer'
  }
  $scope.someAction = function() {
    $scope.someModel.someValue = 'hello human, from parent';
  };
})
.controller('ChildController', function($scope) {
  $scope.childAction = function() {
    $scope.someModel.someValue = 'hello human, from child';
  };
});
```

Live Example[41]

Try clicking on either button. The value always remains in sync.

Note that while this behavior manifests itself most noticeably when using ng-controller, it will also rear its ugly head when using any directive that creates a new child scope by setting the scope property inside its directive definition to true. The following built-in directives do exactly that:

- ng-include
- ng-switch
- ng-repeat
- ng-view
- ng-controller
- ng-if

ng-include

Use ng-include to fetch, compile, and include an external HTML fragment into your current application. The URL of the template is restricted to the same domain and protocol as the application document unless whitelisted or wrapped as trusted values. Furthermore, you'll need to account for Cross-Origin Resource Sharing and Same Origin Policy to ensure your template loads on all browsers. For example, it won't work for cross-domain requests on all browsers and for file:// access on some browsers.

 While developing, you may run Chrome from the command line with chrome --allow-file-access-from-files to disable the CORS error. Only go this route in an emergency (e.g., your boss is standing behind you and everything just broke).

---

[41]http://jsbin.com/aflyeda/1/edit

Use the `onload` attribute within the same element to run an expression when the template is loaded.

Keep in mind that when using `ng-include`, Angular automatically creates a new child scope. If you want to use a particular scope, for instance the scope of `ControllerA`, you must invoke the `ng-controller="ControllerA"` directive on the same DOM element itself; it will not be inherited from the surrounding scope like usual because a new scope is created when the template loads.

Let's look at an example:

```
<div ng-include="/myTemplateName.html"
     ng-controller="MyController"
     ng-init="name = 'World'">
  Hello {{ name }}
</div>
```

ng-switch

We use this directive in conjunction with `ng-switch-when` and `on="propertyName"` to switch which directives render in our view when the given `propertyName` changes. In the following example, when `person.name` is 'Ari' the div below the text field will be shown and the person will have won:

```
<input type="text" ng-model="person.name" />
<div ng-switch on="person.name"></div>
<p ng-switch-default>And the winner is</p>
<h1 ng-switch-when="Ari">{{ person.name }}</h1>
```

Note that we used `ng-switch-default` to output the name of the person until the switch occured.

Live Example[42]

ng-view

The `ng-view` directive sets the view location in the HTML where the router will manage and place the view elements for different routes. We will cover this in depth in the routing chapter.

See the routing chapter for more information.

ng-if

Use `ng-if` to completely remove or recreate an element in the DOM based on an expression. If the expression assigned to `ng-if` evaluates to a false value, then the element is removed from the DOM, otherwise a *clone* of the element is reinserted into the DOM.

---

[42]http://jsbin.com/AVihUdi/2/

ng-if differs from ng-show and ng-hide in that it actually removes and recreates DOM nodes, rather than just showing and hiding them via CSS.

When an element is removed from the DOM using ng-if, its associated scope is destroyed. Furthermore, when it comes back into being, a new scope is created and inherits from its parent scope using prototypal inheritance.

It's also important be aware that ngIf recreates elements using their compiled state. If code inside of ng-if is loaded, is manipulated using jQuery (for example, using .addClass), then is removed because the expression inside the ng-if becomes false, then when the expression later becomes true again, the DOM element and its children will be reinserted into the DOM in their original state, not the state they had when they left the DOM. That means that whatever class was added using jQuery's .addClass will no longer be present.

```
<div ng-if="2 + 2 === 5">
  Won't see this DOM node, not even in the source code
</div>

<div ng-if="2 + 2 === 4">
  Hi, I do exist
</div>
```

Live Example[43]

ng-repeat

Use ng-repeat to iterate over a collection and instantiate a new template for each item in the collection. Each item in the collection is given its own template and therefore its own scope. Furthermore, there are a number of special properties exposed on the local scope of each template instance:

- $index: iterator offset of the repeated element (0..length-1)
- $first: true if the repeated element is first in the iterator
- $middle: true if the repeated element is between the first and last in the iterator
- $last: true if the repeated element is last in the iterator
- $even: true if the iterator position $index is even (otherwise false)
- $odd: true if the iterator position $index is odd (otherwise false)

We'll use $odd and $even in the following example to make a repeating list where even items are red and odd item are blue. Remember that in JavaScript arrays are indexed starting at 0; thus, we use !$even and !$odd to flip the boolean value given by $even and $odd.

---

[43]http://jsbin.com/ezEcamo/1/

```
<ul ng-controller="PeopleController">
  <li ng-repeat="person in people" ng-class="{even: !$even, odd: !$odd}">
    {{person.name}} lives in {{person.city}}
  </li>
</ul>
```

```
.odd {
  background-color: blue;
}
.even {
  background-color: red;
}
```

```
angular.module('myApp', [])
.controller('PeopleController', function($scope) {
  $scope.people = [
    {name: "Ari", city: "San Francisco"},
    {name: "Erik", city: "Seattle"}
  ];
})
```

Live Example[44]

ng-init

Use ng-init to set up state inside the scope of a directive when that directive is invoked.

The most common use case for using ng-init is when creating small examples for educational purposes, like the examples in this chapter.

For anything substantial, create a controller and set up state within a model object.

```
<div ng-init="greeting='Hello'; person='World'">
  {{greeting}} {{person}}
</div>
```

Live Example[45]

{{ }}

---

[44]http://jsbin.com/akuYUkey/1/edit
[45]http://jsbin.com/OZENuhO/1/

```
<div>{{ name }}</div>
```

The {{ }} syntax is a templating syntax that's built into Angular. It creates a binding from the containing $scope to the view. Any time that the $scope changes, the view will update automatically on account of this binding.

Although it doesn't look like a normal directive, it is, in fact, a shortcut for using ng-bind without needing to create an element; therefore, it is most commonly used with inline text.

Be aware that using {{ }} within the visible viewport of the screen while the page loads may cause a flash of unrendered content. To prevent this issue, use ng-bind instead.

```
<body ng-init="greeting = 'Hello World'">
  {{ greeting }}
</body>
```

Live Example[46]

ng-bind

Although we can use the {{ }} template syntax within our views (Angular interpolates these), we can mimic this behavior with the ng-bind directive.

```
<body ng-init="greeting = 'Hello World'">
  <p ng-bind="greeting"></p>
</body>
```

Live Example[47]

When we use the {{ }} syntax, our HTML document loads the element and does not render it immediately, causing a "flash of unrendered content" (FOUC, for short). We can prevent this FOUC from being exposed by using ng-bind and binding our content to the element. The content will then render as the child text node of the element on which ng-bind is declared.

ng-cloak

An alternative to using to using ng-bind to prevent a flash of unrendered content is to use ng-cloak on the element containing {{ }}:

---

[46]http://jsbin.com/ODUxeho/1/edit

[47]http://jsbin.com/esihUJ/1/edit

```
<body ng-init="greeting = 'Hello World'">
  <p ng-cloak>{{ greeting }}</p>
</body>
```

Live Example[48]

ng-bind-template

Similar to the ng-bind directive, we can use the ng-bind-template directive if we want to *bind* multiple expressions to the view.

```
<div
ng-bind-template="{{ message }} {{ name }}">
</div>
```

ng-model

The ng-model directive binds an input, select, textarea, or custom form control to a property on the surrounding scope. It handles and provides validation, sets related CSS classes on the element (ng-valid, ng-invalid, etc.), and registers the control with its parent form.

It binds to the property given by evaluating the expression on the current scope. If the property doesn't already exist on this scope, it will be created implicitly and added to the scope.

We should always use ngModel with a model property on the $scope, not as a raw property on the scope itself. Setting ng-model as a property of the scope will help us avoid overloading properties on the same scope or the inherited scope.

For example:

```
<input type="text"
  ng-model="modelName.someProperty" />
```

The code above is the correct way to think about and practically use ngModel properly.

The bottom line is to always have a . in your ng-models. For in-depth discussion and an example on this topic, see the ng-controller section earlier in this chapter.

---

[48]http://jsbin.com/AJEboLO/1/edit

ng-show/ng-hide

ng-show and ng-hide show or hide the given HTML element based on the expression provided to the attribute. When the expression provided to the ng-show attribute is false the element is hidden. Similarly, when the expression given to ng-hide is true, the element is hidden.

The element is shown or hidden by removing the ng-hide CSS class from, or adding it to, the element. The .ng-hide CSS class is predefined in AngularJS and sets the display style to none (using an !important flag).

```
<div ng-show="2 + 2 == 5">
  2 + 2 isn't 5, don't show
</div>
<div ng-show="2 + 2 == 4">
  2 + 2 is 4, do show
</div>
<div ng-hide="2 + 2 == 5">
  2 + 2 isn't 5, don't hide
</div>
<div ng-hide="2 + 2 == 4">
  2 + 2 isn't 5, do hide
</div>
```

Live Example[49]

ng-change

This directive evaluates the given expression when the input changes. As we're dealing with input, we must use this directive in conjunction with ngModel.

```
<div ng-controller="EquationController">
  <input type="text"
    ng-model="equation.x"
    ng-change="change()" />
  <code>{{ equation.output }}</code>
</div>
```

---

[49]http://jsbin.com/ihOkagE/1/

```
angular.module('myApp', [])
.controller('EquationController', function($scope) {
  $scope.equation = {};
  $scope.change = function() {
    $scope.equation.output
      = Number($scope.equation.x) + 2;
  };
});
```

Live Example[50]

In the above example, we run the `change()` function whenever `equation.x` is changed by entering text into the text field.

ng-form

We use `ng-form` when we need to nest a form within another form. The normal HTML `<form>` tag doesn't allow us to nest our forms, but `ng-form` will.

That means that the outer form is valid when all of the child forms are valid, as well. This fact is especially useful when dynamically generating forms using `ng-repeat`.

Because we cannot dynamically generate the `name` attribute of input elements using interpolation, we need to wrap each set of repeated inputs in an `ng-form` directive and nest these in an outer form element.

The following CSS classes are set automatically, depending on the validity of the form:

- `ng-valid` when form is valid
- `ng-invalid` when form is invalid
- `ng-pristine` when form is pristine
- `ng-dirty` when form is dirty

Angular will not submit the form to the server unless the form has an `action` attribute specified.

To specify which JavaScript method should be called when a form is submitted, use one of the following two directives:

- `ng-submit` on the form element
- `ng-click` on the first button or input field of type submit (input[type=submit])

---

[50]http://jsbin.com/onUXuxO/1/edit

To prevent double execution of the handler, use only the ng-submit or ng-click directives.

In the following examples, we want to dynamically generate a form based on a JSON response from the server. We'll use ng-repeat to loop over the fields we get back from the server. Because we cannot dynamically generate the name attribute, and because we need the name attribute to perform validation, we'll loop over the fields and create a new form for each one.

Because Angular forms that use ng-form instead of form can be nested, and because the parent form is not valid until its child forms are valid, we can both dynamically generate a form with child forms and use validation. Yes, we can have our cake and eat it too.

Let's first view the JSON we're hard coding, as though it came from the server:

```
angular.module('myApp', [])
.controller('FormController', function($scope) {
  $scope.fields = [
    {placeholder: 'Username', isRequired: true},
    {placeholder: 'Password', isRequired: true},
    {placeholder: 'Email (optional)', isRequired: false}
  ];

  $scope.submitForm = function() {
    alert("it works!");
  };
});
```

Now, let's take a look at using that data to generate a dynamic form with validation:

```
<form name="signup_form"
  ng-controller="FormController"
  ng-submit="submitForm()" novalidate>
  <div ng-repeat="field in fields"
       ng-form="signup_form_input">
    <input type="text"
     name="dynamic_input"
     ng-required="field.isRequired"
     ng-model="field.name"
     placeholder="{{field.placeholder}}" />
    <div
      ng-show="signup_form_input.dynamic_input.$dirty &&
      signup_form_input.dynamic_input.$invalid">
      <span class="error"
        ng-show="signup_form_input.dynamic_input.$error.required">
          The field is required.
```

```
      </span>
    </div>
  </div>
  <button type="submit"
    ng-disabled="signup_form.$invalid">
      Submit All
  </button>
</form>
```

```
input.ng-invalid {
  border: 1px solid red;
}
```

```
input.ng-valid {
  border: 1px solid green;
}
```

Live Example[51]

ng-click

Use ng-click to specify a method or expression to run on the containing scope when the element is clicked.

```
<div ng-controller="CounterController">
  <button ng-click="count = count + 1"
          ng-init="count=0">
    Increment
  </button>
  count: {{count}}
  <button ng-click="decrement()">
    Decrement
  </button>
<div>
```

---

[51]http://jsbin.com/UduNeCA/1/edit

```
angular.module('myApp', [])
.controller('CounterController', function($scope) {
  $scope.decrement = function() {
    $scope.count = $scope.count - 1;
  };
})
```

Live Example[52]

ng-select

Use the ng-select directive to bind data to an HTML <select> element. This directive can be used in conjunction with ng-model and ng-options to provide sophisticated and highly performant dynamic forms.

ng-options takes a *comprehension expression* for its attribute value, which is just a fancy way of saying it can take an array or an object and loop over its contents to provide the options available when using the select tag. It comes in one of the following forms:

- for array data sources:
  - label for value in array
  - select as label for value in array
  - label group by group for value in array
  - select as label group by group for value in array track by trackexpr
- for object data sources:
  - label for (key, value) in object
  - select as label for (key, value) in object
  - label group by group for (key, value) in object
  - select as label group by group for (key, value) in object

Let's look at an example of using ng-select:

```
<div ng-controller="CityController">
  <select ng-model="city"
  ng-options="city.name for city in cities">
    <option value="">Choose City</option>
  </select>
  Best City: {{ city.name }}
</div>
```

---

[52]http://jsbin.com/uGipUBU/2/edit

```
angular.module('myApp', [])
.controller('CityController', function($scope) {
    $scope.cities = [
        {name: 'Seattle'},
        {name: 'San Francisco'},
        {name: 'Chicago'},
        {name: 'New York'},
        {name: 'Boston'}
    ];
});
```

Live Example[53]

ng-submit

We use ng-submit to bind an expression to an onsubmit event. This directive also prevents the default action (sending the request and reloading the page), but *only if the form does not contain an action attribute.*

```
<form ng-submit="submit()"
      ng-controller="FormController">
  Enter text and hit enter:
  <input type="text"
         ng-model="person.name"
         name="person.name" />
  <input type="submit"
         name="person.name"
         value="Submit" />
  <code>people={{people}}</code>
  <ul ng-repeat="(index, object) in people">
    <li>{{ object.name }}</li>
  </ul>
</form>
```

[53]http://jsbin.com/iQelOxi/1/edit

```
angular.module('myApp', [])
.controller('FormController', function($scope) {

  $scope.person = {
    name: null
  };

  $scope.people = [];

  $scope.submit = function() {
    if ($scope.person.name) {
      $scope.people.push({name: $scope.person.name});
      $scope.person.name = '';
    }
  };
});
```

Live Example[54]

ng-class

Use ng-class to dynamically set the class of an element by binding an expression that represents all classes to be added. Duplicate classes will not be added. When the expression changes, the previously added classes are removed and only then are the new classes added.

Let's use ng-class to add the class .red to a div whenever a random number drawn is above 5.

```
<div ng-controller="LotteryController">
  <div ng-class="{red: x > 5}"
      ng-if="x > 5">
    You won!
  </div>
  <button ng-click="x = generateNumber()"
      ng-init="x = 0">
    Draw Number
  </button>
  <p>Number is: {{ x }}</p>
</div>
```

---

[54]http://jsbin.com/ONIcAC/1/edit

```
.red {
  background-color: red;
}
```

```
angular.module('myApp', [])
.controller('LotteryController', function($scope) {
  $scope.generateNumber = function() {
    return Math.floor((Math.random()*10)+1);
  }
})
```

Check out the Live Example[55]

ng-attr-(suffix)

When Angular compiles the DOM, it looks for expressions within {{ some expression }} brackets. These expressions are automatically registered with the $watch service and update as part of the normal $digest cycle:

```
<-- updated when `someExpression` on the $scope
  is updated -->
<h1>Hello {{ someExpression }}</h1>
```

Sometimes, however, web browsers are picky about what attributes they allow. SVG is one such instance:

```
<svg>
  <circle cx="{{cx}}"></circle>
</svg>
```

Running the code above will throw an error, telling us we have an invalid attribute. To fix this problem, we can use ng-attr-cx. Notice that the cx is named after the attribute we would like to define. Within the string, we can write an expression with {{ }} and achieve the result we were looking for above.

---

[55]http://jsbin.com/IvEcUci/1/edit

```
<svg>
  <circle ng-attr-cx="{{cx}}"><circle>
</svg>
```

Directives Explained

The goal of this chapter is to explicitly lay out all of the options and capabilities that directives have to offer when building mature client-side applications.

Directive Definition

The simplest way to think about a directive is that it is simply a function that we run on a particular DOM element. The function is expected to provide extra functionality on the element.

For instance, the ng-click directive gives an element the ability to listen for the click event and run an Angular expression when it receives the event. Directives are what makes the Angular framework so powerful, and, as we've seen, we can also create them.

A directive is defined using the .directive() method, one of the many methods available on our application's Angular module.

```
angular.module('myApp')
.directive('myDirective',
function($timeout, UserDefinedService) {
  // directive definition goes here
})
```

The directive() method takes two arguments:

name (string)

The name of the directive as a string that we'll refer to inside of our views.

factory_function (function)

The factory function returns an object that defines how the directive behaves. It is expected to return an object providing options that tell the $compile service how the directive should behave when it is invoked in the DOM.

```
angular.application('myApp', [])
.directive('myDirective', function() {
  // A directive definition object
  return {
    // directive definition is defined via options
    // which we'll override here
  };
});
```

We can also return a function instead of an object to handle this directive definition, but it is best practice to return an object as we've done above. When a function is returned, it is often referred to as the postLink function, which allows us to define the link function for the directive. Returning a function instead of an object limits us to a narrow ability to customize our directive and, thus, is good for only simple directives.

When Angular bootstraps our app, it will register the returned object by the name provided as a string via the first argument. The Angular compiler parses the DOM of our main HTML document looking for elements, attributes, comments, or class names using that name when looking for these directives. When it finds one that it knows about, it uses the directive definition to place the DOM element on the page.

```
<div my-directive></div>
```

To avoid collision with future HTML standards it's best practice to prefix a custom directive with a custom namespace. Angular itself has chosen the ng- prefix, so use something other than that. In the examples that follow, we'll use the my- prefix (e.g., my-directive).

The factory function we define for a directive is only invoked *once*, when the compiler matches the directive the first time. Just like the .controller function, we invoke a directive's factory function using $injector.invoke.

When Angular encounters the named directive in the DOM, it will invoke the directive definition we've registered, using the name to look up the object we've registered. At this point, the directive lifecycle begins, starting with the $compile method and ending with the 'link method. We'll dive into the specifics of this process later in this chapter.

Let's look at all the available options we can provide to a directive definition.

A JavaScript object is made up of keys and values. When the value for a given key is set to a string, boolean, number, array, or object, we call the key a *property*. When we set the key to a function, we call it a *method*.

The possible options are shown below. The value of each key provides the signature of either the method or the type we can set the property to:

```
angular.module('myApp', [])
.directive('myDirective', function() {
  return {
    restrict: String,
    priority: Number,
    terminal: Boolean,
    template: String or Template Function:
      function(tElement, tAttrs) (...},
    templateUrl: String,
    replace: Boolean or String,
    scope: Boolean or Object,
    transclude: Boolean,
    controller: String or
      function(scope, element, attrs, transclude, otherInjectables) { ... },
    controllerAs: String,
    require: String,
    link: function(scope, iElement, iAttrs) { ... },
    compile: return an Object OR
      function(tElement, tAttrs, transclude) {
        return {
          pre: function(scope, iElement, iAttrs, controller) { ... },
          post: function(scope, iElement, iAttrs, controller) { ... }
        }
        // or
        return function postLink(...) { ... }
      }
  };
});
```

Restrict (string)

restrict is an optional argument. It is responsible for telling Angular in which format our directive will be declared in the DOM. By default, Angular expects that we will declare a custom directive as an attribute, meaning the restrict option is set to A.

The available options are as follows:

E (an element)

```
<my-directive></my-directive>
```

A (an attribute, default)

```
<div my-directive="expression"></div>
```

C (a class)

```
<div class="my-directive: expression;"></div>
```

M (a comment)

```
<-- directive: my-directive expression -->
```

These options can be used alone or in combination:

```
angular.module('myDirective', function() {
  return {
    restrict: 'EA' // either an element or an attribute
  };
});
```

In this case, we can declare the directive as an attribute or an element:

```
<-- as an attribute -->
<div my-directive></div>
<-- or as an element -->
<my-directive></my-directive>
```

Attributes are the default and most common form of directive because they will work across all browsers, including older versions of Internet Explorer, without having to register a new tag in the head of the document. See the chapter on Internet Explorer for more information on this topic.

Avoid using comments to declare a directive. This format was originally introduced as a way to create directives that span multiple elements. This approach was especially useful, for example, when using ng-repeat inside a <table> element; however, as of Angular 1.2, ng-repeat provides ng-repeat-start and ng-repeat-end as a better solution to this problem, minimizing the need for the comment form of a directive even more so. If you are curious, however, take a look at the Chrome developer tools elements tab when using ng-repeat to see comments being used under the hood.

Element or Attribute?

Use an element when creating something new on the page that will encapsulate a self-contained piece of functionality. For example, if we're creating a clock (and couldn't care less about supporting old versions of Internet Explorer) we'd make a clock directive and declare it in the DOM like so:

```
<my-clock></my-clock>
```

Doing so tells users of our directive that we're specifying a whole piece of our application. Our clock is not decorating or augmenting a pre-existing clock; instead, it's declaring a whole unit. While we could have used an attribute in this scenario (Angular doesn't care), we've chosen to use an element because it clarifies our intent.

Use an attribute when decorating an existing element with data or behavior. Using our clock example, let's pretend we're interested in an an analog version of the clock:

```
<my-clock clock-display="analog"></my-clock>
```

The choice usually comes down to whether the directive being defined provides the core behavior of a component on the page or will decorate or augment a core directive with optional behavior, state, or anything else one might find while programming in the wild (like analog output for a clock).

The guiding principle here is that the format of a directive tells a story about our applications and reveals the intent of each piece, creating exemplary code that is easy to understand and share with others.

The other distinction that is important to make for a given directive is whether it creates, inherits, or isolates itself from the scope of its containing environment. This child-parent relationship plays another key role in the composition and reusability of our directives, a topic we'll spend more time discussing when we talk about the scope of a directive.

Priority (number)

The priority option can be set to a number. Most directives omit this option, in which case it defaults to 0; however, there are cases where setting a high priority is important and/or necessary. For example, ngRepeat sets this option at 1000 so that it *always* gets invoked before other directives on the same element.

If an element is decorated with two directives that have the same priority, then the first directive declared on the element will be invoked first. If one of the directives has a higher priority than the other, then it doesn't matter which is declared first: The one with the higher priority will *always* run first.

 ngRepeat has the highest priority of any built-in directive. It is always invoked before other directives on the same element. Performance is a key factor here. We'll learn more about performance when we discuss the compile option.

Terminal (boolean)

terminal is a boolean option; it can be set to true or false.

We use the terminal option to tell Angular to stop invoking any further directives on an element that have a lower priority. All directives with the same priority will be executed, however.

As a result, don't further decorate an element if it's already been decorated with a directive that is terminal and has equal or higher priority – it won't be invoked.

An example of such terminal directives are ngView and ngIf. ngIf has a slightly higher priority than ngView. If the ngIf expression resolves to true, then the ngView will execute like normal. If the ngIf expression resolves to false, on the other hand, then ngView will not run as it has a lower priority.

Template (string|function)

template is optional. If provided, it must be set to either:

- a string of HTML
- a function that takes two arguments – tElement and tAttrs – and returns a string value representing the template. The t in tElement and tAttrs stands for template, as opposed to instance. We'll discuss the difference between a template element/attribute and an instance element/attribute when we cover the link and compile options.

Angular treats the template string no differently than any other HTML. It has a scope that can be accessed using double curly markup, like {{ expression }}.

When a template string contains more than one DOM element or only a single text node, it must be wrapped in a parent element. In other words, a root DOM element must exist:

```
template: '\
  <div> <-- single root element -->\
    <a href="http://google.com">Click me</a>\
    <h1>When using two elements, wrap them in a parent element</h1>\
  </div>\
'
```

Furthermore, note the use of backslashes, at the end of each line. We include these so that Angular can parse multi-line strings correctly. In production code, it would be a better choice to use the templateUrl option because multi-lines strings are a nightmare to look at and maintain.

One of the most important features to understand about a template string or templateURL is how it gets its scope. In the beginning_directives chapter, we touched upon how scope is passed into a directive.

templateUrl (string|function)

`templateUrl` is optional. If provided, it must be set to either:

- the path to an HTML file, as a string
- a function that takes two arguments: `tElement` and `tAttrs`. The function must return the path to an HTML file as a string.

In either case, the template URL is passed through the built-in security layer that Angular provides; specifically `$getTrustedResourceUrl`, which protects our templates from being fetched from untrustworthy resources.

By default, the HTML file will be requested on demand via Ajax when the directive is invoked. We should bear two important factors in mind:

- When developing locally, we should run a server in the background to serve up the local HTML templates from our file system. Failing to do so will raise a Cross Origin Request Script (CORS) error.
- Template loading is asynchronous, which means that compilation and linking are suspended until the template is loaded.

Having to wait for a large number of templates to asynchronously load via Ajax can really slow down a client-side application. To prevent such a delay, it's possible to cache one or more HTML templates prior to deploying an application. Caching is a better option in most cases because Angular will not make an Ajax request, thus providing better performance by minimizing the number of requests run. For more information about caching, check out the in-depth discussion on caching here.

After a template has been fetched, Angular caches it in the default `$templateCache` services. In production, we can pre-cache these templates into a JavaScript file that defines our templates so we don't have to fetch the templates over XHR. For more information about how this adjustment works, see the next steps chapter.

replace (boolean)

`replace` is optional. If provided, it must be set to `true`. It is set to `false` by default. That means that the directive's template will be appended as a child node within the element where the directive was invoked:

```
<div some-directive></div>
```

```
.directive('someDirective' function() {
  return {
    template: '<div>some stuff here<div>'
  }
})
```

The result when the directive is invoked will be (remember that this behavior is the default, when replace is false):

```
<div some-directive>
  <div>some stuff here<div>
</div>
```

If we set replace as true:

```
.directive('someDirective' function() {
  return {
    replace: true // MODIFIED
    template: '<div>some stuff here<div>'
  }
})
```

then the result when the directive is invoked will be:

```
<div>some stuff here<div>
```

Directive Scope

In order to fully understand the rest of the options available inside a directive definition object, we'll need to have an understanding of how scope works.

A special object, known as the $rootScope, is initially created when we declare the ng-app directive in the DOM:

```
<div ng-app="myApp"
    ng-init="someProperty = 'some data'"></div>
  <div ng-init="siblingProperty = 'more data'">
    Inside Div Two
  <div ng-init="aThirdProperty"></div>
</div>
```

In the code above, we set three properties on the root scope of our app: `someProperty`, `siblingProperty`, and `anotherSiblingProperty`.

From here on out, every directive invoked within our DOM will:

- directly use the same object,
- create a new object that inherits from the object, or
- create an object that is isolated from the object

The example above shows the first case. The second `div` is a sibling element that has `get` and `set` access to the `$rootScope`. Furthermore, inside this second `div` is another `div` that **also** has `get` and `set` access to the exact same root scope.

Just because a directive is nested within another directive does not necessarily mean its scope has been changed. By default, child directives are given access to the **exact same** scope as their parent DOM nodes. The reason for that can be understood by learning about the `scope` directive option, which is set to `false` by default.

Scope Option (boolean | object)

`scope` is optional. It can be set to `true` or to an object, `{}`. By default, it is set to `false`.

When `scope` is set to `true`, a new scope object is created that prototypically inherits from its parent scope.

If multiple directives on an element provide an isolate scope, only one new scope is applied. Root elements within the template of a directive always get a new scope; thus, for those objects, `scope` is set to `true` by default.

The built-in `ng-controller` directive exists for the sole purpose of creating a new child scope that prototypically inherits from the surrounding scope. It creates a new scope that inherits from the surrounding scope.

Let's amend our last example, with this knowledge in hand:

```
<div ng-app="myApp"
     ng-init="someProperty = 'some data'"></div>
<div ng-init="siblingProperty = 'more data'">
  Inside Div Two: {{ aThirdProperty }}
  <div ng-init="aThirdProperty = 'data for 3rd property'"
       ng-controller="SomeController">
    Inside Div Three: {{ aThirdProperty }}
    <div ng-init="aFourthProperty">
      Inside Div Four: {{ aThirdProperty }}
    </div>
  </div>
</div>
```

If we run the previous code by itself, it fails. This failure occurs because we haven't defined an associated controller in our JavaScript, so let's do that:

```
angular.module('myApp', [])
.controller('SomeController', function($scope) {
  // we can leave it empty, it just needs to be defined
})
```

If we reload the page, we can see that inside the second div, {{ aThirdProperty }} is undefined and therefore outputs nothing. Inside the third div, however, the value we set inside our inherited scope data for a 3rd property is shown.

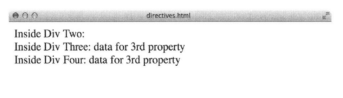

Directives

To further prove the point that this scope flows downwards during inheritance, and not upwards, let's make another child scope and check to see that {{ aThirdProperty }} inherits its value from its parent.

```
<div ng-app="myApp"
    ng-init="someProperty = 'some data'"></div>
<div ng-init="siblingProperty = 'more data'">
  Inside Div Two: {{ aThirdProperty }}
  <div ng-init="aThirdProperty = 'data for 3rd property'"
      ng-controller="SomeController">
    Inside Div Three: {{ aThirdProperty }}
    <div ng-controller="SecondController">
      Inside Div Four: {{ aThirdProperty }}
    </div>
  </div>
</div>
```

We'll need to update our JavaScript so that SecondController is defined:

```
angular.module('myApp', [])
.controller('SomeController', function($scope) {
  // we can leave it empty, it just needs to be defined
})
.controller('SecondController', function($scope) {
  // also can be empty
})
```

To create our own directive whose scope prototypically inherits from the outside world, set the scope property to true:

```
angular.module('myApp', [])
.directive('myDirective', function() {
  return {
    restrict: 'A',
    scope: true
  }
})
```

Now let's use our directive to alter the scope of the DOM:

```
<div ng-app="myApp"
     ng-init="someProperty = 'some data'"></div>
<div ng-init="siblingProperty = 'more data'">
  Inside Div Two: {{ aThirdProperty }}
  <div ng-init="aThirdProperty = 'data for 3rd property'"
       ng-controller="SomeController">
    Inside Div Three: {{ aThirdProperty }}
    <div ng-controller="SecondController">
      Inside Div Four: {{ aThirdProperty }}
      <br>
      Outside myDirective: {{ myProperty }}
      <div my-directive ng-init="myProperty = 'wow, this is cool'">
        Inside myDirective: {{ myProperty }}
      <div>
    </div>
  </div>
</div>
```

Live JS Bin[56]

Now that we understand how surrounding scope and inherited scope work, there remains only one piece to the scope puzzle: isolate scope.

Isolate Scope

Isolate scope is likely the most confusing of the three options available when setting the scope property, but also the most powerful. Isolate scope is based on the ideology present in Object Oriented Programming. Languages like Small Talk and design principles like SOLID have found their way into Angular via directives that use isolate scope.

The main use case for such directives is reusable widgets that can be shared and used in unexpected contexts without polluting the scope around them or having their internal scope corrupted inadvertently.

To create a directive with isolate scope we'll need to set the scope property of the directive to an empty object, {}. Once we've done that, no outer scope is available in the template of the directive:

---

[56]http://jsbin.com/ITEBAF/1/edit

```
<div ng-controller='MainController'>
  Outside myDirective: {{ myProperty }}
   <div my-directive ng-init="myProperty = 'wow, this is cool'">
     Inside myDirective: {{ myProperty }}
   <div>
</div>
```

```
angular.module('myApp', [])
.controller('MainController', function($scope) {})
.directive('myDirective', function() {
  return {
    restrict: 'A',
    scope: {},
    template: '<div>Inside myDirective {{ myProperty }}</div>'
  };
})
```

Live JS Bin[57]

A look at the JS Bin reveals that it seems almost identical to setting scope to true. We can see a difference by making another directive with inherited scope and comparing the two:

```
<div ng-init="myProperty = 'wow, this is cool'">
  Surrounding scope: {{ myProperty }}
   <div my-inherit-scope-directive></div>
   <div my-directive><div>
</div>
```

The JavaScript code:

```
angular.module('myApp', [])
.directive('myDirective', function() {
  return {
    restrict: 'A',
    template: 'Inside myDirective, isolate scope: {{ myProperty }}',
    scope: {}
  };
})
.directive('myInheritScopeDirective', function() {
  return {
```

---

[57]http://jsbin.com/eguDEpa/1/edit

```
    restrict: 'A',
    template: 'Inside myDirective, isolate scope: {{ myProperty }}',
    scope: true
  };
});
```

Live JS Bin[58]

With the most important scope-related concepts out of the way, we *can* **bind** properties on our isolated scope with the outside world, allowing us to *poke holes* through the isolate scopes.

Two-Way Data Binding

Perhaps the most powerful feature in Angular, two-way data binding allows us to bind the value of a property inside the private scope of our directive to the value of an attribute available within the DOM. In the previous chapter on directives we looked at a good example of how ng-model provides two-way data binding with the outside world and a custom directive we created; this example in many ways mirrored the behavior that ng-bind, itself, provides. Review that chapter and practice the example to gain a greater understanding of this important concept.

Transclude

transclude is optional. If provided, it must be set to true. It is set to false by default.

Transclusion is sometimes considered an advanced topic, but once it makes sense it'll fit right in with the rules we've just learned about scope. We'll also see that it's a very powerful addition to our tool set, especially when building customizable chunks of HTML that can be shared with a team, between projects, and with the rest of the Angular community.

Transclusion is most often used for creating reusable widgets. A great example is a modal box or a navbar.

Transclude allows us to pass in an entire template, including its scope, to a directive. Doing so gives us the opportunity to pass in arbitrary content and arbitrary scope to a directive. The transclude option makes it so that the **contents** of the directive have the scope of the outside directive, which gives the template access to the outside scope object.

In order for scope to be passed in, the scope option must be isolated, {}, or set to true. If the scope option is not set, then the scope available inside the directive will be applied to the template passed in.

 Only use transclude: true when you want to create a directive that wraps arbitrary content.

---

[58]http://jsbin.com/0xAlek/1/edit

Transclusion makes it easy to allow users of our directive to customize all these aspects at once by allowing them to provide their own HTML template that has its own state and behavior.

Let's walk through a small example where we provide a reusable directive that others can customize.

Let's create a resuable sidebar box, similar to the sidebars that are popular with WordPress blogs. We want to keep our boxes' styling consistent, but want to reduce the amount of HTML that we have to write for each one.

For instance, let's say we want to create a sidebar box that takes a title and some HTML content, like so:

```
<div sidebox title="Links">
  <ul>
    <li>First link</li>
    <li>Second link</li>
  </ul>
</div>
```

We can create the sidebox directive fairly simply by creating a directive with the transclude option set to true:

```
angular.module('myApp', [])
.directive('sidebox', function() {
  return {
    restrict: 'EA',
    scope: {
      title: '@'
    },
    transclude: true,
    template: '<div class="sidebox">\
      <div class="content">\
        <h2 class="header">{{ title }}</h2>\
        <span class="content" ng-transclude>\
        </span>\
      </div>\
    </div>'
  }
});
```

This code tells the Angular compiler that where it finds the ng-transclude directive is where it should place the content that it has captured from inside the DOM element.

We can reuse this directive with the transclusion to provide a secondary element without needing to worry about the styles and the layout.

For instance, this code will yield us two boxes with consistent styles:

```
<div sidebox title="Links">
  <ul>
    <li>First link</li>
    <li>Second link</li>
  </ul>
</div>
<div sidebox title="TagCloud">
  <div class="tagcloud">
    <a href="">Graphics</a>
    <a href="">AngularJS</a>
    <a href="">D3</a>
    <a href="">Front-end</a>
    <a href="">Startup</a>
  </div>
</div>
```

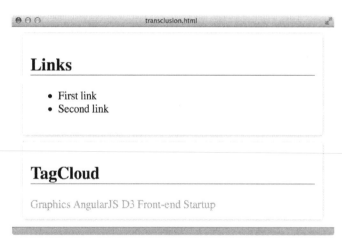

sidebox

If we use the `transclude` option, watching for model property changes from within inside the controller (which we'll look at next) of a directive will not work properly. That is why best practice always recommends using the $watch service from within the link function.

Controller (string | function)

The `controller` option takes a string or a function. When set to a string, the name of the string is used to look up a controller constructor function registered elsewhere in our application:

```
angular.module('myApp', [])
.directive('myDirective', function() {
  restrict: 'A', // always required
  controller: 'SomeController'
})


// elsewhere in our application
// either in the same file or another
// one included by our index.html
angular.module('myApp')
.controller('SomeController', function($scope, $element, $attrs, $transclude) {
  // controller logic goes here
})
```

A controller can be defined inline within a directive by setting the controller function as an anonymous constructor function:

```
angular.module('myApp', [])
.directive('myDirective', function() {
  restrict: 'A',
  controller:
  function($scope, $element, $attrs, $transclude) {
    // controller logic goes here
  }
})
```

While the above example suggests, the arguments that we can pass into a controller are *any* arbitrary injectable angular services. For instance, if we want to pass in the $log service, we can simply inject it into the controller and we can get access to it from within the directive.

The controller option does, however have special services that we can inject in that are specific to directives. These services are:

$scope

The current scope associated with the directive element.

$element

The current element directive element.

$attrs

The attributes object for the current element. For instance, the following element:

```
<div id="aDiv" class="box"></div>
```

has the attribute object of:

```
{
  id: "aDiv",
  class: "box"
}
```

$transclude

A transclude linking function pre-bound to the correct transclusion scope.

This transclude linking function is the function that will run to actually create a clone of the element and manipulate the DOM.

 It goes against the *Angular Way* to manipulate the DOM inside of a controller, but it is possible through the linking function. It is a best practice to only use this transcludeFn inside the compile option.

For example, let's be lazy and say that we just want to add a linktag through the use of a directive. We can do that inside the controller using the $transclude function like so:

```
angular.module('myApp')
.directive('link', function() {
  return {
    restrict: 'EA',
    transclude: true,
    controller:
      function($scope, $element, $transclude, $log) {
      $transclude(function(clone) {
        var a = angular.element('<a>');
        a.attr('href', clone.text());
        a.text(clone.text());
        $log.info("Created new a tag in link directive");
        $element.append(a);
      });
    }
  }
});
```

A directive's controller can often be interchanged with the directive's `link` function. The main use case for a controller is when we want to provide reusable behavior between directives. As the link function is only available inside the current directive, any behavior defined within is not shareable.

 The `link` function provides **isolation** between directives, while the `controller` defines **shareable** behavior.

Because a directive can `require` the controller of another directive, however, controllers are a great place to place actions we may want to use in more than one directive.

The `controller` option attaches a controller to the template of the directive, acting just like `ngController` would if it were the parent scope of the directive's template.

Using the `controller` option is good when we want to expose an API to other directives; otherwise, we can rely on `link` to provide us local functionality for the directive element. It's better to use link when we use `scope.$watch()` or when we're doing any interaction with the live scope of the DOM.

Technically, the `$scope` passed into a controller is passed in before the DOM is actually rendered to the screen. In certain situations, for example when working with transcludes, the scope inside a controller may reflect a different scope than we might expect, and the `$scope` object in such cases is not always guaranteed to update.

 Use the `scope` argument passed into the `link` function when expecting to interact with the instance of the scope on screen.

ControllerAs (string)

The `controllerAs` option enables us to set a controller alias, thus allowing us to publish our controller under this name and giving the scope access to the `controllerAs` name. This step allows us to reference the controller from inside the view and even allows us to not need to *inject* `$scope`.

For instance, we can create a `MainController` that never *injects* `$scope`, like so:

```
angular.module('myApp')
.controller('MainController', function() {
  this.name = "Ari";
});
```

Now, in our HTML, we can simply use this `MainController` without needing to reference the scope at all.

```
<div ng-app ng-controller="MainController as main">
  <input type="text" ng-model="main.name" />
  <span>{{ main.name }}</span>
</div>
```

This option may seem trivial, but it gives us a lot of power in how we can use and create anonymous controllers in our routes and directives. That power allows us to create dynamic objects as controllers that are isolated and easy to test.

For instance, we can create an anonymous controller in a directive, like so:

```
angular.module('myApp')
.directive('myDirective', function() {
  return {
    restrict: 'A',
    template: '<h4>{{ myController.msg }}</h4>',
    controllerAs: 'myController',
    controller: function() {
      this.msg = "Hello World"
    }
  }
});
```

require (string|array)

The require option can be set to a string or an array of strings. The string(s) contain the name of another directive. require is used to inject the controller of the required directive as the fourth parameter of the current directive's linking function.

The string or strings (if it is an array) provided are the names of directives that reside in the current scope of the current directive.

The scope setting will affect what the surrounding scope refers to, be it an isolate scope, an independent scope, or no scope at all. In all cases, the Angular compiler will consult the template of the current directive when looking for child controllers.

Without using the ^ prefix, the directive only looks for the controller on its own element.

```
// ...
restrict: 'EA',
require: 'ngModel'
// ...
```

This directive definition will *only* look for the ng-model="" definition in the local scope of the directive.

```
<!-- Our directive will find the ng-model on the local scope -->
<div my-directive ng-model="object"></div>
```

The string(s) provided to the `require` option may optionally be prefixed with the following options, which change the behavior when looking up a controller:

?

If the required controller is not found on the directive provided, pass `null` to the 4th argument of the `link` function.

^

If we provide the prefix `^`, then the directive will look upwards on its parent chain for the controller in the `require` option.

?^

Combine the behavior of the prior two options where we optionally require the directive and look up the parent chain for the directive.

no prefix

If we pass no prefix, we tell the directive to locate the required controller on the named directive provided and throw an error if no controller (or directive by that name) is found.

Technically, we need to have a controller associated with *anything* we put in the `require` option.

AngularJS Life Cycle

Before our Angular application boots, it sits in our text editor as raw HTML. Once we've booted the app, and the compile and link stages have taken place, however, we're left with a live data-bound application that responds on the fly to changes made by the user on the scope to which our HTML is bound. How does this magic take place, and what do we need to know in order to build effective applications?

There are two main phases that take place.

Compile Phase

The first is called the **compile** phase. During the compile phase, Angular slurps up our initial HTML page and begins processing the directives we declared according to the directive definitions we've defined within our application's JavaScript.

Each directive can have a template that may contain directives, which may have their own templates. When Angular invokes a directive in the root HTML document, it will traverse the template for that directive, which itself may contain directives, each with its own template.

 This tree of templates can go arbitrarily deep and wide, but there is one caveat. While it's true that an element can be backed or decorated (via attributes) with more than one directive and that any directive can contain a template that itself may contain directives with templates, *only the template belonging to the higest-priority directive will be parsed and added to the tree of templates*. The practical advice here is to separate directives that contain templates from those that add behavior. Never further decorate an element with another directive if that element already has a directive that brings its own template. Only the template of the directive with the highest priority will have its template compiled.

Once a directive and its child templates have been *walked* or compiled, a function is returned for the compiled template known as the *template function*. Before the template function for a directive is returned, however, we have the opportunity to modify the compiled DOM tree.

At this point the DOM tree is not data bound, meaning we've got just plain HTML we can manipulate with little to no performance costs. During this phase, built-in directives, such as `ng-repeat` and `ng-transclude`, take advantage of this fact and manipulate the DOM before it has been bound to any scope data.

`ng-repeat`, for example, loops over the array or object it has been given, building out the full representation of the DOM before passing the result off for data binding.

If we're building an unordered list using `ng-repeat`, where each `<li>` is decorated with the `ng-click` directive, this process provides us with performance that is orders of magnitude faster than if we had built the list manually, *especially* as our list approaches 100 elements.

The difference is that instead of cloning an `<li>`, linking it with data, and then repeating that for each item in the loop, we're simply building out the unordered list first, then passing the new version of the DOM (the compiled DOM) to the linking phase, the next phase in the directive life cycle.

Once we have compiled a complete representation of a single directive, we momentarily have access to it via the compile function, whose method signature includes access to the element where the directive was declared (`tElement`) and other attributes provided to that element(`tAttrs`). This compile function returns the template function (mentioned above), which includes the entire parsed tree.

The main takeaway here is that because each directive may have its own template and its own compile function, each directive returns its own template function. The top-level directive that started the chain returns the combined template function of all its children, but anywhere within that tree, we have access to just that branch via the compile function.

Finally, the template function is passed to the link function, where scope, determined by the directive definition rules of each directive in the compiled DOM tree, is applied all at once. This *compile then link* process provides our applications with huge performance gains.

Compile (object | function)

The `compile` option can return an object or a function.

Understanding the `compile` vs `link` option is one of the more advanced topics we'll run across in Angular, and it provides us with considerable context about how Angular really works.

The `compile` option by itself is not explicitly used very often; however, the `link` function is used very often. Under the hood, when we set the link option, we're actually creating a function that will define the `post()` link function so the `compile()` function can define the link function.

Oftentimes, when we set the `compile` function, we're interested in manipulating the DOM before we place the directive on it with live data. Here, it is safe to manipulate HTML, add and remove elements, etc.

 The `compile` option and the `link` option are mutually exclusive. If both are set, then the `compile` option will be expected to return the link function, while the `link` option will simply be ignored.

```
// ...
compile: function(tEle, tAttrs, transcludeFn) {
  var tplEl = angular.element('<div>' +
    '<h2></h2>' +
    '</div>');
  var h2 = tplEl.find('h2');
  h2.attr('type', tAttrs.type);
  h2.attr('ng-model', tAttrs.ngModel);
  h2.val("hello");
  tEle.replaceWith(tplEl);
  return function(scope, ele, attrs) {
    // The link function
  }
}
// ...
```

The template instance and link instance may be different objects if the template has been cloned. Thus, we can **only do DOM transformations** that are safe to do to all cloned DOM nodes within the compile function. Don't do DOM listener registration: That should be done in the linking function.

The compile function deals with transforming the template DOM.

The link function deals with linking scope to the DOM. Before scope is linked to the DOM, we may manually manipulate the DOM. In practice, this manipulation is rather rare when writing custom directives, but there are a few built-in directives that take advantage of this functionality. Understanding the process will help us understand how Angular actually works.

Link

We use the link option to create a directive that manipulates the DOM.

The link function is optional. If the compile function is defined, it returns the link function; therefore, the compile function will overwrite the link function when both are defined. If our directive is simple and doesn't require setting any additional options, we may return a function from the factory function (callback function) instead of an object. When doing so, this function will be the link function.

These two definitions of the directive are **functionally** equal:

```
angular.module('myApp' [])
.directive('myDirective', function() {
  return {
    pre: function(tElement, tAttrs, transclude) {
      // executed before child elements are linked
      // NOT safe to do DOM transformations here b/c the `link` function
      // called afterward will fail to locate the elements for linking
    },
    post: function(scope, iElement, iAttrs, controller) {
      // executed after the child elements are linked
      // IS safe to do DOM transformations here
      // same as the link function, if the compile option here we're
      // omitted
    }
  }
});
```

```javascript
angular.module('myApp' [])
.directive('myDirective', function() {
  return {
    link: function(scope, ele, attrs) {
    return {
      pre: function(tElement, tAttrs, transclude) {
        // executed before child elements are linked
        // NOT safe to DOM transformations here b/c the `link` function
        // called afterward will fail to locate the elements for linking
      },
      post: function(scope, iElement, iAttrs, controller) {
        // executed after the child elements are linked
        // IS safe to do DOM transformations here
        // same as the link function, if the compile option here we're
        // omitted
      }
    }
  }
});
```

When defining the compile function instead of the link function, the link function is the second method we can provide to the object returned, known as the postLink function. In essence, this fact describes precisely what the link function is responsible for. It is invoked after the compiled template has been linked to the scope, and is therefore responsible for setting up event listeners, watching for data changes, and manipulating the live DOM.

The link function has control over the live data-bound DOM, and, as such, performance considerations should be taken into account. Review the section on the life cycle of a directive for more information on performance concerns when choosing to implement something in the compile function versus the link function.

The link function has the following signature:

```javascript
link: function (scope, element, attrs) {
  // manipulate the DOM in here
}
```

If the directive definition has been provided with the require option, the method signature will gain a fourth argument representing the controller or controllers of the required directive:

```
require 'SomeController',
link: function (scope, element, attrs, SomeController) {
  // manipulate the DOM in here, with access to the controller of the
  // required directive
}
```

If the `require` option was given an array of directives, the fourth argument will be an array representing the controllers for each of the `required` directives.

Let's go over each of the arguments available to the link function:

scope

The scope to be used by the directive for registering watches from within the directive.

iElement

The *instance element* is the element where the directive is to be used. We should only manipulate children of this element in the postLink function, since the children have already been linked.

iAttrs

The *instance attributes* are a normalized (pascalCased) list of attributes declared on this element and are shared between all directive linking functions. These are passed as JavaScript objects.

controller

The `controller` argument points to the controller that's defined by the `require` option. If there is no `require` option defined, then this `controller` argument is set as undefined.

The controller is shared among all directives, which allows the directives to use the controllers as a communication channel (public API). If multiple `requires` are set, then this will be an array of controller instances, rather than just a single controller.

ngModel

The `ngModel` usage is a special directive name, as it gives us a deeper API for handling data from within a controller. When we use the `ngModel` attribute from within a directive, it will get access to a special API that deals with data binding, validations, CSS updates, and other things that don't deal with the actual DOM.

The `ngModel` controller, which is injected along with `ngModel` when we use it in our directive, contains several methods. In order to gain access to this `ngModelController`, we must use the `require` option (as we see above):

```
angular.module('myApp')
.directive('myDirective', function() {
  return {
    require: '?ngModel',
    link: function(scope, ele, attrs, ngModel) {
      if (!ngModel) return;
      // Now we have a hold of the
      // ngModelController instance
      // inside of our directive
    }
  };
});
```

 Without passing the require option, the ngModelController will **not** be passed into our directive.

Notice that this directive does **not** have an isolated scope. If we do set the directive to have the isolate scope, then the ngModel value will not update the outer ngModel value: Angular looks up this value outside of the local scope.

In order to set the view value of a scope, we must call the API function ngModel.$setViewValue().

The $setViewValue() function takes a single argument:

value (string) The value is the actual value to which we want to set the ngModel instance. This method updates the local $viewValue on the controller and then passes that value through each of the $parser functions (including all validations).

After the value is parsed and the $parser pipeline has completed its function, the value is assigned to the $modelValue property and handed to the expression provided by the ng-model attribute on the directive.

Finally, once all of these steps have been completed, all of the listeners in the $viewChangeListeners list are called.

Note that simply by calling $setViewValue() alone does not invoke a new digest cycle, so even after we set the $viewValue, we need to trigger a digest when we want the directive to update.

Using the $setViewValue() method is a good idea when creating a custom directive that listens for custom events (for instance, when using a jQuery plugin that has a callback). We'll want to set the $viewValue with the callback change and execute a digest cycle.

```
angular.module('myApp')
.directive('myDirective', function() {
  return {
    require: '?ngModel',
    link: function(scope, ele, attrs, ngModel) {
      if (!ngModel) return;

      $(function() {
        ele.datepicker({
          onSelect: function(date) {
            // set the view and call apply
            scope.$apply(function() {
              ngModel.$setViewValue(date);
            });
          }
        })
      });
    }
  };
});
```

Custom Rendering

It's possible to define how the view actually gets rendered by defining the $render method on the controller. This method will be applied *after* the $parser pipeline has completed.

We should apply this method only sparingly, as it can be disruptive to the *Angular Way*:

```
angular.module('myApp')
.directive('myDirective', function() {
  return {
    require: '?ngModel',
    link: function(scope, ele, attrs, ngModel) {
      if (!ngModel) return;

      ngModel.$render = function() {
        element.html(
          ngModel.$viewValue() || 'None'
        );
      }
    }
  };
});
```

Properties

`ngModelController` has a few properties available that we can examine and even modify to change our view.

$viewValue

The `$viewValue` property holds onto the actual string value that's updated in the view.

$modelValue

The `$modelValue` is the value held by the model. The `$modelValue` and the `$viewValue` can be different, depending upon the `$parser` pipeline.

$parsers

The `$parsers` value is an array of functions that get executed in a pipeline. When the `ngModel` control reads the value from the DOM, this value will be passed into the first `$parser` function. When it's complete, the return value will be passed to the next `$parser`, and so on and so forth.

These are used to sanitize and modify the value. We have described how the validation pipeline works, at a basic level. For more information about creating a `$parser` for validation, head over to the validations chapter.

$formatters

The `$formatters` value is an array of functions that get executed as a pipeline when the model value changes. It is called on the way out of the `$parser` pipeline and is used to format and convert values to display within the bound control.

$viewChangeListeners

The `$viewChangeListeners` value is an array of functions to execute when the view value has changed. Using `$viewChangeListeners` is a way to remove a `$watch` on a value yet retain similar behavior. These functions do **not** need to return a value, as they are ignored.

$error

The `$error` value holds onto the object of errors where the key is the failed validation name and the value is the actual error message.

$pristine

The `$pristine` value is a boolean that tells us whether or not the user has made any changes to the control yet.

$dirty

The $dirty attribute value is the inverse of the $pristine value that tells us whether or not the user has interacted with the control.

$valid

The $valid value tells us if there is no error on the control. It will be true if there are no errors and false if there are.

$invalid

The $invalid value tells us whether or not there is at least one error on the control and is the inverse of the $valid value.

Angular Module Loading

Angular modules, themselves, have the opportunity to configure themselves *before* the module actually bootstraps and starts to run. We can apply different sets of logic during the bootstrap phase of the app.

Configuration

Angular executes blocks of configuration during the provider registration and configuration phases in the bootstrapping of the module. This phase is the only part of the Angular flow that may be modified before the app starts up.

```
angular.module('myApp', [])
  .config(function($provide) {
  });
```

Throughout this book, we use methods that are syntactic sugar around the .config() function and get executed at configuration time. For instance, when we create a factory or a directive on top of the module:

```
angular.module('myApp', [])
.factory('myFactory', function() {
  var service = {};
  return service;
})
.directive('myDirective', function() {
  return {
    template: '<button>Click me</button>'
  }
})
```

Angular executes these helper functions at compile time. They are *functionally equivalent* to:

```
angular.module('myApp', [])
.config(function($provide, $compileProvider) {
  $provide.factory('myFactory', function() {
    var service = {};
    return service;
  });
  $compileProvider.directive('myDirective',
    function() {
      return {
        template: '<button>Click me</button>'
      }
    })
});
```

In particular, it's also important to note that Angular runs these functions in the order in which they are written and registered. That is to say that we cannot inject a provider that has not yet been defined.

 The *only* exception to the rule of in-order definitions is the constant() method. We always place these at the beginning of all configuration blocks.

When writing configuration for a module, it's important to note that there are only a few types of objects that we can *inject* into the .config() function: providers and constants. If we inject any old service into a .config() function, then we might *accidentally* instantiate one before we actually configure it.

The by-product of this strict requirement for configurable services is that we can only inject custom services that are built with the provider() syntax and cannot inject other services.

For more information on how to build with the provider syntax, head over to the services chapter.

These .config() blocks are how we'll custom configure our own services, such as setting API keys and custom URLs.

We can also define multiple configuration blocks, which are executed in order and allow us to focus our configuration in the different phases of the app.

```
angular.module('myApp', [])
.config(function($routeProvider) {
  $routeProvider.when('/', {
    controller: 'WelcomeController',
    template: 'views/welcome.html'
  });
})
.config(function(ConnectionProvider) {
  ConnectionProvider.setApiKey('SOME_API_KEY');
})
```

The config() function takes a single argument:

configFunction (function)   The function that Angular executes on module load.

Run Blocks

Unlike the configuration blocks, run blocks are executed *after* the injector is created and are the first methods that are executed in any Angular app.

Run blocks are the *closest thing in Angular to the main method*. The run block is code that is typically hard to unit test and is related to the general app.

Typically, these run blocks are places where we'll set up event listeners that should happen at the global scale of the app. For example, we'll use the .run() block to set up listeners for routing events or unauthenticated requests.

Let's say that we want to run a function that validates that we have an authenticated user every time that we change our route. The only logical place to set this functionality is in the run method:

```
angular.module('myApp', [])
.run(function($rootScope, AuthService) { $rootScope.$on('$routeChangeStart',
  function(evt, next, current) {
    // If the user is NOT logged in
    if (!AuthService.userLoggedIn()) {
      if (next.templateUrl === "login.html") {
        // Already heading to the login route so no need to redirect
      } else {
        $location.path('/login');
      }
    }
  });
});
```

The run() function takes a single argument:

initializeFn (function)   Angular executes this function after it creates the injector.

Multiple Views and Routing

In a single-page app, navigating from one page view to another is crucial. When apps grow more and more complex, we need a way to manage the screens that a user will see as they navigate their way through the app.

We can already support such management by including template code in line in the main HTML, but not only will this in-line code grow large and unmanageable, it will also make it difficult to allow other developers to join in development.

Rather than including multiple templates in the view (which we could do with the `ng-include` directive), we can break out the view into a layout and template views and only show the view we want to show based upon the URL the user is currently accessing.

We'll break these partial templates into views to be composed inside of a layout template. AngularJS allows us to do that by declaring routes on the `$routeProvider`, a provider of the `$route` service.

Using the `$routeProvider`, we can take advantage of the browser's history navigation and enable users to bookmark and share specific pages, as it uses the current URL location in the browser.

Installation

As of version 1.2, `ngRoutes` has been pulled out of the core of Angular into its own module. In order to use routes in our Angular app, we need to install and reference it in our app.

We can download it from code.angularjs.org[59] and save it in a place that we can reference it from our HTML, like `js/vendor/angular-route.js`.

We can also install it using Bower, which will place it in our usual Bower directory. For more information about Bower, see the Bower chapter.

```
$ bower install --save angular-route
```

We need to reference angular-route in our HTML *after* we reference Angular itself.

```
<script src="js/vendor/angular.js"></script>
<script src="js/vendor/angular-route.js"></script>
```

Lastly, we need to reference the `ngRoute` module as a dependency in our app module:

---

[59]http://code.angularjs.org/

```
angular.module('myApp', ['ngRoute']);
```

Layout Template

To make a *layout* template, we need to change the HTML in order to tell AngularJS where to render the template. Using the `ng-view` directive in combination with the router, we can specify exactly where in the DOM we want to place the rendered template of the current route.

For instance, a layout template might look something like:

```
<header>
  <h1>Header</h1>
</header>
<div class="content">
  <div ng-view></div>
</div>
<footer>
  <h5>Footer</h5>
</footer>
```

In this case, we are placing all of the rendered content in the `<div class="content">`, whereas we're leaving the `<header>` and `<footer>` elements intact on route changes.

The `ng-view` directive is a special directive that's included with the ngRoute module. Its specific responsibility is to stand as a placeholder for $route view content.

It creates its own scope and nests the template inside of it.

 The `ng-view` directive is a terminal directive at a 1000 priority. Angular will **not** run any directives on the element at a lower priority, which is most directives (i.e., all other directives on the `<div ng-view></div>` element are meaningless).

The `ngView` directive follows these specific steps:

- Any time the $routeChangeSuccess event is fired, the view will update
- If there is a template associated with the current route:
    - Create a new scope
    - Remove the last view, which cleans up the last scope
    - Link the new scope and the new template
    - Link the controller to the scope, if specified in the routes
    - Emits the $viewContentLoaded event
    - Run the `onload` attribute function, if provided

Routes

We use one of two methods to declare all application routes in AngularJS: the when method and the otherwise method.

To create a route on a specific module or app, we use the config function.

```
angular.module('myApp', []).
  config(['$routeProvider', function($routeProvider) {
  }]);
```

> We're using special dependency injection syntax here. For more information on this syntax, check out the dependency injection chapter.

Now, to add a specific route, we can use the when method. This method takes two parameters (when(path, route)).

This block shows how can create a single route:

```
angular.module('myApp', []).
  config(['$routeProvider', function($routeProvider) {
    $routeProvider
      .when('/', {
        templateUrl: 'views/home.html',
        controller: 'HomeController'
      });
  }]);
```

The first parameter is the route path, which is matched against the $location.path, the path of the current URL. Trailing or double slashes will still work. We can store parameters in the URL by starting off the name with a colon (for instance, :name). We'll talk about how to retrieve these parameters using the $routeParams.

The second parameter is the configuration object, which determines exactly what to do if the route in the first parameter is matched. The configuration object properties that we can set are controller, template, templateURL, resolve, redirectTo, and reloadOnSearch.

A more complex routing scenario requires multiple routes and a catch-all that redirects a route.

```
angular.module('myApp', []).
  config(['$routeProvider', function($routeProvider) {
    $routeProvider
      .when('/', {
        templateUrl: 'views/home.html',
        controller: 'HomeController'
      })
      .when('/login', {
        templateUrl: 'views/login.html',
        controller: 'LoginController'
      })
      .when('/dashboard', {
        templateUrl: 'views/dashboard.html',
        controller: 'DashboardController',
        resolve: {
          user: function(SessionService) {
            return SessionService.getCurrentUser();
          }
        }
      })
      .otherwise({
        redirectTo: '/'
      });
}]);
```

controller

```
controller: 'MyController'
// or
controller: function($scope) {}
```

If we set the controller property on the configuration object, the controller given will be associated with the new scope of the route. If we pass a string, it associates the registered controller on the module with the new route. If we pass a function, this function will be associated with the template as the controller for the DOM element.

template

```
template: '<div><h2>Route</h2></div>'
```

If we set the template property in the configuration object, Angular will render the HTML template in the ng-view DOM element.

templateUrl

```
templateUrl: 'views/template_name.html'
```

If the templateUrl property is set, then your app will attempt to fetch the view using XHR (utilizing the $templateCache). If it finds the template and can load it, Angular will render the template's contents in the ng-view DOM element.

resolve

```
resolve: {
  'data': ['$http', function($http) {
    return $http.get('/api').then(
      function success(resp) { return response.data; }
      function error(reason) { return false; }
    );
  }]
}
```

If we have set the resolve property, Angular will inject the elements of the *map* into the controller. If these dependencies are promises, they will be resolved and set as a value before the controller is loaded *and* before the $routeChangeSuccess event is fired.

The map object can be a:

- key, where the key is the string name of a dependency that will be injected into the controller
- factory, where the factory can either be a string of the name of a service, a function whose result is injected into the controller, or a promise that is to be resolved (whereupon the resulting value is injected into the controller)

In the example above, resolve sends the $http request off and fills the value of 'data' as the result of the request. The data key of the map above will be injected into our controller, so it can be retrieved in the controller.

redirectTo

```
redirectTo: '/home'
// or
redirectTo: function(route, path, search)
```

If the redirectTo property is set with a string, then the value will change the path and trigger a route change to the new path.

If the redirectTo property is set with a function, the result of the function will be set as the value of the new path, triggering a route-change request.

If the redirectTo property is a function, Angular will call it with one of the following parameters:

1: The route parameters extracted from the current path 2: The current path 3: The current search

reloadOnSearch

If the reloadOnSearch option is set to true (by default), then reload the route when $location.search() is changed. If you set this option to false, then the page won't reload the route if the search part of the URL changes. This tip is useful for nested routing or in-place pagination, etc.

Now we can set up our routes using the when function.

In this example, we're going to set up two routes: a home route and an inbox route. We'll also set the home route as the default route.

```
angular.module('MyApp', []).
  config(['$routeProvider', function($routeProvider) {
    $routeProvider
      .when('/', {
        controller: 'HomeController',
        templateUrl: 'views/home.html'
      })
      .when('/inbox/:name', {
        controller: 'InboxController',
        templateUrl: 'views/inbox.html'
      })
      .otherwise({redirectTo: '/'});
  }]);
```

Above, we've set up these three routes with the when method. If no route matches, then the otherwise method will be called. Using the otherwise method, we've set up a default route of '/'.

When the browser loads the Angular app, it will default to the URL set as the default route. Unless we load the browser with a different URL, the default is the '/' route.

$routeParams

As mentioned above, if we start a route param with a colon (:), AngularJS will parse it out and pass it into the $routeParams. For instance, if we set up a route like so:

```
$routeProvider
  .when('/inbox/:name', {
    controller: 'InboxController',
    templateUrl: 'views/inbox.html'
  })
```

then Angular will populate the $routeParams with the key of :name, and the value of *key* will be populated with the value of the loaded URL.

If the browser loads the URL /inbox/all, then the $routeParams object will look like:

```
{ name: 'all' }
```

As a reminder, to get access to these variables in the controller, we need to inject the `$routeProvider` in the controller:

```
app.controller('InboxController', function($scope, $routeParams) {
  // We now have access to the $routeParams here
});
```

$location Service

AngularJS provides a service that parses the URL in the address bar and gives you access to the route of the current path of your applications. It also gives you the ability to change paths and deal with any sort of navigation.

> The `$location` service provides a nicer interface to the `window.location` JavaScript object and integrates directly with our AngularJS apps.

We'll use the `$location` service whenever we need to provide a redirect internal to our app, such as redirecting after a user signs up, changes settings, or logs in.

The `$location` service does *not* provide access to refreshing the entire page. If we need to refresh the entire page, we need to use the `$window.location` object (an interface to `window.location`).

path()

To get the current path, we can run the `path()` method:

```
$location.path(); // returns the current path
```

To change the current path and redirect to another URL in the app:

```
$location.path('/'); // change the path to the '/' route
```

The path method interacts directly with the HTML5 history API, so the user will be able to press the back button and be returned to the previous page.

replace()

If you want to redirect completely without giving the user the ability to return using the back button (it's useful for times when a redirect occurs after they are redirected, for instance a redirect after login), then AngularJS provides the `replace()` method:

```
$location.path('/home');
$location.replace();
// or
$location.path('/home').replace();
```

absUrl()

If you want to get full URL representation with all segments encoded, use the absUrl() method:

```
$location.absUrl()
```

hash()

To get the hash fragment in the URL, we can use the hash() method:

```
$location.hash(); // return the current hash fragment
```

To change the current hash fragment, we can pass a string parameter into the method. Doing so returns the location object.

```
$location.hash('movies'); // returns $location
```

host()

We can get the host of the current URL by using the host() method:

```
$location.host(); // host of the current url
```

port()

The port of the current URL is available through the port() method:

```
$location.port(); // port of the current url
```

protocol()

The protocol of the current URL is available through the protocol() method:

```
$location.protocol(); // protocol of the current url
```

search()

To get the search part of the current URL, we can use the search() function:

```
$location.search();
```

We can pass in new search parameters, thus modifying the search portion of the URL:

```
// Setting search with an object
$location.search({name: 'Ari', username: 'auser'});
// Setting search with a string
$location.search('name=Ari&username=auser');
```

The search() method takes two parameters:

* search (optional string or object)

The search parameter represents the new search params. A hash object might contain an array of values as well.

* paramValue (optional string)

If the search is a string, then the paramValue will override a single search parameter. If the value is null, then the parameter will be removed.

url()

To get the URL of the current page, we can use the url() method:

```
$location.url(); // String of the url
```

We can set and change the URL using the url() method with parameters. This change modifies the path, search, and hash when called with parameters and returns $location.

```
// Set the new url
$location.url("/home?name=Ari#hashthing")
```

The url() can take two parameters:

* url (optional string)

This is the new URL without the base prefix.

* replace (optional string)

This parameter is the path that we're going to change.

Routing Modes

The routing mode refers specifically to the format of the URL in the browser address bar. The default behavior of the $location service is to route using the hashbang mode.

The routing mode determines what the URL of your site will look like.

Hashbang Mode

Hashbang mode is a trick that AngularJS uses to provide deep-linking capabilities to your Angular apps. In hashbang mode (the fallback for html5 mode), URL paths take a prepended # character. They do not rewrite <a href=""></a> tags and do not require any server-side support. Hashbang mode is the default mode that AngularJS uses if it's not told otherwise.

A hashbang URL looks like:

```
http://yoursite.com/#!/inbox/all
```

To be explicit and configure hashbang mode, it needs to be configured in the config function on an app module.

```
angular.module('myApp', ['ngRoute'])
  .config(['$locationProvider', function($locationProvider) {
    $locationProvider.html5Mode(false);
  }]);
```

We can also configure the hashPrefix, which, in hashbang mode, is the ! prefix. This prefix is part of the fallback mechanism that Angular uses for older browsers. We can also configure this character. To configure the hashPrefix:

```
angular.module('myApp', ['ngRoute'])
  .config(['$locationProvider', function($locationProvider) {
    $locationProvider.html5Mode(false);
    $locationProvider.hashPrefix('!');
  }]);
```

HTML5 Mode

The other routing mode that AngularJS supports is html5Mode. This mode makes your URLs look like regular URLs (except that in older browsers they will look like the hashbang URL). For instance, the same route above in HTML5 mode would look like:

```
http://yoursite.com/inbox/all
```

Inside AngularJS, the $location service uses HTML5's history API, allowing for our app to use the regular URL path. The $location service automatically falls back to using hashbang URLs if the browser doesn't support the HTML5 history API.

One interesting feature of the $location service is that if a modern browser that does support the HTML5 history API loads a hashbang URL, it will rewrite the URL for our users.

In HTML5 mode, Angular takes care of rewriting links when specified in the `<a href=""></a>` tags. That is to say that as Angular compiles your app, it rewrites the `href=""` portion, depending upon the browser's capabilities.

For example, with the tag: `<a href="/person/42?all=true">Person</a>`, a legacy browser's URL will be rewritten to the hashbang URL equivalent: `/index.html#!/person/42?all=true`. In a modern browser, it will see the URL as it was intended.

The back-end server will have to support URL rewriting on the server side. To support HTML5 mode, the server will have to make sure to deliver the `index.html` page for all apps. That ensures that our Angular app will handle the route.

When writing links inside of our Angular app in `html5mode`, we'll never want to use relative links. If you are serving your app using the root, it won't be a problem; however, if you are serving in any other base route, our Angular app won't be able to handle it.

Alternatively, you can set the base URL of your app using the `<base>` tag in the HEAD section of the HTML document:

```
<base href="/base/url" />
```

Routing Events

The $route service fires events at different stages of the routing flow. It's possible to set up event listeners for these different routing events and react.

This functionality is useful particularly when you want to manipulate events based upon routes and is particularly useful for detecting when users are logged in and authenticated.

We need to set up an event listener to listen for routing events. To set it up, we use the $rootScope to listen for the event.

$routeChangeStart

Angular broadcasts $routeChangeStart before the route changes. This step is where the route services begin to resolve all of the dependencies necessary for the route change to happen and where templates and the `resolve` keys are resolved.

```
angular.module('myApp', [])
  .run(['$rootScope', '$location', function($rootScope, $location) {
    $rootScope.$on('$routeChangeStart',
      function(evt, next, current) {
  })
}])
```

The $routeChangeStart event fires with two parameters:

- The next URL to which we are attempting to navigate
- The URL that we are on before the route change

$routeChangeSuccess

Angular broadcasts the $routeChangeSuccess event after the route dependencies have been re-solved.

```
angular.module('myApp', [])
  .run(['$rootScope', '$location', function($rootScope, $location) {
    $rootScope.$on('$routeChangeSuccess', function(evt, next, previous) {
    })
}])
```

The $routeChangeSuccess event fires with three parameters:

- The raw Angular evt object
- The route where the user currently is
- The previous route (or undefined if the current route is the first route)

$routeChangeError

Angular broadcasts the $routeChangeError event if any of the promises are rejected or fail.

```
angular.module('myApp', [])
  .run(['$rootScope', '$location', function($rootScope, $location) {
    $rootScope.$on('$routeChangeError', function(current, previous, rejection) {
    })
}])
```

The $routeChangeError event fires with three parameters:

- The current route information
- The previous route information
- The rejection promise error

$routeUpdate

Angular broadcasts the $routeUpdate event if the reloadOnSearch property has been set to false and we're reusing the same instance of a controller.

Note About Indexing

Web crawlers traditionally have a hard time with fat client-side JavaScript apps. To support web crawlers that run through the app, we need to add a meta tag in the head. This meta tag causes the crawler to request links with an empty *escaped fragment* parameter so that the back end will serve back snippets of HTML.

```
<meta name="fragment" content="!" />
```

Other Advanced Routing Topics

Page Reloading

The $location service does **not** reload the entire page; it simply changes the URL. If we need to cause a full page reload, we have to set the location using the $window service:

```
$window.location.href = "/reload/page";
```

Async Location Changes

If we need to use the $location service outside of the scope life cycle, we have to use the $apply function to propagate the changes throughout the app. That's because the $location service uses the $digest phase as the impetus to start the browser route change, which is how routing events work.

Dependency Injection

In general, there are only three ways an object can get a hold of its dependencies:

1. We can create it internally to the dependent.
2. We can look it up or refer to it as a global variable.
3. We can pass it in where it's needed.

With dependency injection, we're tackling the third way (the other two present other difficult challenges, such as dirtying the global scope and making isolation nearly impossible). Dependency injection is a design pattern that allows for the removal of hard-coded dependencies, thus making it possible to remove or change them at run time.

This ability to modify dependencies at run time allows us to create isolated environments that are ideal for testing. We can replace *real* objects in production environments with mocked ones for testing environments.

Functionally, the pattern *injects* depended-upon resources into the destination when needed by automatically looking up the dependency in advance and providing the destination for the dependency.

As we write components dependent upon other objects or libraries, we will describe its dependencies. At run time, an `injector` will create instances of the dependencies and pass them along to the *dependent* consumer.

```
// Great example from the Angular docs
function SomeClass(greeter) {
  this.greeter = greeter;
}
SomeClass.prototype.greetName = function(name) {
  this.greeter.greet(name)
}
```

 It is never a good idea to create a controller on the global scope like we've done in the sample code above. We're doing it only as an example for simplicity's sake.

At runtime, the `SomeClass` doesn't care *how* it gets the `greeter` dependency, so long as it gets it. In order to get that `greeter` instance into `SomeClass`, the creator of `SomeClass` is responsible for passing in the `SomeClass` dependencies when it's created.

Angular uses the $injector for managing lookups and instantiation of dependencies for this reason. In fact, the $injector is responsible for handling all instantiations of our Angular components, including our app modules, directives, controllers, etc.

When *any* of our modules boot up at run time, the injector is responsible for actually instantiating the instance of the object and passing in any of its required dependencies.

For instance, this simple app declares a single module and a single controller, like so:

```
angular.module('myApp', [])
.factory('greeter', function() {
  return {
    greet: function(msg) { alert(msg); }
  }
})
.controller('MyController',
  function($scope, greeter) {
    $scope.sayHello = function() {
      greeter.greet("Hello!");
    };
});
```

At run time, when Angular instantiates the instance of our module, it looks up the greeter and simply passes it in naturally:

```
<div ng-app="myApp">
  <div ng-controller="MyController">
    <button ng-click="sayHello()">Hello</button>
  </div>
</div>
```

Behind the scenes, the Angular process looks like:

```
// Load the app with the injector
var injector = angular.injector(['ng', 'myApp']);
// Load the $controller service with the injector
var $controller = injector.get('$controller');
var scope = injector.get('$rootScope').$new();
// Load the controller, passing in a scope
// which is how angular does it at runtime
var MyController = $controller('MyController', {$scope: scope})
```

Nowhere in the above example did we describe how to find the greeter; it simply *works*, as the injector takes care of finding and loading it for us.

AngularJS uses an `annotate` function to pull properties off of the passed-in array during instantiation. You can view this function by typing the following in the Chrome developer tools:

```
> injector.annotate(function($q, greeter) {})
["$q", "greeter"]
```

In every Angular app, the `$injector` has been at work, whether we know it or not. When we write a controller without the `[]` bracket notation or through *explicitly* setting them, the `$injector` will *infer* the dependencies based on the name of the arguments.

Annotation by Inference

Angular assumes that the function parameter names are the names of the dependencies, if not otherwise specified. Thus, it will call `toString()` on the function, parse and extract the function arguments, and then use the `$injector` to *inject* these arguments into the instantiation of the object.

The injection process looks like:

```
injector.invoke(function($http, greeter) {});
```

Note that this process will *only* work with non-minified, non-obfuscated code, as Angular needs to parse the arguments intact.

With this JavaScript inference, order is **not** important: Angular will figure it out for us and inject the right properties in the "right" order.

 JavaScript minifiers generally change function arguments to the minimum number of characters (along with changing white spaces, removing new lines and comments, etc.) so as to reduce the ultimate file size of the JavaScript files. If we do not explicitly describe the arguments, Angular will not be able to infer the arguments and thus the required injectable.

Explicit Annotation

Angular provides a method for us to explicitly define the dependencies that a function needs upon invocation. This method allows for minifiers to rename the function parameters and still be able to inject the proper services into the function.

The injection process uses the `$inject` property to annotation the function. The `$inject` property of a function is an array of service names to inject as dependencies.

To use the `$inject` property method, we set it on the function or name.

```
var aControllerFactory =
  function aController($scope, greeter) {
    console.log("LOADED controller", greeter);
    // ... Controller
  };
aControllerFactory.$inject = ['$scope', 'greeter'];
// Greeter service
var greeterService = function() {
  console.log("greeter service");
}
// Our app controller
angular.module('myApp', [])
  .controller('MyController', aControllerFactory)
  .factory('greeter', greeterService);
// Grab the injector and create a new scope
var injector  = angular.injector(['ng', 'myApp']),
  controller  = injector.get('$controller'),
  rootScope   = injector.get('$rootScope'),
  newScope    = rootScope.$new();
// Invoke the controller
controller('MyController', {$scope: newScope});
```

With this annotation style, order is important, as the $inject array must match the ordering of the arguments to inject. This method of injection *does* work with minification, because the annotation information will be packaged with the function.

Inline Annotation

The last method of annotation that Angular provides out of the box is the inline annotation. This syntactic sugar works the same way as the $inject method of annotation from above, but allows us to make the arguments inline in the function definition. Additionally it affords us the ability to not use a temporary variable in the definition.

Inline annotation allows us to pass an array of arguments instead of a function when defining an Angular object. The elements inside this array are the list of injectable dependencies as strings, the last argument being the function definition of the object.

For instance:

```
angular.module('myApp')
  .controller('MyController',
    ['$scope', 'greeter',
      function($scope, greeter) {

}]);
```

The inline annotation method *works* with minifiers, as we are passing a list of strings. We often refer this method as the bracket or array notation [].

$inject API

Although it's relatively rare that we'll need to work directly with the $injector, knowing about the API will give us some good insight into how exactly it works.

annotate()

The annotate() function returns an array of service names that are to be injected into the function when instantiated. The annotate() function is used by the injector to determine which services will be injected into the function at invocation time.

The annotate() function takes a single argument:

* fn (function or array)

The fn argument is either given a function or an array in the bracket notation of a function definition.

The annotate() method returns a single array of the names of services that will be injected into the function at the time of invocation.

```
var injector = angular.injector(['ng', 'myApp']);
injector.annotate(function($q, greeter) {});
// ['$q', 'greeter']
```

Try it in your Chrome Debugger.

get()

The get() method returns an instance of the service and takes a single argument.

* name (string)

The name argument is the name of the instance we want to get.

get() returns an instance of the service by name.

has()

The has() method returns true if the injector knows that a service exists in its registry and false if it does not. It takes a single argument:

- name (string)

The string is the name of the service we want to look up in the injector's registry.

instantiate()

The instantiate() method creates a new instance of the JavaScript type. It takes a constructor and invokes the new operator with all of the arguments specified. It takes two arguments:

- Type (function)

This function is the annotation constructor function to invoke.

- locals (object – optional)

This optional argument provides another way to pass argument names into the function when it is invoked.

The instantiate() method returns a new instance of Type.

invoke()

The invoke() method invokes the method and adds the method arguments from the $injector.

This invoke() method takes three arguments:

- fn (function)

This function is the one to invoke. The arguments for the function are set with the function annotation.

- self (object – optional)

The self argument allows for us to set the this argument for the invoke method.

- locals (object – optional)

This optional argument provides another way to pass argument names into the function when it is invoked.

The invoke() method returns the value that the fn function returns.

ngMin

With the three methods of defining annotations from above, it's important to note that these options all exist when defining a function. In production, however, it is often less convenient to explicitly concern ourselves with order of arguments and code bloat.

The ngMin tool allows us to alleviate the responsibility to define our dependencies explicitly. ngMin is a *pre-minifier* for Angular apps. It walks through our Angular apps and sets up dependency injection for us.

For instance, it will turn this code:

```
angular.module('myApp', [])
.directive('myDirective',
  function($http) {
})
.controller('IndexController',
  function($scope, $q) {
});
```

into the following:

```
angular.module('myApp', [])
.directive('myDirective', [
  '$http',
  function ($http) {
  }
]).controller('IndexController', [
  '$scope',
  '$q',
  function ($scope, $q) {
  }
]);
```

ngMin saves us a lot of typing and cleans our source files significantly.

Installation

To install ngMin, we'll use the npm package manager:

```
$ npm install -g ngmin
```

 If we're using Grunt, we can install the grunt-ngmin Grunt task. If we are using Rails, we
can use the Ruby gem ngmin-rails.

Using ngMin

We can use ngMin in standalone mode at the CLI by passing two arguments: the input.js and the
output.js files or via stdio/stdout, like so:

```
$ ngmin input.js output.js
# or
$ ngmin < input.js > output.js
```

where input.js is our source file and output.js is the annotated output file.

How It Works

At its core, ngMin uses an Abstract Syntax Tree (AST) as it walks through the JavaScript source. With
the help of astral, an AST tooling framework, it rebuilds the source with the necessary annotations
and then dumps the updated source using escodegen.

ngmin expects our Angular source code to consist of logical declarations. If our code uses syntax
similar to the code used in this book, ngMin will be able to parse the source and pre-minify it.

Services

Up until now, we've only concerned ourselves with how the view is tied to $scope and how the controller manages the data. For memory and performance purposes, controllers are instantiated only when they are needed and discarded when they are not. That means that every time we switch a route or reload a view, the current controller gets cleaned up by Angular.

Services provide a method for us to keep data around for the lifetime of the app and communicate across controllers in a consistent manner.

Services are singleton objects that are instantiated only once per app (by the $injector) and lazy-loaded (created only when necessary). They provide an interface to keep together those methods that relate to a specific function.

$http, for instance, is an example of an AngularJS service. It provides low-level access to the browser's XMLHttpRequest object. Rather than needing to dirty the application with low-level calls to the XMLHttpRequest object, we can simply interact with the $http API.

```
// Example service that holds on to the
// current_user for the lifetime of the app
angular.module('myApp', [])
.factory('UserService', function($http) {
  var current_user;

  return {
    getCurrentUser: function() {
      return current_user;
    },
    setCurrentUser: function(user) {
      current_user = user;
    }
  }
});
```

Angular comes with several built-in services with which we'll interact consistently. It will also be useful to make our *own* services for any decently complex application.

AngularJS makes it very easy to create our own services: All we need to do is register the service. Once a service is registered, the Angular compiler can reference it and load it as a dependency for runtime use. The name registry makes it easy to isolate application dependencies for mocks and stubbing in our tests.

Registering a Service

There are several ways to create and register a service with the $injector; we'll explore them later in this chapter.

The most common and flexible way to create a service uses the angular.module API factory:

```
angular.module('myApp.services', [])
  .factory('githubService', function() {
    var serviceInstance = {};
    // Our first service
    return serviceInstance;
  });
```

Although this githubService doesn't do anything very interesting, it is now registered with the AngularJS app using the name githubService as its name.

This service factory function is responsible for generating a single object or function that becomes this service, which will exist for the lifetime of the app. When our Angular app loads the service, the service will execute this function and hold on to the returned value as the singleton service object.

The service factory function can be either a function or an array, just like the way we create controllers:

```
// Creating the factory through using the
// bracket notation
angular.module('myApp.services', [])
  .factory('githubService', [function($http) {
  }]);
```

For instance, this githubService requires access to the $http service, so we'll list the $http service as a dependency for Angular to inject into the function.

```
angular.module('myApp.services', [])
  .factory('githubService', function($http) {
    // Our serviceInstance now has access to
    // the $http service in it's function definition
    var serviceInstance = {};
    return serviceInstance;
  });
```

Now, anywhere that we need to access the GitHub API, we no longer need to call it through $http; we can call the githubService instead and let it handle the complexities of dealing with the remote service.

The GitHub API exposes the activity stream for the user on GitHub (this stream is simply a list of recent events that a user has logged on GitHub). In our service, we can create a method that accesses this API and exposes the resulting set to our API.

To expose a method on our service, we can place it as an attribute on the service object.

```
angular.module('myApp.services', [])
  .factory('githubService', function($http) {
    var githubUrl = 'https://api.github.com';

    var runUserRequest = function(username, path) {
      // Return the promise from the $http service
      // that calls the Github API using JSONP
      return $http({
        method: 'JSONP',
        url: githubUrl + '/users/' +
              username + '/' +
              path + '?callback=JSON_CALLBACK'
      });
    }
    // Return the service object with a single function
    //  events
    return {
      events: function(username) {
        return runUserRequest(username, 'events');
      }
    };
  });
```

The githubService contains a single method that the components in our application can call.

Using Services

To use a service, we need to identify it as a dependency for the component where we're using it: a controller, a directive, a filter, or another service. At run time, Angular will take care of instantiating it and resolving dependencies like normal.

To *inject* the service in the controller, we pass the name as an argument to the controller function. With the dependency listed in the controller, we can execute any of the methods we define on the service object.

```
angular.module('myApp', ['myApp.services'])
.controller('ServiceController',
    function($scope, githubService) {
        // We can call the events function
        // on the object
        $scope.events =
          githubService.events('auser');
});
```

With the new githubService injected into our ServiceController, it is now available for use just like any other service.

Let's set up our example flow to call the GitHub API for a GitHub username that we define in our view. Just as we saw in the data binding section, we'll *bind* the username property to the view.

```
<div ng-controller="ServiceController">
  <label for="username">
    Type in a GitHub username
  </label>
  <input type="text"
         ng-model="username"
         placeholder="Enter a GitHub username" />
  <ul>
    <li ng-repeat="event in events">
      <!--
        event.actor and event.repo are returned
        by the github API. To view the raw
        API, uncomment the next line:
      -->
      <!-- {{ event | json }} -->
      {{ event.actor.login }} {{ event.repo.name }}
    </li>
  </ul>
</div>
```

Now we can *watch* for the $scope.username property to react to how we've changed the view, based on our bi-directional data binding.

```
.controller('ServiceController',
    function($scope, githubService) {
    // Watch for changes on the username property.
    // If there is a change, run the function
    $scope.$watch('username', function(newUsername) {
      // uses the $http service to call the
      // GitHub API and returns the resulting promise
      githubService.events(newUsername)
        .success(function(data, status, headers) {
          // the success function wraps
          // the response in data
          // so we need to call data.data to
          // fetch the raw data
          $scope.events = data.data;
        })
    });
});
```

Since we are returning the $http promise, we can call the .success method on the return as though we are calling $http directly.

Using $watch in the controller as above is not recommended. We're using this example only for simplicity's sake. In production, we would wrap this functionality into a directive and set the $watch function there instead.

In this example, you'll notice that there is a delay before the input field changes. If we don't include this delay, we'll end up calling the GitHub API for every keystroke that is entered into the input, which is obviously not what we want.

To introduce this delay, we're using the built-in $timeout service. To use the $timeout service, we inject it into our controller just like we injected the githubService into the controller:

```
app.controller('ServiceController',
  function($scope, $timeout, githubService) {
});
```

It's conventional to inject any Angular services before our own custom services.

Now we can use the $timeout service in the controller. The $timeout service, in this case, cancels any network requests that would otherwise be running and gives us a *350* millisecond delay between changes in the input field. In other words, if there is a delay of 350 milliseconds between keyboard strokes, we'll assume the user is done typing and we can start the GitHub request:

```
app.controller('ServiceController',
  function($scope, $timeout, githubService) {
    // The same example as above, plus
    // the $timeout service
    var timeout;
    $scope.$watch('username', function(newUserName) {
      if (newUserName) {
        // If there is a timeout already
        // in progress
        if (timeout) $timeout.cancel(timeout);
        timeout = $timeout(function() {
          githubService.events(newUserName)
            .success(function(data, status) {
              $scope.events = data.data;
            });
        }, 350);
      }
    });
  });
```

Since we began this app, we've only looked at how services can bundle similar functionality together. Using services is also the canonical way to share data across several controllers.

For instance, if our application requires authentication from a back-end service, we might want to create a SessionsService that handles user authentication and holds onto a token passed by the back-end service. When any part of our application wants to make an authenticated request, it can use the SessionsService to get the access token.

If our application has a settings page where we set the user's GitHub username, we'll want to share the username with the other controllers in our application.

To share data across controllers, we need to add a method to our service that stores the username. Remember, the service is a singleton service that lives for the lifetime of the app, so we can store the username safely inside of it.

```
angular.module('myApp.services', [])
  .factory('githubService', function($http) {
    var githubUrl = 'https://api.github.com',
        githubUsername;

    var runUserRequest = function(path) {
      // Return the promise from the $http service
      // that calls the Github API using JSONP
      return $http({
```

```
      method: 'JSONP',
      url: githubUrl + '/users/' +
           githubUsername + '/' +
           path + '?callback=JSON_CALLBACK'
    });
  }
  // Return the service object with two methods
  //   events
  // and setUsername
  return {
    events: function() {
      return runUserRequest('events');
    },
    setUsername: function(username) {
      githubUsername = username;
    }
  };
});
```

Now, we have a setUsername method in our service that enables us to set the username for the current GitHub user.

In any controller in our application, we can inject the githubService and call events() without concerning ourselves with whether or not we have the right username on our scope object.

```
angular.module('myApp', ['myApp.services'])
.controller('ServiceController',
  function($scope, githubService) {
      $scope.setUsername =
        githubService.setUsername;
});
```

Options for Creating Services

While the most common method for registering a service with our Angular app is through the factory() method, there are some other APIs we can take advantage of in certain situations to shorten our code.

The five different methods for creating services are:

- factory()
- service()

- constant()
- value()
- provider()

factory()

As we've seen, the factory() method is a quick way to create and configure a service.

The factory() function takes two arguments:

- name (string)

This argument takes the name of the service we want to register.

- getFn (function)

This function runs when Angular creates the service.

```
angular.module('myApp')
.factory('myService', function() {
  return {
    'username': 'auser'
  }
});
```

The getFn will be invoked **once** for the duration of the app lifecycle, as the service is a singleton object. As with other Angular services, when we define our service, getFn can take an array or a function that will take other injectable objects.

The getFn function can return anything from a primitive value to a function to an object (similar to the value() function).

```
angular.module('myApp')
.factory('githubService', [
  '$http', function($http) {
    return {
      getUserEvents: function(username) {
        // ...
      }
    }
}]);
```

service()

If we want to register an instance of a service using a constructor function, we can use service(), which enables us to register a constructor function for our service object.

The service() method takes two arguments:

- name (string)

This argument takes the name of the service instance we want to register.

- constructor (function)

Here is the constructor function that we'll call to instantiate the instance.

The service() function will instantiate the instance using the new keyword when creating the instance.

```
var Person = function($http) {
  this.getName = function() {
    return $http({
      method: 'GET',
      url: '/api/user'
    });
  };
};
angular.service('personService', Person);
```

provider

These factories are all created through the $provide service, which is responsible for instantiating these providers at run time.

A provider is an object with a $get() method. The $injector calls the $get method to create a new instance of the service. The $provider exposes several different API methods for creating a service, each with a different intended use.

At the root of all the methods for creating a service is the provider method. The provider() method is responsible for registering services in the $providerCache.

Technically, the factory() function is shorthand for creating a service through the provider() method wherein we assume that the $get() function is the function passed in.

The two method calls are functionally equivalent and will create the same service.

```
angular.module('myApp')
.factory('myService', function() {
  return {
    'username': 'auser'
  }
})
// This is equivalent to the
// above use of factory
.provider('myService', {
  $get: function() {
    return {
      'username': 'auser'
    }
  }
});
```

Why would we ever need to use the `.provider()` method when we can just use the `.factory()` method?

The answer lies in whether we need the ability to externally configure a service returned by the `.provider()` method using the Angular `.config()` function. Unlike the other methods of service creation, we **can** *inject* a special attribute into the `config()` method.

Let's say we want to configure our `githubService` with our URL in advance of the application starting up:

```
// register the service using `.provider`
angular.module('myApp', [])
.provider('githubService', function($http) {
  // default, private state
  var githubUrl = 'https://github.com'

  setGithubUrl: function(url) {
    // change default via .config
    if (url) { githubUrl = url }
  }
  method: JSONP, // override me, if you want

  $get: function($http) {
    self = this;
    return $http({
      method: self.method,
      url: githubUrl +
```

```
        '/events'
    });
  }
});
```

The idea here is that, by using the `.provider()` method, we have more flexibility when using our service in more than one app, when sharing our service across applications, or when sharing with the community.

With the example above, the `provider()` method creates an additional provider with the string 'Provider' appended to it that *can* be injected into the `config()` function.

```
angular.module('myApp', [])
.config(function(githubServiceProvider) {
  githubServiceProvider
    .setGithubUrl("git@github.com");
})
```

If we want to be able to configure the service in the `config()` function, we must use `provider()` to define our service.

The `provider()` method registers a provider for a service. It takes two arguments:

* name (string)

The `name` argument is a string that we use as the key in the `providerCache`. This argument makes the `name` + Provider available as the provider for the service. The `name` will be used as the name of an instance of the service.

For instance, if we define a service as `githubService`, then the provider will be available as `githubServiceProvider`.

* aProvider (object/function/array)

The `aProvider` argument can take a few different forms:

If the `aProvider` argument is a function, then the function is called through dependency injection and is responsible for returning an object with the `$get` method.

If the `aProvider` argument is an array, then it's treated just like a function with inline dependency injection annotation. It will expect the last argument to be a function that returns an object with the `$get` method.

If the `aProvider` argument is an object, then it is expected to have a `$get` method.

The `provider()` function returns an object that is a registered provider instance.

The most *raw* method of creating a service is by using the `provider()` API directly:

```
// Example of creating a provider directly on the
// module object.
angular.module('myApp', [])
.provider('UserService', {
  favoriteColor: null,
  setFavoriteColor: function(newColor) {
    this.favoriteColor = newColor;
  },
  // the $get function can take injectables
  $get: function($http) {
    return {
      'name': 'Ari',
      getFavoriteColor: function() {
        return this.favoriteColor || 'unknown';
      }
    }
  }
});
```

Creating a service in this way, we must return an object that has the $get() function defined; otherwise, it will result in an error.

We can instantiate the service with the injector (although it's unlikely that we'll ever instantiate it directly, as Angular apps do it on their own – see under the hood):

```
// Get the injector
var injector = angular.module('myApp').injector();
// Invoke our service
injector.invoke(
  ['UserService', function(UserService) {
    // UserService returns
    // {
    //   'name': 'Ari',
    //   getFavoriteColor: function() {}
    // }
}]);
```

Using .provide() is very powerful and gives us the ability to use and share our services across our applications.

It is also important for us to know about the constant() and value() methods when creating services.

constant()

It's possible to register an existing value as a service that we can later *inject* into other parts of our app as a service. For instance, let's say we want to set an *apiKey* for a back-end service. We can store that constant value using constant().

The constant() function takes two arguments:

- name (string)

This argument is the name with which to register the constant.

- value (constant value)

This argument gives the value to register as the constant.

The constant() method returns a registered service instance.

```
angular.module('myApp')
.constant('apiKey', '123123123')
```

We can now *inject* this value into a configuration function just like any other service:

```
angular.module('myApp')
.controller('MyController',
  function($scope, apiKey) {
      // We can use apiKey as a constant
      // string as 123123123 set from above
      $scope.apiKey = apiKey;
});
```

 The constant is not *interceptable* by the decorator.

value()

If the return value of the $get method in our service is a constant, we don't need to define a full-blown service with a more complex method. We can simply use the value() function to register the service.

The value() method accepts two arguments:

- name (string)

Once again, this argument gives the name with which we want to register the value.

- value (value)

We'll return this value as the injectable instance.

The value() method returns a registered service instance for the name given.

```
angular.module('myApp')
.value('apiKey', '123123123');
```

When to Use Value or Constant

The major difference between the value() method and the constant() method is that you can *inject* a *constant* into a config function, whereas you cannot inject a *value*.

Conversely, with *constants*, we're unable to register service objects or functions as the value.

Typically, a good rule of thumb is that we should use value() to register a service object or function, while we should use constant() for configuration data.

```
angular.module('myApp', [])
.constant('apiKey', '123123123')
.config(function(apiKey) {
  // The apiKey here will resolve to 123123123
  // as we set above
})
.value('FBid', '231231231')
.config(function(FBid) {
  // This will throw an error with
  // Unknown provider: FBid
  // because the value is not accessible by
});
```

decorator()

The $provide service gives us a way to intercept the service instance creation. Decorating our services enables us to extend services or replace them with something else entirely.

Decorators, themselves, are very powerful in that we can not only provide decorations for our own services, but we can intercept, interrupt, and even replace functionality in the core Angular services. In fact, a lot of the core Angular testing functionality is built using $provide.decorator().

Use-cases for decorating services might include extending a service to cache external data requests to localStorage or wrapping a service in debugging or tracing wrappers for development purposes.

For instance, let's say that we want to provide logging calls to our previously defined githubService. Rather than modifying the original service, we can *decorate* it using a decorator() function.

The decorator() function takes two arguments:

- name (string)

Here we pass the name of the service to decorate.

- decoratorFn (function)

We give the function that we'll invoke at the time of service instantiation. The function is called with injector.invoke, which allows us to *inject* services into it.

In order to decorate a service, we need to *inject* the $delegate, which is the original service instance that we can decorate.

For instance, to add a decorator function to our above custom githubService to add a timestamp to every call, we can add a decorator function like the following:

```
var githubDecorator = function($delegate, $log) {
  var events = function(path) {
    var startedAt = new Date();
    var events = $delegate.events(path);
    var result = $delegate.locate();
    // Events is a promise
    events.always(function() {
      $log.info("Fetching events" +
          " took " +
          (new Date() - startedAt) + "ms");
    });
    return result;
  }
```

```
  return {
    events: events
  };
};

angular.module('myApp')
.config(function($provide) {
  $provide.decorator('githubService',
    githubDecorator);
});
```

Communicating with the Outside World: XHR and Server-Side Communication

AngularJS web apps are entirely client-side applications. As we've seen, we can write AngularJS applications without integrating with a back end **at all** and still have a dynamic, responsive web app.

Without a back end, we are limited to only showing information that we have at load time. Angular provides us several methods if we want to integrate our AngularJS app with information from a remote server.

Using $http

We can directly call out using the built-in $http service. The $http service is simply a wrapper around the browser's raw XMLHttpRequest object.

The $http service is a function that takes a single argument: a configuration object that is used to generate a HTTP request. The function returns a promise that has two helper methods: success and error.

 See the $http config object section in this chapter for details on the available options.

The most basic usage of the method looks like:

```
$http({
  method: 'GET',
  url: '/api/users.json'
}).success(function(data, status, headers, config) {
  // This is called when the response is
  // ready
}).error(function(data, status, headers, config) {
  // This is called when the response
  // comes back with an error status
});
```

Notice that the $http object looks like we are passing in a callback method to call when the response comes back. This observation is not accurate: The method actually returns a promise.

When this promise is returned, we can return the result of the $http method as a variable and chain other promises atop it to resolve when the HTTP has resolved.

We'll use this technique quite often when we build services so that they can return a promise instead of requiring a callback.

```
var promise = $http({
  method: 'GET',
  url: '/api/users.json'
});
```

Since the $http method returns a promise object, we can use the then method to handle the callback when the response is ready. If we use the then method, we'll get a special argument that represents the response object for both success and error. Then receives optionally 2 functions as a parameter. Otherwise, we can use the success and error callbacks instead.

```
promise.then(function(resp) {
  // resp is a response object
}, function(resp) {
    // resp with error
});
// OR we can use the success/error methods
promise.success(function(data, status, headers, config) {
  // Handle successful responses
});
// error handling
promise.error(function(data, status, headers, config) {
  // Handle non-successful responses
});
```

If the response status code is between 200 and 299, the response is considered successful, and the success callback will be called. Otherwise, the error callback will be invoked.

 Note that if the response results in a redirect, the XMLHttpRequest will follow it, and the error callback will not be called.

Note that we have the ability to use the then() method or the success() and error() methods on the HttpPromise. The difference between using the then() method and the convenience helpers is that the success() and error() functions contain a destructured representation of the response object, which the then() method receives in whole.

When we call the $http method, it won't actually execute until the next $digest loop runs. Although most of the time we'll be calling $http inside of an $apply block, we can also execute the method outside of the Angular digest loop.

To execute an $http function outside of the $digest loop, we need to wrap it in an $apply block. That will force the digest loop to run, and our promises will resolve as we expect them to.

```
$scope.$apply(function() {
  $http({
    method: 'GET',
    url: '/api/users.json'
  });
});
```

Shortcut Methods

The $http service also provides handy methods that allow us to shorten any method calls that don't require more customization than a URL and a method name (or data with POST or PUT requests).

These shortcut methods allow us to modify the above $http GET call to:

```
// Shortened GET request
$http.get('/api/users.json');
```

get()

This method is the shortcut for sending a GET request.

The get() function accepts two parameters:

- url (string)

A relative or absolute URL specifying the destination of the request.

- config (optional object)

This object is an optional configuration object.

The get() method returns a HttpPromise object.

delete()

This method is the shortcut for sending a DELETE request.

The delete() function accepts two parameters:

- url (string)

This parameter gives a relative or absolute URL specifying the destination of the request.

- config (optional object)

This object is an optional configuration object.

The delete() method returns a HttpPromise object.

head()

This method is the shortcut for sending a HEAD request.

The head() function accepts two parameters:

- url (string)

This string is a relative or absolute URL specifying the destination of the request.

- config (optional object)

This object is an optional configuration object.

The head() method returns a HttpPromise object.

jsonp()

This method is the shortcut for sending a JSONP request.

The jsonp() function accepts two parameters:

- url (string)

This string is a relative or absolute URL specifying the destination of the request. In order to send the JSONP request, it must contain the string JSON_CALLBACK. For instance:

```
$http
.jsonp("/api/users.json?callback=JSON_CALLBACK");
```

- config (optional object)

This object is an optional configuration object.

The `jsonp()` method returns a `HttpPromise` object.

post()

This method is the shortcut for sending a POST request.

The `post()` function accepts three parameters:

- url (string)

This string is a relative or absolute URL specifying the destination of the request.

- data (object or string)

This object contains the request data content.

- config (optional object)

This object is an optional configuration object.

The `post()` method returns a `HttpPromise` object.

put()

This method is the shortcut for sending a PUT request.

The `put()` function accepts three parameters:

- url (string)

This string is a relative or absolute URL specifying the destination of the request.

- data (object or string)

This object contains the request data content.

- config (optional object)

This object is an optional configuration object.

The `put()` method returns a `HttpPromise` object.

Configuration Object

When we call the $http service as a method, we pass it a configuration object, which is used to describe how to craft the XMLHttpRequest object. For instance, we can call the $http service as a method like so:

```
$http({
  method: "GET",
  url: "/api/users.json",
  params: {
    "username": "auser"
  }
})
```

It can contain the following keys:

method (string)

This key is the HTTP method we use to make the request. It should be one of the following: 'GET', 'DELETE', 'HEAD', 'JSONP', 'POST', 'PUT'.

url (string)

This string is the absolute *or* relative URL of the resource that is being requested.

params (map of strings/objects)

This key is the map of strings or objects that will be turned into the query string after the URL. If the value is **not** a string, it will be JSONified.

```
// Will params into ?name=ari
$http({
  params: {"name": "ari"}
})
```

data (string/object)

This object contains the data that will be sent as the message data.

headers (object)

This object is the map of strings for functions that return strings representing HTTP headers to send with the request. If the return value of the function is null, the header will **not** be sent.

xsrfHeaderName (string)

This string is the name of the HTTP header to populate with the XSRF token.

xsrfCookieName (string)

This string contains the name of the cookie that holds the XSRF token.

transformRequest (function/array of functions)

This function or array of functions takes the HTTP request body and headers and returns their transformed versions. We generally use it to serialize data before it is sent to the server.

The function looks like:

```
function(data, headers)
```

transformResponse (function/array of functions)

This function or array of functions takes the HTTP response body and headers and returns their transformed versions. We generally use it to deserialize data after it has received returned data.

The function looks like:

```
function(data, headers) {}
```

cache (boolean/Cache object)

If this boolean value is true, then the default $http cache will cache the GET request. If it is a cache object built with $cacheFactory, then Angular will use this new cache to cache the response.

timeout (number/promise)

This key is a timeout in milliseconds *or* a promise that should abort the request when the promise is resolved.

withCredentials (boolean)

If this boolean value is true, then the withCredentials flag on the XHR request object will be set.

By default, CORS requests will not set any cookies. The withCredentials flag sets a custom header called Access-Control-Allow-Credentials, which makes the request with any cookies from the remote domain in the request.

responseType (string)

The `responseType` option sets the `XMLHttpRequestResponseType` property on the request. It can be set to one of the different types of available HTTP response types:

- "" (string – default)
- "arraybuffer" (ArrayBuffer)
- "blob" (blob object)
- "document" (HTTP document)
- "json" (JSON object parsed from a JSON string)
- "text" (string)
- "moz-blob" (Firefox to receive progress events)
- "moz-chunked-text" (streaming text)
- "moz-chunked-arraybuffer" (streaming ArrayBuffer)

Response Object

The response object that Angular passes to the `then()` method contains four properties:

- data (string/object)

This data represents the transformed response body (if any transformations are defined).

- status (number)

This number is the HTTP status code of the response.

- headers (function)

This function is the header getter function that takes a single parameter to get the header value for the header name. For instance, to get the header of X-Auth-ID, we can call the function, like so:

```
$http({
  method: 'GET',
  url: '/api/users.json'
}).then(resp) {
  // Fetch the X-Auth-ID
  resp.headers('X-Auth-ID');
}
```

- config (object)

This object is the full, generated configuration object that was used to generate the original request.

Caching HTTP Requests

By default, the $http service does not cache requests in a local cache. We can enable caching per request by passing either a boolean or a cache instance in our $http requests.

```
$http.get('/api/users.json', { cache: true })
.success(function(data) {})
.error(function(data) {});
```

The first time that we send this $http request, the $http service will send a GET request to /api/users.json. The *next* time that we send this GET request, instead of making the HTTP GET request, it will pull the request out of the cache.

By passing true, for this particular request, Angular will use the default cache using the $cacheFactory, which Angular creates for us automatically at bootstrap time.

 For more information on working directly with Angular caching, check out the caching chapter.

For more custom control of the cache that Angular uses, we can pass a custom cache instead of true in the request.

For instance, for a Least Recently Used (or LRU) cache, we pass the cache like so:

```
var lru = $cacheFactory('lru', {
  capacity: 20
});
// $http request
$http.get('/api/users.json', { cache: lru })
.success(function(data) {})
.error(function(data) {});
```

Now, the latest 20 unique requests will be cached. The 21st most recent unique request will cause the Least Recently Used request to be removed from the cache.

It gets a tad cumbersome to pass a custom cache every single time (even in a service). We can set a default cache for all $http requests across our application in the .config() function of our app:

```
angular.module('myApp')
.config(function($httpProvider, $cacheFactory) {
  $httpProvider.defaults.cache =
    $cacheFactory('lru', {
      capacity: 20
    });
});
```

Every single request will now use our custom LRU cache.

Interceptors

Anytime that we want to provide global functionality on all of our requests, such as authentication, error handling, etc., it's useful to be able to provide the ability to intercept all requests before they pass to the server and back from the server.

For instance, in authentication, if the server returns a response code with 401, we likely would want to kick the user out to a login page.

Angular provides a way for us to handle responses at the global level using *interceptors*.

Interceptors, although the term sounds scary, are basically *middleware* for the $http service that allow us to inject logic into the existing flow of the app.

At their core, interceptors are service factories (see services for more information about services) that we register through the $httpProvider by adding them to the $httpProvider.interceptors array.

There are four types of interceptors – two success interceptors and two rejection interceptors:

- request

Angular calls the request interceptor with the $http config object. It can modify the config object or create a new one, and it is responsible for returning the updated config object or a promise that resolves a new config object.

- response

Angular calls the response interceptor with the $http response object. The function can modify the response or create a new one. It's responsible for returning the response or a promise that resolves a new response object.

- requestError

Angular calls this interceptor when the previous request interceptor throws an error or is resolved with a rejection.

- responseError

We receive this error when the previous respone interceptor throws an error or is resolved with a rejection.

To create an interceptor, we use the .factory() method on our module and add one or more of the four methods to our service.

```
angular.module('myApp')
.factory('myInterceptor',
  function($q) {
    var interceptor = {
      'request': function(config) {
        // Successful request method
        return config; // or $q.when(config);
      },
      'response': function(response) {
        // successful response
        return response; // or $q.when(config);
      },
      'requestError': function(rejection) {
        // an error happened on the request
        // if we can recover from the error
        // we can return a new request
        // or promise
        return response; // or new promise
        // Otherwise, we can reject the next
```

```
        // by returning a rejection
        // return $q.reject(rejection);
      },
      'responseError': function(rejection) {
        // an error happened on the request
        // if we can recover from the error
        // we can return a new response
        // or promise
        return rejection; // or new promise
        // Otherwise, we can reject the next
        // by returning a rejection
        // return $q.reject(rejection);
      }
    };

    return interceptor;
});
```

We then need to **register** our interceptor with the $httpProvider in a .config() function:

```
angular.module('myApp')
.config(function($httpProvider) {
  $httpProvider.interceptors.push('myInterceptor');
});
```

Configuring the $httpProvider

Using the .config() option, we can add certain HTTP headers to every request, which is useful when we want to send authentication headers alongside every request or set a response type, etc.

The default headers sent for *every* single request live in the $httpProvider.defaults.headers.common object. The common default headers are:

```
Accept: application/json, text/plain, * / *
```

We can change or augment these headers using our .config() function for *every* request, like so:

```
angular.module('myApp')
.config(function($httpProvider) {
  $httpProvider.defaults.headers
    .common['X-Requested-By'] = 'MyAngularApp';
});
```

We can also manipulate these defaults at run time using the `defaults` property of the `$http` object. For instance, to add a property for dynamic headers, we can set the header property like so:

```
$http.defaults
  .common['X-Auth'] = "RandomString";
```

 This functionality can be achieved by either using a request transformer or, for a single request, by setting the `headers` option in the `$http` request.

It's also possible to manipulate the requests that are sent on only either POST or PUT requests. The default headers that are sent for all POST requests are:

```
Content-Type: application/json
```

We can change or augment the POST headers in our `config()` function, like so:

```
angular.module('myApp')
.config(function($httpProvider) {
  $httpProvider.defaults.headers
    .post['X-Posted-By'] = 'MyAngularApp';
});
```

We can do the same for all PUT requests. The default headers sent for PUT requests are:

```
Content-Type: application/json
```

We can change or augment the PUT headers in our `config()` function, like so:

```
angular.module('myApp')
.config(function($httpProvider) {
  $httpProvider.defaults.headers
    .put['X-Posted-By'] = 'MyAngularApp';
});
```

Using $resource

Angular comes with another very handy optional service called the $resource service. This service creates a resource object that allows us to intelligently work with RESTful server-side data sources; it comes in handy when dealing with back ends that support the RESTful data model out of the box.

 Representational state transfer, or REST for short, is a method of intelligently serving data from a back-end web service. For more information about REST, check out the Wikipedia article[60] on it.

The $resource service is incredibly useful and will abstract away a lot of complexities that come with setting up a meaningful interaction with a back-end server, provided it supports the RESTful data model.

The $resource service allows us to turn our $http requests into simple methods like save or update. Rather than requiring us to be repetitive or to write tedious code, we can use the $resource method to handle it for us.

Installation

The ngResource module is an optional Angular module that adds support for interacting with RESTful back-end data sources. Since the ngResource module is not built into Angular by default, we need to install it and reference it inside of our app.

We can download it from code.angularjs.org[61] and save it in a place that we can reference it from our HTML, like js/vendor/angular-resource.js.

We can also install it using Bower, which places it in our usual Bower directory. For more information about Bower, see the bower chapter.

```
$ bower install --save angular-resouce
```

We need to reference this module in our HTML *after* we reference Angular itself.

---

[60]http://en.wikipedia.org/wiki/Representational_State_Transfer

[61]http://code.angularjs.org/

```
<script src="js/vendor/angular.js"></script>
<script src="js/vendor/angular-resource.js"></script>
```

Lastly, we need to reference the ngResource module as a dependency in our app module:

```
angular.module('myApp', ['ngResource']);
```

Now we're ready to use the $resource service.

Using $resource

The $resource service itself is a factory that creates a resource object. The returned $resource object has methods that provide a high-level API to interact with back-end servers.

```
var User = $resource('/api/users/:userId.json',
  {
    userId: '@id'
  }
);
```

$resource returns a resource class object with a few methods for default actions. We can think of the User object as an interface to our RESTful back-end services.

This resource class object itself contains methods that allow us to interact indirectly with our back-end services.

By default, this object generates five methods that allow us to interact with a collection of resources or to generate an instance of a resource object. It creates two methods that are HTTP GET-based methods and three that are non-GET methods.

HTTP GET Methods

The two HTTP GET methods it creates expect the following three parameters:

- params (object)

These are the parameters that are sent with the request. They can be named parameters in the URL, or they can be query parameters.

- successFn (function)

This function is the callback function that will be called upon a successful HTTP response.

- errorFn (function)

This callback function is called upon a non-successful HTTP response.

get(params, successFn, errorFn)

The get method sends a GET request to the URL and expects a JSON response.

Without specifying a named parameter, such as above, the get() request is generally used to get a single resource.

```
// Issues a request to:
//  GET /api/users
User.get(function(resp) {
  // Handle successful response here
}, function(err) {
  // Handle error here
});
```

If the named parameter is passed into the parameters (in our example, this parameter is id), then the get() method will send a request to the URL with the id in the URL:

```
// Issues a request to:
//  GET /api/users/123
User.get({
  id: '123'
}, function(resp) {
  // Handle successful response here
}, function(err) {
  // Handle error here
});
```

query(params, successFn, errorFn)

The query method sends a GET request to the URL and expects a collection of resource objects as a JSON response array.

```
// Issues a request to:
//  GET /api/users
User.query(function(users) {
  // The first user in the collection
  var user = users[0];
});
```

The only major difference between the query() method and the get() method is that Angular expects the query() method to return an array.

HTTP Non-GET Methods

The three HTTP non-GET methods it creates expect the following four parameters:

- params (object)

These are the parameters that are sent with the request. They can be named parameters in the URL, or they can be query parameters.

- postData (object)

This object is the payload sent with the request.

- successFn (function)

This callback function is called upon a successful HTTP response.

- errorFn (function)

This callback function is called upon a non-successful HTTP response.

save(params, payload, successFn, errorFn)

The save method sends a POST request to the URL and uses the payload to generate the request body. The save() method is used to create a new resource on the server.

```
// Issues a request to:
//  POST /api/users
//  with the body {name: 'Ari' }
User.save({}, {
  name: 'Ari'
}, function(response) {
  // Handle a successful response
}, function(response) {
  // Handle a non-successful response
});
```

delete(params, payload, successFn, errorFn)

The delete method sends a DELETE request to the URL and *can* use the payload to generate the request body. It is used to remove an instance from the server.

```
// Issues a request to:
//  DELETE /api/users
User.delete({}, {
  id: '123'
}, function(response) {
  // Handle a successful delete response
}, function(response) {
  // Handle a non-successful delete response
});
```

remove(params, payload, successFn, errorFn)

The remove method is synonymous with the delete() method and primarily exists because delete is a reserved word in JavaScript that can cause problems when we use in Internet Explorer.

```
// Issues a request to:
//  DELETE /api/users
User.remove({}, {
  id: '123'
}, function(response) {
  // Handle a successful remove response
}, function(response) {
  // Handle a non-successful remove response
});
```

$resource instances

When the methods above return data, they wrap the response in a prototype class that adds convenience methods on the instances.

The three instance methods that are available on the instance objects are:

- $save()
- $remove()
- $delete()

These methods are the same as the resource counterpart except that they are called on a single resource instead of on a collection.

These three methods can be called on the instances themselves. For instance:

```
// Using the $save() instance methods
User.get({id: '123'}, function(user) {
  user.name = 'Ari';
  user.$save(); // Save the user
});
// This is equivalent to the collection-level
// resource call
User.save({id: '123'}, {name: 'Ari'});
```

$resource Instances Are Asynchronous

With all these methods, it's important to note that when they are invoked, the $resource object immediately returns an empty reference to the data. This data **is** an empty *reference*, not the actual data, as all these methods are executed asynchronously.

Therefore, a call to get an instance might *look* synchronous, but is actually not. In fact, it's simply a reference to data that Angular *will* fill in automatically when it arrives back from the server.

```
// $scope.user will be empty
$scope.user = User.get({id: '123'});
```

We can wait for the data to come back as expected using the callback method that the methods provide:

```
User.get({id: '123'}, function(user) {
  $scope.user = user;
});
```

Additional Properties

The $resource collections and instances have two special properties that enable us to interact with the underlying resource definitions.

- $promise (promise)

The $promise property is the original promise that is created for the $resource. This property is particularly useful when using it in conjunction with the $routeProvider.when() resolve property.

If the request is successful, the promise is resolved with the resource instance or collection object. If the request is unsuccessful, then the promise is resolved with the HTTP response object, without the resource property.

- $resolved (boolean)

The $resolved property is a boolean that turns true upon the *first* server interaction (regardless of whether or not it's successful).

Custom $resource Methods

Although the $resource service provides five methods, it is extensible enough for us to add our own custom methods to the resource object.

To create a custom method on our $resource class object, we can pass a third argument to the resource class that contains an object of a modified $http configuration object as methods.

In the object, the key is the *name* of the method and the value is the $http configuration object.

```
var User = $resource('/api/users/:userId.json',
  {
    userId: '@id'
  },
  {
    sendEmail: {
      method: 'POST'
    },
    allInboxes: {
      method: 'JSONP',
      isArray: true
    }
  }
);
```

With this User resource, the methods sendEmail() and update() are now available on the collection (User resource object), as are the individual instances (as user.$sendEmail() and user.$update()).

$resource Configuration Object

The $resource configuration object is very similar to the $http configuration object (with a few changes).

The value of the object, the action, is the name of the method on the resource object

It can contain the following keys:

method (string)

method refers to the HTTP method we want to use to make the request. It should be one of the following: 'GET', 'DELETE', 'JSONP', 'POST', 'PUT'.

url (string)

A url that overrides the configured url for the route specific to this method.

params (map of string/object)

This key contains the optional set of pre-bound parameters for this action. If any of the values are functions, they will be executed every time we need to fetch a parameter value for a request.

isArray (boolean)

If this isArray key is set to true, then the returned object for this action will be returned as an array.

transformRequest (function/array of functions)

This function or array of functions is a transform function that takes the HTTP request body and headers and returns their transformed versions. It is usually used for serialization.

```
var User = $resource('/api/users/:id', {
  id: '@'
}, {
  sendEmail: {
    method: 'PUT',
    transformRequest: function(data, headerFn) {
      // Return modified data for the request
      return JSON.stringify(data);
    }
  }
});
```

transformResponse (function/array of functions)

This function or array of functions is a transform function that takes the HTTP request body and headers and returns their transformed versions. It is usually used for deserialization.

```
var User = $resource('/api/users/:id', {
  id: '@'
}, {
  sendEmail: {
    method: 'PUT',
    transformResponse: function(data, headerFn)
    {
      // Return modified data for the response
      return JSON.parse(data);
    }
  }
});
```

cache (boolean/cache)

If the `cache` property is set to true, then Angular will use the default `$http` cache to cache GET requests. If the `cache` property is set to an instance of a `$cacheFactory` object, then the cache object will be used to cache GET requests.

If this property is set to false, then no caching will be applied to the `$resource` requests.

timeout (number/promise)

If `timeout` is set to a number, the timeout for this request will take that number of milliseconds. If it's set to a promise, then it will abort the request when the promise is resolved.

withCredentials (boolean)

If this boolean value is true, then the `withCredentials` flag on the XHR request object will be set.

By default, CORS requests do not set any cookies. The `withCredentials` flag sets the customer header `Access-Control-Allow-Credentials`. This makes request send any cookies from the remote domain in the request.

responseType (string)

The `responseType` option sets the `XMLHttpRequestResponseType` property on the request. We can set it to one of these different types of available HTTP response types:

- "" (string – default)
- "arraybuffer" (ArrayBuffer)
- "blob" (blob object)
- "document" (HTTP document)
- "json" (JSON object parsed from a JSON string)
- "text" (string)
- "moz-blob" (Firefox to receive progress events)
- "moz-chunked-text" (streaming text)
- "moz-chunked-arraybuffer" (streaming ArrayBuffer)

interceptor (object)

The interceptor property has two optional methods: either a `response` or a `responseError`. These *interceptors* are called with the `$http` response object, just like normal `$http` interceptors.

$resource Services

We can use the $resource service as the base our own custom services. Building custom services gives us greater overall customization of our app and the ability to abstract the responsibility of communicating to remote services away from our controllers and views.

Finally, we *highly* recommend using $resource from inside a custom service object. Not only does it enable us to abstract away the responsibility of fetching remote services into a single, controllable Angular service, it also disconnects this logic from our controllers, enabling us to keep them clean. Additionally, it allows us to not worry about *how* we are getting data in our controllers.

This disconnection from inside Angular objects also helps to make testing a breeze, as we can stub and mock back-end calls without worrying about actually making the calls to our back end during tests.

To create a service that wraps $resource, we need to *inject* the $resource service into our service object and call the methods like normal.

For instance:

```
angular.module('myApp', ['ngResource'])
.factory('UserService', [
  '$resource', function($resource) {

    return $resource('/api/users/:id', {
      id: '@'
    }, {
      update: {
        method: 'PUT'
      }
    });
}]);
```

$resource API

The $resource service is available through the use of the $resource() method. The method itself takes up to three parameters:

- url (string)

Here, we give the parametrized URL string template with all of the parameters that we need to use to identify the resource (prefixed by the : character). For any parameters we pass in the URL, we can send *named* arguments in as their values:

```
$resource('/api/users/:id.:format', {
  format: 'json',
  id: '123'
})
```

Note that if the parameter before the suffix is empty (:id in our example above), then the URL will collapse into a single . character.

 If we use a server that requires a port as part of the URL – for instance: http://localhost:3000 – we **must** escape the URL pattern using \\. The URL pattern for this back end server would look similar to: $resource('http://localhost\\:3000/api/users/:id.json').

- paramDefaults (optional object)

The second parameter contains the default values for the URL parameters that will be sent with each request. The keys in the object match up with the named parameters. If we pass a key that is not set as a named parameter, then it is passed as a regular query parameter.

For instance, if the URL string passed has the signature of /api/users/:id and we set the default parameters to {id: '123', name: 'Ari' }, then the resulting URL becomes /api/users/123?name=Ari.

We can either pass a static value here, such as we've done above by hard coding it in the default parameter, OR we can set it to pull a dynamic parameter out of the data object.

To set a dynamic parameter, we only need to prefix the value with a '@' character.

- actions (optional object)

The actions object is a hash with declarations of custom actions that can extend the default set of resource actions.

In the object , the *names* of the custom actions as denoted by it's keys, while the values the $http configuration object will be substituted in the URL.

For instance, we can declare a new update action on our resource like so:

```
$resource('/api/users/:id.:format', {
  format: 'json',
  id: '123'
}, {
  update: {
    method: 'PUT'
  }
})
```

Using Restangular

Although Angular on its own is powerful enough to build standalone applications where we pack all important data inside the application, in doing so we would be missing out on one of the nicest features of the framework: its ability to talk with the outside world.

In this section, we're going to talk specifically about an incredibly well-developed and well-thought-out library: **Restangular**.

The What and the Why

Restangular is an Angular service specifically designed simply to fetch data from the rest of the world.

Why not use $http or $resource? Although $http and $resource are built into the framework, they carry limitations with them. Restangular takes a completely different approach to XHR and makes it a pleasant experience.

The complete list of benefits to using Restangular is available on the Restangular README[62], but we'll cover a few benefits here:

Promises

Using promises makes Restangular *feel* more Angular-esque, as it uses and resolves on promises. That enables us to chain together responses just as though we're using the raw $http method.

Promise Unwrapping

You can also use Restangular as $resource works, working with Promises and Objects at the same time in a very easy way.

---

[62]https://github.com/mgonto/restangular

Explicit

The Restangular library includes little to no magic. We don't have to guess how it works or dig up documentation on how to use it.

All HTTP Methods

All *HTTP* methods are supported.

Forget URLs

While $resource requires us to specify the URLs we want to fetch, Restangular doesn't require us to *know* the URLs in advance, nor do we have to specify them all upfront (other than the base URL).

Nested resources

If we want to use nested resources, there's no need to create another instance of the Restangular instance; Restangular will handle it for us.

One resource, not many

Unlike $resource, we only ever need to create one instance of the Restangular resource object.

And there is much, much more.

Installation

Installing Restangular is easy – we have options. We can download the files manually (from GitHub[63]) and include the file locally. If we download the file to our js/vendor directory, then we can include it in our HTML, like so:

```
<script type="test/javascript" src="js/vendor/restangular.min.js"></script>
```

We can include the JavaScript libraries hosted on jsDelivr[64] in our page:

---

[63]https://raw.github.com/jimaek/jsdelivr/master/files/restangular/latest/restangular.min.js

[64]http://www.jsdelivr.com/

```
<script type="text/javascript"
  src="http://cdn.jsdelivr.net/restangular/latest/restangular.js"></script>
<script type="text/javascript"
  src="http://cdn.jsdelivr.net/restangular/latest/restangular.min.js"></script>
```

Alternatively, we can use npm to install Restangular if we're using npm in our project:

```
$ npm install restangular
```

If we've set up Bower for our project, we can also choose to use Bower to install Restangular.

```
$ bower install restangular
```

 Restangular depends on either Lo-Dash or Underscore, so in order to support Restangular, we need to make sure we include one of the two.

If we use bower, Lodash will automatically be downloaded for us.

Otherwise, We can use jsDelivr[65] to include lodash:

```
<script type="text/javascript"
    src="//cdn.jsdelivr.net/lodash/2.1.0/lodash.compat.min.js">
</script>
```

Alternatively, we can download Lo-Dash here[66] or use Bower to install it.

```
bower install --save lodash
```

We also need to include it as a script on the page:

```
<script type="text/javascript"
  src="/js/vendor/lodash/dist/lodash.min.js"></script>
```

Just like any other AngularJS library, we need to include the restangular resource as a dependency for our app module object:

---

[65]http://www.jsdelivr.com/#!lodash

[66]http://lodash.com/

```
angular.module('myApp', ['restangular']);
```

Once we've done that, we'll be able to inject the `Restangular` service into our Angular objects:

```
angular.module('myApp')
.factory('UserService',
  ['Restangular',
    function(Restangular) {
      // Now we have access to the Restangular
      // service our service
  }]);
```

Intro to the Restangular Object

To use Restangular, there are two ways we can create an object to fetch services. We can either set the base route to fetch objects from:

```
var User = Restangular.all('users');
```

Doing so will set all HTTP requests that come from the Restangular service to pull from /users. For instance, calling `getList()` on the above object will fetch from /users:

```
var allUsers = User.getList(); // GET /users
```

It's also possible to fetch nested requests for a single object. Instead of passing only a route, we can pass a unique ID to pull from as well:

```
var oneUser = Restangular.one('users', 'abc123');
```

This code will generate the request /users/abc123 when calling `get()` on it.

```
oneUser.get().then(function(user) {
  // GET /users/abc123/inboxes
  user.getList('inboxes');
});
```

As you can see above, Restangular is smart enough to figure out how to construct URLs based upon the methods that we are calling on the Restangular source object. Sometimes, however, it is convenient to set the URL that we're fetching, especially if our back end doesn't support pure RESTful APIs.

To set the URL for a specific request, we can pass a separate argument using the `allUrl` method:

```
// All URLs on searches will use
// `http://google.com/` as the baseUrl
var searches =
  Restangular.allUrl('one', 'http://google.com/');
// Will send a request to GET http://google.com/
searches.getList();
```

Additionally, we can set the base URL for one particular request, rather than manipulating the entire request using oneUrl:

```
var singleSearch =
  Restangular.oneUrl('betaSearch', 'http://beta.google.com/1');

// Trigger a request to GET http://google.com/1
singleSearch.get();
```

Using Restangular

Now that we have a good handle on the Restangular object, we can get down to using it to make requests.

Once Restangular returns an initial object, we can use several different methods to interact with our back-end API.

Let's say we've created a Restangular object that represents public discussions:

```
var messages = Restangular.all('messages');
```

With this object, we can get a list of all of the messages with the getList() method. This getList() method returns a collection containing methods we can call to work with the specific collection.

```
// allMessages is a promise that will resolve
// into the list of all messages
var allMessages = messages.getList();
```

We can also use the Restangular object to create messages. To create an object, we'll use the post() method.

The post method requires a single object as a parameter and sends a (you guessed it) POST request to the *URL* we've specified. We can also add queryParameters and headers to this request.

```
// POST to /messages
var newMessage = {
  body: "Hello world"
};
messages.post(newMessage);
// OR we can call this on an element
// to create a nested resource
var message = Restangular.one('messages', 'abc123');
message.post('replies', newMessage);
```

Because Restangular returns promises, we can then call methods on the returned data on promises so that we can run a function after the promise has completed.

Restangular returns enhanced promises, so besides being able to call then on them, we can call other special methods like $object. $object returns an empty array (or object) right away, and after the server returns information, that array is filled with new information. This is useful for instance if after we update a collection, we want to refetch the collection on our scope:

```
// Calling then in the promise
messages.post(newMessage).then(function(newMsg) {
  // Setting messages to an empty array first
  // and then fill it once getList is completed
  $scope.messages = messages.getList().$object;
}, function error(reason) {
  // An error has occurred
});
```

We can also remove an object from the collection. Using the remove() method, we can send a DELETE HTTP request to our back end. To send a delete request, we can call the remove() method on an object inside the collection (an element).

```
var message = messages.get(123);
message.remove(); // Send a DELETE to /messages
```

Updating and saving objects is something we'll do quite often. Traditionally, this operation is done with the HTTP method PUT. Restangular supports this functionality out of the box with the method put().

To update an object, we need to query the object, set our new attributes on the instance, and call put() on the object to save the updated attributes in the back end.

> Note that before modifying an object, it's good practice to copy it and then modify the copied object before we save it. Restangular has its own version of copy such that it won't rebind this in the bundled functions. It's good practice to use Restangular.copy() when updating an object.

Now that we have experience working on instances of our collection, let's dig into nested components. Nested components are those that live underneath other components. For instance, for all of the books written by a certain author.

Restangular supports nested resources by default. In fact, we can query a particular instance from our collection for their nested resources.

```
var author = Restangular.one('authors', 'abc123');
// Builds a GET to /authors/abc123/books
var books = author.getList('books');
```

Another cool feature of Restangular is that we're able to call all of this methods (post, put, getList, get, etc.) not only from Restangular created objects with one and all, but also from objects returned from the server. For instance, we can first fetch an author to display in one part of our code, and then get the list of books from it:

```
Restangular.one('authors', 'abc123').then(function(author) {
  $scope.author = author;
});


// Later in the code
// Builds a GET to /authors/abc123/authors
// using $scope.author which is real object returned from the server
$scope.author.getList('books')
```

But What About My HTTP Methods?

Restangular supports, out of the box, *all* HTTP methods. It can support calling GET, PUT, POST, DELETE, HEAD, TRACE, OPTIONS, and PATCH.

```
author.get(); // GET /authors/abc123
author.getList('books'); // GET /authors/abc123/books
author.put(); // PUT /authors/abc123
author.post(); // POST /authors/abc123
author.remove(); // DELETE /authors/abc123
author.head(); // HEAD /authors/abc123
author.trace(); // TRACE /authors/abc123
author.options(); // OPTIONS /authors/abc123
author.patch(); // PATCH /author/abc123
```

Restangular also makes it possible to create custom HTTP methods for cases when our back-end server maps resources differently than we expect.

For instance, if we want to get the author's biography (not a RESTful resource), we can set the URL through the `customMETHOD()` function (where METHOD is replaced by any of the following: GET, GETLIST, DELETE, POST, PUT, HEAD, OPTIONS, PATCH, TRACE).

```
// Maps to GET /users/abc123/biography
author.customGET("biography");
// Or customPOST with a new bio object
// as {body: "Ari's bio"}
// The two empty fields in between are the
// params field and any custom headers
author.customPOST({body: "Ari's Bio"}, // post body
  "biography",    // route
  {},             // custom params
  {});            // custom headers
```

Custom Query Parameters and Headers

We can send custom query parameters or custom headers with each of these methods.

To add custom query parameters, we need to add a JavaScript object as the second parameter to our method call. We can also add a second JavaScript object as a third parameter. Most all of the individual methods that we can call on an element take these two parameters as optional parameters.

With custom query parameters, a post method might look something like:

```
var queryParamObj = { role: 'admin' },
    headerObj = { 'x-user': 'admin' };

messages.getList('accounts', queryParamObj, headerObj);
```

Restangular is incredibly simple to use and gets out of the way so that we can focus on building our app, rather than wrestling with the API.

Configuring Restangular

Restangular is highly configurable and expects us to configure it for our apps. It does come with defaults for every single property, so we don't have to configure it if we don't need to do so.

There are a few different places where we can configure a Restangular service. We can configure it globally or using a custom service.

To configure Restangular for all Restangular usages, regardless of the location it's used in, we can inject the `RestangularProvider` in a `config()` function or inject `Restangular` in a `run()` function.

A good rule of thumb to determine where we should configure our Restangular instances: If we need to use any other service in configuring Restangular, then we should configure it in the run() method, otherwise we'll keep it in the config() method.

Setting the baseUrl

To set the baseUrl for all calls to our backendAPI, we can use the setBaseUrl() method. For instance, if our API is located at /api/v1, rather than at the root of our server.

```
angular.module('myApp')
  .config(function(RestangularProvider) {
    RestangularProvider.setBaseUrl('/api/v1');
  });
```

Adding Element Transformations

We can add any element transformations after Restangular has loaded an element.

Using these elementTransformers, we can add *custom* methods to our Restangular objects after they are fetched.

This method will be called as a callback that will enable us to update or modify the element we fetched after it's been loaded, but before we use it in our Angular objects.

```
angular.module('myApp')
  .config(function(RestangularProvider) {
    // Three parameters:
    // the route
    // if it's a collection - boolean (true/false) or
    // not sending it if you need it for both
    // and the transformer
    RestangularProvider.addElementTransformer('authors',
      false, function(element) {
        element.fetchedAt = new Date();
        return element;
    });
  });
```

There are shortcut methods for only extending a model or a collection. For instance, if we wanted to update only elements that are authors, we can do the following:

```
angular.module('myApp')
  .config(function(RestangularProvider) {
    // Three parameters:
    // the route
    // if it's a collection - boolean (true/false) or
    // not sending it if you need it for both
    // and the transformer
    RestangularProvider.extendModel('authors', function(element) {
        element.getFullName = function() {
            return element.name + ' ' + element.lastName;
        }
        return element;
    });
  });
```

Setting responseInterceptors

Restangular can set responseInterceptors. responseInterceptors are useful for when we want to translate the response we get back from the server. For instance, if our server comes back with the data tucked away in a nested object, we can use a responseInterceptor to dig it out.

 It's important that the getList method always returns an array, so if your response is an object with some metadata and a nested array, we should use the responseInterceptor to get it out.

This responseInterceptor is called after every response we get back from the back end. It is called with the following parameters:

- data - data retrieved from the server
- operation - the HTTP method used
- what - the model that's requested
- url - the relative URL that's being requested
- response - the full server response, including headers
- deferred - the promise for the request

For instance, the following configuration would return an array for getList with the metadata, in case this array is the value of the property with the same name as the route. For example a GET to /customers would return an array like {customers: []}

```
angular.module('myApp')
  .config(function(RestangularProvider) {
    RestangularProvider.setResponseInterceptor(
      function(data, operation, what) {
        if (operation == 'getList') {
          var list = data[what];
          list.metadata = data.metadata;
          return list;
        }
        return data;
    });
});
```

Using requestInterceptors

Restangular supports the other side of the operation, as well: We can work with the data we are going to send to the server before we ever actually send any data back to the server in the first place.

requestInterceptors are useful for times when we need to run manipulations on the object before sending it to the server. For instance, we can't call directly to MongoDB with an _id field, so we have to remove it before it is sent to the back end if we're in a PUT operation.

Tip: We can use requestInterceptors and responseInterceptors together to make a page wide loading. Start loading on every request and stop it each time a response is received.

To set a requestInterceptor, we can use the method setRequestInterceptor(). This method (setRequestInterceptor()) is called with the following parameters:

- element - the element we're sending to the server
- operation - the HTTP method used
- what - the model that's being requested
- url - the relative URL that's being requested

```
angular.module('myApp')
  .config(function(RestangularProvider) {
    RestangularProvider.setRequestInterceptor(
      function(elem, operation, what) {
        if (operation === 'put') {
          elem._id = undefined;
          return elem;
        }
        return elem;
    });
});
```

Custom Fields

Restangular also supports setting custom Restangular fields, which is important for times when we are connecting not to a back-end server, but to a back-end database, such as MongoDB, where the id field doesn't map to an id. When connecting to MongoDB, the id field actually maps to _id.$oid.

```
angular.module('myApp')
  .config(function(RestangularProvider) {
    RestangularProvider.setRestangularFields({
      id: '_id.$oid'
    });
  });
});
```

Catching Errors with errorInterceptors

It's also possible to set errorInterceptors for those times when we want to catch an error from within Restangular. Using the errorInterceptor gives us the ability to halt the flow of the error down to our app.

If we return false from the errorInterceptor, the flow of the promise ends, and our app will never need to deal with handling errors.

It would be a good time to handle dealing with authentication failures at this point, for instance. If any request comes back with a 401, we can use the errorInterceptor to catch it and handle redirecting the user to the login page.

```
angular.module('myApp')
  .config(function(RestangularProvider) {
    RestangularProvider.setErrorInterceptor(
      function(resp) {
        displayError();
        return false; // stop the promise chain
    });
  });
});
```

Setting Parentless

If we're fetching a resource that is **not** nested underneath other nested resources, we can use the setParentless configuration property field to tell Restangular not to build the nested URL structure.

```
angular.module('myApp')
.config(function(RestangularProvider) {
  RestangularProvider.setParentless([
    'cars'
  ]);
});
```

The setParentless() configuration function can take two different types of parameters:

boolean

If this parameter is set to true, all resources are considered 'parentless', and no URL is nested.

array

Only the resources identified by the string in this array will be considered parentless.

Working with Hypermedia

It's a really good practice to only have one point of access to the Backend server (the main URL) and then have each of your models point to its related resources via links.

Restangular supports this really useful practice with selfLink, oneUrl and allUrl.

The first thing we need to do is to configure the selfLink field. Really similar to how we configure the ID, the idea of the selfLink is to set the path to the property in a model that has a link to itself. This will allow us to know to which URL we need to do the PUT or GET if needed.

```
angular.module('myApp')
  .config(function(RestangularProvider) {
    RestangularProvider.setRestangularFields({
      selfLink: 'link.href'
    });
  });
});
```

After configuring this, we can start using this really useful feature.

Let's first fetch the list of all authors, which is the main route for our application.

```
$scope.authors = Restangular.all('authors').getList().$object;
```

Each of this authors has a link to itself in the path we specified before, and it also has a URL that points to the list of books it has. We could use those properties like this:

```
var firstAuthor = authors[0];
firstAuthor.name = "John";

// Does a PUT to /authors/1988-author-1
// That's the url in firstAuthor.link.href
firstAuthor.put()

// GET to /books/for-author/1988-author-1
var books = Restangular.allUrl('books', firstAuthor.books.href).getList().$object;
```

Custom Restangular Services

Finally, we *highly* recommend using Restangular from inside a custom service object. Doing so is particularly useful, as we can configure Restangular on a per-service level with a custom a service. Writing a service will help disconnect the logic to talk to our back-end from within our angular objects and enable our services to handle the load of talking to them directly.

This disconnection from inside Angular objects also helps with making testing a breeze as we can stub and mock back-end calls without worrying about actually making the calls to our back end during tests.

To create a service that wraps Restangular, we simply need to *inject* the Restangular service into our factory and call the methods like normal. Inside this factory, we can create custom configurations by using the withConfig() function.

For instance:

```
angular.module('myApp', ['restangular'])
.factory('MessageService', [
  'Restangular', function(Restangular) {
    var restAngular =
      Restangular.withConfig(function(Configurer) {
        Configurer.setBaseUrl('/api/v2/messages');
    });

    var _messageService = restAngular.all('messages');

    return {
      getMessages: function() {
        return _messageService.getList();
      }
    }
  }
}]);
```

XHR in Practice

Cross-Origin and Same-Origin Policy

Web browsers nearly universally prevent web pages from fetching and executing scripts on foreign domains.

The *same-origin* policy specifically permits scripts to run on pages that originate from the same site. Our browser identifies a page with the same origin by comparing the scheme, hostname, and port number of both pages. There are heavy run restrictions on any other interactions with scripts originating from off-site.

The Cross Origin Resource Sharing (or CORS, for short) is often a source of headaches for fetching data over XHR and dealing with foreign sources.

Fortunately, there are several ways for us to get data that is exposed by external data sources into our app. We'll look at two of these methods and mention a third (that requires a bit more backend support):

- JSONP
- CORS
- Server proxies

JSONP

JSONP is a way to get past the browser security issues that are present when we're trying to request data from a foreign domain. In order to work with JSONP, the server must be able to support the method.

JSONP works by issuing a GET request using a `<script>` tag, instead of using XHR requests. The JSONP technique creates a `<script>` tag and places it in the DOM. When it shows up in the DOM, the browser takes over and requests the script referenced in the `src` tag.

When the server returns the request, it surrounds the response with a JavaScript function invocation that corresponds to a request about which our JavaScript knows.

Angular provides a helper for JSONP requests using the `$http` service. The `jsonp` method of request through the `$http` service looks like:

```
$http
.jsonp("https://api.github.com?callback=JSON_CALLBACK")
.success(function(data) {
  // Data
});
```

When we make this call, Angular places a `<script>` tag on the DOM that might look something like:

```
<script src="https://api.github.com?callback=angular.callbacks._0"
  type="text/javascript"></script>
```

Notice that Angular has replaced the JSON_CALLBACK with a custom function that Angular creates specifically for this request.

When the data comes back from the JSONP-enabled server, it is wrapped in the anonymous function automatically generated by Angular `angular.callbacks._0`.

In this case, the GitHub server will return some JSON wrapped in the callback, and its response might look like:

```
// shortened for brevity
angular.callbacks._0({
  "meta": {
    "X-RateLimit-Limit": "60",
    "status": 200,
  },
  "data": {
    "current_user_url": "https://api.github.com/user"
  }
})
```

When Angular calls the special function, it resolves the `$http` promise.

 When we write our own back-end servers to support JSONP, we need to ensure that, when we respond, we wrap the data inside the function given by the request with `callback`.

When using JSONP, we need to be aware of the potential security risks. First, we're opening up our server to allow a back-end server to call any JavaScript in our app.

A foreign site that we do not control can change its script at any time (or a malicious cracker could), exposing our site for vulnerabilities. The server or a middleman could potentially send extra JavaScript logic back into our page that could expose private user data.

We can only use JSONP to send GET requests, since we're setting a GET request in the `<script>` tag. Additionally, it's tough to manage errors on a script tag. We should use JSONP sparingly and only with servers we trust and control.

Using CORS

In recent years, the W3C has created the CORS specification, or Cross Origin Resource Sharing policy, to replace the JSONP *hack* in a standard way.

The CORS specification is simply an extension to the standard XMLHttpRequest object that allows JavaScript to make cross-domain XHR calls. It does so by *preflighting* a request to the server to effectively ask for permission to send the request.

This *preflight* gives the receiving server the ability to accept or reject any request from all servers, a select server, or set of servers. That means that both the client app and the server app need to coordinate to provide data to the client/server.

The W3C wrote the CORS specification with the intention of abstracting away many of the details from the client-side developer so that it appears as though the request is made in the same way as a same-origin request.

Configuration

To use CORS within Angular, we need to tell Angular that we're using CORS. We use the `.config()` method on our Angular app module to set two options.

First, we need to tell Angular to use the `XDomain`, and we must remove the `X-Requested-With` header from all of our requests.

 The `X-Requested-With` header has been removed from the common header defaults, but it's a good idea to ensure it's been removed anyway.

```
angular.module('myApp')
.config(function($httpProvider) {
  $httpProvider.defaults.useXDomain = true;
  delete $httpProvider.defaults.headers
    .common['X-Requested-With'];
});
```

Now we're ready to make CORS requests.

Server CORS Requirements

Although we will not dive into server-side CORS setup in this chapter (we do in the server communication chapter), it's important that the server we're working with support CORS.

A server supporting CORS must respond to requests with several access control headers:

- Access-Control-Allow-Origin

The value of this header must either echo the origin request header or be a * to allow any and all requests from any origin.

- Access-Control-Allow-Credentials (optional)

By default, CORS requests are **not** made with cookies. If the server includes this header, then we can send cookies along with our request by setting the `withCredentials` option to true.

If we set the `withCredentials` option in our $http request to true, but the server does not respond with this header, then the request will fail and vice versa.

The back-end server must also be able to handle OPTIONS request methods.

There are two types of CORS requests: simple and non-simple.

Simple Requests

Requests are simple if they match one of these HTTP methods:

- HEAD
- GET
- POST

and if they are made with one or many of the following HTTP headers, and no others:

- Accept
- Accept-Language
- Content-Language
- Last-Event-ID
- Content-Type
    - application/x-www-form-urlencoded
    - multipart/form-data
    - text/plain

We categorize these as *simple* requests because the browser can make these types of requests without the use of CORS. Simple requests do NOT require any special type of communication between the server and the client.

A simple CORS request using the $http service looks like any other request:

```
$http
.get("https://api.github.com")
.success(function(data) {
  // Data
});
```

Non-Simple Requests

Non-simple requests are those that violate the requirements for the simple requests. If we want to support PUT or DELETE methods, or if we want to set the specific type of content type in our requests, then we're going to call a non-simple request.

Although, as client-side developers, this request doesn't look any different to us, the browser handles the request differently.

The browser actually sends two requests: the preflight and the request. First, the browser issues a preflight request wherein the server requests permission to make the request. If the permissions have been granted, then the browser can make the actual request.

The browser takes care of handling the CORS request transparently.

Similar to the simple request, the browser will add the Origin header to both of the requests (preflight and the actual request).

Preflight Request

The browser makes the preflight request as an OPTIONS request. It contains a few headers in the request:

- Access-Control-Request-Method

This header is the HTTP method of the actual request. It is always included in the request.

- Access-Control-Request-Headers (optional)

This header is a comma-delimited list of non-simple headers that are included in the request.

The server should accept the request, then we must check if the HTTP method and the headers are valid. If they are, the server should respond with the following headers:

- Access-Control-Allow-Origin

The value of this header must either echo the origin request header or be a * to allow any and all requests from any origin.

- Access-Control-Allow-Methods

This list of allowed HTTP methods is helpful, as we can cache the request in the client, and we don't have to constantly ask for preflights in future requests.

- Access-Control-Allow-Headers

If the `Access-Control-Request-Headers` header is set, then the server should respond with this header.

We expect the server to respond with a 200 response status code if the request is acceptable. If it is, then the second request will be made.

 CORS is **not** a security mechanism; it is simply a standard that modern browsers implement. It's still our responsibility to set up security in our app.

Non-simple requests look exactly like regular requests inside Angular:

```
$http
.delete("https://api.github.com/api/users/1")
.success(function(data) {
  // Data
});
```

Server-Side Proxies

The simplest method for making requests to **any** server, however, is to simply use a back-end server on the same domain (or on a remote server with CORS setup) as a proxy for remote resources.

Rather than making requests to foreign resources through our client-side app, we can simply use our own local server to make and respond to requests for our client-side app.

In this way, we enable older browsers to make requests (only modern browsers implement CORS), without requiring a second request for non-simple CORS requests, and we can use standard browser-level security as it was intended to be used.

In order to use a server-side proxy, we need to set up a local server to handle our requests, which takes care of sending the actual requests.

For more information about setting up a server-side component, read the Server communication chapter.

Working with JSON

JSON, or JavaScript Object Notation, is a data-interchange format that looks a lot like a JavaScript object. In fact, it resolves to one when JavaScript loads it, and Angular will resolve any requests that respond with a JavaScript object in JSON format to a corresponding object for our Angular app.

For instance, if our server returns the following JSON:

```
[
  {"msg": "This is the first msg", state: 1},
  {"msg": "This is the second msg", state: 2},
  {"msg": "This is the third msg", state: 1},
  {"msg": "This is the fourth msg", state: 3}
]
```

When our Angular app receives this data over $http, we can simply reference the data as a JavaScript object:

```
$http.get('/v1/messages.json')
  .success(function(data, status) {
    $scope.first_msg = data[0].msg;
    $scope.first_state = data[0].state;
  });
```

Working with XML

Although Angular transparently handles JSON objects handed back from the server, we can handle other data types as well.

For instance, if our server hands us back XML instead of JSON, we need to massage the data into a JavaScript object.

Luckily, there are some great open-source libraries available, as well as some built-in browser parsers that parse XML into JavaScript objects for us.

For the moment, we'll use the X2JS library, a fantastic open-source library available here[67].

First, we need to make sure we *install* the X2JS library. Let's use Bower to install the library for us:

```
$ bower install x2js
```

and then reference the library from the googlecode.com or from our Bower components:

---

[67]https://code.google.com/p/x2js/

```html
<script type="text/javascript"
  src="https://x2js.googlecode.com/hg/xml2json.js"></script>
<!-- OR -->
<script type="text/javascript"
  src="bower_components/xml2json/xml2json.js"></script>
```

Starting off with our lightweight XML parser, we create a factory that simply parses the XML in the DOM for us.

```javascript
angular.factory('xmlParser', function() {
  var x2js = new X2JS();
  return {
    xml2json: x2js.xml2json,
    json2xml: x2js.json2xml_str
  }
});
```

With this lightweight parsing factory, we can create a transformResponse to parse our XML within our $http requests, such as:

```javascript
angular.factory('Data', [$http, 'xmlParser',
  function($http, xmlParser) {
    $http.get('/api/msgs.xml', {
      transformResponse:
        function(data) {
          return xmlParser.xml2json(data);
        }
    })
});
```

Now, our response will come back as a JSON object, and we can use the response just as though the server returned JSON.

Authentication with AngularJS

In most non-trivial web applications, there are usually protected resources that we want to keep secret from the general public and to which we want to give access only to authenticated users whom we know and trust. These resources can be anything from paid material to administration ability.

Regardless of what we are protecting, the methods that we can use to protect our resources will be similar.

Describing *how* to implement server-side authentication is out of scope of this section; instead, we'll focus on describing *what* our server-side back end needs to do to feature our front-end view.

Then we'll dive right into discussing how to provide client-side authentication protection and discuss potential edge cases for the process.

Server-Side Requirements

First and foremost, we must take the time to secure our server-side API. As we are dealing with uncompiled code being sent by a potentially untrusted source, we cannot count on all of our users to be genuine.

There are generally *two* ways we can handle securing our client-side app:

Server-Side Rendered Views

If we're serving our site through a back-end server that controls all of the HTML, we can use traditional authentication methods and only send the HTML that our client side needs and that the server authenticates.

Pure Client-Side Authentication

We want to be able to build our client side and server side separately and allow the deployment of these components to be naturally separated in production. We therefore need to secure our client-side authentication using the server-side API, but not rely on its authentication.

We're going to implement client-side authentication through token authentication. Our server needs to be able to provide our client app with an auth token.

The token itself should be a random string of numbers and letters that the server side can associate to a particular user session.

 uuid libraries are generally good candidates for generating tokens.

That is, when a user logs into our site, instead of sending a user ID or using any identifiable information, our server side generates a random token and creates an association between the user session and this token.

We expect to send the token with every single client-side request so that we can look up the user by this random string of characters on each one.

Our server side then needs to send the proper status codes for the particular events that we get back, denoting whether or not they are valid, so that our client side can react.

For instance, for all unauthenticated requests, we want our server side to send back a 401 response status code.

The following table is a short list of response status codes that we'll deal with in this section:

Code	Meaning
200	Everything is good
401	Unauthenticated request
403	Forbidden request
404	Page not found
500	Server error

When we encounter these status codes, our app reacts accordingly.

The data flow looks like:

1. Unauthenticated user visits our site.
2. The user tries to access a protected resource and is redirected to the login page. 2a. The user visits the login page manually.
3. The user enters his or her login ID (username or email) and password, and our Angular app makes a POST request to our server with the user's data.
4. Our server looks at the login ID and password and determines whether they are a match.
5. If the login ID matches the password, the server generates a unique token and sends it back alongside the request and a 200 response code. 5a. If the login ID does not match the password, the server responds to the request with a status code of 401.

For an authenticated user (someone who passes along the 5a request path above):

1. The user requests a protected resource path (such as his or her own account page).
2. If the user has not yet logged in, our app redirects the user to the login page. 2a. If the user is logged in, our app makes a request using the unique user token for the session.
3. The server validates this token and returns the appropriate data based on the request.

Client-Side Authentication

In the section above, we've outlined a few behaviors that our authentication scheme needs to handle:

- Redirect on unauthorized page requests
- Capture non-200 responses and act accordingly on any XHR request
- Keep track of the user throughout the page session

To handle redirection on unauthorized page requests, such as when an unauthorized user tries to access a protected resource, we need to determine how to define a protected resource vs. a public one.

There are several ways to handle defining routes as public vs. non-public.

Protected Resources from API

If we're protecting routes that need to operate on protected API calls (i.e., making a protected resource API call to which the server can respond with a 401 response code) in order to load the page, then we can simply rely on $http interceptors to handle the work for us.

To create an $http interceptor that is responsible for responding to unauthenticated API requests, we need to create one that handles responses.

Let's set up our $http response interceptor inside of a .config() block inside our app where we *inject* the $httpProvider:

```
angular.module('myApp', [])
.config(function($httpProvider) {
  // Build our interceptor here
});
```

This interceptor handles both responses and responseErrors and will be called on all requests.

```
angular.module('myApp', [])
.config(function($httpProvider) {
  // Build our interceptor here
  var interceptor =
  function($q, $rootScope, Auth) {
    return {
      'response': function(resp) {
        if (resp.config.url == '/api/login') {
          // Assuming our API server response
          // with the following data:
          // { token: "AUTH_TOKEN" }
          Auth.setToken(resp.data.token);
        }
      },
      'responseError': function(rejection) {
        // Handle errors
        switch(rejection.status) {
          case 401:
            if (rejection.config.url!=='api/login')
              // If we're not on the login page
              $rootScope
                .$broadcast('auth:loginRequired');
            break;
```

```
          case 403:
            $rootScope
              .$broadcast('auth:forbidden');
            break;

          case 404:
            $rootScope
              .$broadcast('page:notFound');
            break;

          case 500:
            $rootScope
              .$broadcast('server:error');
            break;
        }

        return $q.reject(rejection);
      }
    }
  }
});
```

This *auth* interceptor handles a few of the server-side response codes that we can possibly receive from our server on any given request. When the response interceptor takes a 401 response, it $broadcasts an event down the app from the $rootScope so that any child scope (all scopes) can handle the event.

Additionally, this interceptor *saves* the token for any successful 200 request to our /api/login login route.

To actually implement this interceptor for our requests, we need to tell the $httpProvider to include it in its interceptor chain:

```
angular.module('myApp', [])
.config(function($httpProvider) {
  // Build our interceptor here
  var interceptor =
  function($q, $rootScope, Auth) {
    // ...
  }
  // Integrate the interceptor in the
  // request/response chain for $http
  $httpProvider
```

```
        .interceptors.push(interceptor);
});
```

 For more information on $http interceptors, check out the $http interceptors section.

Protected Resources by Route Definition

If we want to always protect all of our paths and/or if we are not making API calls that will protect the route, then we need to monitor our routes and ensure that we have a logged-in user for the routes we are interested in protecting.

In order to monitor our routes, we must set up an event listener on the $routeChangeStart event. This event fires when the route properties start to resolve, but before we've actually changed the route.

 Combined with the interceptors, this approach is more secure. If we don't check for status code, our users may **still** be able to make unprotected requests.

Let's set our listener to focus on this event and check to see if the route itself is defined to be exposed to the current user.

First, we must define some access roles for our application. We can do so by setting a constant in our app such that we can check against these roles on each route.

```
angular.module('myApp', ['ngRoute'])
.constant('ACCESS_LEVELS', {
  pub: 1,
  user: 2
});
```

By setting the ACCESS_LEVELS as a constant, we can *inject* it into both .config() and .run() blocks and can use it throughout our application.

Now, let's use these constants to define access levels for each of our defined routes:

```
angular.module('myApp', ['ngRoute'])
.config(function($routeProvider, ACCESS_LEVELS) {
  $routeProvider
  .when('/', {
    controller: 'MainController',
    templateUrl: 'views/main.html',
    access_level: ACCESS_LEVELS.pub
  })
  .when('/account', {
    controller: 'AccountController',
    templateUrl: 'views/account.html',
    access_level: ACCESS_LEVELS.user
  })
  .otherwise({
    redirectTo: '/'
  })
});
```

Each of the routes above defines its own access_level, which we can check to confirm that the current user is authorized (if necessary) and is of an appropriate user level to access the route.

At this point, there will be a user with one of two states:

- Unauthenticated anonymous user
- Authenticated known user

To authenticate a user, we need to create a service that holds onto the existing user level. We must also let our service work with the local browser cookie store so we can expect that, when logged in, our user will remain logged in while the session is still good.

This small service simply includes some helper functions on top of the user object:

```
angular.module('myApp.services', [])
.factory('Auth',
function($cookieStore, ACCESS_LEVELS) {
  var _user = $cookieStore.get('user');

  var setUser = function(user) {
    if (!user.role || user.role < 0) {
      user.role = ACCESS_LEVELS.pub;
    }
    _user = user;
    $cookieStore.put('user', _user);
```

```
  }

  return {
    isAuthorized: function(lvl) {
      return _user.role >= lvl;
    },
    setUser: setUser,
    isLoggedIn: function() {
      return _user ? true : false;
    },
    getUser: function() {
      return _user;
    },
    getId: function() {
      return _user ? _user._id : null;
    },
    getToken: function() {
      return _user ? _user.token : '';
    },
    logout: function() {
      $cookieStore.remove('user');
      _user = null;
    }
  }
});
```

Now, if our user is authenticated and logged in, we can check on our $routeChangeStart event.

```
angular.module('myApp')
.run(function($rootScope, $location, Auth) {
  // Set a watch on the $routeChangeStart
  $rootScope.$on('$routeChangeStart',
    function(evt, next, curr) {

    if (!Auth.isAuthorized(next.access_level)) {
      if (Auth.isLoggedIn()) {
        // The user is logged in, but does not
        // have permissions to view the view
        $location.path('/');
      } else {
        $location.path('/login');
      }
```

```
    }
  })
});
```

Talking to MongoDB

If we don't have a custom back end, it's also possible to talk directly to a database that exposes a RESTful interface.

Instead of having to build a back end, we can talk directly to Mongo.

 In this example, we're using MongoLab[68], a SAAS service that offers managed MongoDB instances.

In order to talk to MongoDB, we need to set up a few custom configurations for our Restangular objects.

 The following configuration will change the global Restangular objects. If we want to nest this configuration for a single database, then we'll need to create a factory to nest our custom Restangular object.

First, let's set our API key. Since this key won't change across the entire app, we suggest creating it as a constant.

```
angular.module('myApp', ['restangular'])
.constant('apiKey', 'YOUR_API_KEY');
```

We can now inject this API key into other parts of our application. We'll set up our configuration in the config() block on our module.

Using MongoLab, we'll set our baseUrl to the API endpoint:

```
// ...
.config(function(RestangularProvider, apiKey) {
  RestangularProvider
  .setBaseUrl('https://api.mongolab.com/api/1/databases/YOURDB/collections');
});
```

Next, **every** single request we make to our back-end database will require our API key. Restangular makes it easy to add it using the setDefaultRequestParams() method:

---

[68]https://mongolab.com

```
// ...
.config(function(RestangularProvider, apiKey) {
  // ...
  RestangularProvider
  .setDefaultRequestParams({
    apiKey: apiKey
  });
});
```

Next, we need to update the Restangular field to map the custom ID field, provided by MongoDB as `_id.$oid`, to the Restangular `id` field. This update is simple if we use the `setRestangularFields()` function:

```
// ...
.config(function(RestangularProvider, apiKey) {
  // ...
  RestangularProvider.setRestangularFields({
    id: '_id.$oid'
  });
});
```

Lastly, we need to overwrite the `_id` field, which is set by mongo when we are updating a record. Mongo won't let us 'rewrite' the `_id` field, so we can use Restangular to 'fake' setting the field. Since Restangular will call the route to update the element, we don't need to worry about the possibility of the object not being rewritten.

```
// ...
.config(function(RestangularProvider, apiKey) {
  // ...
  RestangularProvider.setRestangularFields({
    id: '_id.$oid'
  });
});
```

For the sake of completeness, here is the entire config block:

```
angular.module('myApp', ['restangular'])
.constant('apiKey', 'API_KEY')
.config(function(RestangularProvider, apiKey) {
  RestangularProvider.setBaseUrl(
    'https://api.mongolab.com/api/1/databases/YOURDB/collections');
    RestangularProvider.setDefaultRequestParams({
      apiKey: apiKey
    })
    RestangularProvider.setRestangularFields({
      id: '_id.$oid'
    });

    RestangularProvider.setRequestInterceptor(
      function(elem, operation, what) {

        if (operation === 'put') {
          elem._id = undefined;
          return elem;
        }
        return elem;
  })
});
```

Promises

Angular's event system (which we discuss in depth in the under the hood chapter) provides a lot of power to our Angular apps. One of the most powerful features it gives us is the automatic resolution of promises.

What's a Promise?

A promise is a method of resolving a value (or not) in an asynchronous manner. Promises are objects that represent the return value or thrown exception that a function may eventually provide. Promises are incredibly useful in dealing with remote objects, and we can think of them as a proxy for our remote objects.

Traditionally, JavaScript uses closures, or callbacks, to respond with meaningful data that is not available synchronously, such as XHR requests after a page has loaded. Rather than depending upon a callback to fire, we can interact with the data as though it has already returned.

Callbacks have worked for a long time, but the developer suffers when using them. Callbacks provide no consistency and no guaranteed call, they steal code flow when depending upon other callbacks, and they generally make debugging incredibly difficult. At every step of the way, we have to deal with *explicitly* handling errors.

Instead of firing a function and hoping to get a callback run when executing asynchronous methods, promises offer a different abstraction: They return a promise object.

For example, in traditional callback code, we might have a method that sends a message from one user to one of the user's friends.

```
// Sample callback code
User.get( fromId, {
  success: function(err, user) {
    if (err) return {error: err};
    user.friends.find(toId, function(err, friend) {
      if (err) return {error: err};
      user.sendMessage(friend, message, callback);
    });
  },
  failure: function(err) {
    return {error: err}
  }
});
```

This callback pyramid is already getting out of hand, and we haven't included any robust error-handling code, either. Additionally, we need to know the order in which the arguments are called from within our callback.

The promised-based version of the previous code might look somewhat closer to:

```
User.get(fromId)
.then(function(user) {
  return user.friends.find(toId);
}, function(err) {
  // We couldn't find the user
})
.then(function(friend) {
  return user.sendMessage(friend, message);
}, function(err) {
  // The user's friend resulted in an error
})
.then(function(success) {
  // user was sent the message
}, function(err) {
  // An error occurred
});
```

Not only is this code more readable; it is also much easier to grok. We can guarantee that the callback will resolve to a single value, rather than having to deal with the callback interface.

Notice that in the first example, we have to handle errors differently from how we handle non-errors. We need to make sure when using callbacks to handle errors, we check if an error is defined in the tradition API response signature (usually with (err, data) being the usual method signature). All of our API methods must implement this same structure.

In the second example, we handle the success and error in the same way. Our resultant object will receive the error in the usual manner. The promise API is specific about resolving or rejecting promises, so we also don't have to worry about our methods implementing a different method signature.

Why Promises?

Escaping from *callback hell* is just one by-product of using promises. The real point of promises is to make asynchronous functions look more like synchronous ones. With synchronous functions, we can capture both return values and exception values as expected.

We can capture errors at any point of the process and bypass future code that relies upon the error of that process. We achieve all of these things without thinking about the benefits of this synchronous code – it's simply in the nature of the code.

Thus, the point of using promises is to regain the ability to do functional composition and error bubbling while maintaining the ability of the code to run asynchronously.

Promises are *first-class* objects and carry with them a few guarantees:

- Only one resolve or reject will ever be called
    - resolve is called with a single fulfillment value
    - reject can be called with a single rejection reason
- If the promise has been resolved or rejected, any handlers depending upon them will still be called
- Handlers will always be called asynchronously

Additionally, we can chain promises and allow the code to process as it would normally run. Exceptions from one promise bubble up through the entire promise chain.

Promises are *always* executed asynchronously; we can use them without worry that they will block the rest of the app.

Promises in Angular

Angular's event loop gives Angular the unique ability to resolve promises in its `$rootScope.$evalAsync` stage (see under the hood for more detail on the run loop). The promises will sit inert until the `$digest` run loop finishes.

This fact allows for Angular to turn the results of a promise into the view without any extra work. It also enables us to assign the result of an XHR call directly to a property on a `$scope` object and think nothing of it.

Let's build an example that will return a list of open pull requests for AngularJS from GitHub.

Play with it[69]

```
<h1>Open Pull Requests for Angular JS</h1>

<ul ng-controller="DashboardController">
  <li ng-repeat="pr in pullRequests">
    {{ pr.title }}
  </li>
</ul>
```

If we have a service that returns a promise (covered in depth in the services chapter), we can simply place the promise in the view and expect that Angular will resolve it for us:

---

[69]http://jsbin.com/UfotanA/3/edit

```
angular.module('myApp', [])
.controller('DashboardController', [
  '$scope', 'UserService',
    function($scope, UserService) {
      // UserService's getFriends() method
      // returns a promise
      User.getFriends(123)
      .then(function(data) {
        $scope.friends = data.data;
      });
}]);
```

Note that the default setting in Angular is no longer automatically unwrapped promises. We can re-enable this form if we really want to by setting the option to true in a .config() function:

```
.config(function($parseProvider) {
  $parseProvider.unwrapPromises(true) ;
});
```

When the asynchronous call to getPullRequests returns, the $scope.pullRequests value will **automatically** update the view.

How to Create a Promise

In order to create a promise in Angular, we can use the built-in $q service. The $q service provides a few methods in its deferred API.

First, we need to inject the $q service into the object where we want to use it.

```
angular.module('myApp', [])
.factory('GithubService', ['$q', function($q) {
  // Now we have access to the $q library
}]);
```

To create a deferred object, we call the method defer():

```
var deferred = $q.defer();
```

The deferred object exposes three methods and the single promise property that we can use to deal with the promise.

- resolve(value)

The resolve function resolves the deferred promise with the value.

```
deferred.resolve({name: "Ari", username: "@auser"});
```

- reject(reason)

This method *rejects* the deferred promise with a reason. It is equivalent to resolving a promise with a rejection.

```
deferred.reject("Can't update user");
// Equivalent to
deferred.resolve($q.reject("Can't update user"));
```

- notify(value)

This method responds with the status of a promises execution.

For example, if we want to return a status from the promise, we can use the notify() function to deliver it.

Let's say that we have several long-running requests that we want to make from a single promise. We can call the notify function to send back a notification of progress:

```
.factory('GithubService', function($q, $http) {
  // get events from repo
  var getEventsFromRepo = function() {
    // task
  }
  var service = {
    makeMultipleRequests: function(repos) {
      var d = $q.defer(),
          percentComplete = 0,
          output = [];
      for (var i = 0; i < repos.length; i++) {
        output.push(getEventsFromRepo(repos[i]));
        percentComplete = (i+1)/repos.length * 100;
        d.notify(percentComplete);
      }

      d.resolve(output);

      return d.promise;
    }
  }
  return service;
});
```

With this `makeMultipleRequests()` function on our `GithubService` object, we will receive a progress notification every time a repo has been fetched and processed.

We can use this notification in our usage of the promise by adding a third function call to the promise usage. For instance:

```
.controller('HomeController',
function($scope, GithubService) {
  GithubService.makeMultipleRequests([
    'auser/beehive', 'angular/angular.js'
  ])
  .then(function(result) {
    // Handle the result
  }, function(err) {
    // Error occurred
  }, function(percentComplete) {
    $scope.progress = percentComplete;
  });
});
```

We can access the promise as a property on the deferred object:

```
deferred.promise
```

A full example of how to create a function that responds with a promise might look similar to the following method on the `GithubService`, as mentioned above.

```
angular.module('myApp', [])
.factory('GithubService', [
  '$q', '$http',
    function($q, $http) {
      var getPullRequests = function() {
        var deferred = $q.defer();
        // Get list of open angular js pull requests from github
        $http.get('https://api.github.com/repos/angular/angular.js/pulls')
        .success(function(data) {
          deferred.resolve(data);
        })
        .error(function(reason) {
          deferred.reject(reason);
        })
        return deferred.promise;
```

```
      }

      return { // return factory object
        getPullRequests: getPullRequests
      };
}]);
```

Now we can use the promise API to interact with the getPullRequests() promise.

View full example[70]

In the case of the service above, we can interact with the promise in two different ways:

- then(successFn, errFn, notifyFn)

Regardless of the success or failure of the promise, then calls either the successFn or the errFn asynchronously as soon as the result is available. The method **always** calls callbacks with a single argument: the result or the rejection reason.

It may call the notifyFn callback zero or more times to provide a progress status indication *before* the promise is resolved or rejected.

The then() method always returns a new promise, which is either resolved or rejected through the return value of the successFn or the errFn. It also serves notifications through the notifyFn.

- catch(errFn)

This method is simply a helper function that allows for us to replace the err callback with .catch(function(reason) {}):

```
$http.get('/user/' + id + '/friends')
.catch(function(reason) {
  deferred.reject(reason);
});
```

- finally(callback)

The finally method allows us to observe the fulfillment or rejection of a promise without modifying the resulting value. The method is useful for when we need to release a resource or run some clean-up, regardless of the success or error of the promise.

We cannot call this method directly, as *finally* is a reserved word in IE JavaScript. To use finally, we have to call it like so:

[70]http://jsbin.com/UfotanA/3/edit

```
promise['finally'](function() {});
```

Angular's $q deferred objects are chainable in that even then returns a promise. As soon as the promise is resolved, the promise that then returns is resolved or rejected.

 These promise chains are how Angular can support $http's interceptors.

The $q service is similar to the original Kris Kowal's Q library:

1. $q is integrated with the Angular $rootScope model, so resolutions and rejections happen quickly inside of Angular.
2. $q promises are integrated with Angular's templating engine, which means that any promises found in the views will be resolved or rejected in the view.
3. $q is tiny and doesn't contain the full functionality of the Q library.

Chaining Requests

The then method returns a new derived promise after the initial promise is resolved. This return gives us the unique ability to attach yet another then on the result of the initial then method.

```
// A service that responds with a promise
GithubService.then(function(data) {
  var events = [];
  for (var i = 0; i < data.length; i++) {
    events.push(data[i].events);
  }
  return events;
}).then(function(events) {
  $scope.events = events;
});
```

In this example, we can create a *chain* of execution that allows us to interrupt the flow of the application based upon more functionality, which we can attach to different results.

This interruption allows us to pause or defer resolutions of promises at any point during the chain of execution.

 This interruption is also how the $http service implements request and response interceptors.

The $q library comes with several different useful methods:

all(promises)

If we have multiple promises that we want to combine into a single promise, we can use the `$q.all(promises)` method to combine them all into a single promise. This single method takes a single argument:

- promises (array or object of promises)

Promises as an array or hash of promises

The `all()` method returns a single promise that will resolve with an array or a hash of values. Each value will correspond to the promises at the same index or key in the promises hash. If **any** of the promises are resolved with a rejection, then the resulting promise will be rejected as well.

defer()

The `defer()` method creates a deferred object. It takes no parameters, and it returns a new instance of a single deferred object.

reject(reason)

This method creates a promise that is resolved with a rejection for a specific reason. It is specifically designed to give us access to forwarding rejection in a chain of promises, which is akin to `throw` in JavaScript. In the same sense that we can *catch* an exception in JavaScript and we can forward the rejection, we need to rethrow the error. We can do so with `$q.reject(reason)`.

This method takes a single parameter:

- reason (constant, string, exception, object)

The reasons for the rejection

The `reject()` method returns a promise that has already been resolved with a rejection and the reason for the rejection.

when(value)

The `when()` function wraps an object that might be a value `then`-able promise into a $q promise. Doing that allows for us to deal with an object that may or may not be a promise.

The `when()` function takes a single parameter:

- value

The value or a promise

The `when()` function returns a promise that we can then use like any other promise.

Server Communication

One of the most powerful components of Angular is its ability to communicate with a server-side back end. Regardless of the back end that we're using, Angular can likely talk to it through an API.

In this chapter, we're going to focus on two types of back ends: custom server-side back ends that we'll develop and server-less back ends using back ends as a service.

Custom Server-Side

In this section, we're going to focus on the process of building a custom server-side application in NodeJS. Although we're going to focus on building this server app in Node, we can build our back end in any server-side language that supports HTTP API routes.

 If you're a Ruby on Rails developer, we've written a book specifically on demonstrating how to use Rails. Check out Riding Rails with AngularJS[71].

To start our Node-backed app, we need to have NodeJS installed.

Install NodeJS

NodeJS is a server-side platform built on the Chrome JavaScript run time. It is an event-driven, non-blocking, lightweight JavaScript run time that enables us to write JavaScript on the server.

To install NodeJS, we can head to nodejs.org[72] and click on the big *Install* button. It will detect and download the appropriate installer for our platform.

i> If for some reason it downloads the wrong package, no problem – we can click on the *Downloads* button and manually select the appropriate package.

We can run the installer and let it run its course. Once it's complete, we'll have the two packages available on the command line:

- node
- npm

node is the Node binary that we'll call to run our Node app, while npm is the Node Package Manager, which we'll use to install Node libraries.

---

[71]http://www.fullstack.io/edu/angular/rails/

[72]http://nodejs.org/

Install Express

We're going to use a web application framework called expressjs that will give us some syntactic sugar around dealing with HTTP. It allows us to only work with the functionality of our web app, as opposed to needing to deal with the nitty gritty details of Node's HTTP server.

Its features are extensive and include providing a clean routing syntax, dynamic middleware, and tons of open-source packages built specifically for Express. Additionally, many well-known companies use it in production.

To install Express, we'll use the npm binary:

```
$ npm install -g express
```

i> We use the -g flag to install the package *globally*. We can omit it if we don't want to install it globally, whereupon it will be installed in the directory node_modules/ within the current directory. We recommend installing it globally, however.

Now, we can use the Express generator to generate our Express app.

```
$ express myApp
```

This line generates a very basic Express app with a set of requirements and a loosely opinionated directory structure.

Running the Express generator

To run our app, we need to install our basic dependencies locally using npm again. This time, we'll use it to install the dependencies set in the package.json locally.

```
$ cd myApp && npm install -d
```

 The -d flag tells npm to install the dependencies locally. This syntax is overly explicit: We can leave the -d off, as it's set to install dependencies locally by default.

Now, let's run the app to make sure everything is working as we expect it should. We can do this simply by running it with the node binary:

```
$ node app.js
```

Running Express

If we open the URL http://localhost:3000 in our web browser, the default page of our Express app shows us that the app has been generated.

Every time we make a change to our app.js file, we need to stop that server and restart it. When in development, this process can be cumbersome, so we suggest using the nodemon server instead of node.js.

To install nodemon, we'll use npm again:

```
$ npm install --save-dev nodemon
```

 The --save-dev flag tells npm to save the package in the devDependencies section of package.json. We recommend using this practice because it helps when introducing multiple developers to a team: We can ensure that the whole team has the *right* dependencies for the codebase.

Instead of using node app.js to start the app, we can replace it with:

```
$ nodemon app.js
```

Every time that we make a change to the app.js file and save it, nodemon restarts our Node app automatically.

The app starts out in app.js. There are two important components to notice in the app.js file: the static path from which static files are served and the routes that are resolved (and how).

```
// ...
app.use(express.methodOverride());
app.use(app.router);
// Line 1
app.use(express.static(path.join(__dirname, 'public')));
// ...
app.get('/', routes.index);
app.get('/users', user.list);
// ...
```

The first line, with the express.static() call, tells Node to look in the public/ directory for any files it may find that match the requested route. For instance, if the requested route is '/users', it would look for a file called 'users'.

The second set of lines (app.get()) matches routes where static files are not found in the public/ directory.

To work with our Angular app, we need to make two modifications to the generated app.js:

First, we swap the lines of the express.static() and the app.router line, like so:

```
// ...
app.use(express.methodOverride());
// Moved this line above the next line
app.use(express.static(path.join(__dirname, 'public')));
app.use(app.router);
// ...
```

Although this swap is not strictly necessary, it will help support HTML5Mode later and will tell Express to prefer the files in the public/ directory above those defined in our app.

Second, we remove the line pointing to the '/' route:

```
// ...
// app.get('/', routes.index); // remove this line
app.get('/users', users.list);
// ...
```

Now we can write our Angular app like normal inside of our public directory.

Calling APIs

Our local Node server now serves our app, so we can call our own APIs, which we'll develop inside of our Express server.

For instance, let's develop an application that records the number of times a user hits a specific button. We need to write two routes:

GET /hits This route returns our total list of hits to the button.

POST /hit This route records a new hit to the button and return us the latest total number of hits.

First, let's build the basic view of our app's index.html page. We'll place this in the public/ directory of our Node app so that if the route requested is either / or /index.html, Express will serve this file as our route:

```
<!doctype html>
<html lang="en" ng-app="myApp">
  <head>
    <title>Node app</title>
    <link rel="stylesheet" href="stylesheets/style.css">
    <script src="bower_components/angular/angular.min.js"></script>
  </head>
  <body>
    <div ng-controller="HomeController">
      <h3>Button hits: {{ hits }}</h3>
      <button ng-click="registerHit()">
        HIT ME, if you dare
      </button>
    </div>
    <script src="javascripts/services.js"></script>
    <script src="javascripts/app.js"></script>
  </body>
</html>
```

Inside of our public/javacscripts/app.js file, we'll add a controller on top of our myApp Angular module:

```
angular.module('myApp', [
  'ngRoute',
  'myApp.services'
])
.controller('HomeController', function($scope, HitService) {
  HitService.count()
  .then(function(data) {
    $scope.hits = data;
  });

  $scope.registerHit = function() {
    HitService.registerHit()
    .then(function(data) {
      $scope.hits = data;
    });
  }
});
```

We'll build an Angular service that is responsible for calling these routes, as we can see in the controller above:

```
angular.module('myApp.services', [])
.factory('HitService', function($q, $http) {
  var service = {
    count: function() {
      var d = $q.defer();
      $http.get('/hits')
      .success(function(data, status) {
        d.resolve(data.hits);
      }).error(function(data, status) {
        d.reject(data);
      });
      return d.promise;
    },
    registerHit: function() {
      var d = $q.defer();
      $http.post('/hit', {})
      .success(function(data, status) {
        d.resolve(data.hits);
      }).error(function(data, status) {
        d.reject(data);
      });
```

```
    return d.promise;
  }
}
return service;
});
```

For more information on services, check out the services chapter.

This service exposes two methods that call the routes that we defined above:

- count
- registerHit

Inside our Node app's `app.js` file, we need to register two new routes and create the functionality that defines the routes for us.

These two new Node routes match the service routes that we're calling above:

```
// ...
var hits = require('./routes/hits');
// ...
app.get('/hits', hits.count);
app.post('/hit', hits.registerNew);
// ...
```

The only component left is building the actual back-end, server-side logic that registers the hit count.

In NodeJS, each required module exposes methods through the method `exports`. To expose the two methods `count` and `registerNew` (from above), we need to attach them to the `exports` object inside the `routes/hits.js` file.

Inside of our `routes/hits.js` file, we create a hits store that stores the number of hits in memory, so that if we restart the server, the number of hits will also reset.

```
/*
 * HIT service
 */
var hits = 0;
exports.count = function(req, res){
  res.send(200, {
    hits: hits
  });
}
```

```
exports.registerNew = function(req, res) {
  hits += 1;
  res.send(200, {
    hits: hits
  });
}
```

Now, if we start our Node app and head to the route at `http://localhost:3000`, we will see that we have added the functionality for our Angular app as we expect.

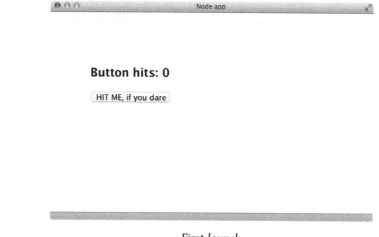

First launch

And after the button has been hit:

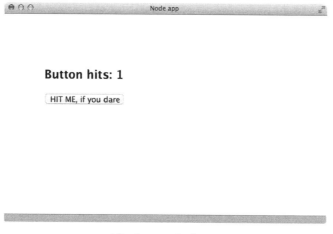

After hitting the button

Server-less with Amazon AWS

One of the biggest benefits to building a single-page app (SPA) is the ability to host flat files rather than needing to build and service a back-end infrastructure.

Most of the applications that we will build, however, need to be powered by a back-end server with custom data. There are a growing number of options that enable developers to focus on building only our front-end code and leave the back end alone.

Amazon recently released a new option that allows us to build server-less web applications from right inside the browser: Amazon AWS JavaScript SDK[73].

Amazon's browser-based (and server-side with NodeJS) SDK allows us to confidently host our applications and interact with production-grade back-end services.

It's now possible to host our application stack entirely on Amazon infrastructure, using S3 to host our application and files, DynamoDB as a NoSQL store, and other web-scale services. We can even securely accept payments from the client side and get all the benefits of the Amazon CDN.

With this release, the JavaScript SDK now allows us to interact with five of the dozens of Amazon AWS services. These five services are:

DynamoDB

This fast, fully managed NoSQL database service allows us to scale to *infinite* size with automatic triplicate replication with secure access controls.

Simple Notification Service (SNS)

This service is a fast, flexible, fully managed push notification service that allows us to push messages to mobile devices as well as other services, such as email or even to Amazon's own Simple Queue Service (SQS).

Simple Queue Service (SQS)

This fast, reliable, fully managed queue service allows us to create huge queues in a well-managed way. We can create large request objects so we can fully decouple our application's components from each other using a common queue.

Simple Storage Service (S3)

This well-known, web-scale, and fully managed data store allows us to store large objects (up to five terabytes) with an unlimited number of objects. We can use S3 to securely store encrypted and protected data all over the world. We'll even use S3 to host our own Angular apps.

---

[73]http://aws.amazon.com/

Security Token Service (STS)

This web service allows us to request temporary and limited privileged credentials for IAM users. We won't cover STS in depth, but it does provide a nice interface for creating limited secure operations on our data.

AWSJS + Angular

In this section, we intend to demonstrate how to get our applications up and running on the AWSJS stack in minutes.

To do so, we're going to create a miniature, bare-bones version of Gumroad[74] to which we will allow our users to upload screenshots. We'll let them sell their screenshots by integrating with the fantastic Stripe[75] API.

> We cannot recommend these two services enough; this mini-demo is not intended to replace their services, only to demonstrate the power of Angular and the AWS API.

To create our product, we need to:

- Allow users to log into our service and store their unique emails
- Allow users to upload files that are associated with them
- Allow users to click on images, and present those users with an option to buy the uploaded image
- Take credit card charges and accept money directly from a single-page Angular app

Getting Started

Let's start with a standard structured index.html:

---

[74]https://gumroad.com/
[75]http://stripe.com

```html
<!doctype html>
<html>
  <head>
    <script
      src="https://ajax.googleapis.com/ajax/libs/angularjs/1.2.6/angular.min.js">
    </script>
    <script
      src="http://code.angularjs.org/1.2.6/angular-route.min.js"></script>
    <link rel="stylesheet" href="styles/bootstrap.min.css">
  </head>
  <body>
    <div ng-view></div>
    <script src="scripts/app.js"></script>
    <script src="scripts/controllers.js"></script>
    <script src="scripts/services.js"></script>
    <script src="scripts/directives.js"></script>
  </body>
</html>
```

In this standard Angular template, we're not loading anything crazy. We're loading the base Angular library, as well as ngRoute and our custom application code.

Our application code is also standard. Our scripts/app.js file simply defines an Angular module with a single route /:

```javascript
angular.module('myApp', [
  'ngRoute',
  'myApp.services',
  'myApp.directives'])
.config(function($routeProvider) {
  $routeProvider
  .when('/', {
    controller: 'MainController',
    templateUrl: 'templates/main.html',
  })
  .otherwise({
    redirectTo: '/'
  });
});
```

Our scripts/controllers.js file creates controllers from the main module:

```
angular.module('myApp')
.controller('MainController', function($scope) {

});
```

And our `scripts/services.js` and `scripts/directives.js` files are simple, as well:

```
// scripts/services.js
angular.module('myApp.services', []);
```

```
// scripts/directives.js
angular.module('myApp.directives', [])
```

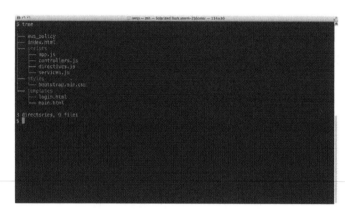

Angular Structure

Introduction

The AWS ecosystem is huge and used in production all over the world. The gross number of useful services that Amazon runs makes it a fantastic platform on top of which to power our applications.

Historically, the APIs have not always been the easiest to use and understand, so we hope to address some of that confusion here.

Traditionally, we'd use a signed request with our applications utilizing the client_id or secret access key model. Since we're operating in the browser, it's not a good idea to embed our `client_id` and our `client_secret` in the browser, where anyone can see it. (It's not much of a secret anyway if it's embedded in clear text, right?)

Luckily, the AWS team has provided us with an alternative method of identifying and authenticating our site to give access to the AWS resources.

The first step to creating an AWS-based Angular app is to set up this relatively complex authentication and authorization that we'll use throughout the process.

Currently (at the time of this writing), the AWS JS library integrates cleanly with three authentication providers:

- Facebook
- Google Plus
- Amazon Login

In this section, we'll be focusing on integrating with the Google+ API to host our login, but the process is very similar for the other two authentication providers.

Installation

First things first, we need to *install* the files in our index.html. Inside of our index.html, we need to include the AWS-SDK library and the Google API library.

We'll modify our index.html to include these libraries:

```
<!doctype html>
<html>
  <head>
    <script
      src="http://code.angularjs.org/1.2.6/angular.min.js"></script>
    <script
      src="http://code.angularjs.org/1.2.6/angular-route.min.js"></script>
    <script
      src="https://sdk.amazonaws.com/js/aws-sdk-2.0.0-rc4.min.js"></script>
    <link rel="stylesheet" href="styles/bootstrap.min.css">
  </head>
  <body>
    <div ng-view></div>
    <script src="scripts/app.js"></script>
    <script src="scripts/controllers.js"></script>
    <script src="scripts/services.js"></script>
    <script src="scripts/directives.js"></script>
    <script type="text/javascript" src="https://js.stripe.com/v2/"></script>
    <script type="text/javascript">
      (function() {
        var po = document.createElement('script');
        po.type = 'text/javascript';
```

```
        po.async = true;
        po.src = 'https://apis.google.com/js/client:plusone.js?onload=onLoadCallba\
ck';

        var s = document.getElementsByTagName('script')[0];
        s.parentNode.insertBefore(po, s);
      })();
    </script>
  </body>
</html>
```

Now, notice that we added an onload callback for the Google JavaScript library and we **did not** use the ng-app to bootstrap our application. If we let Angular automatically bootstrap our application, we'll run into a race condition where the Google API may not be loaded when the application starts.

That non-deterministic nature of our application will make the experience unusable, so instead, we will manually bootstrap our app in the onLoadCallback function.

To manually bootstrap the application, we add the onLoadCallback function to the window service. Before we can call to bootstrap Angular, we need to be sure that the Google login client is loaded.

The Google API client, or gapi, is included at run time and is set by default to lazy-load its services. By telling the gapi.client to load the oauth2 library in advance of starting our app, we avoid any potential mishaps as a consequence of the oauth2 library being unavailable.

```
// in scripts/app.js
window.onLoadCallback = function() {
  // When the document is ready
  angular.element(document).ready(function() {
    // Bootstrap the oauth2 library
    gapi.client.load('oauth2', 'v2', function() {
      // Finally, bootstrap our angular app
      angular.bootstrap(document, ['myApp']);
    });
  });
}
```

With the necessary libraries available and our application ready to be bootstrapped, we can set up the authorization part of our app.

Running

As we are using services that depend upon our URL to be an expected URL, we need to run a server, rather than simply loading the HTML in our browser.

We recommend using the incredibly simple Python SimpleHTTPServer to serve a directory of files:

```
$ python -m SimpleHTTPServer 9000
```

Now we can load the URL `http://localhost:9000/` in our browser.

User Authorization/Authentication

First, we need to get a `client_id` and a `client_secret` from Google so that we'll be able to actually interact with the Google Plus login system.

To get an app, head over to the Google APIs console[76] and create a project.

Create a Google Plus project

Open the project by clicking on the name, and click on the *APIs & auth* nav button. From here, we need to enable the `Google+ API`. Find the *APIs* button and click on it. Find the `Google+ API` item and click the OFF to ON slider.

Enable Google+ API

Once that's set, we need to create and register an application and use its application ID to make authenticated calls.

---

[76]https://developers.google.com/console

Find the `Registered apps` option and click on it to create an app. Make sure to select the Web Application option when it asks about the type of application.

Create a registered application

Once that is set, we reach the application details page. Select the `OAuth 2.0 Client ID` dropdown and take note of the application's Client ID. We'll use this ID in a few minutes.

Lastly, add the localhost origin to the WEB ORIGIN of the application thus ensuring that we can develop using the API locally:

Registered app details

Next, we need to create a Google+ login directive. This Angular directive will enable us to add a customized login button to our app with a single file element.

> For more information about directives, check out our directives chapter.

We're going to have two pieces of functionality attached to our Google login: an element that we'll attach to the standard Google login button and a custom function that we'll run after the button has been rendered.

The final directive will look like the following in `scripts/directives.js`:

```
angular.module('myApp.directives', [])
.directive('googleSignin', function() {
  return {
    restrict: 'A',
    template: '<span id="signinButton"></span>',
    replace: true,
    scope: {
      afterSignin: '&'
    },
    link: function(scope, ele, attrs) {
      // Set standard google class
      attrs.$set('class', 'g-signin');
      // Set the clientid
      attrs.$set('data-clientid',
        attrs.clientId+'.apps.googleusercontent.com');
      // build scope urls
      var scopes = attrs.scopes || [
        'auth/plus.login',
        'auth/userinfo.email'
      ];
      var scopeUrls = [];
      for (var i = 0; i < scopes.length; i++) {
        scopeUrls.push('https://www.googleapis.com/'+scopes[i]);
      };

      // Create a custom callback method
      var callbackId = "_googleSigninCallback",
          directiveScope = scope;
      window[callbackId] = function() {
        var oauth = arguments[0];
        directiveScope.afterSignin({oauth: oauth});
        window[callbackId] = null;
      };

      // Set standard google signin button settings
      attrs.$set('data-callback', callbackId);
      attrs.$set('data-cookiepolicy', 'single_host_origin');
      attrs.$set('data-requestvisibleactions',
        'http://schemas.google.com/AddActivity')
      attrs.$set('data-scope', scopeUrls.join(' '));

      // Finally, reload the client library to
```

```
    // force the button to be painted in the browser
    (function() {
      var po = document.createElement('script');
      po.type = 'text/javascript';
      po.async = true;
      po.src = 'https://apis.google.com/js/client:plusone.js';
      var s = document.getElementsByTagName('script')[0];
      s.parentNode.insertBefore(po, s);
    })();
  }
 }
});
```

Although this directive is long, it's fairly straightforward. We're assigning the Google button class `g-signin`, attaching the Client ID based on an attribute we pass in, building the scopes, etc.

One unique part of this directive is that we're creating a custom callback on the window object. Effectively, this object allows us to *fake* the callback method we need to call in JavaScript when we make the function, allowing us to actually make the call to the local `afterSignin` action instead.

We then clean up the global object, because we're allergic to global state in AngularJS.

With our directive primed and ready to go, we can include the directive in our view. We're going to call the directive in our view like so, replacing the `client-id` and the `after-signin` attributes on the directive with our own:

> Make sure to include the `oauth` parameter exactly as it's spelled in the `after-signup` attribute. We must call the parameter this way due to how Angular directives call methods with parameters inside of directives.

```
<h2>Signin to ngroad</h2>
<div google-signin
  client-id='CLIENT_ID'
  after-signin="signedIn(oauth)"></div>
<pre>{{ user | json }}</pre>
```

> The user data in the example is the returned access_token for our login (if we log in). It is **not** saved on our servers, it is not sensitive data, and it will disappear when we leave the page.

Finally, we need our button to *actually* cause an action, so we need to define the `after-signin` method `signedIn(oauth)` in our controller.

This `signedIn()` method kills off the authenticated page for us in our real application.

 This method would be an ideal place to set a redirect to a new route (for instance, the `/dashboard` route for authenticated users).

```
angular.module('myApp')
.controller('MainController',
  function($scope) {
    $scope.signedIn = function(oauth) {
      $scope.user = oauth;
    }
});
```

UserService

Before we dive a bit deeper into the AWS side of things, let's create ourselves a `UserService` that is responsible for holding on to our new user. This `UserService` will handle the bulk of the work for interacting with the AWS back end and will keep a copy of the current user.

Although we're not quite ready to attach a back end, we can start building it out to handle holding on to a persistent copy of the user instance.

In our `scripts/services.js`, we create the beginnings of our `UserService`:

```
angular.module('myApp.services', [])
.factory('UserService', function($q, $http) {
  var service = {
    _user: null,
    setCurrentUser: function(u) {
      if (u && !u.error) {
        service._user = u;
        return service.currentUser();
      } else {
        var d = $q.defer();
        d.reject(u.error);
        return d.promise;
      }
    },
    currentUser: function() {
      var d = $q.defer();
      d.resolve(service._user);
```

```
    return d.promise;
  }
};
return service;
});
```

Although this setup is a bit contrived for the time being, we want the functionality to set the currentUser as a permanent fixture in the service.

> Remember, services are singleton objects that live for the duration of the application lifecycle.

Now, instead of simply setting our user in the return of the signedIn() function, we can set the user to the UserService:

```
angular.module('myApp')
.controller('MainController',
  function($scope) {
    $scope.signedIn = function(oauth) {
      UserService.setCurrentUser(oauth)
      .then(function(user) {
        $scope.user = user;
      });
    }
});
```

For our application to work, we need to hold onto actual user emails so we can provide a better method of interacting with our users and hold onto some persistent, unique data per user.

We use the gapi.client.oauth2.userinfo.get() method to fetch the user's email address rather than holding onto the user's access_token (and other various access details).

In our UserService, we need to update our currentUser() method to include this functionality:

```
// ...
},
currentUser: function() {
  var d = $q.defer();
  if (service._user) {
    d.resolve(service._user);
  } else {
    gapi.client.oauth2.userinfo.get()
    .execute(function(e) {
      service._user = e;
    })
  }
  return d.promise;
}
// ...
```

All Aboard AWS

Now, as we said when we first started this journey, we need to set up authorization with the AWS services.

> If you don't have an AWS account, head over to aws.amazon.com[77] and grab an account. It's free and quick.

First things first: Let's create an IAM role. IAM, or AWS's Identity and Access Management service, is one of the reasons why the AWS services are so powerful. With IAM, we can create fine-grain access controls over our systems and data.

Unfortunately, the flexibility and power of IAM also make it a bit more complex, so we'll walk through creating it here and make it as clear as we can.

Let's create the IAM role by heading to the IAM console[78] and clicking on the Roles navigation link.

We have to click the *Create New Role* button to give our new role a name. We'll call ours the google-web-role.

---

[77]http://aws.amazon.com/
[78]https://console.aws.amazon.com/iam/home?region=us-east-1#roles

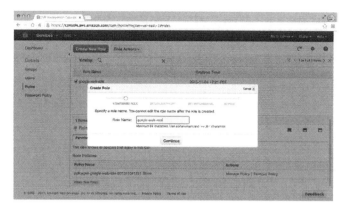

Create a new role

Next, we need to configure the IAM role to be a *Web Identity Provider Access* role type so we can manage our new role's access to our AWS services.

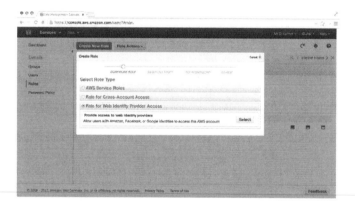

Set the role type

Remember the CLIENT ID that we created above with Google? In the next screen, select Google from the dropdown and paste the CLIENT ID into the Audience box.

This step unites our IAM role and our Google app so that our application can call out to AWS services with an authenticated Google user.

Google auth

We then click through the *Verify Trust* (the next screen, which shows the raw configuration for AWS services) and create the policy for our applications.

The Policy Generator is the easiest method of getting up and running quickly to build policies. At this point, we must set what actions our users can and cannot take.

We're going to make an effort to be very specific with regard to the actions that our users may take:

S3

On the specific bucket (`ng-newsletter-example`, in our example app), we're going to allow our users to take the following actions:

* GetObject
* ListBucket
* PutObject

The Amazon Resource Name (ARN) for our S3 bucket is:

```
arn:aws:s3:::ng-newsletter-example/*
```

DynamoDB

For two specific table resources, we'll allow the following actions:

* GetItem
* PutItem
* Query

The Amazon Resource Name (ARN) for our DynamoDB tables are the following:

```
[
  "arn:aws:dynamodb:us-east-1:<ACCOUNT_ID>:table/Users",
  "arn:aws:dynamodb:us-east-1:<ACCOUNT_ID>:table/UsersItems"
]
```

 Your

The final version of our policy can be found here[79].

Adding the IAM policy

For more information on the confusing ARN numbers, check out the relevant Amazon documentation here[80].

One final piece of information that we need to hold onto is the Role ARN. We can find this Role ARN on the summary tab of the IAM user in our IAM console.

Take note of this string – we'll set it in a moment.

---

[79]http://d.pr/9Obg

[80]http://docs.aws.amazon.com/general/latest/gr/aws-arns-and-namespaces.html

Role ARN

Now that we're finally done with creating our IAM user, we can move on to integrating it inside of our Angular app.

AWSService

Let's move the root of our application for integrating with AWS into its own service, the AWSService, and build it out.

Since we're going to need to have the ability to custom configure our service at configure time, we want to create it as a provider.

> Remember, the *only* service type that we can *inject* into the .config() function is the .provider() type.

First, we create the stub of our provider in scripts/services.js:

```
// ...
.provider('AWSService', function() {
  var self = this;
  self.arn = null;

  self.setArn = function(arn) {
    if (arn) self.arn = arn;
  }

  self.$get = function($q) {
    return {}
  }
});
```

We can already see that we'll need to set the `Role ARN` for this service such that we can attach the proper user to the correct services.

Setting up our `AWSService` as a provider as we've done above enables us to set the following in our `scripts/app.js` file:

```
angular.module('myApp',
  ['ngRoute', 'myApp.services', 'myApp.directives']
)
.config(function(AWSServiceProvider) {
  AWSServiceProvider
    .setArn(
      'arn:aws:iam::<ACCOUNT_ID>:role/google-web-role');
})
```

Now, we can carry on with the `AWSService` and not worry about overriding our `Role ARN`. Creating the provider makes sharing amongst our different applications incredibly easy, rather than writing custom glue code every time.

At this point, our `AWSService` doesn't really do anything yet. The last thing we need to do is ensure that we're giving access to our actual users who log in.

This final step is where we need to tell the AWS library that we have an authenticated user that can operate as our IAM role.

We create this `credentials` as a promise that will eventually resolve; that way, we can define the different portions of our application without needing to bother checking if the credentials have been loaded – we simply use the `.then()` method on promises.

Let's modify the `$get()` method in our service by adding a method called `setToken()` that creates a new set of `WebIdentityCredentials`:

```
// ...
self.$get = function($q) {
  var credentialsDefer = $q.defer(),
      credentialsPromise = credentialsDefer.promise;
  return {
    credentials: function() {
      return credentialsPromise;
    },
    setToken: function(token, providerId) {
      var config = {
        RoleArn: self.arn,
        WebIdentityToken: token,
        RoleSessionName: 'web-id'
```

```
      }
      if (providerId) {
        config['ProviderId'] = providerId;
      }
      self.config = config;
      AWS.config.credentials =
        new AWS.WebIdentityCredentials(config);
      credentialsDefer
        .resolve(AWS.config.credentials);
    }
  }
}
// ...
```

Now, when we get our `oauth.access_token` back from our login through Google, we just need to pass in the `id_token` to this function, which will take care of the AWS config setup.

Let's modify the `UserService` service such that we call the `setToken()` method:

```
// ...
.factory('UserService', function($q, $http) {
  var service = {
    _user: null,
    setCurrentUser: function(u) {
      if (u && !u.error) {
        AWSService.setToken(u.id_token);
        return service.currentUser();
      } else {
        var d = $q.defer();
        d.reject(u.error);
        return d.promise;
      }
    },
    // ...
```

Starting on Dynamo

In our application, we want to associate any images that one user uploads to that unique user. To create that association, we'll create a Dynamo table that stores our users and another that stores the association between the user and the user's uploaded files.

To start interacting with Dynamo, we first need to instantiate a Dynamo object. We do so inside of our `AWSService` service object, like so:

```
// ...
setToken: function(token, providerId) {
  // ...
},
dynamo: function(params) {
  var d = $q.defer();
  credentialsPromise.then(function() {
    var table = new AWS.DynamoDB(params);
    d.resolve(table);
  });
  return d.promise;
},
// ...
```

As we discussed earlier, by using promises inside of our service objects, we only need to use the promise .then() API method to ensure that our credentials are set when we start to use them.

You might ask why we're setting params with our dynamo function. Sometimes, we'll want to interact with our DynamoDB with different configurations and different setups. For that interaction, we might need to recreate objects that we've already used once in our page.

Rather than having this duplication around our different AWS objects, we can *cache* these objects using the built-in Angular $cacheFactory service.

$cacheFactory

The $cacheFactory service enables us to create an object if we need it or recycle and reuse an object if we've already needed it in the past.

To start caching, we create a dynamoCache object where we'll store our cached Dynamo objects:

```
// ...
self.$get = function($q, $cacheFactory) {
  var dynamoCache = $cacheFactory('dynamo'),
      credentialsDefer = $q.defer(),
      credentialsPromise = credentialsDefer.promise;

  return {
  // ...
```

Back in our dynamo method, we can draw from the cache if the object exists inside of it, or we can set it to create the object when necessary:

```
// ...
dynamo: function(params) {
  var d = $q.defer();
  credentialsPromise.then(function() {
    var table =
      dynamoCache.get(JSON.stringify(params));
    if (!table) {
      var table = new AWS.DynamoDB(params);
      dynamoCache.put(JSON.stringify(params), table);
    };
    d.resolve(table);
  });
  return d.promise;
},
// ...
```

Saving Our currentUser

The point at which a user logs in and we fetch his or her email is a good place for us to add the user to our user's database.

To create a dynamo object, we need to use the promise API method .then() again, this time outside of the service. We create an object that enables us to interact with the User's table we'll create in the Dynamo API console.

> We need to manually create these Dynamo tables the first time we run our app as it's insecure to give access to our web users the ability to create dynamo tables.

To create a Dynamo table, let's head to the Dynamo console[81] and find the Create Table button.

We want to create a table called Users with a primary key type of Hash. The Hash Attribute Name will be the primary key that we'll use to get and put objects on the table. For this demo, we'll use the string: User email.

---

[81]https://console.aws.amazon.com/dynamodb/home

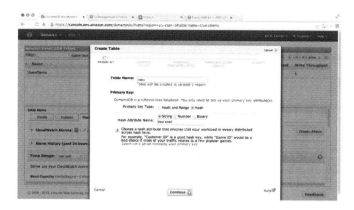

Create the Users Dynamo table

As we click through the next two screens, we will set up a basic alarm by entering our email. Although this step isn't 100% necessary, it's easy to forget that our tables are up; without being reminded, we might just end up leaving them up forever.

Once we've clicked through the final review screen and click create, we'll have a brand new Dynamo table where we will store our users.

While we are at the console, we need to create the *join* table. This table joins the user and the items the users uploads.

We must go back and find the Create Table button again to create a table called `UsersItems` with a primary key type of `Hash and Range`. For this table, The Hash Attribute Name will also be `User email` and the Range Attribute Name will be `ItemId`.

Setting up our table in this way allows us to query for any users who have created items based on email.

The rest of the options that are available on the next screens are optional, and we can click through the rest.

At this point, we have two `dynamo` tables available.

Back to our `UserService`, we first query the table to see if the user is already saved in our database; if not, we have to create an entry in our Dynamo database.

```
var service = {
  _user: null,
  UsersTable: "Users",
  UserItemsTable: "UsersItems",
  // ...
  currentUser: function() {
    var d = $q.defer();
    if (service._user) {
      d.resolve(service._user);
    } else {
```

```
  // After we've loaded the credentials
AWSService.credentials().then(function() {
  gapi.client.oauth2.userinfo.get()
  .execute(function(e) {
    var email = e.email;
    // Get the dynamo instance for the
    // UsersTable
    AWSService.dynamo({
      params: {TableName: service.UsersTable}
    })
    .then(function(table) {
      // find the user by email
      table.getItem({
        Key: {'User email': {S: email}}
      }, function(err, data) {
          if (Object.keys(data).length == 0) {
            // User didn't previously exist
            // so create an entry
            var itemParams = {
              Item: {
                'User email': {S: email},
                data: { S: JSON.stringify(e) }
              }
            };
            table.putItem(itemParams,
              function(err, data) {
                service._user = e;
                d.resolve(e);
            });
          } else {
            // The user already exists
            service._user =
              JSON.parse(data.Item.data.S);
            d.resolve(service._user);
          }
      });
    });
  });
}
return d.promise;
},
```

```
// ...
```

Although it looks like a lot of code, it simply does a find or create by username on our DynamoDB.

At this point, we can finally check out what's happening back in our view.

In our templates/main.html file, let's add a container that simply shows the login form if there is no user and shows the user details if there is a user.

We do so with simple ng-show directives and our new google-signin directive.

```
<div class="container">
  <h1>Home</h1>
  <div ng-show="!user" class="row">
    <div class="col-md-12">
      <h2>Signup or login to ngroad</h2>
      <div google-signin
        client-id='395118764200'
        after-signin="signedIn(oauth)"></div>
    </div>
  </div>
  <div ng-show="user">
    <pre>{{ user | json }}</pre>
  </div>
</div>
```

Once our view is set up, we can work with logged-in users inside the second <div> (in production, it's a good idea to make it a separate route).

Uploading to S3

Now that we have our logged-in user stored in Dynamo, it's time we build out our file upload functionality, storing files directly on S3.

First and foremost, let's take a shallow dive into CORS. CORS, or Cross-Origin Resource Sharing, is a security feature supported by modern browsers that allow us to make requests to foreign domains using a standard protocol.

Luckily, the AWS team has made supporting CORS incredibly simple. If we're hosting our site on S3, we don't even need to set up CORS (other than for development purposes).

To enable CORS on a bucket, head to the S3 console[82] and find the bucket that we're going to use for file uploads. For this demo, we're using the ng-newsletter-example bucket.

---

[82]https://console.aws.amazon.com/s3/home

Once we've located the bucket, let's click on it, load the Properties tab, and pull open the Permissions option. From there, we click on the *Add CORS configuration* button and pick the standard CORS configuration.

Enable CORS on an S3 bucket

We want to create a simple file upload directive that kicks off a method using the HTML5 File API to handle the file upload. That way, when the user selects a file, the file upload will start immediately.

To handle the file selection directive, we create a simple directive that binds to the change event and calls a method after the file has been selected.

The directive is simple:

```
// ...
.directive('fileUpload', function() {
  return {
    restrict: 'A',
    scope: { fileUpload: '&' },
    template: '<input type="file" id="file" /> ',
    replace: true,
    link: function(scope, ele, attrs) {
      ele.bind('change', function() {
        var file = ele[0].files;
        if (file) scope.fileUpload({files: file});
      })
    }
  }
})
```

We can use this directive in our view like so:

```
<!-- ... -->
<div class="row"
  <div class="col-md-12">
    <div file-upload="onFile(files)"></div>
  </div>
</div>
```

Now, when the file selection has been made, it calls the method onFile(files) in our current scope.

> Although we're creating our own file directive here, we recommend checking out the
> ngUpload[83] library for handling file uploads.

Inside the onFile(files) method, we want to handle the file upload to S3 and save the record to our Dynamo database table. Instead of placing this functionality in the controller, we want to remember to be nice Angular citizens and place it in our UserService service.

First, we need to make sure we have the ability to get an S3 JavaScript object just like how we made the dynamo available.

```
// ...
var dynamoCache = $cacheFactory('dynamo'),
    s3Cache = $cacheFactory('s3Cache');
// ...
return {
  // ...
  s3: function(params) {
    var d = $q.defer();
    credentialsPromise.then(function() {
      var s3Obj = s3Cache.get(JSON.stringify(params));
      if (!s3Obj) {
        var s3Obj = new AWS.S3(params);
        s3Cache.put(JSON.stringify(params), s3Obj);
      }
      d.resolve(s3Obj);
    });
    return d.promise;
  },
// ...
```

This method works in the same way that our Dynamo object creation works, giving us direct access to the S3 instance object, as we'll see shortly.

---

[83]https://github.com/twilson63/ngUpload

Handling File Uploads

To handle file uploads, we need to create a method called `uploadItemForSale()` in our `UserService`. For the sake of planning, in terms of our functionality, we want to:

- Upload the file to S3
- Get a signedUrl for the file
- Save this information to our database

We're going to be using our current user throughout this process, so we must start by ensuring that we have our user and get an instance:

```javascript
// in scripts/services.js
// ...
},
Bucket: 'ng-newsletter-example',
uploadItemForSale: function(items) {
  var d = $q.defer();
  service.currentUser().then(function(user) {
    // Handle the upload
    AWSService.s3({
      params: {
        Bucket: service.Bucket
      }
    }).then(function(s3) {
      // We have a handle of our s3 bucket
      // in the s3 object
    });
  });
  return d.promise;
},
// ...
```

The handle of the S3 bucket gives us the ability to create a file to upload. AWS requires three parameters when uploading to S3:

- Key - The key of the file object
- Body - The file blob itself
- ContentType - The type of file

Luckily for us, all of this information is available on the file object when we get it from the browser.

```
// ...
// Handle the upload
AWSService.s3({
  params: {
    Bucket: service.Bucket
  }
}).then(function(s3) {
  // We have a handle of our s3 bucket
  // in the s3 object
  var file = items[0]; // Get the first file
  var params = {
    Key: file.name,
    Body: file,
    ContentType: file.type
  }

  s3.putObject(params, function(err, data) {
    // The file has been uploaded
    // or an error has occurred during the upload
  });
});
// ...
```

By default, S3 uploads files in a protected form. It prevents us from uploading and making the files available to the public without some work. This *feature* ensures that anything we upload to S3 will be protected, and it forces us to make conscious choices about what files are public and which are not.

With that in mind, let's create a temporary URL that expires after a given amount of time. In our ngroad marketplace, this URL will provide a time expiry on each of the items that are available for sale.

In any case, to create a temporary URL, we fetch a `signedUrl` and store that in our join table for User's Items:

```
// ...
s3.putObject(params, function(err, data) {
  if (!err) {
    var params = {
      Bucket: service.Bucket,
      Key: file.name,
      Expires: 900*4 // 1 hour
    };
    s3.getSignedUrl('getObject', params,
      function(err, url) {
        // Now we have a url
    });
  }
});
});
// ...
```

Finally, we can save our User's object along with the file they uploaded in our Join table:

```
// ...
s3.getSignedUrl('getObject', params,
  function(err, url) {
    // Now we have a url
    AWSService.dynamo({
      params: {TableName: service.UserItemsTable}
    }).then(function(table) {
      var itemParams = {
        Item: {
          'ItemId': {S: file.name},
          'User email': {S: user.email},
          data: {
            S: JSON.stringify({
              itemId: file.name,
              itemSize: file.size,
              itemUrl: url
            })
          }
        }
      };
      table.putItem(itemParams, function(err, data) {
        d.resolve(data);
      });
```

```
    });
});
// ...
```

This method is available in its entirety here[84].

We can use this new method inside of our controller's `onFile()` method, which we can write to be similar to:

```
$scope.onFile = function(files) {
  UserService.uploadItemForSale(files)
  .then(function(data) {
    // Refresh the current items for sale
  });
}
```

Querying Dynamo

Ideally, we want to be able to list all the products a certain user has available for purchase. In order to set up a listing of the available items, we will use the `query` API.

The Dynamo query API is a tad esoteric and can be considerably confusing at first glance.

 The Dynamo query documentation is available at docs.aws.amazon.com[85].

Basically, we're going to match object schemes using a comparison operator, such as `equal`, `lt` (less than), `gt` (greater than), or any of several more. Our join table's key is the `User email` key, so we're going to match this key against the current user's email as the query key.

As we did with our other APIs related to users, we create a method inside of our `UserService` to handle this querying of the database:

---

[84]https://gist.github.com/auser/7316267#file-services-js-L98

[85]http://docs.aws.amazon.com/amazondynamodb/latest/APIReference/API_Query.html

```
// ...
itemsForSale: function() {
  var d = $q.defer();
  service.currentUser().then(function(user) {
    AWSService.dynamo({
      params: {TableName: service.UserItemsTable}
    }).then(function(table) {
      table.query({
        TableName: service.UserItemsTable,
        KeyConditions: {
          "User email": {
            "ComparisonOperator": "EQ",
            "AttributeValueList": [
              {S: user.email}
            ]
          }
        }
      }, function(err, data) {
        var items = [];
        if (data) {
          angular.forEach(data.Items, function(item) {
            items.push(JSON.parse(item.data.S));
          });
          d.resolve(items);
        } else {
          d.reject(err);
        }
      })
    });
  });
  return d.promise;
},
// ...
```

In the above query, the `KeyConditions` and `"User email"` are required parameters.

Showing the Listing in HTML

To show our user's images in HTML, we simply assign the result of our new `itemsForSale()` method to a property of the controller's scope:

```
var getItemsForSale = function() {
  UserService.itemsForSale()
  .then(function(images) {
    $scope.images = images;
  });
}
// Load the user's list initially
getItemsForSale();
```

Now we can easily iterate over the list of items using the `ng-repeat` directive:

```
<!-- ... -->
<div ng-show="images">
  <div class="col-sm-6 col-md-4"
    ng-repeat="image in images">
    <div class="thumbnail">
      <img ng-click="sellImage(image)"
          data-ng-src="{{image.itemUrl}}" />
    </div>
  </div>
</div>
```

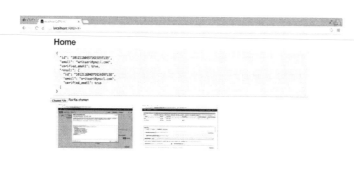

Image listing

Selling Our Work

The final component of our AWS-powered demo app that we need to create is the ability to create sales from our single-page app.

To start handling and accepting payments, we'll create a `StripeService` that handles creating charges for us. Since we'll want to support configuring Stripe in the `.config()` method in our module, we'll need to create a `.provider()`.

The service itself is incredibly simple, as it leverages the `Stripe.js` library to do the heavy lifting.

```
// ...
.provider('StripeService', function() {
  var self = this;

  self.setPublishableKey = function(key) {
    Stripe.setPublishableKey(key);
  }

  self.$get = function($q) {
    return {
      createCharge: function(obj) {
        var d = $q.defer();

        if (!obj.hasOwnProperty('number') ||
            !obj.hasOwnProperty('cvc') ||
            !obj.hasOwnProperty('exp_month') ||
            !obj.hasOwnProperty('exp_year')
        ) {
          d.reject("Bad input", obj);
        } else {
          Stripe.card.createToken(obj,
            function(status, resp) {
              if (status == 200) {
                d.resolve(resp);
              } else {
                d.reject(status);
              }
          });
        }

        return d.promise;
      }
    }
  }
});
```

If you do not have a Stripe account, get one at stripe.com[86]. Stripe is an incredibly developer-friendly payment processing gateway, which makes it ideal for our use in building our ngroad marketplace.

Once we have an account, we want to find our Account Settings page and locate the API Keys page. Our first order of business is to find the publishable key (either the test one, which won't actually make charges, or the production version) and take note of it.

In our scripts/app.js file, we just add the following line and replace the 'pk_test_YOUR_KEY' publishable key with our own.

```
// ...
.config(function(StripeServiceProvider) {
  StripeServiceProvider
    .setPublishableKey('pk_test_YOUR_KEY');
})
```

Using Stripe

When a user clicks on an image he or she likes, we open a form in the browser that takes credit card information. We want to set the form to submit to an action on our controller called submitPayment().

Notice that above, where we have the thumbnail of the image, we include an action when the image is clicked that calls the sellImage() action with the image.

Implementing the sellImage() function in the MainController looks like:

```
// ...
$scope.sellImage = function(image) {
  $scope.showCC = true;
  $scope.currentItem = image;
}
// ...
```

Now, when the image is clicked, the showCC property will be true and we can show the credit card form. We've included an incredibly simple one here:

---

[86]http://stripe.com

```
<div ng-show="showCC">
  <form ng-submit="submitPayment()">
    <span ng-bind="errors"></span>
    <span>Card Number</span>
    <input type="text"
            ng-minlength="16"
            ng-maxlength="20"
            size="20"
            data-stripe="number"
            ng-model="charge.number" />
    <span>CVC</span>
    <input type="text"
            ng-minlength="3"
            ng-maxlength="4"
            data-stripe="cvc"
            ng-model="charge.cvc" />
    <span>Expiration (MM/YYYY)</span>
    <input type="text"
      ng-minlength="2"
      ng-maxlength="2"
      size="2"
      data-stripe="exp_month"
      ng-model="charge.exp_month" />
    <span> / </span>
    <input type="text"
      ng-minlength="4"
      ng-maxlength="4"
      size="4"
      data-stripe="exp-year"
      ng-model="charge.exp_year" />
    <input type="hidden"
      name="email"
      value="user.email" />
    <button type="submit">Submit Payment</button>
  </form>
</div>
```

We're binding the form almost entirely to the charge object on the scope, which we will use when we make the charge.

The form itself submits to the function submitPayment() on the controller's scope. The submitPayment() function looks like:

```
// ...
$scope.submitPayment = function() {
  UserService
    .createPayment($scope.currentItem, $scope.charge)
  .then(function(data) {
    $scope.showCC = false;
  });
}
// ...
```

The last thing that we'll have to do to be able to *accept charges* is implement the createPayment() method on the UserService.

Now, since we're taking payment on the client side, we're technically not going to be able to process payments; we can only accept the stripeToken. We can set a background process to manage turning the Stripe tokens into actual payments.

Inside of our createPayment() function, we need to call our StripeService to generate the stripeToken. Then, we add the payment to an Amazon SQS queue so that our background process can make the charge.

First, we use the AWSService to access our SQS queues.

Unlike our other services, the SQS service requires a bit more integration to make it work, as the service requires us to have a URL to interact with them. In our AWSService service object, we need to cache the URL that we're working with and create a new object every time time using the generated service object instead. The idea behind the workflow is the exact same, however.

```
// ...
self.$get = function($q, $cacheFactory) {
  var dynamoCache = $cacheFactory('dynamo'),
      s3Cache = $cacheFactory('s3Cache'),
      sqsCache = $cacheFactory('sqs');
// ...
sqs: function(params) {
  var d = $q.defer();
  credentialsPromise.then(function() {
    var url = sqsCache.get(JSON.stringify(params)),
        queued = $q.defer();
    if (!url) {
      var sqs = new AWS.SQS();
      sqs.createQueue(params,
        function(err, data) {
          if (data) {
            url = data.QueueUrl;
```

```
            sqsCache.put(JSON.stringify(params), url);
            queued.resolve(url);
          } else {
            queued.reject(err);
          }
        });
    } else {
      queued.resolve(url);
    }
    queued.promise.then(function(url) {
      var queue =
        new AWS.SQS({params: {QueueUrl: url}});
      d.resolve(queue);
    });
  })
  return d.promise;
}
// ...
```

Now, we can use SQS inside of our `createPayment()` function. One caveat to the SQS service is that it can only send simple messages, such as with strings and numbers. It cannot send objects, so we need to call `JSON.stringify` on any objects we want to pass through the queue.

```
// ...
ChargeTable: "UserCharges",
// ...
createPayment: function(item, charge) {
  var d = $q.defer();
  StripeService.createCharge(charge)
  .then(function(data) {
    var stripeToken = data.id;
    AWSService.sqs(
      {QueueName: service.ChargeTable}
    ).then(function(queue) {
      queue.sendMessage({
        MessageBody: JSON.stringify({
          item: item,
          stripeToken: stripeToken
        })
      }, function(err, data) {
        d.resolve(data);
      })
```

```
  })
}, function(err) {
  d.reject(err);
});
  return d.promise;
}
```

When we submit the form...

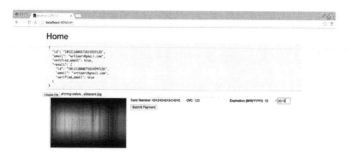

Payment handling

Our SQS queue grows, and we have a payment just waiting to be completed.

SQS queue

Server-less with Firebase

As a client-side framework, Angular alone is not enough to build a full back-end webapp. It's often difficult to know when to sync our data with the back end and how to handle the changes and potential conflicts of data between versions of modified content.

Imagine that we have two instances of our application running at the same time. What if both instances are trying to edit the same data? Without handling this case, we can get into trouble, especially if we're building the front end for a complex web application, like a bank.

Using Firebase, we can easily add a back end to our Angular app. Featured on the Angular.js home page, Firebase is quickly becoming the standard for Angular persistence.

Firebase is a real-time back end for building collaborative, modern applications. Instead of requiring us to focus on building custom request-response models with a server-side component where we manually worry about data synchronization, Firebase lets us get our app up and running in minutes. We can build a data-backed web app entirely in Angular that can scale out of the box and update all clients in real time.

Data that is stored in Firebase is standard schema-less JSON, which makes it incredibly easy to save data models of any type into Firebase. If a device loses network connection, Firebase continues to allow access to locally cached data and seamlessly synchronizes changes with the cloud when the device comes back online.

 The Firebase client libraries and REST API provide easy access to that data from any platform. Although we're focusing specifically on Angular, this fact means that native apps or other server-side apps can reach the data that Angualr has saved.

Three-Way Data Binding With Firebase and Angular

With Angular, rendering content to the browser easy. Firebase is an excellent partner to Angular, as it elegantly handles storing and retrieving data, which is the other major component to production-level web apps.

Angular is great with its two-way data binding between models in JavaScript and the DOM. By syncing our Angular model with Firebase, we synchronize our app's data in the model in real time across all clients. That means that when data changes in one client, these updates immediately persist to Firebase and render across all connected devices.

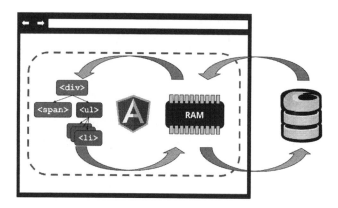

When we update data in any of the three places (View, Model, or Firebase), the changes propagate in real time to the other two across *all* clients.

Getting Started With AngularFire

It's easy to create real-time web applications using Firebase and Angular thanks to the official Angular library, AngularFire. The Firebase team built the AngularFire bindings specifically for integration with Angular applications, as we'll see.

There are only **four** steps to backing our Angular app on Firebase using AngularFire:

1. Sign up and Create a Firebase

Before we can actually save or retrieve any data from Firebase, we need an account. It's free to create one, so let's sign up.

First, we'll head to firebase.com[87] and click on the *Sign up* button (or login if you already have an account):

---

[87]http://firebase.com

Now that we have signed up for an account, we can create our first Firebase. The name we choose will be part of the URL we'll use to reference our Firebase data.

For example, when we create a Firebase with the name of `ng-newsletter`, our Firebase URL will be available at `https://ng-newsletter.firebaseio.com`.

The AngularFire bindings let us associate a Firebase URL with a model or collection of models. These models represent the data that AngularFire will transparently keep in sync across all clients currently using our app.

Angular's two-way data binding keeps the DOM synced to JavaScript variables in memory; Firebase stores those changes and sends them to all listening clients in real time.

> We get this data synchronization **without changing** how we build our Angular app. Very cool!

2. Include the Firebase and AngularFire Libraries

Using AngularFire is as simple as including two JavaScript files in our HTML file: one for Firebase and another for AngularFire.

We need to use Firebase's CDN, so at the top of our index.html file we'll add the following two lines:

```
<script
  src="https://cdn.firebase.com/v0/firebase.js"></script>
<script
  src="https://cdn.firebase.com/libs/angularfire/0.5.0/angularfire.js">
</script>
```

3. Add Firebase As a Dependency

As is usual with any application libraries, we need to set the Firebase library as a dependency for our module. That tells the rest of our application that we can use the Firebase bindings in our app:

```
angular.module("myapp", ["firebase"]);
```

4. Bind a Model to a Firebase URL

By declaring Firebase as a dependency, we now have access to the $firebase service, which allows us to inject it as a dependency into our controllers and services.

```
angular.module('myapp', ['firebase'])
.controller("MyController", ["$scope", "$firebase",
  function($scope, $firebase) {
    // Our controller definition goes here
  }
]);
```

The $firebase service takes a single argument: a Firebase reference.

FirebaseRef (Firebase Reference)

The Firebase reference tells $firebase where the data is stored and how to connect. The $firebase service handles synchronization with Angular and is where we'll call methods to save our changes.

This object has several methods we'll use to interact with our remote data. These methods, detailed below, are all prefixed with the $ symbol (e.g., $add(), $save()) and are available on this object.

> Note that **no** changes to the object result in changes made to the remote data.

To synchronize a local object model to the remote Firebase reference, we use the service method and pass it an instance of the Firebase object. For example, to synchronize the $scope.items model to our ng-newsletter items, we run the following method:

```
angular.module('myApp')
.controller("MyController", function($scope, $firebase) {
  // Firebase URL
  var URL = "https://ng-newsletter.firebase.com";
  // Synchronizing the items on our $scope
  $scope.items = $firebase(new Firebase(URL + '/items'));
});
```

Now, we can simply interact with the $scope.items object to synchronize our Angular models with Firebase.

Data Synchronization

We can synchronize our data back to Firebase by using the following methods provided by the $firebase object.

$add(value)

The $add method takes a single argument of any type. It appends this value as a member of a chronologically ordered list. We can think of this like we're calling .push(value) on to the Firebase reference *array*.

> Note that the Firebase reference object is not really an array, but we can act as though it is.

For example, we can add the string "bar" to the Firebase reference located at the /foo endpoint:

```
$scope.items.$add({foo: "bar"});
```

$remove(key)

The $remove method removes remote child references from Firebase. It takes a single optional argument:

key (optional string)   If we provide a key argument (as a string), the $remove() method will remove the child referenced by that key. If no key is provided, it will remove the entire remote object.

```
$scope.items.$remove("foo"); // Remove the child named "foo".
$scope.items.$remove();      // Remove the entire object.
```

$save(key)

The $save method synchronizes all changes to the local elements with the Firebase data store and pushes them instantly to all listening clients. It takes a single argument:

key (optional string)   If we provide the key argument (string), the $save() method saves changes made to the child element referenced by the key to Firebase. If no key is provided to the $save() method, then all local changes made to the object persist to Firebase.

> The $save() method is most commonly used to save any local changes made to the model.

```
$scope.items.foo = "baz";
$scope.items.$save("foo");  // new Firebase(URL + "/foo") now contains "baz".
```

$child(key)

The $child() method creates a new $firebase object for a child referenced by the provided key. The method takes a single argument:

key (string)   The key string is used to reference the newly created child.

```
var child = $scope.items.$child("foo");
child.$remove();            // Equivalent to calling $scope.items.$remove("foo");
```

$set(value)

The $set() method overwrites the remote value for this object to be the newValue. The $set() method also updates local object version of the object to the value.

It takes a single argument:

value (string)   The value argument is the new value of the local object. The value overwrites the old value, and is subsequently updated to this new value.

```
$scope.items.$set({bar: "baz"});  // new Firebase(URL + "/foo") is now null.
```

Ordering in AngularFire

If we want to sort our remote objects, rather than simply sorting locally with Angular's orderBy filter, we can set the $priority field on a record before calling $save().

```
$scope.items.foo.$priority = 2;
$scope.items.$save("foo");  // new Firebase(URL + "foo")'s priority is now 2.
```

By default, the $firebase service returns a simple JavaScript object. We can convert this object into an array that respects order simply by using the orderByPriority filter.

This filter turns the object returned by the $firebase service into an array and orders by the priority definition defined by Firebase. AngularFire will will set an $id property on each object defined on it which references the keyname of the object.

```
<ul ng-repeat="item in items | orderByPriority">
  <li>
    <input type="text" id="{{item.$id}}" ng-model="item.$priority"/>
    {{item.name}}
  </li>
</ul>
```

Firebase Events

Firebase fires two types of events that we can use to handle custom logic from within our app. We can use the $on() method to attach event handlers for these two event types:

loaded

Firebase fires the loaded event when initial data is received from Firebase, initiated by a connection. It is fired once and only once.

```
$scope.items.$on('loaded', function() {
  console.log("Items loaded");
});
```

change

Firebase fires the change event whenever there is a remote change in the data applied to the local object. For instance, it fires if there is a new task added by another user to our task list.

```
$scope.items.$on('change', function() {
  console.log("A change is afoot");
});
```

Implicit Synchronization

To add automatic, implicit synchronization with a $scope variable, we can call the $bind() method on the object returned by the $firebase service.

The $bind() method automatically establishes a three-way binding so we don't need to explicitly save data to Firebase using the $add() or $save() methods.

```
$scope.items.$bind($scope, "remoteItems");
$scope.remoteItems.bar = "foo";   // new Firebase(URL + "/bar") is now "foo".
```

The $bind() method returns a promise that will resolve when the initial data from the server has been received. The promise will be resolved with an unbind function, which will disassociate the three-way binding when called.

```
$scope.items.$bind($scope, "remote")
.then(function(unbind) {
  unbind();
  $scope.remote.bar = "foo";     // No changes have been made to the remote data.
});
```

The $bind method returns a promise, which resolves when the initial data from the server has been received by AngularFire. The promise will resolve with an unbind function, which disassociates the three-way binding when called. This disassociation is useful for optimizing our site and removing unnecessary watches.

Authentication with AngularFire

Firebase provides a simple, client-side authentication strategy out of the box.

Using Firebase's Simple Login or Custom Login methods, we can easily add user authentication to our application with AngularFire.

Custom Login is most appropriate to use if we have our own server where we want to control our own authentication or if we want to integrate existing authentication with Firebase.

If we want to use Firebase to manage all of our authentication, we can use Simple Login, which supports Facebook, Twitter, GitHub, Persona, and Email/Password authentication.

By defining Firebase as a dependency in our app's module, we have access to the $firebaseAuth service in our controllers and services.

```
angular.module('myApp')
.controller("MyAuthController", function($scope, $firebaseAuth) {
  // Define our controller here
});
```

The $firebaseAuth service method takes two arguments: a Firebase reference and an optional object with options. The object can contain the following properties to customize how the authentication works with Firebase:

- path - This property is the path to which the user will be redirected if the authRequired property is set to true in the $routeProvider and the user is not logged in.
- simple - $firebaseAuth requires inclusion of the firebase-simple-login.js file by default. If this simple value is set to false, this requirement is waived, but only custom login functionality will be enabled, and we cannot use simple auth.
- callback - Firebase calls this function when there is a change in authentication state. We can use this callback as an alternative to events fired on $rootScope, which is the recommended way to handle changes in auth state.

```
angular.module('myApp')
.controller("MyAuthController", function($scope, $firebaseAuth) {
    var ref = new Firebase(URL);
    $scope.auth = $firebaseAuth(ref);
    // $scope.auth.user is null until the user logs in.
});
```

The object that $firebaseAuth() returns contains a single property called user. user is set to null if the user is logged out and changes to an object containing the user's details once he or she is logged in. We cover detecting logins below.

> The contents of the user's detail object will vary depending upon the authentication mechanism used, but at the very least, it will contain a user id and provider name.

Authentication Events

With AngularFire authentication, we have access to several methods for changing a user's authentication state; these methods are $login(), $logout(), and $createUser().

Authentication state in AngularFire is considered global, and each of the authentication methods below will broadcast on the $rootScope. Since nearly all scopes inherit from $rootScope, we can call $scope.on(...) from any controller.

> Global authentication means that we cannot have multiple users logged into the same instance of the application at the same time. For example, global authentication prevents two users from being logged into Gmail at the same time in the same browser instance.

$firebaseAuth:login   A user triggers this event when he or she successfully logs in. It fires with two arguments: an event and user object.

```
$rootScope.$on("$firebaseAuth:login", function(evt, user) {
  console.log("User " + user.id + " successfully logged in!");
});
```

$firebaseAuth:logout   The user triggers the logout event when he or she logs out. The event fires with an event argument.

```
$rootScope.$on("$firebaseAuth:logout", function(evt) {
  console.log("User logged out!");
});
```

$firebaseAuth:error   The error event is triggered when there is an error during either calling $login() or $logout(). This event fires with a single argument: the error.

)

]$login(token, [options])

We use the $login() method to log in a user. We usually use it when a user clicks a login button, like the following:

```
<a href="#"
   ng-hide="auth.user"
   ng-click="auth.$login('persona')">Login</a>
```

The $login() function takes up to two arguments:

tokenOrProvider (string/JWT token)   If we are using Firebase Simple Login, we can simply pass in a provider name, such as 'facebook', or 'persona'. If we want to use the Custom Login flow, then we'll need to pass in a valid JWT token instead.

options (object)   We'll only use the options argument with Simple Login, where the provided options are passed without modification to the Simple Login method.

For a "password" provider, we'll want to provide a username and password as an object.

> For more information about the user object, read the Firebase documentation on AngularFire.com[88].

$logout()

The $logout() method logs out the current user. It takes no arguments.

The $firebaseAuth:logout event will fire, setting the user property to null after the logout is completed. We'll typically attach this method to a logout button:

```
<span ng-show="auth.user">
  {{auth.user.name}} | <a href="#" ng-click="auth.$logout()">Logout</a>
</span>
```

$createUser()

The $createUser() method is useful when we are using the "password" provider with Firebase Simple Login.

The $createUser() method takes three arguments:

email (string) The email with which we want to create the user

password (string) The password with which we want to create the user

callback (function) Firebase calls the callback method after $createUser() has run. It takes two arguments: error and user. If there was an error in the $createUser() method, the error will contain the error message and user will be null. If the error is null, then the user will be defined.

```
auth.createUser(email, password, function(error, user) {
  if (!error) {
    console.log('User Id: ' + user.id + ', Email: ' + user.email);
  }
});
```

Firebase makes it easy to wire up a back end to our Angular app without having to worry about setting up a server or writing a single line of back-end code. AngularFire enables us to create complex, real-time applications that synchronize immediately between our application's model and data stored in Firebase.

To learn more about AngularFire, the source code is available on GitHub[89].

To get an AngularFire app up and running in minutes, clone the angularFire-seed[90] repo.

---

[89]https://github.com/firebase/angularFire
[90]https://github.com/firebase/angularFire-seed

Beyond AngularFire

AngularFire is a great wrapper for interacting with Firebase, but you can certainly interact directly with the Firebase SDK from Angular for more complex operations. Check out the Firebase tutorial[91] to learn more about the advanced capabilities of this sophisticated real-time platform.

---

[91]https://www.firebase.com/tutorial/

Testing

The AngularJS framework encourages writing clean, solid, testable code. This feature is one of the most useful that you get out of the box with Angular.

The Angular team's emphasis on testing is so strong that they built a test runner to make the process easier. In their words:

 JavaScript is a dynamically typed language which comes with great power of expression, but it also comes with almost no help from the compiler. For this reason we feel very strongly that any code written in JavaScript needs to come with a strong set of tests. We have built many features into Angular which makes testing your Angular applications easy. So there is no excuse for not testing.

Why Test?

When building any non-trivial application for any business purpose beyond prototyping (and even then), it's important to be confident about our code. When we have tests backing up our codebase, we can discretely know whether or not our code is working as intended.

Bugs in our code are inevitable, and without tests it's difficult to know where they are; tests make it easy to isolate and eliminate them. They make it easy to onboard other developers and provide working documentation about the code.

Testing is essential if we are to understand what is happening in our app.

Testing Strategies

When building a testing suite to develop Angular apps, it's always good to have a strategy for how and what we are going to test in our app. If we end up not testing anything of substance and write meaningless tests, we'll have gained nothing to give us confidence our apps are functioning properly. Conversely, if we test everything we can possibly think of, we'll end up spending more time writing tests and fixing minor bugs in our test code than we will on our app.

It's important to be realistic about the value we'll get out of the tests we do write and about what we should be testing.

At the end of the day, our tests are both a tool for us to gauge the health of our app and a measuring stick to tell us if we've broken our code when introducing new functionality.

Getting Started Testing

One of the major hurdles in getting started with testing is setting up a test runner that runs tests on our code. JavaScript testing is also a bit more difficult, because it requires us to build automation into browsers.

Building a development testing suite is difficult enough, but what about supporting continuous integration so that new deployments can be automated and we can be confident about the quality of the code before making a new one?

> In software engineering, continuous integration is the practice of merging development working copies of a shared mainline several times a day and running the test suite upon update.

Karma[92] is a testing tool that was built from the ground up to remove the burden of setting up testing and allow us to focus on building our core application logic.

Karma spawns a browser instance (or multiple different browser instances) and runs the tests against the different browser instances to see if the tests pass under different browser environments. Karma communicates with the browsers through socket.io, which enables Karma to keep in constant contact. Thus, Karma provides real-time feedback about what tests are running and gives us a human-readable output that tells us which tests pass and which ones fail or time out.

Karma is capable of communicating with several different browsers natively and removes the need for us to manually test our code in different browsers. For example, it can run the tests in Chrome, IE, and Firefox and spit out the results to your console. We can even hook up to our own native devices (yes, like an iPhone or iPad) to test our code.

Types of AngularJS Tests

There are several different ways to test our Angular apps, depending upon what level of granularity we want to focus on and what features we want to target.

Unit Testing

We can focus on building our tests to isolate specific, isolated components of our code. This approach is called "unit testing", where we test specific units of code for all sorts of different input at different stages and under different conditions.

Unit testing is specifically for testing small, individual units of code, single functions, or small and contained function interactions. It is *not* about testing large feature sets.

The tricky part about unit testing is setting up the isolation of one piece of logic so that we can test it. We'll discuss strategies of accomplishing this isolation later in this chapter.

---

[92]http://karma-runner.github.io/0.10/index.html

When Is Unit Testing the *Right* Choice?

When we're writing our functional code, we're going to create little components of functionality. For instance, in building an application that handles live filtering elements in a list, we're going to build the filtering functionality.

The feature of this *filter* is a 'unit' of functionality that is an ideal case where we'll want to test with a unit test. To be confident that this filter functionality has been implemented and is working as expected, we'll need to isolate the component and test it for different inputs.

> Imagine we're building a rocket ship. We'll want to test each individual part of the ship (e.g., the thrusters, the joystick controls, the oxygen system) to verify the ship is generally working how we expect it to work.

E2E Testing

On the other hand, we can *black-box* test (i.e., perform an end-to-end test on) our application. In an end-to-end (or E2E) test, we test the application from the point of view where we are an end user and know nothing about the underlying components of the system. This method is great for testing large features of the application.

E2E testing works well for testing the user interaction with the page without forcing us to refresh the page manually and test with the browser.

This kind of testing is nothing new, and there are great tools that enable us to set up automated browser testing. We can use tools like PhantomJS or CasperJS for headless browser testing (i.e., without opening a browser) or tools like Karma that will open a real browser and perform all the tests in an iframe.

When Is End-to-End Testing the *Right* Choice?

When we're writing tests of use-case functionality, it's always a good idea to write a test to walk the path of our user. End-to-end testing is great because it maps out the *real* experiences our users will have when using our application.

For instance, when building a user login flow, we test that the user is logged in and redirected to his or her homepage. We don't worry about *how* the user is logged in, just that they are logged in and directed to the proper place.

> Imagine you're building a rocket ship. End-to-end testing doesn't care about the engines or the landing gear, it cares that the rocket takes off and flies your astronauts to space.

Both unit testing and E2E testing are supported out of the box with the Karma test runner.

Note that writing unit tests instead of E2E tests will allow our tests to run extremely quickly. Setting up our tests to run synchronously and using mocking libraries will greatly speed up our testing, as well.

Getting Started

In order to run our tests, we'll need to install the Karma test runner. At this point in the book, you likely already have NodeJS[93] and npm available to you; if you don't, make sure you install them. Once you do, we'll use the npm command to install the Karma tool:

```
$ npm install -g karma
```

To install npm, we'll save our dependencies in the package.json file that lists our dependencies. To set up package.json with **npm** installed, simply run npm init and walk through the wizard.

To start testing our application, we'll need to set up a reasonable structure for both our application code and our test code.

We recommend storing application files in the following format:

```
app/
  index.html
  js/
    app.js
    controllers.js
    directives.js
    services.js
    filters.js
  views/
    home.html
    dashboard.html
    calendar.html
test/
  karma-e2e.conf.js
  karma.conf.js
  lib/
    angular-mocks.js
```

[93]http://nodejs.org

```
    helpers.js
unit/
e2e/
```

The app/ layout is standard, wherein we divide our application code. The test/ directory nests our tests in the appropriate directories that reflect the type of test: unit/ or e2e/.

There are two different Karma configuration files in the test/ directory. Each of these files contains the specific type of test that it will run. As we walk through each type of test, we'll discuss how each Karma configuration should look and how to customize it for our use.

Running a Karma test is simple: karma start path/to/karma.config.js. When the test runner starts up, it will start the browsers listed in the Karma config file.

Running Karma with Chrome and Safari

By default, if not otherwise specified, Karma will watch all the files listed in the Karma configuration. Any time a file changes, Karma will run the appropriate tests.

Initializing Karma Config File

Karma gives us a generator to help us build configuration files. This generator will ask a few questions about how we want to set up our configuration. Each question suggests a default value so it is possible to simply accept all the default values, which we'll do in a moment.

Karma init

The process of setting up testing with unit tests and E2E tests is largely the same. We'll use the `karma init` generator to create `karma.conf.js` configuration files.

Setting Up Unit Testing

First, let's run the `karma init` command with the path of our test file. In this case, we'll build our Karma config in our tests directory:

```
$ karma init test/karma.conf.js
```

For unit testing, we all of the dependencies against which we're running our tests to be available. When building our unit tests with the Karma generator, it's important that our unit tests contain references to code for:

- a testing framework (choose one):
    - Jasmine (default)
    - Mocha
    - QUnit
- custom test configuration (required w/ Mocha)
- any vendor-required code
- our app-specific code
- our test code
- `angular-mocks.js` library for mocking

Unit tests need references to all of the app code that we'll be testing as well as all of the tests that we'll be writing.

For instance, a sample unit test Karma config file might look like the following (comments removed for simplicity):

```
module.exports = function(config) {
  config.set({
    basePath: '..',
    frameworks: ['jasmine'],
    files: [
      'lib/angular.js',
      'lib/angular-route.js',
      'test/lib/angular-mocks.js',
      'js/**/*.js',
      'test/unit/**/*.js'
    ],
    exclude: [],
    port: 8080,
    logLevel: config.LOG_INFO,
    autoWatch: true,
    browsers: ['Safari'],
    singleRun: false
  });
};
```

This config file is similar to the one we'll generate.

Once this file is set, we can run our unit tests like so:

```
$ karma run test/karma.conf.js
```

Alternatively, if we want the tests to run any time the code changes (if we set autoWatch to true):

```
$ karma start test/karma.conf.js
```

Setting Up E2E Testing

To set up end-to-end testing, we'll run the Karma generator with the path of our E2E Karma config file.

```
$ karma init test/karma-e2e.conf.js
```

The E2E tests will use the ng-scenario framework. Unlike unit tests, we do not need to reference all of our library code: These E2E tests run against our server. The ng-scenario framework simply needs to load all of the tests in the browser.

A sample Karma config for E2E tests might look like:

```
module.exports = function(config) {
  config.set({
    basePath: '..',
    frameworks: ['ng-scenario'],
    files: [
      'test/e2e/**/*.js'
    ],
    exclude: [],
    port: 8080,
    logLevel: config.LOG_INFO,
    autoWatch: false,
    browsers: ['Chrome'],
    singleRun: false,
    urlRoot: '/_karma_/',
    proxies: {
      '/': 'http://localhost:9000/'
    }
  });
};
```

Once we've set up this config, we can run our unit tests like so:

```
$ karma run test/karma-e2e.conf.js
```

Alternatively, if we want our tests to run any time the code changes (if we set autoWatch to true):

```
$ karma start test/karma-e2e.conf.js
```

Configuration Options

With Karma, we can choose between many configuration options and customize testing any way we like.

Framework

The generator will ask us which testing framework we'd like to use for tests. Jasmine is the *default* testing framework, but the generator also supports Mocha, QUnit, Jasmine, and others by default.

These testing frameworks all require the installation of an additional npm library. For instance, to use the *Jasmine* framework, we'll need to install the Jasmine plugin.

```
$ npm install --save-dev karma-jasmine
```

 Using the `--save-dev` flag writes the dependency to the `package.json` file and places it under `devDependencies`.

In the configuration file, this takes an array, which allows us to use multiple frameworks. Typically we'll only use one, so this option is usually going to be set as `['jasmine']` or `['mocha']`.

For example:

```
frameworks: ['jasmine'],
```

RequireJS

If the project is using the RequireJS[94] library, then select 'yes' for the question asking to include RequireJS. If the project does include it, then instead of listing all of the files in your Karma config (which we'll see momentarily), we'll want to include our single test file, which will be responsible for loading the specific modules.

RequireJS is a JavaScript file and module loader specifically designed for the browser. It enables us to write JavaScript libraries that `export` a library and use the name of the module to set up a dependency expectation that it will be available when our module loads.

Its main benefits are that:

- It sets up an import process
- It can load nested dependencies
- It enables easy packaging dependencies

In effect, RequireJS allows us to define JavaScript through modules and require those modules in our JavaScript. For instance:

```
define(['jquery', 'underscopre'],
  function($, _) {
    // $ references jQuery
    // _ references underscore
});
```

For more information on how to set up testing, see RequireJS.

---

[94]http://requirejs.org/

Browser Captures

The Karma generator will ask which browsers you want to start automatically to capture their test results. Upon termination of the test runner, Karma will shut down these browsers, as well. We can also test any browser by opening the URL that Karma's web server is listening to (defaults to http://localhost:9876), which is something worth keeping in mind if you want to test Internet Explorer from another machine (or VM) on your local network.

Each browser requires additional plugins to be installed to launch and run the browsers using Karma. We can install these plugins using npm. For instance, to enable Karma to control Chrome, we'll need to install the Chrome launcher plugin:

```
$ npm install --save-dev karma-chrome-launcher
```

If we want to use Safari, we'll need to install the Safari launcher; for Firefox, the firefox launcher; and so on.

```
browsers: ['Chrome', 'Safari'],
```

Source and Test Files

The Karma generator will ask where your JavaScript source and test files are located. This array can contain simple strings and/or objects.

Strings can be patterns (e.g., app/js/**/*.js), or file locations (e.g.,app/js/main.js). These files and patterns are relative to the basePath.

We can also specify files using an object (instead of a string), which is useful when we want to configure certain aspects of a given file path or pattern. In the following example, this object tells Karma to watch the file public/js/watch-me.js for changes, but to not include the file on the page or serve it to a URL:

```
{pattern: 'public/js/watch-me.js', watched: true, included: false, served: false}
```

Note that the reason for using an object is to provide fine-grained control over a file or file pattern; thus, the pattern property is required. The other properties, such as included, have defaults and therefore only need to be set when our pattern deviates from the norm.

Let's discuss each option and its defaults in detail:

pattern The pattern is a regex that match test files, this option can be either a path to a single file or a pattern of files in the same manner that strings are listed above.

watched   If Karma is set to use autoWatch, this boolean specifies whether the file identified will be watched. If it is listed as true, then Karma will run the tests when this file is changed. If it is set to false, these tests will not run.

If watched is not listed as a property in the configuration object, then the files listed in this object will be watched by default (true).

included   This boolean tells Karma to load the file using the ‹script› tag in the browser. If this option is set to true, the browser will load the files. If set to false, we are responsible for loading them manually. We generally use this option in conjunction with RequireJS.

By default, files are set to be included with the ‹script› tag (true).

served   This boolean tells Karma to serve the file through the Karma web server. If it is set to true, the file will be accessible over the web server. If it's set to false, it won't be.

By default, this option is set to true and, thus, the files will be accessible over the webserver.

Ordering

The order in which files are listed matters, so we'll list our libraries before we list our application files as they need to be required. If a pattern is listed, the files are sorted in alphabetical order and included.

Every file that is included is only included once, so if a file is matched more than once in a pattern match, it is only included once.

A full example of the files property:

```
files: [
  // simple strings
  // we can target a single file
  'js/app/vendor/angular/angular.js',
  // or we can target a glob of files in a pattern
  'js/app/*.js',
  // objects
  // when the index.html file changes, we won't
  // run the tests
  {pattern: 'public/index.html', watched: false},
  // And we can set the file to not be included
  // but still be watched
  {pattern: 'public/index.html', included: false}
]
```

exclude

Karma can exclude any files that we don't want included when loading our tests. The exclude option allows us to set a list of files we don't want included by default. This array is useful if you are using RequireJS, for example.

```
exclude: [
  'public/index.html'
]
```

basePath

We can set the root path location where we want relative paths defined in the files and exclude properties by using the basePath option. If the basePath is a relative path, then it will be resolved relative to where the Karma configuration file is (__dirname).

```
basePath: '..',
```

autoWatch

Setting autoWatch to true will trigger karma to execute the configured tests whenever the files in files are changed. It is useful to set this to false when using a continuous integration server where watching file changes are unnecessary.

```
autoWatch: true,
```

captureTimeout

If the browser loads in more time than the captureTimeout (defaults to 60 seconds or 60000 ms), Karma will kill the process and try again. If it fails after three attempts, Karma will give up trying to launch the browser.

```
captureTimeout: 60000
```

colors

Karma's default output will include color. If you do not want to include color output in your terminal, you can disable it by setting the colors property to false:

```
colors: true,
```

hostname

The hostname is localhost by default, but if you want to change it, you can set the hostname property.

```
hostname: '127.0.0.1',
```

logLevel

When something goes wrong or unexpectedly with Karma, it's useful to look at more detailed information from Karma. We can set the level of detailed output by setting the `logLevel` property. When running a continuous integration server, we most likely want to disable logging output entirely.

The possible log values are:

- config.LOG_DISABLE
- config.LOG_ERROR
- config.LOG_WARN
- config.LOG_INFO
- config.LOG_DEBUG

```
logLevel: config.LOG_INFO,
```

port

The default port for Karma's webserver to launch and listen on is 9876. It's possible to customize the port by setting it in the config file.

```
port: 9875,
```

preprocessors

It's possible to tell Karma to preprocess files before any tests are run. Preprocessing can be useful when writing tests in a language like Coffeescript[95]; it obviates the need to process these files manually.

The coffeescript preprocessor is baked-in to Karma by default, but other preprocessors require additional plugins to run via npm.

The preprocessors that are available for Karma that are included are:

- CoffeeScript
- html2js

Other plugins available as preprocessors that can be included via a plugin are:

---

[95]http://coffeescript.org

- coverage
- ng-html2js
- ember

To include one or more of these, we install them with the `npm` command:

```
$ npm install karma-coverage --save-dev
```

To configure which preprocessors are to be used, we set them in the config file map. By default, the file map is set to `{'**/*coffee': 'coffee'}`.

```
preprocessors: {
  '**/*.coffee': ['coffee']
}
```

It's possible to configure some of the preprocessors, as well. Configuration is dependent upon the plugin we're using. To configure CoffeeScript, for example:

```
coffeePreprocessor: {
  options: { bare: true }
}
```

We can also customize the preprocessors using a `customPreprocessor` property:

```
customPreprocessor: {
  mini_coffee: {
    base: 'coffee',
    options: { bare: true }
  }
}
```

proxies

Karma will set up HTTP proxies for us so that when our tests fetch a route, they can fetch it off a remote server. This is useful and required for e2e tests (that use a server).

This object will be a list of key-value pairs that point from a path to a remote server.

```
proxies: {
  '/': 'http://localhost:9000'
}
```

reporters

Reporting from Karma is also customizable: We can set reporters to display all sorts of useful output in the terminal about the state of the tests.

By default, this option is set to ['progress'], which will report the progress of the tests in human-readable form. progress and dots are included by default as reporters for Karma.

We can include other reporters, such as growl and coverage, via npm plugins. We use npm to install these plugins:

```
$ npm install karma-[plugin-name] --save-dev
```

singleRun

If this boolean is set to true, Karma will run the tests once for all the configured browsers; we'll see an exit code of 0 if they all pass and 1 if any tests fail.

This indicator is particularly useful when running our tests on a continuous integration server.

urlRoot

This URL is the base URL where Karma runs. We prefix any of the URLs Karma uses with the urlRoot parameter. It's a good idea to use this option when using a proxy so that calls from our tests don't collide with existing functions on the server.

Using RequireJS

To use RequireJS with Karma, we'll need an additional file after our karma.conf.js config file: the test-main.js file.

- karma.conf.js - responsible for configuring Karma (as we've seen)
- test-main.js - responsible for configuring Require.js for the tests

karma.conf.js

We'll configure karma like normal with the Karma configuration file generator:

```
$ karma init test/karma.conf.js
```

When we are prompted to use Require.js, select yes.

When the generator asks which files you want to be loaded by default, we'll need to select all of the files that Require.js does *not* load. It's safe to only include the `test/test-main.js` file, which we'll create shortly.

When we list the source and tests files, we're choosing all of the files we want to load with `Require.js`. We should list every file that we're loading with `Require.js`. That includes all external libraries, all of our code, and all of our test files.

We need to configure these files with the configuration object and set them so they are not included by default.

At this point, our `karma.conf.js` should be:

```
module.exports = function(config) {
  config.set({
    basePath: '..',
    frameworks: ['jasmine', 'requirejs'],
    files: [
      {pattern: 'app/lib/angular.js', included: false},
      {pattern: 'app/lib/angular-route.js', included: false},
      {pattern: 'app/lib/angular-mocks.js', included: false},
      {pattern: 'app/js/**/*.js', included: false},
      {pattern: 'test/**/*.js', included: false}
      {pattern: 'test/lib/**/*.js', included: false},
      'test/test-main.js'
    ],
    exclude: [
      'js/main.js'
    ],
    reporters: ['progress'],
    port: 9876,
    colors: true,
    logLevel: config.LOG_INFO,
    autoWatch: true,
    browsers: ['Chrome'],
    captureTimeout: 60000,
    singleRun: false
  });
};
```

Notice that we're excluding our `main.js` file, the application file that starts the application.

Since Karma serves files under the `app/js` directory, we're configuring Karma's file server with a starting context for modules that load with a relative path. *Since we want the* `baseUrl` *for our tests to be in the same folder as our source files, we'll need to set the* `basePath` *to the local directory (.).*

test/test-main.js

Our `test-main.js` file will operate as a substitute for our main application file, providing us with the ability to reference our test files without actually kicking off our app.

Karma will include all the files in the array `window.__karma__.files`, so we'll find our test files from here. After we've found our tests, we can configure our RequireJS like normal:

```
var tests = [];
for (var file in window.__karma__.files) {
  if (window.__karma__.files.hasOwnProperty(file)) {
    if (/Spec\.js$/.test(file)) {
      tests.push(file);
    }}}


requirejs.config({
  baseUrl: 'app',
  paths: {
    'jquery': 'lib/jquery',
    'angular': 'lib/angular',
    'angularRoute': 'lib/angular-route',
    'angularMocks': 'lib/angular-mocks',
  },
  shim: {
    'underscore': {
      exports: '_'
    }
  },

  // ask Require.js to load these files (all our tests)
  deps: tests,
  // start test run, once Require.js is done
  callback: window.__karma__.start
});
```

Our tests will look a bit different from those that do not use `RequireJS` by default. We can simply use `RequireJS` like normal and wrap our tests in `define()`. For example:

```
define([
  'app', 'jquery', 'angular',
  'angular', 'angularRoute', 'angularMocks'
  ],
  function() {
    describe('UnitTest: App', function() {
      // just like normal
      it('is defined', function() {
        expect(_.size([1,2,3])).toEqual(3);
      });
    });
});
```

Jasmine

We're going to cover the Jasmine testing framework. Although Karma does support multiple testing frameworks, the default option for Karma is Jasmine.

Jasmine is a *behavior-driven development* framework for testing JavaScript code. Since we'll be working closely with the Jasmine syntax, let's run through an overview of how to write Jasmine-based test suites.

Spec Suite

At the heart of a Jasmine suite is the describe function. This function is a global function defined in the Jasmine suite, so we can call it directly from the test.

The describe() function takes two parameters, a string and a function. The string is a name or description of the spec suite we're setting up. The function encapsulates the test suite.

```
describe('Unit test: MainController', function() {
});
```

We can nest these describe() functions such that we can create a test tree that executes the different conditions that we'll set up throughout the tests:

```
describe('Unit test: MainController', function() {
  describe('index method', function() {
    // Specs go in here
  });
});
```

It's a good idea to group related specs together using the describe() function. When each describe() block runs, the strings will be concatenated together along with the spec's name. Thus, the above example's title would become "Unit test: MainController index method."

These describe() block titles are then appended to the spec title. This step is specifically designed to allow us to read our specs as full sentences, so it's important that we name our tests in readable English.

Defining a Spec

We define a spec by calling the it() function. This function is also a global function defined in the Jasmine test suite, so we can call it directly from our tests.

The it() function takes two arguments: a string title or description of the spec and a function that contains one or more expectations we'll set to test the functionality of our code.

These expectations are functions that, when executed, evaluate to true or false. A test with all true expectations is considered a passing spec, whereas a spec with one or more expectations that evaluate to false is considered a failing test.

A simple test might look like:

```
describe('A spec suite', function() {
  it('contains a passing spec', function() {
    expect(true).toBe(true);
  });
});
```

This single spec's title, as appended to the describe() title, becomes "A spec suite contains a passing spec."

Expectations

When testing our app, we'll want to *assert* that conditions are how we expect them to be at different stages of the app. The tests we'll write will likely read like so: "If we click on this button, then we *expect* this result." For instance, "If we navigate to the home page, then we *expect* the welcome message to be rendered."

We set up expectations using the expect() function. The expect() function takes a single value argument. This argument is called the *actual* value.

To set up an expectation, we chain a *matcher* function that takes a single value argument. This argument is the *expected* value.

These matcher functions implement a boolean comparison between the actual value and the expected value. We can create a negation of the test by calling not before calling the matcher.

```
describe('A spec suite', function() {
  it('contains a passing spec', function() {
    expect(true).toBe(true);
  });
  it('contains another passing spec', function() {
    expect(false).not.toBe(true);
  });
});
```

Jasmine comes with a large set of built-in matchers that we'll use throughout testing our app. It is also incredibly easy to write a custom matcher.

Included Matchers

toBe

The toBe() matcher compares values with the JavaScript operator: ===.

```
describe('A spec suite', function() {
  it('contains passing specs', function() {
    var value = 10,
        another_value = value;
    expect(value).toBe(another_value);
    expect(value).not.toBe(null);
  });
});
```

toEqual

The toEqual() matcher compares values and works for simple literals and variables:

```
describe('A spec suite', function() {
  it('contains a passing spec', function() {
    var value = 10;
    expect(value).toEqual(10);
  });
});
```

toMatch

The toMatch() matcher matches strings with a regular expression:

```
describe('A spec suite', function() {
  it('contains a passing spec', function() {
    var value = "<h2>Header element: welcome</h2>";
    expect(value).toMatch(/welcome/);
    expect(value).toMatch('welcome');
    expect(value).not.toMatch('goodbye');
  });
});
```

toBeDefined

The toBeDefined() matcher compares values against undefined:

```
describe('A spec suite', function() {
  it('contains a passing spec', function() {
    var value = 10,
        undefined_value = undefined;
    expect(value).toBeDefined();
    expect(undefined_value).not.toBeDefined();
  });
});
```

toBeUndefined

The toBeUndefined() matcher does the exact opposite as the toBeDefined() matcher:

```
describe('A spec suite', function() {
  it('contains a passing spec', function() {
    var value = 10,
        undefined_value = undefined;
    expect(undefined_value).toBeUndefined();
    expect(value).not.toBeUndefined();
  });
});
```

toBeNull

The toBeNull() matcher compares values against the null value:

```
describe('A spec suite', function() {
  it('contains a passing spec', function() {
    var value = null,
        not_null_value = 10;
    expect(value).toBeNull();
    expect(not_null_value).not.toBeNull();
  });
});
```

toBeTruthy

The toBeTruthy() matcher compares values for boolean casting of a truthy value:

```
describe('A spec suite', function() {
  it('contains a passing spec', function() {
    var value = 10,
        undefined_value;
    expect(value).toBeTruthy();
    expect(undefined_value).not.toBeTruthy();
  });
});
```

toBeFalsy

The toBeFalsy() matcher compares values for boolean casting testing of a falsy value:

```
describe('A spec suite', function() {
  it('contains a passing spec', function() {
    var value = 10,
        undefined_value;
    expect(undefined_value).toBeFalsy();
    expect(value).not.toBeFalsy();
  });
});
```

toContain

The toContain() matcher looks for an item in an array:

```
describe('A spec suite', function() {
  it('contains a passing spec', function() {
    var arr = [1,2,3,4];
    expect(arr).toContain(4);
    expect(arr).not.toContain(12);
  });
});
```

toBeLessThan

The toBeLessThan() matcher sets an expectation that compares a numerical value to be less than the expected:

```
describe('A spec suite', function() {
  it('contains a passing spec', function() {
    var value = 10;
    expect(value).toBeLessThan(20);
    expect(value).not.toBeLessThan(5);
  });
});
```

toBeGreaterThan

The toBeGreaterThan() matcher sets an expectation that compares a numerical value to be more than the expected:

```
describe('A spec suite', function() {
  it('contains a passing spec', function() {
    var value = 30;
    expect(value).toBeGreaterThan(40);
    expect(value).not.toBeGreaterThan(20);
  });
});
```

toBeCloseTo

The `toBeCloseTo()` matcher compares a value to be close to another value within a specified precision level:

```
describe('A spec suite', function() {
  it('contains a passing spec', function() {
    var value = 30.02;
    expect(value).toBeCloseTo(30, 0);
    expect(value).not.toBeCloseTo(20, 2);
  });
});
```

toThrow

The `toThrow()` matcher tests on whether or not a function throws an exception:

```
describe('A spec suite', function() {
  it('contains a passing spec', function() {
    expect(function() {
      return a + 10;
    }).toThrow();
    expect(function() {
      return 2 + 10;
    }).not.toThrow();
  });
});
```

Creating Custom Matchers

Jasmine makes it incredibly easy to create our own matchers for more complex situations in our code. To create a matcher, we can call the `addMatcher()` function inside a Jasmine block with a function that takes the value:

```
describe('A spec suite', function() {
  this.addMatchers({
    toBeLessThanOrEqual: function(expected) {
      return this.actual <= expected;
    }
  });
});
```

We can then call this toBeLessThanOrEqual() matcher in any of tests that are defined in our test suite.

Setup and Teardown

Rather than setting up our test conditions manually in every test, we can use the beforeEach method to run a group of setup functions. The beforeEach() function takes a single argument: a function that is called once before each spec is run. It can be used in a describe block, like so:

```
describe('A spec suite', function() {
  var message;
  beforeEach(function() {
    message = "hello ";
  });
  it('should say hello world', function() {
    expect(message + "world").toEqual("hello world");
  });
  it('should say hello ari', function() {
    expect(message + "ari").toEqual("hello ari");
  });
});
```

We can also reset conditions (e.g., clearing a database or flushing all requests from a mock using the afterEach() function). Similarly to the beforeEach() function, it takes a single argument: a function to be executed after each spec is run.

```
describe('A spec suite', function() {
  var count;
  afterEach(function() {
    count = 0;
  });
  it('should add one to count', function() {
    count += 1;
    expect(count).toEqual(1);
  });
  it('should check for the reset value', function() {
    expect(count).toEqual(0);
  });
});
```

These beforeEach and afterEach methods are chained when inside nested describe blocks, so we can set up complex test trees without duplicating our code.

End-to-End Introduction

When we are end-to-end testing, we are going to use the Angular scenario runner. The Angular scenario runner simulates user interactions so that we can more accurately assess the status of the application.

When we write scenario tests, we'll describe how the application should behave from different stages. Just like in unit testing, we'll use Jasmine to set up our expectations and behavior.

We will work directly with the scenario runner API to control our browsers as they work through the application tests. The API allows us to run the browser through many various actions, including entering data into input fields, selecting elements, navigating the browser, controlling browser flow, and more.

The core fundamental API method we'll use is the browser() method. This method returns an object to which we'll be able to chain methods in order to control the browser.

The scenario runner works by opening a browser window with an iframe embedded in it. This iframe is where Karma runs our app tests and tracks the success or failures of the scenario runner.

Navigating Pages

To load a URL into the test browser frame, we use the navigateTo function, which takes a single argument: the URL to load.

```
browser().navigateTo(url)
```

We can also dynamically load a URL by calling a function to find the URL. This call is common for cases when we don't know the destination URL when we're writing a test or checking the outcome of a certain action, for instance.

```
browser().navigateTo(title, function() {
  // return the dynamic url here;
  return '/';
});
```

Reload the Page

We can refresh the currently loaded page in the test frame:

```
browser().reload()
```

Handling the Window Object

We can get the current href of the currently loaded page in the test frame:

```
browser().window().href()
```

To get the path of the currently loaded page in the test frame, we use the following:

```
browser().window().path()
```

To get the current search of the page loaded in the test frame, we execute:

```
browser().window().search()
```

We can get the latest hash of the currently loaded page in the test frame like so:

```
// The hash is returned without the #
browser().window().hash();
```

Location, Location, Location

To get the current $location.url() of the page loaded in the test frame, we use:

```
browser().location().url()
```

We can get the $location.path() of the currently loaded page in the test frame in this way:

```
browser().location().path()
```

It's also easy to get the $location.search() of the current page like so:

```
browser().location().search()
```

Finally, we can get the hash of the current page, as well:

```
browser().location().hash()
```

Setting Expectations

To actually verify that our application does work the way we expect it to act, we'll need to set up expectations that assert a certain state. We can do this with a combination of the E2E and scenario APIs.

Using expect(), we *assert* that the value of a given *future* object matches the matcher. Anything given back by the scenario API is a future object that the scenario runner will resolve, and we're validating that the eventual value will result in what is expected.

```
expect(browser().location().path())
  .toBe('/')
// Or negate the expectation with not()
expect(browser().location().path())
  .not().toBe('/home')
```

Interacting with the Content

End-to-end testing is particularly powerful because we are *actually* loading the page our users will see, so we can peek into the result that they see and verify that it looks right and works according to our expectations.

We can select elements, enter values into input fields, click on buttons, verify content is where it should be, run through repeaters, etc.

To select an element on a page, we use the element() API method. This API method takes two parameters:

- selector - the jQuery HTML element selector
- label - a string of text used for output in the browser or terminal

```
element("form", "the signup form")
```

With this element selected, we can execute methods to query the state of the it on the page. To check the number of elements that match a certain jQuery selector:

```
element("input", "input elements").count()
```

To click on an element (for instance, on a submit button), we can call:

```
element("button", "submit button").click()
```

We can run a function on a certain jQuery selector using the `query()` function.

```javascript
// select all links on the page
element("a", "all links").query(
  // all of the links will be passed to the
  // function as elements
  function(elements, done) {
    // Do what we'd like with each element
    angular.forEach(elements, function(ele) {
      expect(ele.attr('ng-click'))
        .toBeDefined();
    });
    done(); // Tell the scenario runner we are done
  });
```

We can look at each element and set different expectations on the jQuery attributes.

We can fetch or set the value of an element:

```javascript
element("button", "submit button").val()
// Or set
element("button", "submit button").val("Enter")
```

We can fetch or set the text:

```
// The text of a block of html
element("h1", "header").text()
// Or set
element("h1", "header").text("Header text")
```

We can get or fetch the HTML of an element:

```
// HTML of the html
element("h1", "header").html()
// Or set
element("h1", "header").html("<h2>New header</h2>")
```

To set or fetch the height:

```
// Height of an element
element("div", "signup box").height()
// To set
element("div", "signup box").height('200px')
```

To fetch or set the innerHeight:

```
// innerHeight of an element
element("div", "signup box").innerHeight()
// To set
element("div", "signup box").innerHeight('190px')
```

To set or fetch the outerHeight:

```
// outerHeight of an element
element("div", "signup box").outerHeight()
// To set
element("div", "signup box").outerHeight('210px')
```

To set or fetch the width:

```
// width of the element
element("div", "signup box").width()
// Setting
element("div", "signup box").width('300px')
```

To set or fetch the innerWidth:

```
// innerWidth of the element
element("div", "signup form").innerWidth()
// Setting
element("div", "signup form").innerWidth('200px')
```

To set or fetch the outerWidth:

```
// outerWidth of the element
element("div", "signup form").outerWidth()
// Setting
element("div", "signup form").outerWidth('305px')
```

To set or fetch the position of the element:

```
// The position of the element
element(".logo", "our logo").position()
// Or
element(".logo", "our logo").position("absolute")
```

To get or set the scrollLeft:

```
// The scrollLeft value of the element
element("#signup_form", "signup form").scrollLeft()
// Setting
element("#signup_form", "signup form").scrollLeft(0)
```

To get or set the scrollTop value, where you can force the browser to scroll to a specific element:

```
// The scrollTop value of the element
element("#signup_form", "signup form").scrollTop()
// Setting
element("#signup_form", "signup form").scrollTop(0)
```

To fetch or set the offset:

```
// The element's offset
element("#signup_form", "signup form").offset()
// Setting
element("#signup_form", "signup form").offset(0);
```

We can also query and/or change the value of an element in a jQuery selector. We can get an attribute (with attr):

```
element("div", "signup box").attr('width')
// To set it
element("div", "signup box").attr('width', '100%')
```

We can fetch a property (with prop)

```
element("div", "signup box").prop('width')
// To set it
element("div", "signup box").prop('width', '100%')
```

And we can fetch CSS (with css):

```
element("div", "signup box").css('border-color')
// To set it
element("div", "signup box").css('border-color', 'red')
```

We can interact with the content in different ways than simply by fetching the element using element(). Angular's scenario runner includes a few different helper methods that enable us to both query and interact with the rendered DOM.

We can investigate Angular's understanding of different elements in which we're interested. We can select them, find bindings, interact with input elements, and query the page for testing native Angular bindings.

Selecting Elements on the Page

One of the lowest-level helpers the scenario runner sets up for us is the using() function. The using() method allows us to target specific elements using jQuery-style element selectors.

```
it('does not test anything yet', function() {
    // Target a specific element
    using('.input_email').binding('email');
});
```

The using() method takes up to two parameters:

jQuery selector   We use this selector to choose the element on the page.

Label (string optional)   This string is a label that the runner uses to identify the selector in the output of our tests.

Interacting with the Angular Binding

The scenario runner includes a way for us to query into the bindings that Angular set up, which enables us to query into our Angular bindings on the DOM and select the *first* binding for the specific element.

For instance, if we have HTML where the property name on the $scope element is available on the DOM:

```
<input type="text" ng-model="name" />
```

We can query for this specific binding in the scope by using the binding() method:

```
it('should update the name', function() {
  using('.form').input('name').enter('Ari');
  expect(
    using('.form').binding('name')
  ).toBe('Ari');
});
```

The binding() method takes a single argument:

- name (string)

This string is the name of the binding for the DOM element we're interested in querying.

Interacting with Input Elements

We can interact with input elements on our page, as well. If we want to enter text into a text box, check a checkbox, or select a value for an option element, we can using the input() method.

The input() method itself returns an object that allows us to call methods to interact with the element. It takes a single argument:

- name (string)

The name of the corresponding ng-model name.

The available methods that we can call on the input field are:

enter() The enter() method enters a value into an input field.

Given the HTML:

```
<input type="text" ng-model="name" />
```

We can enter 'Ari' into the input with:

```
input('name').enter('Ari');
```

check()   The check() method checks a checkbox input field.
Given the HTML:

```
<input type="checkbox" ng-model="save" />
```

we can check the save checkbox by calling:

```
input('name').check();
```

select()   The select() method selects a given value for a radio button.
Given the HTML:

```
<input type="radio" ng-model="color" value="red" />
<input type="radio" ng-model="color" value="blue" />
<input type="radio" ng-model="color" value="yellow" />
```

we can select the radio button with the following test:

```
input('color').select('red');
```

val()   Lastly, we can get the current value of the input field simply by calling .val() on the input element. We'll use this to check the current value of the specific input element.

```
input('color').select('red');
input('color').val(); // This will be "red"
```

Option Inputs

It's also easy to select a specific option value for a given option input field. We'll use the select() method to enable us select one option over another option in a selection tag.

Given the HTML:

```
<select ng-model="color"
      ng-options="c.name for c in colors">
    <option value="">Pick your favorite color"</option>
</select>
```

and the JavaScript:

```
select('color')
```

The `select()` method returns an object with a method that we can use to select a single option from the select input. It also gives us the ability to select multiple inputs for multi-selects.

option() The `option()` method allows us to select a single value from the list.

```
select('color').option('red');
```

The `option()` method takes a single argument:

- value (string)

The value argument is a single string that selects the input with the given value.

options() The `options()` method allows us to select multiple values from a multi-select option.

```
select('color').options('Ghostbusters', 'Titanic');
```

The `options()` method takes any number of arguments to select the values from the option field as necessary:

- values (list of strings)

These are the values to select from the multi-select.

Repeating Repeating Elements Elements

Angular makes it incredibly easy to build DOM elements for lists through the ng-repeat directive, and the Angular scenario enables us to easily test these repeating directives.

The repeater() function itself returns an object with several methods we can use to query a list of elements in our view. It accepts up to two arguments:

- selector (string)

The jQuery selector points to the selector of the elements in which we are interested.

- label (optional string)

The label is a string used in test outputs.

The available methods that we can call on the list of elements returned by the repeater are as listed below. For each of these tests, we'll use the following HTML as example HTML:

```
<table id="phonebook">
  <tr ng-repeat="person in people">
    <td>{{ person.name }}</td>
    <td>{{ person.email }}</td>
  </tr>
</table>
```

The methods are as follows:

count()   The count() method returns the number of rows in the repeater that match the jQuery selector in the DOM.

```
repeater('#phonebook tr').count();
```

The count method takes no arguments and simply returns a single integer.

column()   The column() method returns an array containing the values in the column that have the given binding in the repeater matching the jQuery selector in the DOM.

```
repeater('#phonebook tr')
  .column('person.name');
```

The `column()` method takes a single argument:

- binding (string)

This binding is for the specific element of the repeater. It is the name of the binding that is rendered in the element.

row() The `row()` method returns an array containing the values in the row that have the the given bindings in the repeater matching the given jQuery selector in the DOM.

```
repeater("#phonebook tr").row(0);
```

The `row()` method takes a single argument:

- index (integer)

The `index` is the number of the row from which to return the given bindings.

Mocking and Test Helpers

Before we can start writing tests, we need to understand a core feature of testing: **mocking**. Mocking in testing is an old concept that allows us to define simulated objects that mimic the behavior of real objects under controlled circumstances.

AngularJS provides its own mocking library called `angular-mocks`; it is available as the `angular-mocks.js` file. Mocking objects are specifically designed to be used in unit testing.

To set up a `mock` object in a unit test, we need to make sure we're including the `angular-mocks.js` file in our Karma configuration.

We must ensure that our `test/karma.conf.js` file contains the `angular-mocks.js` in the `files` array. Once the dependency is included, we can create a mock reference to the Angular module.

For example, in this common unit test setup, we'll create a `describe` execution context wherein we call `angular.mock.module` before every test runs in our `describe` context:

```
describe('myApp', function() {
  // Mock our 'myApp' angular module
  beforeEach(angular.mock.module('myApp'));

  it('...')
});
```

Note that we can also just call `module` because the function `angular.mock.module` is published on the window interface for global access.

After we have set up our mock Angular module, we can *inject* any of the services connected to that module into our test code.

With the tests, we need to *inject* the dependencies just as Angular will at run time. In our unit tests, this step is necessary because it's important that we isolate the functionality we want to test.

To inject a dependency, we use the `angular.mock.inject` method in a `beforeEach` function call, similarly to how we did so above.

```
describe('myApp', function() {
  var scope;

  // Mock our 'myApp' angular module
  beforeEach(angular.mock.module('myApp'));
  beforeEach(angular.mock.inject(function($rootScope) {
    scope = $rootScope.$new();
  });
  it('...')
});
```

Similarly to the `module` function, the `inject` function is also available on the `window` object for global access, so we can just call `inject`.

In this test, as in almost all of our unit tests, we'll want to save a reference to an instance of the object with which we're working (in the above example, we're saving scope). That way, we can work with the reference of the object in all of our `it()` clauses.

Oftentimes, we'll want to store the reference as the same name as we're injecting into our test. For example, if we are testing a service, we can inject the service and store a reference to it using a slightly different naming scheme. We want to enclose the injected service in _ underscores to cause the injector to ignore the name when it's injected.

```
describe('myApp', function() {
  var myService;

  // Mock our 'myApp' angular module
  beforeEach(module('myApp'));
  beforeEach(inject(function(_myService_) {
    myService = _myService_;
  });
  it('...')
});
```

Mocking the $httpBackend

Angular also comes with a built-in $httpBackend mocking library so that we can mock any external XHR requests in our app and avoid making expensive $http requests in our tests.

The $httpBackend service is a *Fake HTTP back-end* implementation that allows us to isolate and specify conditions that external servers might be in such that we can determine exactly how our app behaves under different circumstances.

Using the $httpBackend, we can verify that a request is made, stub responses, stub calls, and set assertions that verify how we expect our app to behave based on the response of the remote server. We'll use the $httpBackend solely in unit tests.

 It is possible to use the $httpBackend service in end-to-end testing, but doing so will generally not test the app fully, because we are no longer using our real server.

Testing with the $httpBackend works simply by hijacking the dependency injection chain: We inject the mock $httpBackend instead of the real $httpBackend service that makes the actual HTTP requests by the $http service. In this way, we don't need to change our app at all to support testing it.

Flushing HTTP Requests

When in production, the $httpBackend responds to requests asynchronously, which is fundamentally difficult to set up in testing environments. Thus, we need to manually flush any pending requests at the end of our tests so that we can clean the execution environment, yet still keep the asynchronous behavior of the $httpBackend.

The $httpBackend contains two methods for setting up a mock back-end system to handle HTTP responses; these two methods are expect and when, and they have different use cases.

Typically, in a unit test we'll want to ensure that all of the requests we set up with expectations run at the end of each test and throw an exception if they don't. Additionally, we'll want to ensure that there are no outstanding requests pending at the end of each test.

We can take care of these two cases with two methods in an afterEach block:

```
// ...
afterEach(function() {
  $httpBackend.verifyNoOutstandingExpectation();
  $httpBackend.verifyNoOutstandingRequest();
});
```

There are cases when we want to reset all of the request expectations we've set. These cases occur when we want to reuse the same instance of $httpBackend inside of a multiple-phase test.

We can reset them with the resetExpectations() method:

```
// ...
it('should be a multiple-phase test', function() {
  // ...
  $httpBackend.resetExpectations();
  // ...
});
```

expect

The expect method sets up a request expectation and is used to both make assertions about the requests the application makes and define responses for them. The test will fail if the expected requests are not made or they are incorrectly made. These request expectations are used to set up an assertion that a request has been made.

The expect method takes two required arguments and two additional optional arguments:

- method

The string HTTP method, like 'GET' or 'POST'

- url

The HTTP URL where we're expecting the call

- data (optional)

The HTTP request body or function that receives a data string and returns true if the data is expected (or a JavaScript object to send the body in JSON format)

- headers (optional)

The HTTP headers or function that will receive the header object and return true if the headers match the expectation

The `expect` method returns an object with a `respond` method that controls how the matched request is handled inside the tests.

```
describe('Remote tests', function() {
  var $httpBackend, $rootScope, myService;

  beforeEach(inject(
      function(
        _$httpBackend_, _$rootScope_, _myService_) {
    $httpBackend = _$httpBackend_;
    $rootScope = _$rootScope_;
    // myService is a service that makes HTTP
    // calls for us
    myService = _myService_;
  }));

  it('should make a request to the backend', function() {
    // Set an expectation that myService will
    // send a GET request to the route
    // /v1/api/current_user
    $httpBackend.expect('GET', '/v1/api/current_user')
      .respond(200, {userId: 123});
    myService.getCurrentUser();
    // Important to flush requests
    $httpBackend.flush();
  });
});
```

The `$httpBackend.expect` method has several helper functions that allow us to be more descriptive of the expectation we're setting:

`expectGET()` creates a new request expectation for a GET method. `expectGET()` takes two arguments:

- url - an HTTP URL
- headers - (optional) HTTP headers

```
// ...
$httpBackend.expectGET("/v1/api/current_user")
```

expectHEAD() creates a new request expectation for a HEAD method. It accepts two arguments:

- url - an HTTP URL
- headers - (optional) HTTP headers

```
// ...
$httpBackend.expectHEAD("/v1/api/current_user")
```

expectJSONP() creates a new request expectation for a JSONP request. It accepts a single argument:

- url - an HTTP URL

```
// ...
$httpBackend.expectJSONP("/v1/api/current_user")
```

expectPATCH() creates a new request expectation for PATCH requests. It accepts three arguments:

- url - an HTTP URL
- data - (optional) an HTTP request body or a function that receives the data string and returns true if the data returned is as expected. Or it returns an object if the request body is in JSON format
- headers - (optional) HTTP headers

```
// ...
$httpBackend.expectPATCH("/v1/api/current_user")
```

expectPOST() creates a new request expectation for POST requests. It accepts three arguments:

- url - an HTTP URL
- data - (optional) an HTTP request body or a function that receives the data string and returns true if the data returned is as expected. Or it returns an object if the request body is in JSON format
- headers - (optional) HTTP headers

```
// ...
$httpBackend.expectPOST("/v1/api/sign_up", {'userId': 1234});
```

expectPUT() creates a new request expectation for PUT requests. It takes three arguments:

- url - an HTTP URL
- data - (optional) an HTTP request body or a function that receives the data string and returns true if the data returned is as expected. Or it returns an object if the request body is in JSON format
- headers - (optional) HTTP headers

```
// ...
$httpBackend.expectPUT("/v1/api/user/1234", {'name': 'Ari'});
```

expectDELETE() creates a new request expectation for DELETE requests. It takes two arguments:

- url - an HTTP URL
- headers - (optional) HTTP headers

```
// ...
$httpBackend.expectDELETE("/v1/api/user/123")
```

requestHandler

Our expect() methods all return a requestHandler object that has a single function: respond. The respond method gives us the ability to set up a response for the mocked HTTP request.

The requestHandler response function is a function that can take one of two forms:

The first form allows us to set a response code, response data, headers, or all three.

```
// ...
$httpBackend.expectGET("/v1/api/current_user")
  // Respond with a 200 status code
  // and the body "success"
  .respond(200, 'Success');
  // Or only return data
  .respond("Fail");
  // Or only headers
  .respond({'X-RESPONSE', 'Failure'});
```

The second form enables us to set a request handler function that is executed upon the successful execution of the request. Instead of returning data, we'll return a function handler that can return an array containing the response status code, response data, and response headers.

```
// ...
$httpBackend.expectGET("/v1/api/current_user")
  // Respond with a 200 status code
  // and the body "success"
  .respond(function(method, url, data, headers) {
    return [200, "DATA", {"header1": "Header1"}];
  });
```

when

The $httpBackend also has the when method that differs from the expect method in that it doesn't create an expectation for a request at all. In fact, its purpose is primarily to create a fake back end for an app and return fake data.

Unlike expectations, when using when(), every single request that matches the URL can be handled by a single when definition. Additionally, a response is required when using when, whereas with expect a response is not required.

The when() method is great for setting up back-end definitions that are common for all tests (e.g., when testing a controller that is using the resolve property that depends upon foreign data being loaded).

The when() function takes two required arguments and two additional optional requirements:

- method

The string HTTP method, like 'GET' or 'POST'

- url

The HTTP URL where we're expecting the call

- data (optional)

The HTTP request body or function that receives a data string and returns true if the data is expected (or a JavaScript object to send the body in JSON format)

- headers (optional)

The HTTP headers or function that will receive the header object and return true if the headers match the expectation

```
// ...
$httpBackend.when('GET', "/v1/api/current_user")
  // Respond with a 200 status code
  // and the body "success"
  .respond(200, 'success');
```

Similar to the expect method, we have the same helper methods that make the use of when more descriptive:

whenGET() creates a new back-end definition for a GET method. whenGET() takes two arguments:

- url - an HTTP URL
- headers - (optional) HTTP headers

```
// ...
$httpBackend.whenGET("/v1/api/current_user")
  .respond(200, {userId: 123});
```

whenHEAD() creates a new back-end definition for a HEAD method. It accepts two arguments:

- url - an HTTP URL
- headers - (optional) HTTP headers

```
// ...
$httpBackend.whenHEAD("/v1/api/current_user")
  .respond(200);
```

whenJSONP() creates a new back-end definition for a JSONP request. It accepts a single argument:

- url - an HTTP URL

```
// ...
$httpBackend.whenJSONP("/v1/api/current_user")
  .respond({userId: 123});
```

whenPOST() creates a new back-end definition for POST requests. It accepts three arguments:

- url - an HTTP URL
- data - (optional) an HTTP request body or a function that receives the data string and returns true if the data returned is as expected. Or it returns an object if the request body is in JSON format
- headers - (optional) HTTP headers

```
// ...
$httpBackend.whenPOST("/v1/api/sign_up",
  {'userId': 1234})
  .respond(200);
```

whenPUT() creates a new back-end definition for PUT requests. It takes three arguments:

- url - an HTTP URL
- data - (optional) an HTTP request body or a function that receives the data string and returns true if the data returned is as expected. Or it returns an object if the request body is in JSON format
- headers - (optional) HTTP headers

```
// ...
$httpBackend.whenPUT("/v1/api/user/1234", {'name': 'Ari'});
```

whenDELETE() creates a new back-end definition for DELETE requests. It takes two arguments:

- url - an HTTP URL
- headers - (optional) HTTP headers

```
// ...
$httpBackend.whenDELETE("/v1/api/user/123")
  .respond(200);
```

Testing an App

With our testing harness set up, we can start testing the different components of our app. Any part of our module that has logic that may change is a good candidate for testing. *Does a route work the way we expect? Does the page contain specific content? Does the controller code execute?*

We're going to focus on testing different components of our app, the most common places to test our app, and tips and tricks for testing the various components.

We'll cover testing the following components of our app:

- Routes
- Requests and page content
- Controllers
- Services and Factories
- Filters
- Templates and views
- Directives
- Resources
- Animations

For each component, we'll look at our options for testing, and then we'll run through how to test it with the available methods.

For most of our tests, the base code that we'll start with looks like:

```
describe('NAME', function() {
});
```

Testing Routes

When we test our routes, we want to set up a test to ensure that our app properly routes the request to the route that we're interested in. We need to check where the route works and whether it's found or a 404. We'll check to make sure the routing events are fired and whether the template that we expect is actually loaded.

We can use either unit testing or end-to-end testing to test routes. Since our routes will change page locations (URL) and page content, we'll need to check if the route has been loaded, if the page has been found, and what's in between.

To test these routes, let's assume we have the following simple routing code set up:

```
angular.module('myApp', ['ngRoute'])
  .config(function($routeProvider) {
    $routeProvider
      .when('/', {
        templateUrl: 'views/main.html',
        controller: 'HomeController'})
      .when('/login', {
        templateUrl: 'views/login.html',
        controller: 'LoginController'})
      .otherwise({redirectTo '/'});
  })
```

Unit Testing Routes

In order to set up our unit tests so that they can test our routing code, we need to do a few things:

- Inject the $route, $location, and $rootScope services
- Set up a mock back end to handle XHR fetching template code
- Set a location and run a $digest lifecycle

We want to store a copy of the three services we'll use in our tests (location, route, and rootScope) so we can later reference these services in our tests.

```
describe('Routes test', function() {
  // Mock our module in our tests
  beforeEach(module('myApp'));

  var location, route, rootScope;
  beforeEach(
    inject(_$location_, _$route_, _$rootScope_) {
      location = _$location_;
      route = _$route_;
      rootScope = _$rootScope_;
    });
  // Our test code will go here
});
```

Now that we have our services injected into the controller, we set a mock back end to handle fetching the templates from the templateUrl. We can use the $httpBackend to create an assertion that determines a specific template will be fetched:

```
describe('Routes test', function() {
  // Mock our module in our tests
  beforeEach(module('myApp'));

  var location, route, rootScope;
  beforeEach(inject(
    function(_$location_, _$route_, _$rootScope_) {
      location = _$location_;
      route = _$route_;
      rootScope = _$rootScope_;
    }));
  describe('index route', function() {
    beforeEach(inject(
      function($httpBackend) {
        $httpBackend.expectGET('views/home.html')
          .respond(200, 'main HTML');
      }));
      // Our tests will code here
  });
});
```

Our test code is all set up – now we can start writing our tests!

In order to test the router with unit tests, we need to mimic how the router works in production. The router works with the digest lifecycle, wherein after the location is set, it takes a single digest loop cycle to process the route, transform the page content, and finish the routing. Knowing that, we need to account for the change in paths in our test.

Inside our test, we're going to test two states of the application in the index route:

- When a user navigates to the index page, they are shown the index page with the proper controller
- When a user navigates to an unknown route, they are taken to the index page as defined by our otherwise function.

We can test the conditions by setting up our $location service to pass the paths. In order to trigger the location request, we'll run a digest cycle (on the $rootScope) and check that the controller is as expected (in this case, the 'HomeController').

```
it('should load the index page on successful load of /',
function() {
  location.path('/');
  rootScope.$digest(); // call the digest loop
  expect(route.current.controller)
    .toBe('HomeController')
});
it('should redirect to the index path on non-existent
  route', function() {
  location.path('/definitely/not/a/_route');
  rootScope.$digest();
  expect(route.current.controller)
    .toBe('HomeController')
});
```

To run these tests, we need to make sure we have our Grunt server running:

```
$ cd myApp
$ grunt server
```

If we run `karma start karma.conf.js` in our app file, we will see immediate output in our terminal.

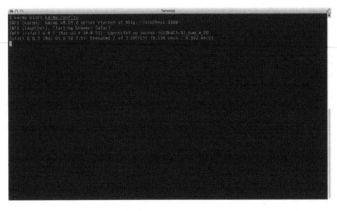

Unit testing routes

We did a lot of work to set up our routes test, and we only tested one route location. Since we are testing flow changes for our user features, we can shuffle this work off to the application and test it more rigorously in end-to-end testing.

End-to-end Route Testing

With end-to-end testing, we don't need to mock any part of Angular: We're black-box testing the app. In this way, we can just describe how we want our app to behave and write our tests accordingly.

In writing our end-to-end tests, we need to think about how the user navigates around our application. Our tests should be readable in that we're sending our user to a particular page and describing what they should experience in our app.

Our base test for all of our end-to-end tests will simply be:

```
describe('E2E: NAME', function() {
  // Our tests will go here
});
```

That's it. We're going to use the browser() API function to modify the source of the iframe inside our browser.

To test our index route, we'll point our browser to the index route and ensure that the location is, in fact, at the index page.

```
describe('E2E: Routes', function() {
  it('should load the index page', function() {
    browser().navigateTo('/#/');
    expect(browser().location().path()).toBe('/');
  });
});
```

To run this test, we need to make sure that our Grunt server is running:

```
$ cd myApp
$ grunt server
```

Now we'll run Karma:

```
$ karma start karma-e2e.conf.js
```

Here, we'll see immediate output in our terminal. If the test is successful, we'll see that it passes all of its tests. If not, it will report its failures to you.

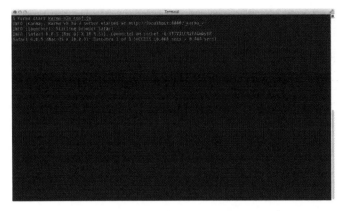

End-to-end testing routes in our terminal

We can also use the browser to debug our end-to-end tests. When we started `karma`, a browser opened in the background. Open the browser and click on the debug button in the top right corner. Clicking this button opens a new page that shows us all of our tests, including a list of the ones that pass and a list of the ones that fail. When we're developing tests, it's useful to use our browser as a reference to debug our application and tests.

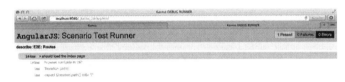

Visual representation of our tests in browser

Testing Page Content

When we're testing, we want to ensure the page content is rendered correctly by our browser. We will need to assert that certain content gets delivered in the browser and eventually to our users.

Unit testing content in the browser won't give us much insight into the state of the application, as we don't have direct access to browser content in unit testing.

We can confirm that the controllers are executing the expected functions and set assertions that confirm the content will load, which we will cover in depth.

End-to-end Testing Page Content

End-to-end testing, on the other hand, is ideal for setting up expectations for loaded HTML. With end-to-end testing, every part of the application responsible for executing a successful browser request will fire.

To set up end-to-end content testing, we set up our test like normal:

```
describe('E2E: Content', function() {
});
```

We're going to set up two scenarios in this route test:

- That we have a link to the login route at our index page
- That we can click on the link, and it will bring us to the login page

In our first test, we're simply testing that there IS a login button on our page. We'll set an assertion that we have a login button to click.

In our index.html, suppose we have the following content:

```
<div id="authorize">
  <a id="login" class="radius" href="#/login">Try it! Sign in</a>
</div>
```

Inside of this first test, we'll just confirm that we have the element that matches the text in the button:

```
it('should have a sign up button', function() {
  browser().navigateTo('/#/');
  expect(
    element("a#login").html()
  ).toEqual("Try it! Sign in");
});
```

Now, we want to ensure that clicking on this link brings our users to the login page. We'll set up another test that asserts that if we click on the link our new location is at the login route:

```
it('should show login when clicking sign in', function() {
  browser().navigateTo('/#/');
  element("a#login", "Sign in button").click();
  expect(browser().location().path())
    .toBe('/login');
});
```

Lastly, if we have a user to test against, we can set up our test to fill out our login form simply by selecting the input elements and setting their value.

```
it('should be able to fill in the user info',
  function() {
    browser().navigateTo('/#/');
    element("a#login", "Sign in button").click();
    input("user.email").enter("ari@fullstack.io");
    input("user.password").enter('123123');
    element('form input[type="submit"]').click();
    expect(browser().location().path())
      .toBe('/dashboard');
});
```

Content loading tests

Testing Controllers

Our controllers contain the business logic of our application. The controller is where the $scope marries the controller to the view. Since we're going to do most of the work of updating the views of our application in our controllers, we want to set up tests to ensure that their behavior executes as expected.

Unit Testing Controllers

When we're unit testing controllers, we need to set up our tests to mimic the behavior of Angular.

In setting up our unit tests, we need to make sure we:

- Set up our tests to mock the module
- Store an instance of the controller with an instance of a known scope
- Test our expectations against the scope

To instantiate a new controller instance, we need to create a new instance of a scope from the $rootScope with the $new() method. This new instance will set up the scope inheritance that Angular uses at run time.

With this scope, we can instantiate a new controller and pass the scope in as the $scope of the controller.

```
describe('Unit controllers: ', function(){
  // Mock the myApp module
  beforeEach(module('myApp'));
  describe('FrameController', function() {
    // Local variables
    var FrameController, scope;
    beforeEach(inject(
      function($controller, $rootScope) {
        // Create a new child scope
        scope = $rootScope.$new();
        // Create a new instance of the FrameController
        FrameController = $controller('FrameController',
          { $scope: scope });
    }));

  // Our tests go here
  });
});
```

With our test set up, we have both an instance of our FrameController as well as the $scope for the controller. Now we can use that scope to test the scope on the FrameController.

In our FrameController, we have a clock that ticks with the current time at the top of the app. We also have access to a user and his or her time zone.

The relevant parts of the controller code look like:

```
angular.module('myApp.controllers', [])
  .controller('FrameController',
    function($scope, $timeout) {
      $scope.time = {
        today: new Date()
      };
      $scope.user = {
        timezone: 'US/Pacific'
      }
      var updateClock = function() {
        $scope.time.today = new Date();
      };
      var tick = function() {
        $timeout(function() {
          $scope.$apply(updateClock);
          tick();
        }, 1000);
      }
      tick();
  });
```

 Our `FrameController` is purposefully simplified for focus on the test. To see the entire test suite for the sample app, take a look at the code that accompanies this book.

We'll test two features of our controller:

- The time is defined
- The user is defined and has a time zone

```
// Testing the FrameController values
it('should have today set', function() {
  expect(scope.time.today).toBeDefined();
});

it('should have a user set', function() {
  expect(scope.user).toBeDefined();
});
```

End-to-End Testing Controllers

The result of end-to-end testing our controllers will look very similar to that of our tests where we test that the page content renders as expected: We're testing that all of the functions in the controller actually fire.

To test whether or not a page has been rendered, we can load the page in question in the browser and test if the content we expect has been rendered in the view.

The boilerplate for our end-to-end tests looks like:

```
describe('E2E controllers: ', function() {
  // Our tests go here
});
```

With our test set up, we can add our specs. We're going to test that the date (or at least a portion of it) exists on the page, as well as the time zone.

```
beforeEach(function() {
  browser().navigateTo('/#/');
});

it('should have the date in the browser', function() {
  var d = new Date();
  expect(
    element("#time h1").html()
  ).toMatch(d.getFullYear());
});

it('should have the user timezone in the header', function() {
  expect(
    element('header').html()
  ).toMatch('US/Pacific');
});
```

It is convenient to know if our timeout function has been called inside our controller. We can confirm that we are, in fact, setting the timeout to be called using the Jasmine helper createSpy.

If we modify our beforeEach() function (see above), we can include the $timeout service in our controller.

```
var FrameController, scope, timeout;
beforeEach(inject(
  function($controller, $rootScope) {
    scope = $rootScope.$new();
    timeout = jasmine.createSpy('timeout');
    FrameController = $controller('FrameController', {
      $scope: scope,
      $timeout: timeout
    });
}));
```

Now, in our tests, we can set an expectation that the service is, in fact, called:

```
it('should set the clock a foot', function() {
  expect(timeout).toHaveBeenCalled();
});
```

Testing Services and Factories

Services are easy to test: They are isolated objects that offer localized functionality. Since they are singleton objects, we can create these objects in isolation and test their behavior.

Unit Testing Services

Unit testing services is pretty easy, as we only need to inject our services into our tests.

Starting with the simple example, suppose we have the service that provides a version:

```
angular.module('myApp.services', [])
  .value('version', '0.0.1');
```

In this case, our *service* provides a single string value. We can inject the version service into the current test.

Our test boilerplate for this unit test looks like:

```
describe('Unit: services', function() {
  beforeEach(module('myApp'));
});
```

 Up until now, we've been implicitly calling the $injector service. This example shows how to use it explicitly.

To isolate the test, we nest this test into a describe() block and inject our version service in a beforeEach() block.

```
describe('version', function() {
  var version;
  beforeEach(inject(function($injector) {
    // use the $injector to get the version service
    version = $injector.get('version');
  }));

  it('should have the version as a service',
    function() {
      // set our expectation on the version service
      expect(version).toEqual('0.0.1');
  });
});
```

As we can see, testing services is really simple; however, our services are not always this simple. In our sample app, we're interacting with the googleApi; this service is a bit more complex.

Here is the full source for the googleServices.googleApi service:

```
// Our google services module
angular.module('googleServices', [])
  .factory('googleApi',
    function($window, $document, $q, $rootScope) {
      // Create a defer to encapsulate the loading of
      // our Google API service.
      var d = $q.defer();

      // After the script loads in the browser, we're going
      // to call this function, which in turn will resolve
      // our global defer which enables the
      $window.bootGoogleApi = function(keys) {
        // We need to set our API key
        window.gapi.client.setApiKey(keys.apiKey);
        $rootScope.$apply(function() {
          d.resolve(keys);
        });
      };

      // Load client in the browser
      var scriptTag = $document[0].createElement('script');
      scriptTag.type = 'text/javascript';
      scriptTag.async = true;
      scriptTag.src =
```

```
      'https://apis.google.com/js/client:plusone.js?onload=onLoadCallback';
    var s = $document[0].getElementsByTagName('body')[0];
    s.appendChild(scriptTag);

    // Return a singleton object that returns the
    // promise
    return {
      gapi: function() { return d.promise; }
    }
  });
```

The service itself returns us an object containing a single function that returns a promise. The promise will be resolved once the Google API has been loaded and is ready on the page.

To set out our expectations for this service, we need to use the Jasmine method spyOn to create a spy on the method we're calling and to set up an expectation that it is actually called.

We'll set up our tests to run against the Google API in an isolated describe() block:

```
describe('googleServices', function() {
  var googleApi, resolvedValue;

  beforeEach(inject(function($injector) {
    // Fetch the defined googleApi from our service
    googleApi = $injector.get('googleApi');
    // Create a spy for the gapi function
    // that tells us it's been called, but doesn't
    // prevent the actual function from being called
    spyOn(googleApi, 'gapi')
      .andCallThrough();
    // Use the actual function's resolve to
    // set the resolved value
    googleApi.gapi().then(function(keys) {
      resolvedValue = keys;
    });
  }));

  describe('googleApi', function() {
    // Our tests go here
  });
});
```

We can also inject the googleApi service above by name, as the inject() function uses the same syntax as the $injector. The above call would change to inject(function(googleApi)) instead.

361

 By using the andCallThrough() method, our test will wait for the gapi object to be present on the window. We can stub these requests by using a different method, andCallFake().

```
var q;
beforeEach(inject(function($injector) {
  // Fetch the defined googleApi from our service
  googleApi = $injector.get('googleApi');
  // Get the $q object
  q = $injector.get('$q');
  // Create a spy for the gapi function
  // and mock the actual response
  spyOn(googleApi, 'gapi')
    .andCallFake(function() {
      var d = q.defer(); // fake the deferred function
      setTimeout(function() {
        resolvedValue = {
          clientId: '12345'
        }
      }, 100);
      return d.promise;
    });
  // Use the actual function's resolve to
  // set the resolved value
  googleApi.gapi().then(function(keys) {
    resolvedValue = keys;
  });
}));
```

Now, we can use our spy to determine if the function has actually been called.

Our first test in this describe() block simply tests that the method exists and is a function. This test is useful if we're still working on the API and we change the method name or signature.

To set up tests for waiting for a promise to resolve, we use a Jasmine helper, waitsFor(). It takes a single parameter: a function that provides a true or false response for when the method can continue. We'll set it up to wait a maximum of .5 seconds, at most:

```
describe('googleApi', function() {
  beforeEach(function() {
    // pause the spec for up to
    // half a second while we are waiting for
    // the resolvedValue to be resolved
    waitsFor(function() {
      return resolvedValue !== undefined;
    }, 500);
  });

  it('should have a gapi function', function() {
    expect(
      typeof(googleApi.gapi)
    ).toEqual('function');
  });
});
```

Now we can set expectations for the return values of the service and assert that they are equal to our assumptions:

```
it('should call gapi', function() {
  expect(googleApi.gapi.callCount)
    .toEqual(1);
});
```

```
it('should resolve with the browser keys', function() {
  expect(resolvedValue.clientId)
    .toBeDefined();
});
```

End-to-End Testing Services

Since services interact with our front end through our controllers, it's not effective to specifically test services with end-to-end testing. We can, however, test that services resolve their promises and that the results populate the view.

For instance, we can test that a service populates a list of events in the view. In an /events page, where we are showing a list of events, we can assert that we actually are listing out the number of events we expect with the details that we expect:

```
beforeEach(function() {
  browser().navigateTo('/#/events');
});

it('should show 10 events', function() {
  expect(
    repeater('.event_listing li').count()
  ).toBe(10);
});
```

Testing Filters

Filters are also easy to test: They are isolated functionality. The filter's job is specifically to limit or manipulate output, so we'll set assertions on the output of the filter functions.

Unit Testing Filters

It is simple to unit test filters. First, we need to get access to the filter, which we can do simply by injecting the $filter service into our tests. That will give us access to looking up the filter in the process:

```
describe('Unit: Filter tests', function() {
  var filter;

  // Mock our module in our tests
  beforeEach(module('myApp'));
  beforeEach(inject(function($filter) {
    filter = $filter;
  }));
});
```

With this access to the filter, it's simply a matter of setting expectations on the output of the filter.

```
it('should give us two decimal points',
  function() {
    expect(filter('number')(123, 2)).toEqual('123.00');
});
```

End-to-End Testing Filters

We can also test the output of our filters in the view using end-to-end testing. End-to-end testing is slightly different from using unit tests to test our code, as we're focused on what the end user sees rather than the output of our filter function specifically.

In order to set up a filter test, we'll have our browser load the page(s) where we are testing our filter, and we'll interact with the filter itself.

For instance, given the case where we have a live search with an ng-repeat:

```
<input ng-model="search.$" type="text" placeholder="Search filter" />
<table id="emailTable">
  <tbody>
    <tr ng-repeat="email in emails | filter:search.$">
      <td>{{ $index + 1 }}</td>
      <td>{{ email.from }}</td>
      <td>{{ email.subject | capitalize }}</td>
    </tr>
  </tbody>
</table>
```

where our *emails* data looks like:

```
[
  {
    from: 'ari@fullstack.io',
    subject: 'ng-book and things'
  },
  {
    from: 'ari@fullstack.io',
    subject: 'Other things about ng-book and angular'
  },
  {
    from: 'ted@google.com',
    subject: 'Conference speaking gig'
  }
];
```

Here, we'll test two filters: the live search filter where we set an expectation against the ng-repeat and on the subject line (to ensure it's capitalized).

To ensure that the live search is working, we need to enter a value into the input field and ensure that the field changes to what we expect.

```
it('should filter on the search', function() {
  expect(repeater('#emailTable tbody tr')).count()
    .toBe(3);
  // things shows up in two of our emails
  input('search.$').enter('things');
  expect(repeater('#emailTable tbody tr')).count()
    .toBe(2);
});
```

We can see that when we set a different input for the `search.$` field, the `ng-repeat` changes from 3 to 2.

We can also test our own filter (the `capitalize` filter) to ensure it's working as expected:

```
it('should capitalize the subject line', function() {
  expect(
    repeater('#emailTable tbody tr:first')
      .column('email.subject')
    ).toEqual(["Ng-book and things"]);
});
```

Testing Templates

When we test templates, we're looking to ensure that the proper content template is loaded and that the correct data inside the template shows up in the view.

Unit Testing Templates

Since our templates are tied directly to the view, unit testing components *inside* the view doesn't make a lot of sense: We're making assertions upon the completion of multiple components to build the view.

We can make an assertion that the template is loaded properly. To make that, we need to set up our test to expect a request to the home template and execute a view change to test that it is, in fact, loaded.

```
describe('Unit: Templates', function() {
  var $httpBackend,
        location,
        route,
        rootScope;

  beforeEach(module('myApp'));
  beforeEach(inject(
    function(_$rootScope_, _$route_, _$httpBackend_, _$location_){
      location = _$location_;
      rootScope = _$rootScope_;
      route = _$route_;
      $httpBackend = _$httpBackend_;
  }));

  afterEach(function() {
    $httpBackend.verifyNoOutstandingExpectation();
    $httpBackend.verifyNoOutstandingRequest();
  });

  // Our tests will go here
});
```

Now, we can set up our tests to reflect the expectation that our templates do load when we navigate to different parts of the app.

```
it('loads the home template at /', function() {
  $httpBackend.expectGET('templates/home.html')
    .respond(200);
  location.path('/');
  rootScope.$digest(); // call the digest loop
  $httpBackend.flush();
});

it('loads the dashboard template at /dashboard', function() {
  $httpBackend.expectGET('templates/dashboard.html')
    .respond(200);
  location.path('/dashboard');
  rootScope.$digest(); // call the digest loop
  $httpBackend.flush();
});
```

Notice that we're not actually returning a template into our tests (.respond(200) instead of .respond(200, "<div></div>div>")). Since we're only verifying that the template is being loaded on our requests, we don't need to worry about *what* shows up, just that it does.

End-to-end testing is where we'll verify that the view looks how it's supposed to look in end-to-end tests.

End-to-End Testing Templates

When testing the view in end-to-end testing, we want to focus our attention on the actual data being loaded in the view, rather than on whether the template simply loads up. These tests will give us a better picture of what our users will actually see when the view loads.

We'll test the content of the view when it's in our user's view.

To test our templates, we'll test that the view contains our expected HTML and that it does not load other parts of our app.

```
describe('E2E: Views', function() {
  beforeEach(function() {
    browser().navigateTo('#/');
  });

  it('should load the home template', function()
  {
    expect(
      element('#emailTable').html()
    ).toContain('tbody');
  });

  it('should not load the dashboard template',
  function() {
    expect(
      element('#dashboard').count()
    ).toBe(0);
  });
});
```

Making assertions on view templates is very straightforward.

Testing Directives

Directives are the root of the Angular workflow. Since most of the interaction that we do within our Angular apps is working on directives, testing directive functionality is one of the most important components to test, especially when we build larger components.

When we're testing our directives, we'll want to test that the directive does *actually* get loaded into the view and that it behaves as we expect it to behave on the $scope in the DOM.

In unit testing, we focus on testing the functionality of the directive, while in end-to-end testing, we're able to verify that we're using the directive properly.

Unit Testing Directives

Unit testing directives requires that we set up a test to ensure that the directive renders as we expect it. We'll want to set expectations that bindings are set up properly, that errors are thrown when we expect them to be thrown, and that the view shows the full directive as expected.

In this test, we'll work with the following directive:

```
angular.module('myApp')
.directive('notification', function($timeout) {
  var html = '<div class="notification">' +
               '<div class="notification-content">' +
                 '<p>{{ message }}</p>' +
               '</div>' +
             '</div>';
  return {
    restrict: 'A',
    scope: { message: '=' },
    template: html,
    replace: true,
    link: function(scope, ele, attrs) {
      scope.$watch('message', function(n, o) {
        if (n)
          $timeout(function() {
            ele.addClass('ng-hide');
          }, 2000);
      });
}}});
```

In order to unit test our directives, we need to expose them to the view. Similar to how we test our controllers, we need to manually place the directive in an element that we'll create (in a manner similar to how Angular places the directive in the first place).

```
describe('Unit: Directives', function() {
  var ele, scope;
  // Load our app
  beforeEach(module('myApp'));
  // Our tests will go here
});
```

Now, in order to load the directive into the view, we need to compile the HTML content and apply the bindings that Angular automatically runs for us in the production.

```
describe('Unit: Directives', function() {
  var ele, scope;
  // Load our app
  beforeEach(module('myApp'));
  beforeEach(inject(function($compile, $rootScope) {
    scope = $rootScope;
    ele = angular.element(
      '<div notification message="note"></div>'
    );
    $compile(ele)(scope);
    scope.$apply();
  }));

  // Our tests will go here
});
```

Notice that we're creating an element that calls the directive, just like when we place it into the DOM. Then we need to compile the element and run the digest loop to effectively *place* the element in our fake DOM.

All we have to do to test the directive is interact with it as though it is in our DOM. In order to make any changes to any bindings in the directive, we need to force a digest loop to run.

In our directive, we're attaching a binding to the message property of the scope, so when we change it, we'll need to do it within an $apply() call:

```
// ... test setup
it('should display the welcome text', function() {
  scope.$apply(function() {
    scope.note = "Notification message";
  });

  expect(
    ele.html()
  ).toContain("Notification message");
});
```

End-to-End Testing Directives

When E2E testing directives, we're not primarily concerned with the functionality of the directives – we're testing what the user sees and does in the overall view.

As we're simply testing the view, end-to-end testing of directives looks similar to testing templates.

```
describe('E2E: directives', function() {

  beforeEach(function() {
    browser().navigateTo('/');
  });

  it('should have the welcome message', function() {
    expect(
      element('.notification', 'Notification').html()
    ).toContain('Notification message');
  });
});
```

Testing Events

When we're using events in our app, especially events that cause interaction to happen in the DOM, we'll want to set up tests that ensure the actual event is fired and that it gets the expected event data.

We'll also want to set up tests that set expectations for what happens when an event is caught in the browser. We want to see whether our reaction to the event is operating how we expect it to respond.

Unit Testing Events

When we're unit testing that events are fired, we're interested to know that they are actually called and that the *right* events are actually called. Second, we're mostly interested to know that the handlers have the data they need.

Setting up event testing is incredibly easy using the spyOn() Jasmine helper.

Imagine that we're testing a controller that is firing an $emit function. With this function, we can set up an expectation that our event is fired and that it's called with any arguments in which we're interested.

First, as usual, we need to set up our tests such that we'll have access to the controller's scope:

```
describe('myApp', function() {
  var scope;
  beforeEach(angular.mock.module('myApp'));
  beforeEach(angular.mock.inject(function($rootScope) {
    scope = $rootScope.$new();
  });
});
```

With setup, we can simply set a spyOn() call on the scope for the $emit or $broadcast event.

```
// ...
});
it('should have emit called', function() {
  spyOn(scope, "$emit");
  scope.closePanel();  // for example
                       // or any event that
                       // causes the emit to
                       // be called
  expect(scope.$emit)
    .toHaveBeenCalledWith("panel:closed",
      panel.id);
});
```

We can also test the events that are we set an $on() listener that the gets called after an event is fired. To execute the $broadcast method, we can simply call $broadcast on the scope and set an expectation for the changes in the scope that the event will cause.

```
// ...
it('should set the panel to closed state',
  function() {
    scope.$broadcast("panel:closed", 1);
    expect(scope.panel.state).toEqual("closed");
});
```

End-to-End Testing Events

End-to-end testing events being called is fairly easy: We'll simply test that the functionality the event causes is firing as we expect.

Continuous Integration for Angular

Angular's Karma works wonderfully with continuous integration services. Continuous integration services, or CI for short, allows our app a *gateway* for deployment and allows us to be confident that every check-in of our code is working as expected.

Continuous integration servers are used by developers and large and small companies all over the world, and it's a good idea to learn how to set them up. Both JenkinsCI[96] and TravisCI[97] easily integrate with Karma, and we strongly encourage our readers to use them.

Protractor

The new end-to-end testing framework, called `Protractor`, will eventually replace the current framework as the default framework.

Unlike the Angular scenario runner, Protractor is built on WebDriver[98], which is an API for controlling browsers, written as extensions.

WebDriver has controller extensions for IE, Chrome, Safari, FireFox, and more to give us options and a variety of browsers to test against. This has many benefits, including being more stable and quicker.

Protractor, like the Angular scenario runner, implements Jasmine as its test scaffolding so we don't need to learn a completely new testing framework to use it.

Protractor itself can be installed as a standalone runner or it can be embedded into our tests as a library.

Installation

We can install Protractor with npm:

```
$ npm install -g protractor
```

---

[96]http://jenkins-ci.org/
[97]https://travis-ci.org/
[98]https://code.google.com/p/selenium/wiki/WebDriverJs

The -g tells npm to install protractor globally.

Unlike the Angular scenario runner, Protractor requires a separate standalone server to be running at http://location:4444 (we can configure this location).

Luckily, Protractor itself comes with a tool that eases the installation of a Selenium server.

In order to access the script, we'll need to install Protractor locally in the top-level directory of the Angular app we want to test.

```
$ npm install protractor
```

Then we can run the Selenium installation script located in the local node_modules/ directory:

```
$ ./node_modules/protractor/bin/install_selenium_standalone
```

This script will download the files required to run Selenium itself and build a start script and a directory with them.

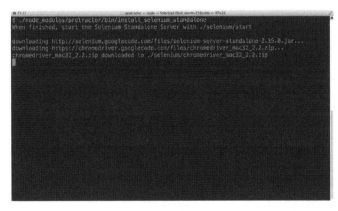

Install Selenium

When this script is finished, we can start the standalone version of Selenium with the Chrome driver by executing the start script:

```
$ ./selenium/start
```

Install Selenium

 If you are having trouble running your Selenium installation, try updating the ChromeDriver by downloading the latest version here[99].

Now we can use Protractor to connect to our Selenium server running in the background.

Configuration

Protractor, like Karma, requires a configuration script to run that tells the Protractor runner how to connect to Selenium, which browser(s) to use, and where the test files are located.

The easiest way to create a configuration file is by copying the reference configuration file from the Protractor install:

```
$ cp ./node_modules/protractor/referenceConf.js protractor_conf.js
```

This reference file includes all of the options available for running Protractor.

Configuration Options

Protractor includes several options that allow us to configure how we are running Protractor with our spec files.

seleniumServerJar (string)

By setting the seleniumServerJar as the path to the standalone Selenium server, we can tell Protractor to launch the Selenium server when we run the test.

This setting is useful when we're running continuous integration (CI) tests, but the startup time of Selenium is slow, so this is quite inefficient for development time.

---

[99]http://chromedriver.storage.googleapis.com/index.html

seleniumPort (integer)

The port on which to start the Selenium server, if Protractor is to start the server.

chromeDriver (string)

The path of the ChromeDriver to start as the `webdriver.chrome.driver` when starting the Selenium server. Protractor attempts to find the ChromeDriver using the `PATH` environment variable if this is null.

seleniumArgs (array)

The strings in this array are additional arguments that we can manually pass to the Selenium server on boot.

sauceUser / sauceKey (string)

If the `sauceUser` and `sauceKey` are set, then the Selenium server will not start, and the tests will run remotely using SauceLabs[100], a cloud testing service.

seleniumAddress (string)

This string is the address of a running Selenium server if we're running our own. For instance, if we start the Selenium server using the included script, this string would be set to: `http://localhost:4444/wd/hub`.

allScriptsTimeout (integer)

This integer is the timeout for each script to run in the browser. That is, if a script takes longer than this time to complete, it will be killed and reported as a failure.

specs (array)

This array of strings is the location of the specs to run. These can be relative, absolute filepaths, or patterns to match.

```
specs: [
  'spec/*_spec.js',
],
```

capabilities (object)

This object contains the key-value pairs of capabilities to be passed to the webdriver instance.

---

[100]https://saucelabs.com/

```
capabilities: {
  'browserName': 'chrome'
}
```

baseUrl (string)

This string is the base URL for our application. If our tests use relative paths, these paths will be appended to this string.

```
baseUrl: 'http://localhost:9000'
```

rootElement (string)

This string is the selector for the element that houses the Angular app. It defaults to body, but if we include the Angular app as a descendant of the <body> element, then we need to include this option.

onPrepare (string/function)

This function runs after Protractor has been started and is ready to run, but before *all* of the specs are executed. It can also be a file that contains code to be run before the specs are executed.

The onPrepare option is useful for setting up Jasmine or Protractor, for instance:

```
onPrepare: function() {
  // For example, adding a Jasmine reporter:
  jasmine.getEnv()
  .addReporter(new jasmine.JUnitXmlReporter(
    'outputdir/', true, true)
  );
},
```

params (object)

The params object will be passed directly to the Protractor instance, and we can access this object inside our tests. We can put any arbitrary values inside of this params object.

jasmineNodeOpts (object)

The jasmineNodeOpts specifies the options to be passed to the Jasmine Node instance. The full list of options for jasmineNodeOpts can be found at https://github.com/juliemr/minijasminenode[101].

---

[101]https://github.com/juliemr/minijasminenode

Writing Tests

Protractor uses Jasmine by default and, thus, the tests that we'll write are very similar to those that we can write with karma with a few key differences.

Protractor exposes a few global variables that we can use in our tests:

browser

This variable is a wrapper around the instance of the webdriver. We'll use it for navigation and page information.

element

The element function helps us find and interact with elements on the page that we're testing.

Remember: The return value of element is **not** a DOM element; it's an instance of ElementFinder, which is an object that acts over webdriver. We can use this object to interact with our objects on the page using methods such as sendKeys and click.

The full API is extensive; more documentation can be found at the documentation page that can be found on Github:

https://github.com/angular/protractor/blob/master/docs/api.md[102]

by

This option is the collection of element locater strategies. We can use it to find elements by CSS selectors, IDs, or even attributes that are bound via ng-model.

by.binding   This option allows us to search for elements that are bound either by ng-bind or by the template notation {{ }}

by.model   We can use by.model to search for input elements that are bound by ng-model.

by.repeater   We can search for elements that contain the directive ng-repeat.

by.id   by.id allows us to search for elements by their CSS ID.

by.css   We can search for elements by their CSS selector using by.css.

Since we'll select by CSS selectors often, Protractor binds the global variable of $ to the function element.by.css as a convenience.

---

[102]https://github.com/angular/protractor/blob/master/docs/api.md

protractor

This option is the Protractor namespace that wraps the webdriver namespace. It contains static variables and classes.

Combining these global variables, we can write efficient end-to-end tests.

 Protractor assumes we are testing Angular apps and expects Angular to be present on the page. If it's not found, it will throw an error.

We **can** load non-Angular pages by dipping down into the lower-level webdriver instance using the `browser.driver` object.

For instance, let's say we want to test the basic example on the AngularJS homepage:

```
describe('angularjs homepage', function() {
  it('should greet the named user', function() {
    // Load the AngularJS homepage.
    browser.get('http://www.angularjs.org');

    element(by.model('yourName'))
        .sendKeys('Julie');

    var greeting =
      element(by.binding('yourName'));

    expect(greeting.getText())
      .toEqual('Hello Julie!');
  });
});
```

Page Objects

To make our tests more readable, we can use the `webdriver` concept of `Page Objects`. Page Objects are basically classes that allow us to wrap specific page functionality into a clean interaction.

For instance, we can wrap a page like:

```
var AngularHomepage = function() {
  this.nameInput = element(by.model('yourName'));
  this.greeting = element(by.binding('yourName'));

  this.get = function() {
    browser.get('http://www.angularjs.org');
  };

  this.setName = function(name) {
    this.nameInput.sendKeys(name);
  };
};
```

Now we can clean up our tests like so:

```
describe('angularjs homepage', function() {
  it('should greet the named user', function() {
    var angularHomepage = new AngularHomepage();
    angularHomepage.get();

    angularHomepage.setName('Julie');

    expect(angularHomepage.greeting.getText()).toEqual('Hello Julie!');
  });
});
```

Events

In cases where the components of our web application are loosely connected, such as when we require user authentication and handle authorization, it's not always feasible to handle the immediate communication without coupling our components together.

For example, if our back end responds to a request with a status code of 401 (indicative of an unauthorized request), we expect that our web app won't allow our user to stay connected to the current view. In this case, we'd want our app to redirect the user to a login or signup page.

Given this logic, we cannot tell our controllers to set a new location from the outside. We also want this specific functionality to space across multiple scopes so we can protect multiple scopes using the same behavior.

We need another way to communicate between them.

Angular's scopes are hierarchical in nature: They can naturally communicate back and forth through parent-child relationships. Oftentimes, however, our scopes don't share variables, and they often perform completely different functions from each other, regardless of their place in the parent tree.

For these cases, we have the ability to communicate between our scopes by propagating events up and down the chain.

What are Events

Just as the browser responds to browser-level events, such as a mouse click or a page scroll, our Angular app can respond to Angular events. This fact gives us the advantage of being able to communicate across our application inside nested components that are not built with other components in mind.

 Note that the Angular event system does not share the browser event system, meaning that, by design, we can only listen for Angular events, not DOM events on scopes.

We can think of events as snippets of information propagated across an application that generally (optionally) contain information about what's happening inside of that application.

Event Propagation

Since scopes are hierarchical, we can pass events up or down the scope chain.

A generally good rule of thumb for choosing the event passing method that we'll use is to look at the scope from which we're firing the event. If we want to notify the entire event system (thus allowing any scope to handle the event), we'll want to broadcast downwards.

On the other hand, if we want to alert a global module (so to speak), we'll end up needing to alert our higher-level scopes ($rootScope, for instance), and we'll need to pass an event upwards.

 It's a good idea to limit the number of notifications sent to the global level, particularly because events, although very powerful, introduce complexity into our apps.

For example, when we're routing, the 'global' app state needs to know at which page the app is currently set, while, on the other hand, if we're communicating between a tab directive to its child pane directives, we'll need to send the event downwards.

Bubbling an Event Up with $emit

To dispatch an event to travel up the scope chain (from child scopes to parent scopes), we'll use the $emit() function.

```
// Send an event that our user logged in
// with the current user
scope.$emit('user:logged_in', scope.user);
```

Within an $emit() event function call, the event bubbles up from the child scope to the parent scope. All of the scopes above the scope that fires the event will receive notification about the event.

We use $emit() when we want to communicate changes of state from within our app to the rest of the application. If we want to communicate with our $rootScope then we need to $emit() the event.

The $emit() method takes two arguments:

name (string)

The name of the event to emit

args (set)

A set of arguments passed into the event listeners as objects

The $emit() method returns an event object (see event object for details on the event object).

Any exception that is emitted from any of the listeners passes into the $exceptionHandler service.

Sending an Event Down with $broadcast

To pass an event downwards (from parent scopes to child scopes), we use the $broadcast() function.

```
// hold on, cart is checking out
// so all directives below should disable
// themselves while the cart is checking out
scope.$broadcast('cart:checking_out', scope.cart);
```

On the $broadcast() method, every single child scope that registers a listener will receive this message. The event propagates to all directives and indirect scopes of the current scope and calls every single listener all the way down.

We **cannot** cancel events sent using the $broadcast() method.

The $broadcast() method itself takes two parameters:

name (string)

The name of the event to emit

args (set)

A set of arguments passed into the event listeners as objects

The $broadcast() method returns an event object (see event object for details on the event object).

Any exception that is emitted from any of the listeners passes into the $exceptionHandler service.

Events

Listening

To listen for an event, we can use the $on() method. This method registers a listener for the event bearing a particular name. The event name is simply the event type fired in Angular.

For instance, we can listen for the event that fires when a route change process is triggered:

```
scope.$on('$routeChangeStart',
  function(evt, next, current) {
    // A new route has been triggered
});
```

Whenever the event $routeChangeStart (which is broadcasted when the route is going to be changed) fires, the listener (the function) is called.

Angular passes in the evt object as the first parameter to any event that we are listening for, be it our own custom events or built-in Angular services.

Event Object

The event object has the following attributes:

targetScope (scope object)

This attribute is the scope emitting or broadcasting the event.

currentScope (scope object)

This object contains the current scope that is handling the event.

name (string)

This string is the name of the event that was fired and that we are handling.

stopPropagation (function)

The stopPropagation() function cancels any further event propagation for events that are fired through $emit.

preventDefault (function)

The preventDefault function sets the flag of defaultPrevented to true. Although we cannot stop event propagation, we can tell our child scopes that we don't need to handle the event (i.e., that we can safely ignore them).

defaultPrevented (boolean)

Calling preventDefault() sets defaultPrevented to true.

The $on() function returns a de-registration function that we can call to cancel the listener.

Core Services Riding on Events

The Angular core framework sends events that we listen for and upon which we can act. We'll use these events to provide our custom Angular objects the ability to interact with our app at different levels of global state.

There are several events that we call with $emit(), sending their events upward, and several more that we call as $broadcast() events.

Core System $emitted Events

The following events are emitted from directives upward to scopes containing the directive invocation. We can use $on() to listen to these methods in any scope above the chain:

```
$scope.$on('$includeContentLoaded',
  function(evt) {
});
```

$includeContentLoaded

The $includeContentLoaded event fires from the ngInclude directive when the ngInclude content is reloaded.

$includeContentRequested

The $includeContentRequested event is emitted on the scope from which the ngInclude is called. This is emitted every single time that the ngInclude content is requested.

$viewContentLoaded

The $viewContentLoaded event is emitted on the current ngView scope every single time that ngView content is reloaded.

Core System $broadcasted Events

$locationChangeStart

The $locationChangeStart event is fired when Angular starts to update the browser's location based upon a mutation set by the $location service (through $location.path(), $location.search(), etc.).

$locationChangeSuccess

The $locationChangeSuccess event is broadcasted from the $rootScope if and only if we have not prevented the $locationChangeStart event when the location of the browser changes successfully.

$routeChangeStart

The $routeChangeStart event kicks off from the $rootScope before a route change occurs. It is at this point that the route services start to resolve all of the dependencies needed for the route change to occur.

This process usually involves fetching view templates and any resolve dependencies on the route property.

$routeChangeSuccess

The $routeChangeSuccess event is broadcasted from the $rootScope after all of the route dependencies are resolved following $routeChangeStart.

The ngView directive uses the $routeChangeSuccess event to know when to instantiate the controller and render the view.

$routeChangeError

The $routeChangeError event is fired if any of the resolve properties on the route object are rejected (i.e., if they fail). This event is broadcasted from the $rootScope.

$routeUpdate

The $routeUpdate is broadcasted from the $rootScope if the reloadOnSearch property on the $routeProvider has been set to false *and* the same instance of a controller is being used.

$destroy

The $destroy event is broadcasted on the scope **before** the scope is destroyed. This sequence gives the children scopes a chance to clean themselves up before the parent scope is actually removed.

For instance, if we have a $timeout running in our controller, we don't want this event to continuously fire even if the containing controller no longer exists.

```
angular.module('myApp')
.controller('MainController', function($scope, $timeout) {
    var timer;
    var updateTime = function() {
      $scope.date = new Date();
      timer = $timeout(updateTime, 1000);
    }
    // Start updating time
    timer = $timeout(updateTime, 1000);

    // Clean up the timer before we kill this
    // controller
    $scope.$on('$destroy', function() {
      if (timer) { $timeout.cancel(timer); }
    });
});
```

Architecture

When learning Angular, one of the most confusing adjustments we need to make is learning *how to think* about structuring the application. Although we cannot prescribe a structure, as it is the developer's prerogative to choose one, we can share what has worked for us.

Directory Structure

AngularJS is so packed with options that it can be difficult to determine how to structure our web apps as they grow over time. Where is the most logical place to put our controllers? Should we contain all of the logic of our services in a single file or should we break them out?

When building an Angular app of any size, we can usually best make our structuring choices by considering the tools that we're going to use when building the app and the current size of the project. We should always build with the expectation that our project will grow.

We suggest creating the following directory structure for our applications, where we keep our application files in the `scripts/` directory, each separated out by its function type with a main `app.js` file.

Recommended directory structure

 We also suggest using a tool like Grunt to concatenate our files together in a single file for production.

Every Angular object should have its own file, named appropriately for its function. For instance, the logical place for a `MainController` object would be in the `scripts/controllers/main.js` file. A `myFilter` object belongs in the `scripts/filters/myFilter.js`.

Employing this structure is beneficial because each file is small and directed on its functionality and because it enables multiple developers to efficiently work together on the app.

Additionally, we suggest mirroring the scripts directory in a `test/` folder at the root directory when we write tests for our application, like so:

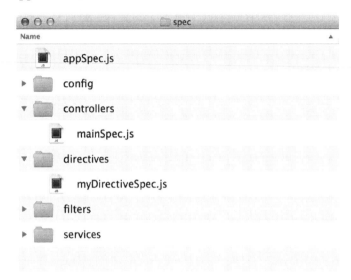

Recommended test directory structure

We suggest this structure when building a single-module application. When building an app composed of multiple modules, we'll include a `modules/` directory with a similar structure as the top level structure.

Modules

A module is the kernel of functionality for Angular apps. Modules contain all of the code that we write for our specific app and, thus, tend to grow huge in a monolithic way. Although this tendency isn't bad (modules are a great way to reduce global scope noise), we can divide our modules.

There are several differing opinions about when to create a module and when to nest functionality in a global module. Both of the following methods are valid ways to break up our functionality by modules:

Modularize on Functionality

The most obvious method for breaking up our app by modules is to divide the modules by type.

We need to inject these modules as dependencies for our main app, which makes it incredibly easy to set up tests for each module type and also isolates and subdivides the functionality that we'll need to account for when writing specs.

For instance, we can create a module for each Angular object type:

```
angular.module('myApp.directives', []);
angular.module('myApp.services', []);
angular.module('myApp.filters', []);
// Often time we'll want to use our services
// inside of our controllers, so we'll inject
// those into our 'myApp.controllers' module
angular.module('myApp.controllers', [
  'myApp.services'
]);
angular.module('myApp', [
  'myApp.directives',
  'myApp.controllers',
  'myApp.filters',
  'myApp.services'
]);
```

One issue with this method is that it sometimes leaves us with a bunch of incredibly small modules. This outcome won't hurt performance, but it can be cumbersome to develop.

Modularize on Routes

Another method we can use to break up our app is to divide our modules by route. This breakdown allows us to write isolated tests that focus on the functionality per route. Modularizing by route can make more sense, depending upon the project; it allows us to divide our functionality efficiently when we're dealing with a lot of independent routes.

For instance:

```
angular.module('myApp.home', []);
angular.module('myApp.login', []);
angular.module('myApp.account', []);
angular.module('myApp', [
  'myApp.home',
  'myApp.login',
  'myApp.account'
]);
```

This modularization makes sense specifically when we're dealing with large numbers of routes and/or when we don't have too much cross-over between routes.

Controllers

When naming a controller, it's conventional to use the name of the controller – beginning with a capital letter – and `Controller`. For example,

```
angular.module('myApp')
.controller('someController', function($scope) {
  // This is NOT conventional
})
.controller('SomeController', function($scope) {
  // This is the conventional way to
  // write a controller
})
```

Scope creep can be one of the most confusing aspects of the Angular framework where we have a lot of functionality defined on our $scope in our controllers. As we're writing our web apps, we'll sometimes find that the size of of controllers is growingly wildly out of control.

We can reduce the size of our controllers by shifting the responsibility of handling the DOM and methods away from them. Moving functionality into custom directives greatly reduces the need to create functions that determine whether we need to expose a particular view or format a value.

Since we're `binding` values on the $scope inside of the view, the controller doesn't need to be responsible for holding onto the value states we need for a particular DOM object.

For instance, we can remove the method in the controller that deals with showing values.

Let's say we have a single login page that shows either a login form or a registration form depending upon a state a user has chosen. We can call the page `showLoginForm`:

```
angular.module('myApp')
.controller('LoginController', function($scope) {
  // Show login form if true and show
  // registration form if false
  $scope.showLoginForm = true;
  $scope.sendLogin = function() {}
  $scope.sendRegister = function() {}
});
```

In our HTML, we might set the functionality of the `LoginController` in the following format:

```
<div ng-show="showLoginForm">
  <form ng-submit="runLogin()"></form>
</div>
<div ng-show="!showLoginForm">
  <form ng-submit="runRegister()"></form>
</div>
```

Although this example is particularly trivial (we only have one extra variable in our $scope), the number of these values can grow exponentially large as our views grow increasingly complex.

We can remove the value by using a directive. For instance:

```
angular.module('myApp')
.directive('loginForm', function() {
  return {
    scope: {
      onLogin: '&',
      onRegister: '&'
    },
    templateUrl: '/templates/loginRegForms.html',
    link: function(scope, ele, attrs) {
      scope.showLoginForm = true;
      scope.submitLogin = function() {
        scope.onLogin({user: scope.loginUser});
      }
      scope.submitRegister = function() {
        scope.onRegister({user: scope.newUser});
      }
    }
  }
});
angular.module('myApp')
.controller('LoginController', function($scope) {
  $scope.sendLogin = function() {}
  $scope.sendRegister = function() {}
});
```

We can call this directive in our view as we would with any directive:

```
<div login-form
    on-login="sendLogin(user)"
    on-register="sendRegister(user)"></div>
```

With our view variable safely tucked away in the directive, we no longer need to hold onto the view conditional in our controller. It's a best practice to keep our controllers thin; using directives allows us to do so efficiently.

Additionally, isolating our login routes inside of a directive, as above, also makes it very easy to test their functionality.

Sharing Data between Controllers

In Angular, we can share data between two controllers in a few different ways. We can nest our controllers underneath the same parent controller and allow each controller to independently modify the values of the parent controller's $scope attribute, *or* we can share a value inside of a service.

It's preferable to hold onto data inside of a service, but the more efficient method can depend upon the situation. For instance, inside of a dialog box, it makes sense for us to hold onto the data that the dialog box is showing inside of a parent controller.

Directives

Knowing when to write a directive is as important as to knowing when not to write one. More often than not, it's generally a good idea to write a directive.

It's always better to err on the side of using directives over not using directives. As we've seen above, they reduce the amount of clutter inside of our controller.

It's also much simpler to test directives than to test controllers.

Directives do not always need to have a view template. Oftentimes, they can simply serve as a shim to handle dealing with data underneath the view. The ngModelController is an example of when this functionality comes in handy.

Testing

We **always** encourage testing inside of our apps. We constantly strive to write unit tests for any piece of functionality that has any level of complexity. These tests allow us to feel confident about our code, no matter how small. Focusing on unit tests also enables us to be efficient with time and to focus on functionality.

Once we're confident we have tested the API of our Angular apps with unit tests, we can start to write end-to-end tests. End-to-end tests can be brittle and dependent upon the view, so we usually leave them until later in the development process. Not only that, but end-to-end tests generally run much more slowly than unit tests, so writing unit tests first allow us to focus on functionality with the same momentum as the development process.

We encourage writing tests for ALL parts of our apps. For more information about testing, check out the extensive testing chapter.

Angular Animation

The Angular team created the `ngAnimate` module to give our Angular apps hooks into providing CSS and JavaScript.

There are several ways to make animations in an Angular app:

- Using CSS3 Animations
- Using JavaScript animations
- Using CSS3 Transitions

In this chapter, we aim to discuss these three methods of animating and provide a solid understanding of how we can power our own custom animations.

Installation

As of 1.2.0, animations are no longer part of the core of Angular; they exist in their own module. In order to include animations in our Angular app, we need to install and reference this module in our app.

We can download it from code.angularjs.org[103] and save it in a place that we can reference it from our HTML, like `js/vendor/angular-animate.js`.

We can also install it using Bower, which will place it in our usual Bower directory. For more information about Bower, see the Bower chapter.

```
$ bower install --save angular-animate
```

We'll need to reference this library in our HTML *after* we reference Angular itself.

```
<script src="js/vendor/angular.js"></script>
<script src="js/vendor/angular-animate.js"></script>
```

Lastly, we'll need to reference the `ngAnimate` module as a dependency in our app module:

---

[103]http://code.angularjs.org/

```
angular.module('myApp', ['ngAnimate']);
```

Now we are ready to take on animations with AngularJS.

How It Works

The $animate service itself, by default, applies two CSS classes to the animated element for each animation event (see below).

The $animate service supports several built-in Angular directives that automatically support animation without the need for any extra configuration. It is also flexible enough to enable us to build our own animations for our directives.

All of the pre-existing directives that support animation do so through monitoring events provided on those directives. For instance, when a new ngView *enters* and brings new content into the browser, this event is called the *enter* event for ngView. When ngHide is ready to show an element, the remove event is fired.

The following is a list of directives and the events that each fires at different states. We will use these events to define how our animations will work in each state.

Directive	Events
ngRepeat	enter, leave, move
ngView	enter, leave
ngInclude	enter, leave
ngSwitch	enter, leave
ngIf	enter, leave
ngClass or class="..."	add, remove
ngShow	add, remove (.ng-class)
ngHide	add, remove

The $animate service attaches specific classes based upon the events that the directive emits. For structural animations (like enter, move and leave) the CSS classes that are applied are in the form of ng-[EVENT] and ng-[EVENT]-active.

For class-based animations (like ngClass) the animation classes are in the form [CLASS]-add, [CLASS]-add-active, [CLASS]-remove, [CLASS]-remove-active.

Finally for ngShow and ngHide only the .ng-hide class is added or removed and its form is the same as for ngClass: .ng-hide-add, .ng-hide-add-active, .ng-hide-remove, .ng-hide-remove-active.

Automatically Added Classes

The directives that fire the enter event receive a class of .ng-enter when the DOM is updated. Angular then adds the ng-enter-active class, which triggers the animation. ngAnimate automatically detects the CSS code to determine when the animation is complete.

When the event is done, Angular removes both classes from the DOM element, enabling us to define animatable properties to the DOM elements.

If the browser does *not* support CSS transitions or animations, then the animation will start and end immediately, and the DOM will end up at its final state with no CSS transitions or animation classes applied.

The same convention applies for all of the supported structural animation events: enter, leave and move. The class-based animation events have a slightly different form (as mentioned above).

Using CSS3 Transitions

Using CSS3 transitions is by far the easiest way to include animations in our app, and it works for all browsers except IE9 and earlier versions.

Browsers that do not support CSS3 transitions gracefully fall back to the non-animated version of the app.

To do **any** CSS animation, we need to make sure we include the classes we'll be working with to the DOM element we're interested in animating.

For instance, in the following demo, we'll look at animating this element:

```
<div class="fade-in"></div>
```

CSS3 transitions are fully class-based, which means that as long as we have classes that define the animation in our HTML, the animation will be animated in the browser.

In order for us to achieve animations with classes, we need to following the Angular CSS naming conventions to define our CSS transitions.

CSS transitions are effects that let an element gradually change from one style to another style. To define an animation, we must specify the property we want to add an animation to as well as specify the duration of effect.

For instance, this code adds a transition effect on the all of the properties on DOM elements with the .fade-in class for a two-second duration.

```
.fade-in {
  transition: 2s linear all;
  -webkit-transition: 2s linear all;
}
```

With this transition and timing set, we can define properties on different states of the DOM element.

```
.fade-in:hover {
  width: 300px;
  height: 300px;
}
```

With ngAnimate, Angular starts our directive animations by adding two classes to each animation event: the initial ng-[EVENT] class and, shortly thereafter, the ng-[EVENT]-active class.

To automatically allow the DOM elements from above to transition with Angular animation, we modify the initial .fade-in example from above to include the initial state class:

```
.fade-in.ng-enter {
  opacity: 0;
}
.fade-in.ng-enter.ng-enter-active {
  opacity: 1;
}
```

> To actually *run* the animation, we need to include the CSS animation definition. In this definition, we need to include **both** the duration and the element attributes that we're going to modify.
>
> .fade-in.ng-enter { transition: 2s linear all; -webkit-transition: 2s linear all; }

We can also place the transition properties on the base CSS class (the ".fade-in" instead of specifying it for each animation that will take place.

```
.fade-in {
  -webkit-transition: 2s linear all;
  transition: 2s linear all;
}
.fade-in.ng-enter {
  opacity: 0;
}
.fade-in.ng-enter.ng-enter-active {
  opacity: 1;
}
.fade-in.ng-leave {
  opacity: 1;
}
.fade-in.ng-leave.ng-leave-active {
  opacity: 0;
}
```

Using CSS3 Animations

CSS3 animations are more extensive and more complex than CSS3 transitions. They are supported by all major browsers except IE9 and earlier versions of IE. With CSS3 animations, we use the same initial class `ng-[EVENT]`, but we don't need to define animation states in the `ng-[EVENT]-active` state, because our CSS rules will handle the rest of the block.

We create the animation in the `@keyframes` rule. Within the CSS element where we define the `@keyframes` rule, we define the CSS styles that we want to manipulate.

When we want to animate the DOM element, we use the `animation:` property to bind the `@keyframe` CSS property, which applies the animation to the CSS element.

 When we bind the animation to the CSS element, we need to specify both the name of the animation as well as the duration.

 Remember to add the animation duration: If we forget to add the duration of the animation, the duration will default to 0, and the animation will not run.

To create our `@keyframes` rule, we need to give our keyframe a name and set the time periods of the where the properties should be throughout the animation.

```
@keyframes firstAnimation {
  0% {
    color: yellow;
  }
  100% {
    color: black;
  }
}
/* For Chrome and Safari */
@-webkit-keyframes firstAnimation {
  /* from is equivalent to 0% */
  from {
    color: yellow;
  }
  /* from is equivalent to 100% */
  to {
    color: black;
  }
}
```

 Using the keyword from is equivalent to setting the percentage to 0%. Using the keyword to is equivalent to setting the percentage to 100%.

We are not limited to 0% and 100%: We can provide animations in steps, such as at 10%, 15%, etc.

To assign this @keyframe property to the classes we want to animate, we use the animation keyword, which applies the animation to the elements targeted by that CSS selector.

```
.fade-in:hover {
  -webkit-animation: 2s firstAnimation;
  animation: 2s firstAnimation;
}
```

With ngAnimate, we bind the firstAnimation value to any elements that are targeted with the .fade-in class. Angular applies and removes the .ng-enter class for us automatically, so we can simply attach our event to the .fade-in.ng-enter class:

```
.fade-in.ng-enter {
  -webkit-animation: 2s firstAnimation;
  animation: 2s firstAnimation;
}
```

Staggering CSS Transitions / Animations

The ngAnimate comes bundled up with an additional feature to space-out simultaneous animations by a specified delay. This means that if 10 items are entered into a ngRepeat list then each item can be inserted X milliseconds after the last one. The effect produced from this is known as a stagger effect and ngAnimate handles this out of the box for CSS transitions and animations.

Staggering CSS transitions

Following the format of structuring CSS transition code for ng-enter and ng-enter-active an additional CSS class can also be placed in to provide the stagger delay. With the CSS code below, we can add a stagger effect to our .fade-in class using CSS transitions.

```
.fade-in.ng-enter-stagger {
  -webkit-transition-delay:200ms;
  transition-delay:200ms;

  /* safeguard to prevent accidental CSS inheritance */
  -webkit-transition-duration:0;
  transition-duration:0;
}
```

The code below will perform a 200 millisecond pause between each successive item being animated in. Notice, however, that there is another CSS property which specifies the **duration** and sets it to **zero**. Why? This is here as a safeguard to prevent accidental CSS inheritance from the base CSS class. Otherwise, without this safeguard in place the staggering effect could be silently ignored.

But what does this mean for our .fade-in class? Well let's imagine that we're using a ngRepeat element that uses that exact .fade-in class.

```
<div ng-repeat="item in items" class="fade-in">
  Item: #1 -- {{ item }}
</div>
```

Each time a series of items is inserted into the list then the stagger delay will kick in. Item #1 will be inserted right away, #2 will go in 200ms after, #3 400ms after and so on.

Staggering CSS animations

CSS animations are also supported and follow the exact same naming CSS convention as mentioned above for staggering CSS transitions. The only difference is that instead of using `transition-delay`, `animation-delay` is used instead (for obvious reasons). Here's what the `.fade-in` class would look like if CSS animations were used for the stagger effect.

```
.fade-in.ng-enter-stagger {
  -webkit-animation-delay:200ms;
  animation-delay:200ms;

  /* css stagger animations also needs to be here */
  -webkit-animation-duration:0;
  animation-duration:0;
}
```

Since the CSS keyframe animation does not take place until a reflow occurs (when the browser repaints the screen) there may be a slight flicker or the element itself may appear not to be animated briefly until the stagger kicks in. This is because the `from` or `0%` animation hasn't started yet since the keyframe animation hasn't been triggered. To work around this, additional CSS styling can be placed in the CSS class where the keyframe animation is assigned.

```
.fade-in.ng-enter {
  /* pre-reflow styling */
  opacity:0;

  -webkit-animation: 2s firstAnimation;
  animation: 2s firstAnimation;
}

.fade-in.ng-enter-stagger { ... }

@keyframes firstAnimation { ... }
@-webkit-keyframes firstAnimation { ... }
```

What directives support staggering animations?

Simple. All of them do, but they're only available when two or more of the same animation event, within the same parent container, are triggered at the same time. So when 10 items are inserted into a ngRepeat list then a stagger effect occurs. This means that if ngClass is placed on a ngRepeat element and the ngClass value changes for each item within the list then a stagger effect can be rendered for the class-changing animation.

Stagger animations can also be triggered inside of custom directives. Simply make a call using the $animate service a few times in a row and a stagger animation will be up for grabs. Do ensure that the parent element is the same for each animation as well as the className value for each element being animated.

Using JavaScript Animations

JavaScript animation is different from the previous two Angular animation methods in that we set properties on the DOM element directly using JavaScript.

All major browsers that enable JavaScript support JavaScript animation, so it's a good choice if we want to offer animations on browsers that don't support CSS transitions and animations.

Here, instead of manipulating our CSS to animate elements, we update our JavaScript to handle running animations for us.

The `ngAnimate` module adds the `.animation` method to the module API; this method presents an interface on which we can build our animations.

The `animation()` method takes two parameters:

*   classname (string)

This classname will match the class of the element to animate. For our examples thus far, the animation should be named: `.fade-in`.

*   animateFun (function)

The animate function is expected to return an object that includes functions for the different events that the directive fires (where it's used).

See the $animate API docs for detailed documentation on these functions.

```
angular.module('myApp', ['ngAnimate'])
.animation('.fade-in', function() {
  return {
    enter: function(element, done) {
      // Run animation
      // call done when the animation is complete
      return function(cancelled) {
        // close or cancellation callback
      }
    }
  }
});
```

The $angular service calls these functions for the element specified. Inside of these functions, we are free to do what we will with the element. The only requirement is that we call the callback function done() when we are done with the animation.

Inside of these functions, we can return an end function that will be called when the animation is complete OR when the animation has been canceled.

When the animation is triggered, $animate looks for the matching animation function for the event. If it finds a function that matches the event, it executes it, otherwise it will skip the animation entirely.

Fine-tuning animations

Depending on how complex the application, ngAnimate and the underlying animation code may need to be tweaked around.

Filtering out CSS classes

By default, ngAnimate will automatically attempt to animate every element that passes through the $animate service. But don't worry, only the elements that contain the CSS classes that are registered with CSS or JavaScript animations will actually animate.

Despite this system working, having to check every possible CSS class may slow things down on low-powered devices. Therefore, with the release angular.js version 1.2.6, ngAnimate provides a configuration setting for the $animate provider to filter out any possible animation operations on elements that do not contain any matching CSS classes against the given regular expression.

```
myModule.config(function($animateProvider) {
  //a regular expression is the only valid parameter
  $animateProvider.classNameFilter(/\banimate-/);
});
```

Now with the provided regular expression, /animated/, only CSS classes starting with animate will be processed for animation. As a result, our .fade-in animation won't work anymore and it will need to be renamed to .animate-fade-in to actually animate.

Animating Built-In Directives

Animating ngRepeat

The ngRepeat directive fires the events:

Action	Event name
An item was inserted to the list of items	enter
An item was removed to the list of items	leave
An item was moved in the list of items	move

For these three examples, we work with the HTML as follows:

```
<div ng-controller="HomeController">
  <ul>
    <li class="fade-in" ng-repeat="r in roommates">
      {{ r }}
    </li>
  </ul>
</div>
```

Let's assume that the HomeController is defined as such:

```
angular.module('myApp', ['ngAnimate'])
.controller('HomeController', function($scope) {
  $scope.roommates = [
    'Ari', 'Q', 'Sean', 'Anand'
  ];
  setTimeout(function() {
    $scope.roommates.push('Ginger');
    $scope.$apply(); // Trigger a digest

    setTimeout(function() {
      $scope.roommates.shift();
      $scope.$apply(); // Trigger digest
    }, 2000);
  }, 1000);
});
```

In these examples, we have a list of roommates comprising four elements. After a second, we add a fifth. Two seconds later, we remove the first element.

CSS3 Transitions

To animate items in the ngRepeat list, we need to make sure to add the CSS class that will present the initial state of the element and the class that will define the final state for both states: enter and edit.

We can start by defining the animation properties on the initial class(es):

```
.fade-in.ng-enter,
.fade-in.ng-leave {
  transition: 2s linear all;
  -webkit-transition: 2s linear all;
}
```

Now, we can simply define the stages of the initial and final CSS properties in the animation. Here, we fade the element in with green text and turn the text black at the final stage of the enter animation. In the leave (item removal) animation, we reverse the properties:

```
.fade-in.ng-enter {
  opacity: 0;
  color: green;
}
.fade-in.ng-enter.ng-enter-active {
  opacity: 1;
  color: black;
}
.fade-in.ng-leave {}
.fade-in.ng-leave.ng-leave-active {
  opacity: 0;
}
```

CSS3 Keyframe Animation

When using keyframe animation, we don't need to define start and end classes; instead, we define only a single selector that includes the animation CSS key.

We can start by defining the animation properties for the keyframes:

```
@keyframes animateView-enter {
  from {opacity:0;}
  to {opacity:1;}
}
@-webkit-keyframes animateView-enter {
  from {opacity:0;}
  to {opacity:1;}
}
@keyframes animateView-leave {
  from {opacity: 1;}
```

```
  to {opacity: 0;}
}
@-webkit-keyframes animateView-leave {
  from {opacity: 1;}
  to {opacity: 0;}
}
```

With the keyframe set, we can simply attach the animation to the CSS classes that ngAnimate has added:

```
.fade-in.ng-enter {
  -webkit-animation: 2s fade-in-enter-animation;
  animation: 2s fade-in-enter-animation;
}
.fade-in.ng-leave {
  -webkit-animation: 2s fade-in-leave-animation;
  animation: 2s fade-in-leave-animation;
}
```

JavaScript Animation

When animating with JavaScript, we need to define the enter and leave properties on our animation description object.

```
angular.module('myApp')
.animation('.fade-in', function() {
  return {
    enter: function(element, done) {
      // Raw animation without jQuery
      // This is much simpler with jQuery
      var op = 0, timeout,
        animateFn = function() {
          op += 10;
          element.css('opacity', op/100);
          if (op >= 100) {
            clearInterval(timeout);
            done();
          }
        };

      // Set initial opacity to 0
      element.css('opacity', 0);
```

```
      timeout = setInterval(animateFn, 100);
    },
    leave: function(element, done) {
      var op = 100,
          timeout,
          animateFn = function() {
            op-=10;
            element.css('opacity', op/100);
            if (op <= 0) {
              clearInterval(timeout);
              done();
            }
          };
      element.css('opacity', 100);
      timeout = setInterval(animateFn, 100);
    }
  }
});
```

Animating ngView

The ngView directive fires the events:

Action	Event name
New content is ready for the view	enter
Existing content is ready to be hidden	leave

For these three examples, we work with the HTML as follows:

```
<a href="#/">Home</a>
<a href="#/two">Second view</a>
<a href="#/three">Third view</a>
<div class="animateView" ng-view></div>
```

As we're working with the ng-view directive, we're working with routes inside of Angular. For more information about routes, check out the routing chapter. The download for angular-routing is here[104].

For the following examples, we can set our routes as:

---

[104]http://code.angularjs.org/1.2.6/angular-route.js

```
angular.module('myApp', ['ngAnimate', 'ngRoute'])
.config(function($routeProvider) {
  $routeProvider.when('/', {
    template: '<h2>One</h2>'
  }).when('/two', {
    template: '<h2>Two</h2>'
  }).when('/three', {
    template: '<h2>Three</h2>'
  });
})
```

The three routes in these examples each show a different view.

CSS3 Transitions

To animate items in the ngView list, we need to add the CSS class that will define the initial state of the element and the class that will define the final state for both states: enter and edit.

```
.animateView.ng-enter,
.animateView.ng-leave {
  transition: 2s linear all;
  -webkit-transition: 2s linear all;
}
```

Now, we can simply define the stages of the initial and final CSS properties in the animation. Here, we fade the element in with green text and turn the text black at the final stage of the enter animation. In the leave (item removal) animation, we reverse the properties:

```
.animateView.ng-enter {
  opacity: 0;
  color: green;
}
.animateView.ng-enter.ng-enter-active {
  opacity: 1;
  color: black;
}
.animateView.ng-leave {}
.animateView.ng-leave.ng-leave-active {
  opacity: 0;
}
```

CSS3 Keyframe Animation

Let's start by adding the @keyframe animations that we define for the animation.

```
@keyframes animateView-enter {
  from {opacity:0;}
  to {opacity:1;}
}
@-webkit-keyframes animateView-enter {
  from {opacity:0;}
  to {opacity:1;}
}
@keyframes animateView-leave {
  from {opacity: 1;}
  to {opacity: 0;}
}
@-webkit-keyframes animateView-leave {
  from {opacity: 1;}
  to {opacity: 0;}
}
```

All we need to do to apply the animation is include the `animation` CSS style on our class:

```
.animateView.ng-enter {
  -webkit-animation: 2s animateView-enter;
  animation: 2s animateView-enter;
}
.animateView.ng-leave {
  -webkit-animation: 2s animateView-leave;
  animation: 2s animateView-leave;
}
```

JavaScript Animation

First, we need to download[105] and include jQuery in the head of the document.

When animating with JavaScript, we need to define the `enter` and `leave` properties on our animation description object.

---

[105]http://jquery.com/download/

```
angular.module('myApp')
.animation('.animateView', function() {
  return {
    enter: function(element, done) {
      // Example to show how to animate
      // with jQuery. Note, this requires
      // jQuery to be included in the HTML
      $(element).css({
        opacity: 0
      });
      $(element).animate({
        opacity: 1
      }, done);
    },
    leave: function(element, done) {
      done();
    }
  }
});
```

Animating ngInclude

The ngInclude directive fires these events:

Action	Event name
New content is ready for the view	enter
Existing content is ready to be hidden	leave

For these three examples, we work with the HTML as follows:

```
<div ng-init="template.url='/home.html'"
    ng-controller="HomeController">
  <button ng-click="template.url='/home.html'">
    Home
  </button>
  <button ng-click="template.url='/second.html'">
    Second
  </button>
  <button ng-click="template.url='/third.html'">
    Third
```

```
  </button>
  <div class="animateInclude"
       ng-include="template.url">
  </div>
</div>
```

We also include the inline templates (for demo purposes) in our page. Alternatively, we could set these views to be fetched from a remote server.

```
<script type="text/ng-template" id="/home.html">
  Home Template
</script>
<script type="text/ng-template" id="/second.html">
  Second Template
</script>
<script type="text/ng-template" id="/third.html">
  Third Template
</script>
```

CSS3 Transitions

To animate items in ngInclude, we need to add the CSS class that will define the initial state of the element and the class that will define the final state for both states: enter and edit.

```
.animateInclude.ng-enter,
.animateInclude.ng-leave {
  transition: 2s linear all;
  -webkit-transition: 2s linear all;
}
```

Now, we can simply define the stages of the initial and final CSS properties in the animation. Here, we fade the element in with green text and turn the text black at the final stage of the enter animation. In the leave (item removal) animation, we reverse the properties:

```
.animateInclude.ng-enter {
  opacity: 0;
  color: green;
}
.animateInclude.ng-enter.ng-enter-active {
  opacity: 1;
  color: black;
}
.animateInclude.ng-leave {}
.animateInclude.ng-leave.ng-leave-active {
  opacity: 0;
}
```

CSS3 Animations

We start by defining the @keyframe animations that define the animation in CSS:

```
@keyframes animateInclude-enter {
  from {opacity:0;}
  to {opacity:1; color: green}
}
@-webkit-keyframes animateInclude-enter {
  from {opacity:0;}
  to {opacity:1; color: green}
}
@keyframes animateInclude-leave {
  from {opacity: 1;}
  to {opacity: 0; color: black}
}
@-webkit-keyframes animateInclude-leave {
  from {opacity: 1;}
  to {opacity: 0; color: black}
}
```

All we need to do to apply the animation is include the animation CSS style on our classes:

```css
.animateInclude.ng-enter {
  -webkit-animation: 2s animateInclude-enter;
  animation: 2s animateInclude-enter;
}
.animateInclude.ng-leave {
  -webkit-animation: 2s animateInclude-leave;
  animation: 2s animateInclude-leave;
}
```

JavaScript Animation

When animating with JavaScript, we need to define the enter and leave properties on our animation description object.

```javascript
angular.module('myApp')
.animation('.animateInclude', function() {
  return {
    enter: function(element, done) {
      // Example to show how to animate
      // with jQuery. Note, this requires
      // jQuery to be included in the HTML
      $(element).css({
        opacity: 0
      });
      $(element).animate({
        opacity: 1
      }, done);
    },
    leave: function(element, done) {
      done();
    }
  }
});
```

Animating ngSwitch

The ngSwitch directive fires the following events:

Action	Event name
New content is ready for the view	enter
Existing content is ready to be hidden	leave

The ngSwitch directive is similar to our previous examples. For these examples, we work with the following HTML that uses the ng-switch directive:

CSS3 Transitions

To animate items in ngSwitch, we need to add the CSS class that will define the initial state of the element and the class that will define the final state for both states: enter and edit.

```
.animateSwitch.ng-enter,
.animateSwitch.ng-leave {
  transition: 2s linear all;
  -webkit-transition: 2s linear all;
}
```

Now, we can simply define the stages of the initial and final CSS properties in the animation. Here, we fade the element in with green text and turn the text black at the final stage of the enter animation. In the leave (item removal) animation, we reverse the properties:

```
.animateSwitch.ng-enter {
  opacity: 0;
  color: green;
}
.animateSwitch.ng-enter.ng-enter-active {
  opacity: 1;
  color: black;
}
.animateSwitch.ng-leave {}
.animateSwitch.ng-leave.ng-leave-active {
  opacity: 0;
}
```

CSS3 Animations

Let's start by adding the @keyframe animations that we'll define for the animation.

```
@keyframes animateSwitch-enter {
  from {opacity:0;}
  to {opacity:1; color: green}
}
@-webkit-keyframes animateSwitch-enter {
  from {opacity:0;}
  to {opacity:1; color: green}
}
@keyframes animateSwitch-leave {
  from {opacity: 1;}
  to {opacity: 0; color: black}
}
@-webkit-keyframes animateSwitch-leave {
  from {opacity: 1;}
  to {opacity: 0; color: black}
}
```

All we need to do to apply the animation is include the `animation` CSS style on our classes:

```
.animateSwitch.ng-enter {
  -webkit-animation: 2s animateSwitch-enter;
  animation: 2s animateSwitch-enter;
}
.animateSwitch.ng-leave {
  -webkit-animation: 2s animateSwitch-leave;
  animation: 2s animateSwitch-leave;
}
```

JavaScript Animation

When animating with JavaScript, we need to define the `enter` and `leave` properties on our animation description object.

```
angular.module('myApp')
.animation('.animateSwitch', function() {
  return {
    enter: function(element, done) {
      // Example to show how to animate
      // with jQuery. Note, this requires
      // jQuery to be included in the HTML
      $(element).css({
        opacity: 0
```

```
    });
    $(element).animate({
      opacity: 1
    }, done);
  },
  leave: function(element, done) {
    done();
  }
}
});
```

Animating ngIf

The `ngSwitch` directive fires the following events:

Action	Event name
Fired after ngIf contents change and the new DOM element is injected in	enter
Fired just before the ngIf contents are removed	leave

For the following `ngIf` examples, we're going to work with this HTML:

CSS3 Transitions

To animate items in `ngIf`, we need to add the CSS class that will define the initial state of the element and the class that will define the final state for both states: enter and edit.

```
.animateNgIf.ng-enter,
.animateNgIf.ng-leave {
  transition: 2s linear all;
  -webkit-transition: 2s linear all;
}
```

Now, we can simply define the stages of the initial and final CSS properties in the animation. Here, we fade the element in with green text and turn the text black at the final stage of the enter animation. In the `leave` (item removal) animation, we reverse the properties:

```
.animateNgIf.ng-enter {
  opacity: 0;
  color: green;
}
.animateNgIf.ng-enter.ng-enter-active {
  opacity: 1;
  color: black;
}
.animateNgIf.ng-leave {}
.animateNgIf.ng-leave.ng-leave-active {
  opacity: 0;
}
```

CSS3 Animations

Let's start by adding the @keyframe animations that we'll define for the animation.

```
@keyframes animateNgIf-enter {
  from {opacity:0;}
  to {opacity:1;}
}
@-webkit-keyframes animateNgIf-enter {
  from {opacity:0;}
  to {opacity:1;}
}
@keyframes animateNgIf-leave {
  from {opacity: 1;}
  to {opacity: 0;}
}
@-webkit-keyframes animateNgIf-leave {
  from {opacity: 1;}
  to {opacity: 0;}
}
```

All we need to do to apply the animation is include the animation CSS style on our classes:

```
.animateNgIf.ng-enter {
  -webkit-animation: 2s animateNgIf-enter;
  animation: 2s animateNgIf-enter;
}
.animateNgIf.ng-leave {
  -webkit-animation: 2s animateNgIf-leave;
  animation: 2s animateNgIf-leave;
}
```

JavaScript Animation

When animating with JavaScript, we need to define the enter and leave properties on our animation description object.

```
angular.module('myApp')
.animation('.animateNgIf', function() {
  return {
    enter: function(element, done) {
      // Example to show how to animate
      // with jQuery. Note, this requires
      // jQuery to be included in the HTML
      $(element).css({
        opacity: 0
      });
      $(element).animate({
        opacity: 1
      }, done);
    },
    leave: function(element, done) {
      done();
    }
  }
});
```

Animating ngClass

It's possible to animate based upon behvavior that happens when classes are changed in the view. When a CSS class changes (such as in the ngShow and ngHide directives), $animate notices and triggers animations for both when the classes are added and when the old ones are removed.

Instead of using the naming convention for entering, we can use a new CSS convention for ngClass whereby we postfix the new class as: [CLASSNAME]-add and [CLASSNAME]-remove'.

Similar to the enter events above, the [CLASSNAME]-add-active and the [CLASSNAME]-remove-active will get added by ngAnimate at the appropriate times for the specific event.

When we are animating on these classes, the animation is fired **first**, and the final class is added only when the animation is complete. When a class is removed, the class remains on the element until the animation is complete.

The ngClass directive fires the following events:

Action	Event name
After ngClass evaluates to a truthy value and before the class has been added	add
Fired just before the class is removed	remove

For the following ngClass examples, we're going to work with the HTML:

CSS3 Transitions

To animate items in ngClass, we need to add the CSS class that will define the initial state of the element and the class that will define the final state for both states: enter and edit.

```
.animateMe.grown-add,
.animateMe.grown-remove {
  transition: 2s linear all;
  -webkit-transition: 2s linear all;
}
```

Now, we can simply define the stages of the initial and final CSS properties in the animation.

```
.grown {font-size: 50px;}
.animateMe.grown-add {
  font-size: 16px;
}
.animateMe.grown-add.grown-add-active {
  font-size: 50px;
}
.animateMe.grown-remove {}
.animateMe.grown-remove.grown-remove-active {
  font-size: 16px;
}
```

CSS3 Animations

Let's start by adding the `@keyframe` animations that we'll define for the animation. Here, we add a background color to highlight the text. We also define the `remove` animation for pulling the highlight from the text:

```
@keyframes animateMe-add {
  from {font-size: 16px;}
  to {font-size: 50px;}
}
@-webkit-keyframes animateMe-add {
  from {font-size: 16px;}
  to {font-size: 50px;}
}
@keyframes animateMe-remove {
  to {font-size: 50px;}
  from {font-size: 16px;}
}
@-webkit-keyframes animateMe-remove {
  to {font-size: 50px;}
  from {font-size: 16px;}
}
```

All we need to do to apply the animation is include the `animation` CSS style on our classes:

```
.animateMe.grown-add {
  -webkit-animation: 2s animateMe-add;
  animation: 2s animateMe-add;
}
.animateMe.grown-remove {
  -webkit-animation: 2s animateMe-remove;
  animation: 2s animateMe-remove;
}
```

JavaScript Animation

When animating with JavaScript, we need to define the `addClass` and `removeClass` properties on our animation description object.

```
angular.module('myApp')
.animation('.animateMe', function() {
  return {
    addClass: function(ele, clsName, done)
    {
      // Example to show how to animate
      // with jQuery. Note, this requires
      // jQuery to be included in the HTML
      if (clsName === 'grown') {
        $(ele).animate({
          'font-size': '50px'
        }, 2000, done);
      } else { done(); }
    },
    removeClass: function(ele, clsName, done)
    {
      if (clsName === 'grown') {
        $(ele).animate({
          'font-size': '16'
        }, 2000, done);
      } else { done(); }
    }
  }
});
```

Animating ngShow/ngHide

The ngShow and ngHide directives use the .ng-hide class when showing or hiding elements. It's possible to add animations to the time between showing and hiding DOM elements.

When we are animating on these classes, the animation is fired **first**, and the final .ng-hide is added to the DOM element only when the animation is complete.

Because the ng-hide directive is still applied to the DOM element when we're removing the ng-hide class, we never get see our animation until it's complete. Thus, we need to tell the CSS to display our class and not cascade.

The ngShow and ngHide directives fire the events:

Action	Event name
After ngClass evaluates to a truthy value and before the class has been added	add
Fired just before the class	remove

Action	Event name
is removed	

For the following `ngHide` examples, we're going to work with this HTML:

CSS3 Transitions

To animate items in `ngHide`, we need to add the CSS class that will define the initial state of the element and the class that will define the final state for both states: enter and edit.

```
.animateMe.ng-hide-add,
.animateMe.ng-hide-remove {
  transition: 2s linear all;
  -webkit-transition: 2s linear all;
  display: block !important;
}
```

Notice the last line in this CSS block: It tells the CSS to render this class and no other fallback class property for the `display` property. Without this line, the element won't show.

Now, we can simply define the stages of the initial and final CSS properties in the animation.

```
.animateMe.ng-hide-add {
  opacity: 1;
}
.animateMe.ng-hide-add.ng-hide-add-active
{
  opacity: 0;
}
.animateMe.ng-hide-remove {
  opacity: 0;
}
.animateMe.ng-hide-remove.ng-hide-remove-active {
  opacity: 1;
}
```

CSS3 Animations

Let's start by adding the `@keyframe` animations that we'll define for the animation. Here, we add a background color to highlight the text. We also define the `remove` animation for pulling the highlight from the text:

```css
@keyframes animateMe-add {
  from {opacity: 1;}
  to {opacity: 0;}
}
@-webkit-keyframes animateMe-add {
  from {opacity: 1;}
  to {opacity: 0;}
}
@keyframes animateMe-remove {
  from {opacity:0;}
  to {opacity:1;}
}
@-webkit-keyframes animateMe-remove {
  from {opacity:0;}
  to {opacity:1;}
}
```

All we need to do to apply the animation is include the `animation` CSS style on our classes:

```css
.animateMe.ng-hide-add {
  -webkit-animation: 2s animateMe-add;
  animation: 2s animateMe-add;
}
.animateMe.ng-hide-remove {
  -webkit-animation: 2s animateMe-remove;
  animation: 2s animateMe-remove;
  display: block !important;
}
```

JavaScript Animation

When animating with JavaScript, we need to define the `addClass` and `removeClass` properties on our animation description object.

```
angular.module('myApp')
.animation('.animateMe', function() {
  return {
    addClass: function(ele, clsName, done)
    {
      // Example to show how to animate
      // with jQuery. Note, this requires
      // jQuery to be included in the HTML
      if (clsName === 'ng-hide') {
        $(ele).animate({
          'opacity': 0
        }, 2000, done);
      } else { done(); }
    },
    removeClass: function(ele, clsName, done)
    {
      if (clsName === 'ng-hide') {
        $(ele).css('opacity', 0);
        // Force the removal of the ng-hide
        // class so we can actually show the
        // animation
        $(ele).removeClass('ng-hide');
        $(ele).animate({
          'opacity': 1
        }, 2000, done);
      } else { done(); }
    }
  }
});
```

Building Custom Animations

The $animate service provides hooks for us to implement our own custom animation inside of our directives. After injecting the $animate service into our own apps, we can use the exposed events to trigger associated functions on the $animate object for each event.

To get started with animations in our own directives, we need to *inject* the $animate service in our directives.

```
angular.module('myApp', ['ngAnimate'])
.directive('myDirective', function($animate) {
  return {
    template: '<div class="myDirective"></div>',
    link: function(scope, ele, attrs) {
      // Add animations here
      // for instance:
      $animate['addClass'](element, 'ng-hide');
    }
  }
});
```

Now, we can bind events to the directive and start showing our animations.

With our directive set up, we can create an `animation` that corresponds with our directive calling the $animate function.

```
angular.module('myApp')
.animation('.scrollerAnimation', function() {
  return {
    animateFun: function(element, done) {
      // We are free to do what we want inside
      // this function, but we must call
      // done to let angular know we're done
      // animating
    }
  }
});
```

The $animate service exposes several methods that provide *hooks* into the animation events for the built-in directives. These events that are exposed as hooks in the $animate service are:

- enter
- leave
- move
- addClass
- removeClass

The $animate service provides these events as functions that give us control to work with custom animations from within our own directives.

addClass()

The addClass() method triggers a custom animation event based on the 'className' variable and attaches the 'className' value to the element as a CSS class. When adding a class to a DOM element, the $animate service adds a suffix to the className with -add to allow for us to set up animation.

 If there are no CSS transitions or keyframe animations defined on the CSS selector ([className]-add), ngAnimate won't trigger the animation, it will only add the class.

The addClass() method takes three parameters:

- element (jQuery/jqLite element)

The element that we're animating

- className (string)

The CSS class that we're animating and attaching to the element

- done (function)

The callback function called when the animation is complete

```
angular.module('myApp', ['ngAnimate'])
.directive('myDirective', function($animate) {
  return {
    template: '<div class="myDirective"></div>',
    link: function(scope, ele, attrs) {
      ele.bind('click', function() {
        $animate.addClass(ele, 'greenlight');
      });
    }
  }
});
```

Calling the addClass() method runs through the following steps:

1. Runs any JavaScript-defined animations on the element
2. The [className]-add class is added to the element
3. $animate scans the CSS styles for transition/animation duration and delay properties

4. The [className]-add-active class is added to the element's classList (triggering the CSS animation)
5. $animate waits for the defined duration to complete
6. The animation ends, and $animate removes the two added classes [className]-add and [className]-add-active
7. The className class is added to the element
8. The done() callback function is fired (if defined)

removeClass()

The removeClass() method triggers a custom animation event based on the className and removes the CSS class provided by the CSS className value. When removing a class on a DOM element, the $animate service adds a suffix to the className with -remove to allow us to set up animation.

 If there are no CSS transitions or keyframe animations defined on the CSS selector: [className]-remove, then ngAnimate won't trigger the animation, it will only add the class.

The removeClass() method takes three parameters:

- element (jQuery/jqLite element)

The element we're animatin

- className (string)

The CSS class we're animating and removing from the element

- done (function)

The callback function called when the animation is complete

```
angular.module('myApp', ['ngAnimate'])
.directive('myDirective', function($animate) {
  return {
    template: '<div class="myDirective"></div>',
    link: function(scope, ele, attrs) {
      ele.bind('click', function() {
        $animate.addClass(ele, 'greenlight');
      });
    }
  }
});
```

A call to the removeClass() animation function kicks off the following steps:

1. Runs any JavaScript-defined animations on the element
2. The [className]-remove class is added to the element
3. $animate scans the CSS styles for transition/animation duration and delay properties
4. The [className]-remove-active class is added to the element's classList (triggering the CSS animation)
5. $animate waits for the defined duration to complete
6. The animation ends, and $animate removes the three classes [className], [className]-add and [className]-add-active
7. The done() callback function is fired (if defined)

enter()

The enter() method appends the element to its parent element in the DOM and then runs the enter animation. When the animation has started, the $animation service adds the classes ng-enter and ng-enter-active, giving the directive a chance to set up the animation.

The enter() method can take up to four parameters:

- element (jQuery/jqLite element)

The element we're animating.

- parent (jQuery/jqLite element)

The parent element of the element that is the focus of our enter animation.

- after (jQuery/jqLite element)

This is the sibling element of the element that will be the focus of the enter animation.

- done (function)

The callback function called when the animation is complete (if defined).

```
angular.module('myApp', ['ngAnimate'])
.directive('myDirective', function($animate) {
  return {
    template: '<div class="myDirective">' +
              '<h2>Hi</h2></div>',
    link: function(scope, ele, attrs) {
      ele.bind('click', function() {
        $animate.enter(ele, ele.parent());
      });
    }
  }
});
```

A call to the enter() animation function kicks off the following steps:

1. The element is inserted into the parent element or beside the after element
2. $animate runs any JavaScript-defined animations on the element
3. The .ng-enter class is added to the element's classList
4. $animate scans the CSS styles for transition/animation duration and delay properties
5. The .ng-enter-active class is added to the element's classList (triggers the animation)
6. $animate waits for the defined duration to complete
7. The animation ends, and $animate removes both of the classes .ng-enter and .ng-enter-active from the element
8. The done() callback function is fired (if defined)

leave()

The leave() method runs the leave animation. When it's done running, it removes the element from the DOM. When the animation has started, it adds the .ng-leave and .ng-leave-active classes to the element.

The leave() method takes two parameters:

- element (jQuery/jqLite element)

The element we're animating

- done (function)

The callback function called when the animation is complete (if defined)

```
angular.module('myApp', ['ngAnimate'])
.directive('myDirective', function($animate) {
  return {
    template: '<div class="myDirective">' +
              '<h2>Hi</h2></div>',
    link: function(scope, ele, attrs) {
      ele.bind('click', function() {
        $animate.leave(ele);
      });
    }
  }
});
```

A call to the leave() animation function kicks off the following steps:

1. $animate runs any JavaScript-defined animations on the element
2. The .ng-leave class is added to the element's classList
3. $animate scans the CSS styles for transition/animation duration and delay properties
4. The .ng-leave-active class is added to the element's classList (triggers the animation)
5. $animate waits for the defined duration to complete
6. The animation ends, and $animate removes both of the classes .ng-leave and .ng-leave-active from the element
7. The element is removed from the DOM
8. The done() callback function is fired (if defined)

move()

The move() function fires the move DOM animation. Before the animation starts, the $animate service either appends the element into the parent container or adds the element directly after the element, if present. Once the animation has started, .ng-move and .ng-move-active are added for the duration of the animation.

The move() method takes four parameters:

- element (jQuery/jqLite element)

The element we're animating

- parent (jQuery/jqLite element)

The parent element of the element that is the focus of the move animation

- after (jQuery/jqLite element)

This is the sibling element of the element that will be the focus of the enter animation.

- done (function)

The callback function called when the animation is complete (if defined)

```
angular.module('myApp', ['ngAnimate'])
.directive('myDirective', function($animate) {
  return {
    template: '<div class="myDirective">' +
             '<h2>Hi</h2></div>',
    link: function(scope, ele, attrs) {
      ele.bind('click', function() {
        $animate.move(ele, ele.parent());
      });
    }
  }
});
```

A call to the move() animation function kicks off the following steps:

1. The element is moved into the parent element or beside the after element
2. $animate runs any JavaScript-defined animations on the element
3. The .ng-move class is added to the element's classList
4. $animate scans the CSS styles for transition/animation duration and delay properties
5. The .ng-move-active class is added to the element's classList (triggers the animation)
6. $animate waits for the defined duration to complete
7. The animation ends, and $animate removes both of the classes .ng-move and .ng-move-active from the element
8. The done() callback function is fired (if defined)

Integrating with Third-Party Libraries

Animate.css

The Animate.css library provides a bunch of cool, fun, cross-browser animations. It's a great library that gives us a lot of power without requiring us to do much work.

Luckily, the Angular community has provided a slick method of including the `Animate.css` classes into our Angular app. To use the `Animate.css` shim, download the `animate.css` and `animate.js` files from https://github.com/yearofmoo/ngAnimate-animate.css[106]. We just need to reference both of them in our HTML, like so:

```
<!-- In the HEAD of our HTML -->
<link rel="stylesheet" type="text/css" href="css/animate.css">
<!-- In the BODY of our HTML -->
<script type="text/javascript" src="js/vendor/animate.js"></script>
```

Now, instead of requiring `ngAnimate` as a dependency for our app, we can simply include the file `ngAnimate-animate.css` as a dependency. This substitution works because the `ngAnimate-animate.css` module requires the `ngAnimate` module by default.

With this switch set, we can simply reference our animate classes with the `ng-class` directive. For instance:

```
<div class="animateMe"
    ng-class="{'dn-fade':dn_fade}">
</div>
```

For a list of every animation possibility, check out the README[107].

TweenMax/TweenLite

TweenLite and TweenMax are slick, fantastic libraries that were modeled after the ActionScript animation properties. To use them, we need to make sure we download the Greensock library.

Download it from Greensock[108], and store it in a place accessible to your `index.html`. We recommend storing it in `js/vendor/TweenMax.min.js`. We then need to make sure to reference the TweetMax library in our page:

```
<script type="text/javascript" src="js/vendor/TweetMax.min.js"></script>
```

With that set up, we're all ready to go. To include the Greensock animations in our app, we need to set up our animations to use JavaScript. In this way, there is little to no integration code necessary beyond simply animating with JavaScript:

---

[106]https://github.com/yearofmoo/ngAnimate-animate.css

[107]https://github.com/yearofmoo/ngAnimate-animate.css/blob/master/README.md

[108]http://www.greensock.com/

```
angular.module('myApp', ['ngAnimate'])
.animation('scrollAside', function($window) {
  return {
    enter: function(element, done) {
      TweenMax.set(element, {
        position: 'relative'
      });
      TweenMax.to(element, 1, {
        opacity: 0,
        width: 0
      });
      $window.setTimeout(done, 2000);
    }
  }
});
```

The Digest Loop and $apply

Let's take a peek at how Angular works underneath the hood. How do we get this *magical* data binding to work in only a few lines of code? It's important that we understand how the `$digest` loop works and how to use the `$apply()` method.

In the *normal* browser flow, a browser executes callbacks that are registered with an event when that event occurs (e.g., clicking on a link).

Events are fired when the page loads, when an `$http` request comes back, when the mouse moves or a button is clicked, etc.

When an event is fired/triggered, JavaScript creates an event object and executes any functions listening for the specific events with this event object. This callback method then runs inside the JavaScript function, which returns to the browser, potentially updating the DOM.

 No two events can run at the same time. The browser waits until one event handler finishes before the next handler is called.

In non-Angular JavaScript, we can attach a function callback to the click event on a div. Any time that a click event is found on an element, the function callback runs:

```
var div = document.findElementById("clickDiv");
div.addEventListener("click",
  function(evt) {
    console.log("evt", evt);
  });
```

 Open the Chrome developer tools, and copy and paste the previous code inside of any web page and click around the page.

Any time the browser detects a *click*, the browser calls the function registered with the addEventListener on the document.

When we mix Angular into the flow, it extends this normal browser flow to create an *Angular context*. The Angular context refers specifically to code that runs *inside* the Angular event loop, referred to as the `$digest` loop. To understand the *Angular context*, we need to look at exactly what goes on inside of it. There are two major components of the `$digest` loop:

- The $watch list
- The $evalAsync list

$watch List

Every time we track an event in the view, we are registering a callback function that we expect to be called when an event happens in the page. Recall our first example:

```
<!DOCTYPE html>
<html ng-app>
<head>
  <title>Simple app</title>
  <script
    src="https://ajax.googleapis.com/ajax/libs/angularjs/1.2.6/angular.js">
    </script>
</head>
<body>
  <input ng-model="name" type="text" placeholder="Your name">
  <h1>Hello {{ name }}</h1>
</body>
</html>
```

Any time a user updates the input field, {{ name }} changes in the UI. This change happens because we bind the input field in the UI to the $scope.name property. In order to update the view, Angular needs to *track* the change. It does so by adding a *watch* function to the $watch list.

Properties that are on the $scope object are *only* bound if they are used in the view. In the case above, we've added a single function to the $watch list.

Remember: For *all* UI elements that are bound to a $scope object, a $watch is added to the $watch list.

These $watch lists are resolved in the $digest loop through a process called dirty checking.

Dirty Checking

Dirty checking is a simple process that boils down to a very basic concept: It checks whether a value has changed that hasn't yet been synchronized across the app.

 The dirty checking strategy is commonly used in plenty of different applications, beyond Angular. Game engines, database engines, and Object Relational Mappers (ORMs) are some examples of such systems.

Our Angular app keeps track of the values of the current watches (in the watch object, for those who are curious). Angular walks down the $watch list, and, if the updated value has *not* changed from the old value, it continues down the list. If the value *has* changed, the app records the new value and continues down the $watch list.

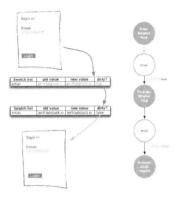

Digest loop

Once Angular has run through the entire $watch list, if any value changed, the app will fall back into the $watch loop until it detects that nothing has changed.

Why run the loop all over again? If we update a value in the $watch list that updates another value, Angular won't detect the update unless we rerun the loop.

If the loop runs ten times or more, our Angular app throws an exception, and the app dies. If Angular doesn't throw this exception, our app could launch into an infinite loop, with bad results.

 In future versions of Angular, the framework will use the native browser specification Object.observe(), which will speed up the *dirty checking* process considerably.

$watch

The $watch method on the $scope object sets up a dirty check on every call to $digest inside the Angular event loop. The Angular $digest loop always returns if it detects changes on the expression.

The $watch function itself takes two required arguments and a third optional one:

- watchExpression

The watchExpression can either be a property of a scope object or a function. It runs on **every** call to $digest in the $digest loop.

If the watchExpression is a string, Angular evaluates it in the context of the $scope. If it is a function, then Angular expects it to return the value that should be watched.

- listener/callback

The callback listener function is only called when the current value of the watchExpression and the previous value of the expression are not equal (except during initialization on the first run).

- objectEquality (optional)

The objectEquality parameter is a comparison boolean that tells Angular to check for strict equality.

The $watch function returns a *deregistration* function for the listener that we can call to *cancel* Angular's watch on the value.

```
// ...
var unregisterWatch =
  $scope.$watch('newUser.email',
    function(newVal, oldVal) {
      if (newVal === oldVal) return; // on init
});
// ...
// later, we can unregister this watcher
// by calling
unregisterWatch();
```

If we are done watching the newUser.email in this example, we can clean up our watcher by calling the *deregistration* function it returns.

For instance, let's say we want to parse an input field value from a full name to split on spaces and find a simple first and last name. Given that our view looks like:

```
<input type="text" ng-model="full_name" placeholder="Enter your full name" />
```

 We should **never** use $watch in a controller: It makes it difficult to test the controller. We're making an allowance here for the sake of illustration, and we'll move these watches into services later.

We want to set up a $watch listener on the full_name property and detect any changes to the value. We also want to set the $watch function on the full_name property.

```
angular.module("myApp")
.controller("MyController", ['$scope', function($scope) {
  $scope.$watch('full_name', function(newVal, oldVal, scope) {
    // the newVal of the full_name will be available here
    // while the oldVal is the old value of full_name
  });
}]);
```

In our example, we're setting an AngularJS expression that tells our Angular app to "watch the full_name property for any potential changes on it, and run the function if you detect any changes".

The listener function is called once on initialization, so the first time around, the value of newVal and oldVal will be undefined (and will be equal). That being the case, it's generally good to check inside the expression if we're in the initialization phase or if there is an update to the previous value. We can easily accomplish this check inside the function, like so:

```
$scope.$watch('full_name',
  function(newVal, oldVal, scope) {
    if (newVal === oldVal) {
      // This will run only on the initialization of the watcher
    } else {
      // A change has occurred after initialization
    }
  });
```

The $scope.$watch() function sets up a watchExpression on the $scope for 'full_name'.

$watchCollection

Angular also allows us to set shallow watches for object properties or elements of an array and fire the listener callback whenever the properties change.

Using $watchCollection allows us to detect when there are changes on an object or array, which gives us the ability to determine when items are added, removed, or moved in the object or array. $watchCollection works just like the normal $watch works in the $digest loop, and we can treat it as a normal $watch.

The $watchCollection() function takes two parameters:

  • obj (string/function)

This object is the one to watch. If a string is passed in, it will be evaluated as an Angular expression. If a function is passed in, it will be called with the current scope, and will be expected to return the value to watch.

- listener (function)

This callback function will be fired when the collection changes. Similar to the $watch function, this function will be called with the new collection fired from the $watch, the old collection (a copy of the previous collection), and the scope within which it will be executed.

The $watchCollection() function returns a *deregistration* function that, when called, cancels our $watch on the collection.

```
$scope.$watchCollection('names',
  function(newNames, oldNames, scope) {
    // Our names collection has changed
});
```

The $digest Loop in a Page

Let's take a look at the $digest loop process inside of a web page. We'll first assume that we have a (very insecure) login page that features a single name field that lets us log in with a single form validation.

 We do not recommend this insecure form of authentication.

```
<h2>Sign in</h2>
<input
  type="text"
  placeholder="Your name"
  ng-model="name"
  ng-minlength='3' />
<input type="submit"
    ng-click="login()"
    value="Login" />
```

With the *name* bound in the view through the ng-model directive, Angular sets up an implicit *watcher* to bind the value of the input field to the current $scope.

When the user enters a character into the form, the Angular context kicks in and begins iterating through the $$watchers (the $watch list).

In this case, the $watch list consists of a single element: $scope.name. Since the user has changed the input field by a single character, the watch function will execute on the $scope.name binding. This action triggers the validations and formatters to run on the value (because of the ng-model binding) before we exit the $digest loop.

Since a value *has* changed in the digest loop, Angular will need to rerun the loop to confirm that it did not change any other values on the scope.

 Why run the digest loop again? If we have a value called $scope.full_name that consists of $scope.first_name + $scope.last_name, any change to either of these values will change $scope.full_name, so the loop needs to run again to ensure that nothing else has changed.

Since changing the $scope.name attribute does not change any other attribute in the $scope, the $digest loop exits, and the browser repaints the DOM which refreshes the view.

After the user has entered their name in the input field and click on the submit button. This will cause a slightly different flow to happen.

ng-click *binds* the browser's native click event to the DOM element. When that DOM element receives the click event, the ng-click directive calls $scope.$apply(), and we enter the $digest loop.

$evalAsync List

The $evalAsync() method is a way to schedule running expressions on the current scope at some time in the future. The second operation that the $digest loop runs is executing the $$asyncQueue. We can get access to this work queue with the $evalAsync() method.

Throughout the $digest loop, the queue empties between each loop through the dirty checking lifecycle, which means two things for any function called with $evalAsync:

- The function will execute sometime *after* the function that called it.
- At least *one* $digest cycle will be performed after the expression is executed.

The $evalAsync() method takes a single argument:

- expression (string/function)

This expression is what we want to execute on the current scope. If a string is passed, it will $eval the expression on the scope.

If a function is passed, it will execute the function with the scope that is passed in as it's executed.

```
$scope.$evalAsync('attribute',
  function(scope) {
    scope.foo = "Executed"
});
```

Some particulars to consider when using $evalAsync:

- If a directive calls $evalAsync() directly, it will run *after* Angular has manipulated the DOM, but *before* the browser renders.
- If a controller calls $evalAsync(), it will run *before* Angular has manipulated the DOM and before the browser renders (we'll never really want to apply this order of events).

We will want to use the $evalAsync() function any time that we want an action to execute outside the execution context of another action in Angular.

We might use it instead of a setTimeout() function, where it might cause a flicker after the browser re-renders the view.

$apply

The $apply() function executes an expression inside of the Angular context from outside of the Angular framework. For instance, if we implement a setTimeout() or are using a third-party library and we want the event to run **inside** the Angular context, we must use $apply().

The $apply() function takes one optional argument:

- expression (string/function)

The expression argument optionally takes a string or a function and executes it inside the current scope.

If a string is passed, then $apply() will first call $eval() on the string, forcing Angular to $eval() the string on the local scope context.

If a function is passed, the function will be executed on the scope passed into the function.

The $exceptionHandler service will catch and handle any exception that the $eval() method throws. Lastly, the $apply() method directly calls the $digest loop.

```
// Ways to call apply
// with a string to be eval'd
$scope.$apply('message = "Hello World"');
// With a function that is passed a scope
$scope.$apply(function(scope) {
  // Execute this function with the scope
  scope.message = "Hello World";
});
// With a function that ignores the scope
$scope.$apply(function() {
  $scope.message = "Hello World";
});
// Or just force the $digest loop to run
// by calling it at the end of our operation
$scope.$apply();
```

Simply said, using $scope.$apply() is a way to gain access to the Angular context from outside of it.

If we call $apply() when an event is fired, we run it through the Angular event loop. If we don't call $apply(), we don't execute the function in the event loop, and it runs outside of the Angular context.

When to Use $apply()

We can generally count on any directive that Angular provides and that is available in the view to call $apply() for us. Any of the ng-[event] directives (like ng-click, ng-keypress, etc) will call $apply().

We can also depend on a lot of built-in Angular services to call $digest() for us, as well. The $http service calls $apply() after the XHR request is done to trigger updating the return value (promise).

Any time that we are handling an event manually, using a third-party framework (e.g., jQuery, the Facebook API), or calling setTimeout(), we want to use the $apply() function to tell Angular to rerun the $digest loop.

> We generally advise *against* using $apply() in a controller, because doing so makes it difficult to test, and because if we have to use $apply() or $digest() in a controller, we're probably making things more difficult than they should be.

When integrating jQuery with Angular (an action generally considered *dirty*), we **need** to use $apply(), because Angular is not aware of events that execute outside of the Angular context. For instance, when using a jQuery plugin (e.g., the datepicker), we need to use $apply to transfer the value from jQuery into our Angular app.

Here, we can build a simple directive (we'll dive deep into building these in the directives chapter), and use the datepicker jQuery plugin function on the element.

The datepicker plugin exposes an event onSelect that fires when the user picks a date. In order to gain access to the date that the user picks *inside* of our Angular app, we need to run the datepicker callback inside the $apply() function.

 The ele.datepicker() function is a property function made available on the DOM element by the jQuery datepicker plugin. In order to make it work, we need to make sure we include jQuery and the jQuery datepicker plugin on the page.

 The ctrl.$setViewValue() function is made available to the directive when using ng-model on a DOM element. For more information, read the controllers chapter.

```
app.directive('myDatepicker', function() {
  return function(scope, ele, attrs, ctrl) {
    $(function() {
      // call datepicker on the element
      ele.datepicker({
        dateFormat: 'mm/dd/yy',
        onSelect: function(date) {
          scope.$apply(function() {
            ctrl.$setViewValue(date);
          });
        }
      })
    });
  }
});
```

Demystifying Angular

At their core, AngularJS web apps load in the browser the same way that non-AngularJS apps do; however, they do run slightly differently. The browser loads the AngularJS library as it is building the DOM (as it ordinarily loads any JavaScript libraries).

When the browser fires the `DOMContentLoaded` event, Angular goes to work. It starts by looking for the `ng-app` directive (for more information on the `ng-app` directive, see the Directives explained chapter).

 AngularJS also starts initializing when the angular.js script is loaded *if* the `document.readyState` is set to `complete`. This fact is useful if we want to dynamically link the AngularJS script.

If the browser finds the `ng-app` directive in the DOM, the app is *automatically* bootstrapped for us. If it doesn't find the directive, Angular expects us to bootstrap the app manually.

To manually bootstrap an AngularJS app, we can use the Angular method `bootstrap()`. It makes sense to manually bootstrap an application in some relatively rare cases. For instance, let's say we want to run an AngularJS app after some other library code runs or we are dynamically creating an element on the fly.

To manually bootstrap an app, we can bootstrap it, like so:

```
var newElement = document.createElement("div");
angular.bootstrap(newElement, ['myApp']);
```

 If there is no `ng-app` directive found in the DOM *and* we have not manually bootstrapped our app, AngularJS does not run. Forgetting `ng-app` can definitely cause some serious issues.

If there is no application specified in the `ng-app` attribute, Angular loads the app without a specific module. If one is specified, Angular loads the module associated with the directive.

Using `ng-app` without specifying a module:

```
<html ng-app>
</html>
```

Using `ng-app` with a specified module:

```
<html ng-app="moduleName">
</html>
```

Angular uses the value of the ng-app directive to configure the $injector service (we cover this service in depth in the dependency injection chapter).

Once the application is loaded, the $injector creates the $compile service alongside the app's $rootScope.

Following the $rootScope's creation, the $compile service takes over. It links the $rootScope with the existing DOM and starts to compile the DOM beginning from where the ng-app directive is set as the root.

How the View *Works*

When the browser gets its HTML in the normal web flow, it receives the HTML and parses it into a DOM tree. Each element in the DOM tree, called a DOM element, will build a bunch of nodes. The browser is then responsible for laying the DOM tree structure out.

When the browser fetches scripts (from the <script> tag), it pauses the parsing and waits until the script is retrieved (it's possible to modify this behavior, but this behavior is the default).

When the angular.js script is retrieved, it is executed and it sets up an event listener to listen for the DOMContentLoaded event.

The DOMContentLoaded event is fired when the HTML document has been completed loaded and parsed.

When the event is detected, Angular looks for the ng-app directive and creates the several necessary components it needs to run (i.e., the $injector, the $compile service, and the $rootScope), then it starts parsing the DOM tree.

Compilation Phase

The $compile service traverses the DOM and collects all of the directives that it finds. It then combines all of their linking functions into a single linking function.

This *linking* function is then used to link the compiled template to the $rootScope (the scope attached to the ng-app DOM element).

It *finds* the directives in the DOM by looking through the attributes, comments, classes, and the DOM element name.

```
<span my-directive></span>
<span class="my-directive"></span>
<my-directive></my-directive>
<!-- directive: my-directive -->
```

 For more in-depth directive coverage, check out the directives chapter.

The $compile service walks the DOM tree looking for DOM elements with *directives* declared on them. When it encounters a DOM element with one or more directives, it orders the directives (based upon their priority), then uses the $injector service to find and collect the directive's compile function and execute it.

The compile function in directives is the appropriate time to do any DOM transformations or inline templating, as it creates a *clone* of the template.

```
// Returns a linking function
var linkFunction = $compile(appElement);
// Calls the linking function, attaching
// the $rootScope to the domElement
linkFunction($rootScope);
```

After the compile method runs, per node, the $compile service calls the linking functions. The linking functions set up watches on the directives that are bound to the enclosing scopes. This action creates the *live-view*.

Finally, after the $compile service is complete, the AngularJS run time is ready to go.

Run time

In a normal browser flow, the event loop waits for events (like the mouse moving, clicking, a keypress, etc). As these events occur, they are placed on the browser's event queue. If any function handlers are set to react to the event, they are are called with the event as a parameter.

```
ele.addEventListener('click', function(event) {});
```

The event loop is augmented a bit with Angular, as Angular provides its own event loop. Directives themselves register event listeners so that when events are fired, the directive function is run in AngularJS $digest loop.

 The Angular event loop is called the $digest loop. The $digest loop is composed of two small loops: the evalAsync loop and the $watch list.

When the event is fired, it is called within the context of the directive, which is in the AngularJS context. Functionally, AngularJS calls the directive within an $apply() method on the containing scope. Angular kicks off this entire process when it starts its $digest cycle on the $rootScope, propagating to all of the child scopes.

When Angular falls into the $digest loop, it waits for the $evalAsync queue to empty before it hands the callback execution context back to the browser. The $evalAsync is used to schedule any work that needs to be run outside of the current stack frame, but before the browser renders.

Additionally, the $digest loop waits for the for the $watch expression list, an array of potential expressions that *may* change during the previous iteration. *If* a change is detected, then the $watch function is called, and the $watch list is run over again to ensure that nothing has changed.

Note that for any changes detected in the $watch list, AngularJS runs through the list again to ensure that nothing has changed.

Once the $digest loop settles down and no potential changes are detected, the execution leaves the Angular context and passes normally back to the browser, where the DOM will be rendered.

This entire flow happens between every browser event, which is why Angular can be so powerful. It is also possible to inject events from the browser into the AngularJS flow.

Essential AngularJS Extensions

One of the most popular and highly supported AngularJS plugins is the the AngularUI framework.

AngularUI

AngularJS itself is packed full of out-of-the-box features that we can use to build an expressive AngularJS app without relying on separate libraries; however, the **very active** AngularJS community has built some great libraries that we can take advantage of to maximize the power of our apps.

In this section, we're covering several different and most commonly used components of the AngularUI[109] library.

The AngularUI library has been broken out into several modules so that, rather than including the entire suite, we can pick and choose the components that we're interested in using.

As we walk through the different components, we'll need to ensure that we install each of the different components with which we are going to work.

Installation

For each component, we can either download the individual JavaScript library and place it in our application path *or* we can use Bower[110] to complete our installation. We at ng-newsletter.com[111] recommend using Bower. For the purposes of this chapter, we'll cover installing each module only with Bower.

ui-router

One of the most useful libraries that the AngularUI library gives us is the `ui-router`. It's a routing framework that allows us to organize our interface by a state machine, rather than a simple URL route.

---

[109]http://angular-ui.github.io/

[110]http://bower.io/

[111]http://ng-newsletter.com

Installation

To install the ui-router library, we can either download the release[112] or use Bower to install the library.

Make sure you have Bower installed globally:

```
$ npm install bower -g
```

Use Bower to install the angular-ui library:

```
$ bower install angular-ui-router --save
```

We'll need to make sure we link the library to our view:

```
<script type="text/javascript"
  src="app/bower_components/angular-ui-router/release/angular-ui-router.js">
</script>
```

And we'll need to inject the ui.router as a dependency in our app:

```
angular.module('myApp', ['ui.router'])
```

Now, unlike the built-in ngRoute service, the ui-router can nest views as it works based off states, rather than simply a url.

Instead of using the ng-view directive as we do with the ngRoute service, we'll use the ui-view directive with ngRoute.

When dealing with routes and states inside of ui-router, we're mainly concerned with in which state the application and at which route the web app currently stands.

```
<div ng-controller="DemoController">
  <div ui-view></div>
</div>
```

Just like ngRoute, the templates we define at any given state are placed inside of the <div ui-view></div> element. Each of these templates can include its own ui-view, as well. This fact allows us to have *nested* views inside our routes.

To define a route, we use the .config method, just like normal, but instead of setting our routes on $routeProvider, we set our *states* on the $stateProvider.

---

[112]http://angular-ui.github.io/ui-router/release/angular-ui-router.js

```
.config(function($stateProvider, $urlRouterProvider) {
  $stateProvider
    .state('start', {
      url: '/start',
      templateUrl: 'partials/start.html'
    })
});
```

This step assigns the *state* named start to the state configuration object. The state configuration object, or the stateConfig, has similar options to the route configuration object, which gives us the ability to configure the states of our application.

template, templateUrl, templateProvider

These are the three ways to set up templates on each of the views:

- template - a string of HTML content or a function that returns HTML
- templateUrl - a string URL path to a template or a function that returns a URL path string
- templateProvider - a function that returns an HTML content string

For instance:

```
$stateProvider.state('home', {
  template: '<h1>Hello {{ name }}</h1>'
});
```

controller

Just like in ngRoute, we can either associate an already-registered controller with a URL (via a string) or we can create a controller function that operates as the controller for the state.

If there is no template defined (in one of the previous options), the controller will **not** be created.

resolve

We can resolve a list of dependencies that we will inject into our controller using the resolve functionality. In ngRoute, the resolve option allows us to resolve promises before the route is actually rendered. Inside angular-route, we have a bit more freedom as to how we can use this option.

The resolve option takes an object where the keys are the names of the dependencies to inject into the controller and the values are the factories that are to be resolved.

If a string is passed, then angular-route tries to match an existing registered service. If a function is passed, the function is injected, and the return value of the function is the dependency. If the function returns a promise, it is resolved *before* the controller is instantiated and the value (just like ngRoute) is injected into the controller.

```
$stateProvider.state('home', {
  resolve: {
    // This will return immediately as the
    // result is not a promise
    person: function() {
      return {
        name: "Ari",
        email: "ari@fullstack.io"
      }
    },
    // This function returns a promise, therefore
    // it will be resolved before the controller
    // is instantiated
    currentDetails: function($http) {
      return $http({
        method: 'JSONP',
        url: '/current_details'
      });
    },
    // We can use the resulting promise in another
    // resolution
    facebookId: function($http, currentDetails) {
      $http({
        method: 'GET',
        url: 'http://facebook.com/api/current_user',
        params: {
          email: currentDetails.data.emails[0]
        }
      })
    }
  },
  controller: function($scope, person,
                currentDetails, facebookId) {
    $scope.person = person;
  }
})
```

url

The url option assigns a unique URL for the state of the application. The url options gives us the same features of deep linking, while navigating around the app by state, rather than simply by URL.

This option is similar to the ngRoute URL, but can be considered a major upgrade, as we'll see in a moment.

The basic route can be specified like so:

```
$stateProvider
  .state('inbox', {
    url: '/inbox',
    template: '<h1>Welcome to your inbox</h1>'
  });
```

When the user navigates to /inbox, the app transitions into the inbox state, and we fill the main ui-view directive with the contents of the template (<h1>Welcome to your inbox</h1>).

The URL can take several different options and we can set the basic parameters in the url like in ngRoute:

```
$stateProvider
  .state('inbox', {
    url: '/inbox/:inboxId',
    template: '<h1>Welcome to your inbox</h1>',
    controller: function($scope, $stateParams) {
      $scope.inboxId = $stateParams.inboxId;
    }
  });
```

The app captures :inboxId as the second component in the URL. For instance, if the user transitions to /inbox/1, $stateParams.inboxId becomes 1 (as $stateParams will be {inboxId: 1}).

We can also use a different syntax if you prefer:

```
url: '/inbox/{inboxId}'
```

The path must match the URL exactly. Unlike ngRoute, if the user navigates to /inbox/, the above path *will* work; however, when navigating to /inbox the state will not be activated in the example configuration above.

The path also enables us to use regex inside of parameters so we can set a rule to match against our route. For instance:

```
// Match only inbox IDs that contain
// 6 hexidecimal digits
url: '/inbox/{inboxId:[0-9a-fA-F]{6}}',
// Or
// match every URL at the end of `/inbox`
// to `inboxId` (a catch-all)
url: '/inbox/{inboxId:.*}'
```

Note, we cannot use regex capture groups inside the route: The route resolver will not be able to resolve the route.

We can even specify query parameters in our route:

```
// will match a route such as
// /inbox?sort=ascending
url: '/inbox?sort'
```

Nested Routing

We can use the `url` parameter to use appended routes to provide for nested routes. This option enables us to support having multiple `ui-views` inside our page and our templates. For instance, we can nest individual routes inside of our `/inbox` route above.

```
$stateProvider
  .state('inbox', {
    url: '/inbox/:inboxId',
    template: '<div><h1>Welcome to your inbox</h1>\
              <a ui-sref="inbox.priority">Show priority</a>\
              <div ui-view></div>\
              </div>',
    controller: function($scope, $stateParams) {
      $scope.inboxId = $stateParams.inboxId;
    }
  })
  .state('inbox.priority', {
    url: '/priority',
    template: '<h2>Your priority inbox</h2>'
  });
```

Our first route matches as we expect (see above). We now have a second route, a child route that matches underneath the parent `inbox` route (because we specified it as a child using the `.` syntax).

- `/inbox/1` matches the first state
- `/inbox/1/priority` matches the second state.

With this syntax, we can support a nested URL inside of the parent route. The `ui-view` inside of the parent view resolves to the `priority` inbox.

params

The params option is an array of parameter names or regexes. We **cannot** combine this option with the `url` option. When the state becomes active, these parameters will be populated in the `$stateParams` service.

views

Our ability to set multiple *named* views inside of a state is a particularly powerful feature of `ui-router`. Inside of a single view, we can define multiple views that we reference inside of a single template.

> If we set the `views` parameter, then the state's `templateUrl`, `template`, and `templateProvider` are ignored. If we want to include a parent template in our routes, we need to create an abstract template that contains an abstract template.

Let's say we have a view that looks like:

```
<div>
  <div ui-view="filters"></div>
  <div ui-view="mailbox"></div>
  <div ui-view="priority"></div>
</div>
```

We can now create *named* views that fill each of these individual templates. Each of the subviews can contain its own templates, controllers, and resolve data using the `resolve` keyword.

```
$stateProvider
  .state('inbox', {
    views: {
      'filters': {
        template: '<h4>Filter inbox</h4>',
        controller: function($scope) {}
      },
      'mailbox': {
        templateUrl: 'partials/mailbox.html'
      },
      'priority': {
        template: '<h4>Priority inbox</h4>',
        resolve: {
          facebook: function() {
            return FB.messages();
          }
        }
      }
    }
  });
```

abstract

An abstract template can never be directly activated, but can set up descendants that are activated.

We can use an abstract template to provide a template wrapper around multiple named views, or to pass $scope objects to descendant children. We can use them to pass around resolved dependencies or custom data or simply to nest several routes under the same 'url' (e.g., have all routes under the /admin URL).

Setting up an abstract template is just like setting up a regular state, except that we set the abstract property:

```
$stateProvider
  .state('admin', {
    abstract: true,
    url: '/admin',
    template: '<div ui-view></div>'
  })
  .state('admin.index', {
    url: '/index',
    template: '<h3>Admin index</h3>'
  })
  .state('admin.users', {
```

```
  url: '/users',
  template: '<ul>...</ul>'
});
```

onEnter, onExit

Angular calls these callbacks when we are transitioning into or out of views (respectively). For both options, we can set a function we want to call. These functions have access to the resolved data.

These callbacks give us the ability to trigger an action on a new view or before we head out to another state. Using them is a good way to launch an "Are you sure?" modal view or request that a user log in before he or she heads into this state.

data

We can attach arbitrary data to our state configObject. This option is similar to the resolve property, except that this data will **not** be injected into the controller, nor will promises be resolved.

This option can be particularly useful when passing data to child states from a parent state.

Events!

Like the ngRoute service, the angular-route service fires events at different times during the state lifecycle.

We can attach functions to these events inside of our application by listening on the $scope. All of the following events are fired on the $rootScope, so we can listen to these events on any of our $scope objects.

State Change Events

We can listen to the events as follows:

```
$scope.$on('$stateChangeStart',
function(evt, toState, toParams, fromState, fromParams), {
  // We can prevent this state from completing
  evt.preventDefault();
});
```

The events that may be fired are as follows:

$stateChangeStart This event is fired when the transition from one state to another **begins**.

$stateChangeSuccess   This event is fired when the transition from one state to the next is **completed.**

$stateChangeError   This event is fired when an error occurs during the transition. It is usually caused by either a template that cannot be resolved or a resolve promise failing to resolve.

View Load Events

The ui-router provides events at the view loading stage.

$viewContentLoading   This event is fired when the view begins loading and before the DOM is rendered.

We can listen to this event like so:

```
$scope.$on('$viewContentLoading',
function(event, viewConfig){
    // Access to all the view config properties.
    // and one special property 'targetView'
    // viewConfig.targetView
});
```

$viewContentLoaded   This event is fired after the view has been loaded and after the DOM is rendered.

$stateParams

Above, we used the $stateParams to pick out the different params options from the URL parameters. The service is how we'll handle data from different components of our URL.

For instance, if we have a URL in our inbox state that looks like:

```
url: '/inbox/:inboxId/messages/{sorted}?from&to'
```

And our user finds their way to the route:

```
/inbox/123/messages/ascending?from=10&to=20
```

Then our $stateParams object results in:

```
{inboxId: '123', sorted: 'ascending', from: 10, to: 20}
```

$urlRouterProvider

Just like ngRoute, we have access to a route provider with which we can build rules around what happens when a particular URL is activated.

The states that we create are responsible for handling activating themselves at different URLs, so the $urlRouterProvider is not necessary to manage activating and loading states. It does come in handy when we want to manage events that happen outside of the scope of our states, such as with redirection or authentication.

We can use the $urlRouterProvider in our module's config function.

when() The when function takes two parameters: the incoming path that we want to match and the path that we want to redirect to (or a function that is invoked when the path is matched).

To set up redirection, we need to set the when method to take a string.

For instance, if we want to redirect an empty route to our /inbox route:

```
.config(function($urlRouterProvider) {
  $urlRouterProvider.when('', '/inbox');
});
```

If we pass a function, it will be invoked when the path has matched. The handler can return one of three values:

- **falsy** - This value tells the $urlRouter that the rule didn't match, and it should try finding a different state that does match. It can be useful if we want to ensure a user has valid access to a URL.
- **a string** - The $urlRouter will treat a string value as a redirect URL.
- **truthy or undefined** - This value lets the $urlRouter know that we've handled the URL.

otherwise() Just like the otherwise() method in ngRoute, the otherwise() method here redirects a user if no other routes are matched. This method is a good way to create a *default* URL, for instance.

The otherwise() method takes a single parameter: either a string or a function.

If we pass in a string, any invalid or unmatched routes will be redirected to the string as a specified URL.

If we pass in a function, it will be invoked if no other route is matched, and we'll be responsible for handling the return.

```
.config(function($urlRouterProvider) {
  $urlRouterProvider.otherwise('/');
  // or
  $urlRouterProvider.otherwise(
    function($injector, $location) {
      $location.path('/');
    });
});
```

rule() If we want to bypass any of the URL matching or want to do some route manipulation before other routes, we can use the rule() function.

We must return a valid path as a string when using the rule() function.

```
.config(function($urlRouterProvider){
  $urlRouterProvider.rule(
    function($injector, $location) {
      return '/index';
    });
})
```

Create a Wizard

Why does it matter if we use a new, more powerful router than the built-in ngRoute provider?

One useful case in which we might want to use ui-router is when we want to create a signup wizard for our users.

Using ui-router, we'll create a quick signup service with a single controller to handle the signup.

First, we need to create a view for the app:

```
<div ng-controller="WizardSignupController">
  <h2>Signup wizard</h2>
  <div ui-view></div>
</div>
```

Inside of this view, we house our signup views. Next, in our signup wizard, we need three stages:

- **start** - At this stage, we take the user's name and introduce him or her to our signup wizard.
- **email** - Here, we accept the user's email.
- **finish** - At this point, the user completes our signup process, and we show them a complete page.

In a *real* app, the **finish** stage would likely send the registration data back to a server and handle real registration. Here, we have no back end, so we'll just show the view.

Our signup process depends on the `wizardapp.controllers` module where we will write the containing controller: `WizardSignupController`.

```
angular.module('wizardApp', [
  'ui.router',
  'wizardapp.controllers'
]);
```

Our `WizardSignupController` simply houses the `$scope.user` object, which we carry with us through the signup process, as well as the signup action.

```
angular.module('wizardapp.controllers', [])
.controller('WizardSignupController',
  function($scope, $state) {
    $scope.user = {};
    $scope.signup = function() {}
});
```

The wizard process logic houses the majority of the work. We want to set up this logic in the `config()` function of our app:

```
angular.module('wizardApp', [
  'ui.router', 'wizardapp.controllers'
  ])
.config(function($stateProvider, $urlRouterProvider) {
  $stateProvider
    .state('start', {
      url: '/step_1',
      templateUrl: 'partials/wizard/step_1.html'
    })
    .state('email', {
      url: '/step_2',
      templateUrl: 'partials/wizard/step_2.html'
    })
    .state('finish', {
      url: '/finish',
      templateUrl: 'partials/wizard/step_3.html'
    });
});
```

With these options set up, we have our basic flow all done. Now, if the user navigates to the route /step_1, they'll be directed to the beginning of the flow. Although it might make sense for our entire flow to take place at the root URL (i.e., /step_1), we might want to house that in a sublocation (/wizard/step_1, for instance).

To do so, we set up an abstract state that will house the rest of our steps.

```
.config(function($stateProvider, $urlRouterProvider) {
  $stateProvider
    .state('wizard', {
      abstract: true,
      url: '/wizard',
      template: '<div><div ui-view></div></div>'
    })
    .state('wizard.start', {
      url: '/step_1',
      templateUrl: 'partials/wizard/step_1.html'
    })
    .state('wizard.email', {
      url: '/step_2',
      templateUrl: 'partials/wizard/step_2.html'
    })
    .state('wizard.finish', {
      url: '/finish',
      templateUrl: 'partials/wizard/step_3.html'
    });
});
```

Now, instead of having our routes at a top level, we can nest them safely inside our /wizard URL.

We also want to attach an action at the end of the signup process that calls the signup function on our parent controller WizardSignupController. We'll set a controller on the final step of the wizard process that calls the function on the $scope. Because our entire wizard is encapsulated in our WizardSignupController, we'll be able to use the nested scope property of scopes like normal.

```
.state('wizard.finish', {
  url: '/finish',
  templateUrl: 'partials/wizard/step_3.html',
  controller: function($scope) {
    $scope.signup();
  }
});
```

ui-utils

The UI Utils library is a powerful utility package that makes a lot of custom extensions available to your project without needing to reinvent the wheel.

Below, we present a few notable features that the ui-utils library gives us:

Installation

```
$ bower install --save angular-ui-utils
```

We need to ensure that we include the library in our HTML template. Each component of the ui-utils library is built as an individual module, so we need to include each one independently.

mask

When we want to take a credit card or a phone number (or any other input that requires a specific format), we can present a clean UI that tells our users they're giving us clean input.

We need to ensure we include the mask.js library in our HTML:

```
<script type="text/javascript"
  src="app/bower_components/angular-ui-utils/modules/mask/mask.js"></script>
```

and set the ui-mask as a dependency for our app:

```
angular.module('myApp', ['ui.mask'])
```

Now, we can specify input masks using the ui-mask directive. The ui-mask directive takes a single format string that follows these formatting rules:

- A - any letter
- 9 - any number
- * - any alphanumeric character.

For instance, to format a credit card number in an input, we might set the ui-mask directive to look like:

```
<input name="ccnum" ui-mask="9999 9999 9999 9999"
  ng-model="user.cc" placeholder="Credit card number" />
```

 The ui-mask is similar to how Angular input does not consider input valid until its validations are all satisfied.

Note that this input only supports credit cards for which the input mask matches 9999-9999-9999-9999. With a bit more work, we can support other card types.

In the same sense, we can format an input field with characters or any alphanumeric character.

ui-event

Just like the other modules, we need to include the event.js library in our HTML:

```
<script type="text/javascript"
  src="app/bower_components/angular-ui-utils/modules/event/event.js"></script>
```

and we need to include the ui.event as a dependency for our app:

```
angular.module('myApp', ['ui.event'])
```

The ui-event module is great to use when we want to handle events that are not natively supported by AngularJS. For instance, if we want the user to double click on an element or handle a blur event, we'd have to write a wrapper around the native browser event of double click. The ui-event module is simply a wrapper around native events, so we can use it to respond to any event that is fired by the browser on any element.

For instance, let's say we want to reveal an image after the user double-clicks on another image. We simply set the ui-event directive to a key-value pair populated with the event name and the action to take when the element catches the event.

For instance, in our HTML, we can set a double-click dblclick event to call a showImage() function on our controller:

```
<img src="/images/ui/ginger.png"
  ui-event="{dblclick:'showImage()'}" />
```

and in our controller, we can write our method on the scope like normal:

```
.controller('DemoController', function($scope) {
  $scope.showImage = function() {
    $scope.shouldshowImage = !$scope.shouldshowImage;
  }
});
```

Since the ui-event directive is simply a wrapper around native browser events, we can use it to mimic any browser event on any element.

For instance, if we want to capture a blur or focus event on an element, we can use the ui-event directive to capture it for us.

Let's say we want to provide some helpful tips for filling out a form. We can set actions on the focus event and the blur event to show and reveal these help tips.

For instance, if we have a form that includes *name* and *email* input fields, we can attach functions to our blur and focus events to show help events on those input fields.

```
<form name="form">
  <input type="text" name="name" placeholder="Your name"
    ui-event="{focus: 'showNameHelp=true',
            blur: 'showNameHelp=false'}"
    />
  <input type="email" name="email" placeholder="Your email"
    ui-event="{focus: 'showEmailHelp=true',
            blur: 'showEmailHelp=false'}"
    />
</form>
```

With these events set on the input fields, we can show our help fields depending on which field the user is focused on (using ng-show and ng-hide).

ui-format

We need to ensure that we include the format.js library in our HTML:

```
<script type="text/javascript"
    src="app/bower_components/angular-ui-utils/modules/format/format.js"></script>
```

and set ui.format as a dependency for our app:

```
angular.module('myApp', ['ui.format'])
```

The `format` library is a wrapper around different ways to handle working with string tokens. It enables us to work directly with tokens we expect in our app that are variable.

We can use this token replacement with the format library either with an array or a key-value/javascript object. For instance:

```
{{ "Hello $0" | format: 'Ari' }}
```

Alternatively, we can bind the name to a variable on our scope and use the `format` library to present it in a clean format. Let's say we have a controller that looks like:

```
angular.module('myApp', ['ui.format'])
.controller('FormatController', function($scope) {
  $scope.name = 'Ari';
});
```

We can format the input against that bound variable on the `$scope`:

Although this code isn't particularly interesting (and this functionality comes out of the box with Angular), it becomes more interesting when we want to manipulate text on a key-value basis.

For instance, we can format a string based on the keys of an object we have. Let's say we have an object with `name` and `email` attributes:

```
.controller('FormatController', function($scope) {
  $scope.person = {
    name: 'Ari',
    email: 'ari@fullstack.io'
  }
});
```

We can change our HTML to include object keys as `tokens` which allow us to transform our markup to match against the keys as tokens:

```
{{ "Hello :name. Your email is :email" | format: person }}
```

The `format` module is particularly useful when working with translations or `i18n` support (for more on translations, check out our translations chapter).

Mobile Apps

Mobile apps are **not** the *next frontier* for software developers – they're already here. There are already 1.2 billion mobile web app users, and that number is growing rapidly (Wikipedia[113]). Soon, the number of mobile devices will exceed the number of people on the planet. At the rate at which the number of mobile devices is growing, it's estimated that 5.1 billion people will be using mobile phones by 2017.

For us as app developers, it's important that we develop for mobile technology if we want to stay relevant. With AngularJS, we have some great support for mobile, written by both the Angular team and the community.

In this section, we're going to work through these two different ways to give our users a mobile experience for our app:

- Responsive web apps
- Native with Cordova

Responsive Web Apps

The easiest way to support mobile with Angular is by using the tools we already know and love – HTML and CSS– to create a mobile-ready Angular app. Since Angular apps are already based on HTML, making our designs and interaction responsive is only a matter of building the architecture that will support different devices.

Interaction

For the desktop, the ability to create interactions is already available to us through the ng-click and family directives.

Beginning with Angular version 1.2.0, we now have the ability to use touch events using the new ngTouch module. Since ngTouch is not built into the core Angular library, we need to install it.

---

[113]http://en.wikipedia.org/wiki/List_of_countries_by_number_of_mobile_phones_in_use

Installation

We can install ngTouch in any of several ways. The simplest way to install the ngTouch module is by downloading the source from angularjs.org[114].

Find the extras in the download section, then we can download and store the ng-touch.js file into an accessible location in our app.

Alternatively, we can use Bower to install angular-touch:

```
$ bower install angular-touch --save
```

Either way, we need to reference the library in our index.html as a script:

```
<script src="/bower_components/angular-touch/angular-touch.js"></script>
```

Finally, we need to include ngTouch as a dependency in our app:

```
angular.module('myApp', ['ngTouch']);
```

Now we're ready to take advantage of the ngTouch library.

ngTouch

Mobile browsers work slightly differently than desktop browsers when dealing with click events. Mobile browsers detect a *tap* event then wait about 300 ms to detect any other taps (i.e., they wait to find out if we're double-tapping the device). After this delay, the browser fires a click event.

This delay can make our apps feel incredibly unresponsive. Instead of dealing with the click event, we can detect touch events instead.

The ngTouch library seamlessly handles this functionality for us through the ng-click directive and takes care of calling the *correct* click event for us. This so-called fast click event will be called.

> After the *fast* click has been called, the browser's delayed click is called secondarily, causing a 'double' action. ngTouch takes care of removing this browser delay on ng-click events.

Using the ngClick directive on mobile devices works the exact same way on mobile browsers as it does on desktop browsers:

---

[114]http://angularjs.org/

```
<button ng-click="save()">Save</button>
```

ngTouch also introduces two new directives: *swipe* directives. These swipe directives allow us to capture user swipes, either left or right across the screen. These are useful for situations where we want the user to be able to swipe through a photo gallery photo or to a new portion of our app.

The ngSwipeLeft directive detects when an element is swiped from the right to the left, while the ngSwipeRight directive detects when an element is swiped from the left to the right.

> One of the nice features the ngSwipe* directives give us is that they work both with touch-based devices as well as with mouse clicking and dragging.

Using the ngSwipe* directives is easy. For instance, let's say we have a list of emails and we want to reveal actions for each email, like the popular mobile email client MailboxApp.

We can easily implement that functionality using these swipe directives on our list of elements. When we are showing our list of emails, we enable swiping in one direction to show the actions we can take on that particular mail item.

When we are showing actions for the mail item, we enabled swiping in the other direction to hide the actions we can take.

```
<ul>
  <li ng-repeat="mail in emails">
    <div
      ng-show="!mail.showActions"
      ng-swipe-left="mail.showActions=true">
      <div class="from">
        From: <span>{{ mail.from }}</span>
      </div>
      <div class="body">
        {{ mail.body }}
      </div>
    </div>
    <div
      ng-show="mail.showActions"
      ng-swipe-right="mail.showActions=false">
      <ul class="actions">
        <li><button>Archive</button></li>
        <li><button>Trash</button></li>
      </ul>
    </div>
  </li>
</ul>
```

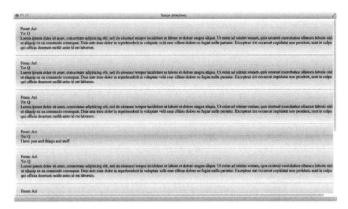

Swipe directives example

$swipe Service

For more *custom* touch-based animations, we can use the $swipe service directly. The $swipe service is a service that abstracts the details of hold-and-drag swiping behavior.

The $swipe service has a single method called bind(). This bind() method takes an element to which it binds the swipe actions as well as an object with four event handlers.

These event handlers are called with an object that contains the coordinates object, like so: { x: 200, y: 300 }.

The four events handlers handle the following events:

- start

The start event is fired on either a mousedown or a touchstart event. After this event, the $swipe service sets up watches for touchmove and mousemove events. These events are only fired until the **total** distance moved exceeds a small distance (to prevent accidental swipes).

Once this distance has been surpassed, one of two events happens:

- If the vertical delta is greater than the horizontal, the browser takes over as a scroll event.
- If the horizontal delta is greater than the vertical delta, the action is considered a swipe, and our move and end events are set to follow the swipe.
- move

The move event is called on mousemove and touchmove events only after the $swipe service has determined that a swipe is, in fact, in progress.

- end

The end event is fired when the touchend or a mouseup event has finished and after the move event has been fired.

- cancel

The cancel event is called on either a touchcancel or when we begin scrolling after the start event instead.

For instance, we can create a directive that enables swiping between slides that might control a projector screen. To handle swiping on the mobile control, we use the $swipe service to handle our custom logic for how to display the UI layer.

```
angular.module('myApp')
.directive('mySlideController', ['$swipe',
  function($swipe) {

    return {
      restrict: 'EA',
      link: function(scope, ele, attrs, ctrl) {
        var startX, pointX;

        $swipe.bind(ele, {
          'start': function(coords) {
            startX = coords.x;
            pointX = coords.y;
          },
          'move': function(coords) {
            var delta = coords.x - pointX;
            // ...
          },
          'end': function(coords) {
            // ...
          },
          'cancel': function(coords) {
            // ...
          }
        });
      }
    }
}]);
```

angular-gestures and Multi-Touch Gestures

`angular-gestures` is an Angular module that gives us the ability to handle multi-touch actions in our Angular apps. It is based on the very popular and well-tested Hammer.js[115] library.

The Hammer.js library gives us a bunch of events common to touchscreen events:

- Tap
- DoubleTap
- Swipe
- Drag
- Pinch
- Rotate

The `angular-gestures` library enables us to use these events using Angular directives. For instance, all of the following directives are available to us:

- hmDoubleTap : 'doubletap',
- hmDragStart : 'dragstart',
- hmDrag : 'drag',
- hmDragUp : 'dragup',
- hmDragDown : 'dragdown',
- hmDragLeft : 'dragleft',
- hmDragRight : 'dragright',
- hmDragEnd : 'dragend',
- hmHold : 'hold',
- hmPinch : 'pinch',
- hmPinchIn : 'pinchin',
- hmPinchOut : 'pinchout',
- hmRelease : 'release',
- hmRotate : 'rotate',
- hmSwipe : 'swipe',
- hmSwipeUp : 'swipeup',
- hmSwipeDown : 'swipedown',
- hmSwipeLeft : 'swipeleft',
- hmSwipeRight : 'swiperight',
- hmTap : 'tap',
- hmTouch : 'touch',
- hmTransformStart : 'transformstart',
- hmTransform : 'transform',
- hmTransformEnd : 'transformend'

---

[115]http://eightmedia.github.io/hammer.js/

angular-gestures Installation

To install the `angular-gestures` library in our app, we need to include the `gestures.js` (or `gestures.min.js`) library in our page.

We can either download the `gestures.js` files directly from the GitHub page[116] or we can use Bower to install it.

To install `angular-gestures` using Bower, we can install it with the following command:

```
$ bower install --save angular-gestures
```

Lastly, we need to set `angular-gestures` as a dependency for our Angular app:

```
angular.module('myApp', ['angular-gestures']);
```

Using angular-gestures

From here, Angular gestures are really easy to use. Gestures are just Angular directives, so we use them the same way we use any other directives in our app.

Let's say we want to allow users to rotate, pinch, and zoom photos in a photo gallery. We can use the Hammer.js library to handle this functionality for us.

In this example, we'll set a *random* translation on the element only for *double taps*. To do that, we need to set up our HTML using the `hm-tap` directive.

```html
<div id="photowrapper">
  <div class="cardProps"
       hm-tap="tapped($event)">
    <div class="tradingcard">
      <img src="/img/ari.jpeg" alt="" />
      <span>Ari</span>
    </div>
    <div class="tradingcard">
      <img src="/img/nate.jpeg" alt="" />
      <span>Nate</span>
    </div>
  </div>
</div>
```

There is nothing incredibly special about this HTML other than the fact that we have a directive called `hm-tap`. This `angular-gestures` directive handles what happens when someone taps the image.

---

[116]https://github.com/wzr1337/angular-gestures

Hammer.js directives can take Angular expressions – so we can call functions on or run actions inside of them (like ng-click, for example) – and Hammer.js options.

In the example above, we're calling a function that we'll define on our $scope as tapped(). We've defined this function as:

```
$scope.tapped = function($event) {
  var ele = $event.target;
  var x = Math.floor(Math.random() * 200) + 1,
      y = Math.floor(Math.random() * 100) + 1,
      z = Math.floor(Math.random() * 6) + 1,
      rot = Math.floor(Math.random()*360)+1;
  $(ele).css({
    'transform':
      "translate3d("+x+"px,"+y+"px,"+z+"px)" +
      "rotate("+rot+"deg)"
  });
}
```

The angular-gestures library gives us access to the event through a special argument called $event. We'll use the event's target ($event.target) to determine which element our user clicks on and then we can go crazy and do all sorts of neat tricks with the element.

Native Applications with Cordova

Cordova is a free, open-source framework that allows us to create mobile apps using standard web APIs instead of native code. It enables us to write mobile applications using HTML, JavaScript, CSS, and AngularJS instead of needing to write Objective-C or Java (for iOS or Android, respectively).

Cordova

Cordova exposes native device access through JavaScript APIs that allow us to run device-specific operations, such as getting the native location or using the camera. Cordova is designed natively with plugin architecture, so we can take advantage of Cordova community-built plugins, such as native audio access or barcode scanning plugins.

One of the benefits of using Cordova is that we can reuse our Angular app code to support the mobile environment. Of course, there are a few issues that we'll deal with, such as performance and native component access.

Installation

Cordova itself is distributed as an npm package, so we can use npm to install it.

> If you don't yet have npm installed, first make sure you install node. For information on installing NodeJS, read the Next Steps chapter.

```
$ npm install -g cordova
```

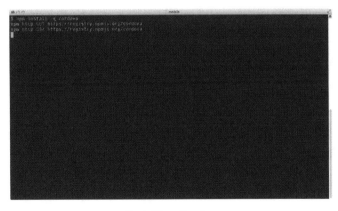

Installing Cordova

The Cordova package includes a generator that will create our app and make it Cordova-ready.

Getting Started with Cordova

Getting started with Cordova is simple. We use the generator to create the starting point of our Cordova app. Let's call the app GapApp.

The generator takes up to three parameters:

- project-directory (required)

The directory where we'll create the app

- package-id

The ID of the project (the package name in reverse-domain style)

- name

The package name (name of the application)

```
$ cordova create gapapp io.fullstack.gapapp "GapApp"
```

This line sets up a directory called gapapp (identified by the first parameter) with a package ID io.fullstack.gapapp and the project name GappApp.

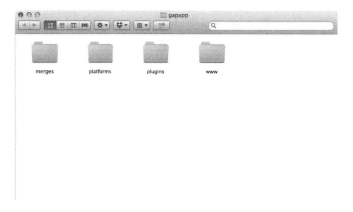

Cordova file structure

The Cordova team has broken Cordova into plugins so that we don't need to include any platforms we won't be building for; this breakdown makes it easier to develop support for other platforms. That means that we need to add to our project any platforms for which we're interested in developing.

For this project, we can assume the rest of these commands are run from *inside* the project directory:

```
$ cd gapapp/
```

We'll be building for iOS (although the process is the same for other platforms). To add iOS as a platform, simply add it to the project using the following Cordova command:

```
$ cordova platform add ios
```

> For this command to work, we need to ensure that we have the iOS SDK installed using XCode. Download the iOS SDK and XCode at developer.apple.com[117].

Once you have that set, build the basic app:

---

[117]https://developer.apple.com/

```
$ cordova build ios
```

Now, due to some intricacies with Apple's developer tools, we will have to build the app ourselves to get it to run on our local iOS simulator.

Let's navigate to our app directory, where we'll find the platforms directory. Inside of it, we'll find the io/ directory that was created for us by the platform add command above.

Generated project

In XCode, open the project that we created with said command. Make sure the simulator is shown in the platform identifier at the top of XCode.

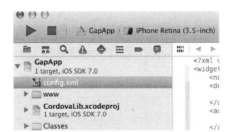

Build in XCode

Click run.

Once you have done so, we should see the basic Cordova app start to run in our simulator.

Barebones Cordova app

Development Workflow with Cordova

Cordova powers the PhoneGap project, which has been accepted into the Apache Foundation. The project itself includes a command-line tool that we'll use to interact with our native app, from creation to deployment.

Platforms

At this point, we've created our app and added a platform (in this case, iOS).

> Available platforms for the Cordova app vary depending on which development environment we're using. On a Mac, the available platforms are:

- iOS
- Android
- Blackberry10
- Firefox OS

For a Windows machine, we can develop for the following platforms:

- Android
- Windows Phone 7
- Windows Phone 8
- Windows8
- Blackberry10
- Firefox OS

If we forget which platforms are available, we can run the platforms command to check which are available and installed:

```
$ cordova platforms ls
```

To add a platform, we can use the `platform add` command (as we've done above):

```
$ cordova platform add android
```

To remove one, we can use the `rm` or `remove` command:

```
$ cordova platform rm blackberry10
```

Plugins

Cordova is built to be incredibly modular, with the expectation that we will install all of the non-core components with the plugin system. To add a plugin to our project, we'll use the `plugin add` command:

```
$ cordova plugin add\
  https://git-wip-us.apache.org/repos/asf/cordova-plugin-geolocation.git
```

We can list the current plugins that we have installed using the `plugins ls` command:

```
$ cordova plugins ls
[ 'org.apache.cordova.geolocation' ]
```

Finally, we can remove a plugin using the `plugin rm` command:

```
$ cordova plugins rm org.apache.cordova.geolocation
```

Building

By default, Cordova creates a skeleton project that houses the web-view files in the www/ directory in the project directory. When Cordova builds the project, it copies these files and places them in their platform-specific directories.

To build the app, we use another Cordova command, the `build` command:

```
$ cordova build
```

Without specifying any platform to build for, this command will build for all of the platforms we've listed in our project.

We can limit the scope by building only for specific platforms, such as:

```
$ cordova build ios
$ cordova build android
```

> The `build` command ensures that the necessary platform-specific code is set so our app can be compiled. In effect, we're doing the same thing as calling `cordova prepare && cordova compile`.

Emulating and Running

Cordova also makes it possible to run an emulator to simulate running the app on a device. Doing so is, of course, only possible if an emulator is installed and set up on our local development environment.

Assuming our emulator is set up in our development environment, we can tell Cordova to launch and install the app in our emulator:

```
$ cordova emulate ios
```

> For iOS, we may have to build the project (as we did above) using XCode if the emulator environment is not set up on our machine.

It's also possible to run the application on a particular device by using the `run` command instead. The `run` command launches the application on a device or on the emulator if no device is found and available.

```
$ cordova run ios
```

In Development

It can be cumbersome to make a change to one part of our app and then recompile the app to see the changes reflected therein. To help expedite the process of developing the web app side of the app, we can use the `serve` command to serve a local version of our `www/` folder to a web browser.

```
$ cordova serve ios
Static file server running at
  => http://0.0.0.0:8000/
CTRL + C to shutdown
```

Now, we can use our web browser and navigate to the URL:

`http://localhost:8000/ios/www/index.html`.

Our app's `www/` folder is being served through HTTP, so we can build it and watch it change as we make changes to the app.

When we make changes, we need to make sure we rebuild the app:

```
$ cordova build ios
```

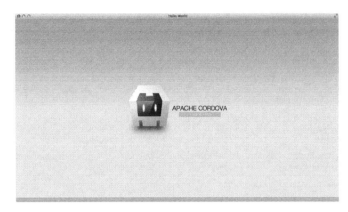

Building using Safari

Angular Cordova Service

When our Cordova app is ready, the device has connected, and everything is ready to go, Cordova fires the browser event called deviceready.

With Angular, we can either bootstrap the app *after* this event has been fired or we can use promises to handle our logic after the deviceready event has been fired.

To bootstrap the app after we've received the deviceready event, we need to set an event listener for the event and then manually call bootstrap on our app:

```
angular.module('myApp', []);

var onDeviceReady = function() {
    angular.bootstrap( document, ['myApp']);
}
document.addEventListener('deviceready',
onDeviceReady);
```

We prefer to use an alternative method of listening for the deviceready event that uses promises to set up execution bindings for after the deviceready event has been fired.

We set up an Angular module that listens for the deviceready event. We can also use a service that listens for the deviceready event and resolves our promises depending on whether the event has been fired.

```
angular.module('fsCordova', [])
.service('CordovaService', ['$document', '$q',
  function($document, $q) {

    var d = $q.defer(),
        resolved = false;

    var self = this;
    this.ready = d.promise;

    document.addEventListener('deviceready', function() {
      resolved = true;
      d.resolve(window.cordova);
    });

    // Check to make sure we didn't miss the
    // event (just in case)
    setTimeout(function() {
      if (!resolved) {
        if (window.cordova) d.resolve(window.cordova);
      }
    }, 3000);
}]);
```

Now, we set the fsCordova as a dependency for our module:

```
angular.module('myApp', ['fsCordova'])
// ...
```

We can use the CordovaService to determine if Cordova is, in fact, ready, and we can set our logic to depend upon the service being ready:

```
angular.module('myApp', ['fsCordova'])
.controller('MyController',
  function($scope, CordovaService) {
    CordovaService.ready.then(function() {
      // Cordova is ready
    });
});
```

Including Angular

With the bare Cordova app, we only have a bare JavaScript app that hides and displays the JavaScript view in `js/index.js`.

We can introduce Angular into the workflow very simply. As we are building a native app, including Angular from a CDN is not ideal; instead, we'll include the necessary components directly into the app.

We can use Bower for more complex setups, but for the time being, we'll keep it simple.

To get our Angular app building, we need to download Angular from angularjs.org[118] and store it in a directory accessible by our `index.html`. We recommend `www/js/vendor/angular.js`.

Once that's set, we can start building our Angular app. We need to include the JavaScript file in our `www/index.html`.

```
<script type="text/javascript" src="js/vendor/angular.js"></script>
```

Now we can replace all of the contents of the `js/index.js` file with our Angular app and develop our app like normal.

Development Workflow

When building our app, we'll use the following workflow:

- Start our local server (Cordova serve [platform])
- Edit our app
- Rebuild our app (Cordova build [platform])

This flow, although somewhat cumbersome, is how we'll edit our app.

If our app doesn't rely on the Cordova platform, we can edit outside of the simulator and in our web browser. In this case, we can work specifically with building our app, instead of needing to rebuild and redeploy the app.

Building with Yeoman

We can use Yeoman[119] to build a production-ready version of our app. Yeoman is a collection of build scripts that is the officially supported build process for Angular apps. For more information on Yeoman, check out the Yeoman section in the Next Steps chapter.

To install Yeoman, the Angular generator, and the Cordova generator:

---

[118]http://angularjs.org/
[119]http://yeoman.io

```
$ npm install -g yo
$ npm install -g generator-angular
$ npm install -g cordova
```

In order to get Yeoman working with Cordova, we'll need to make a few adjustments to the flow we describe above.

First, we want to create a Cordova app like normal.

```
$ cordova create gapapp io.fullstack.gapapp "GapApp"
```

This line creates the folder gapapp/ in our local directory like normal.

Generating our app

Next, let's change into the directory and add our platform:

```
$ cd gapapp/
$ cordova platform add ios
```

This step creates a platform folder that we'll work with in a minute to get the actual gapapp working locally in both our emulator and our device.

The first thing that we need to do is set up our Yeoman app in our directory and make a few minor changes to the default configuration:

```
$ yo angular
```

We'll go through the normal Yeoman questions to let the process complete and build our directory like normal.

When this process is done, we will have our Yeoman app in the app/ directory. This location is where we'll do all of our work when it comes to building our mobile app.

In our toolchain, we'll use the following workflow to build our app:

- Write code
- Test our code (Angular testing)
- Run our code in the emulator (optional)
- Test our code on a running device (optional)

The Yeoman build tool takes care of the first two tasks. The second two are the tasks that we'll build now.

Cordova works by including the www/ directory into the compiled apps, so any modifications we make to the files in the www/ directory will be wrapped into the compiled application after we build it.

Modifying Yeoman to Work with Cordova

Yeoman assumes a different structure by default where it builds our application into a folder called dist/. We'll modify this build directory to build into the www/ directory.

First, we must save the www/config.xml file that the Cordova creat command built. We want to copy or move this file from the www/ into the app/ directory:

```
$ cp www/config.xml app/
```

Now, we want to copy this config.xml file back over to our www/ directory when Yeoman builds it.

To change the default directory in which Yeoman builds our app, we find the Yeoman section in our Gruntfile.js and change the dist: key from dist to www:

```
// ...
grunt.initConfig({
  yeoman: {
    app: require('./bower.json').appPath || 'app',
    dist: 'www' // <~ Change this to www
  },
  watch: {
    // ...
```

Next, we need to tell Yeoman to include the config.xml file in the list of files it copies over. Luckily, this process is incredibly easy: We only need to add a single string to the list of paths in the copy task.

Inside the copy:dist configuration, add the extension xml to the glob string that lists the files to copy over:

```
  // ...
},
copy: {
  dist: {
    files: [{
      expand: true,
      dot: true,
      cwd: '<%= yeoman.app %>',
      dest: '<%= yeoman.dist %>',
      src: [
        '*.{ico,png,txt,xml}', // <~ Add xml
        '.htaccess',
        // ...
```

With these two commands in place, we can now build our app with Yeoman, which will build our application inside the app/ directory as well as the www/ directory.

```
$ grunt build
```

This command sets up our basic app to work with Yeoman, but not with any of the dev tools we want to use to actually build our mobile app.

Fixing the Yeoman Build

Note that when we're developing our applications, we cannot fetch remote resources from a CDN. The default Yeoman build sets up our scripts to load from the Google CDN. Therefore, we must modify the index.html template slightly so that we don't load jquery and angular from the CDN by surrounding the script tags inside a usemin build script, like so:

```
<!--
  Add the following line and the endbuild line
  after the script tags
-->
<!-- build:js scripts/library.js -->
<script src="bower_components/jquery/jquery.js"></script>
<script src="bower_components/angular/angular.js"></script>
<!-- endbuild -->
```

Building the Mobile Part

To build our mobile app with our Yeoman tools, we can add a few more task definitions to Grunt to make the processes of building, testing, and deploying to our devices a breeze.

Cordova has two different binaries to build our app: a local builder inside the `platforms/` directory (to actually compile the native application) and a global binary (to build our application from the root directory created by the Cordova create command).

To build our application *normally*, we can simply run the Cordova build command from the root directory. Cordova will handle copying the `www/` directory into the appropriate location for the different platforms.

```
$ cordova build
```

We can create a task to do the same for us so we can simply use `grunt` like normal. To support this, we need to install a Grunt library called `grunt-shell`. We can use `npm` to handle installing this library for us:

```
$ npm install --save-dev grunt-shell
```

Next, we need to define our configuration for the shell commands. We're going to create two commands: one to emulate our app on our computer's mobile device simulator and one to deploy to our actual device.

```
uglify: {
  // ...
},
shell: {
  build: {
    command: 'cordova build'
  },
  emulate: {
    command: 'cordova build'
  }
}
// ...
```

These commands are very similar right now, as in both commands we want to tell Cordova to actually build the application first.

Next, we need to use the *local* Cordova command to emulate or run our application. The *local* Cordova command can be found in our location platforms path for each type of platform.

For instance, we have a local `emulate` command in the iOS directory because we've added the iOS platform in `platforms/ios/cordova/emulate`. If we add an Android platform, we'll find the Cordova command inside the Android platform directory at `platforms/android/cordova/emulate`.

We want to build a helper function to help us find these local Cordova commands. At the top of the Gruntfile, let's add the following command:

```
module.exports = function (grunt) {
  var path = require('path'),
      cordova = require('cordova');

  var cordova_cmd = function(cmd) {
    var target = grunt.option('target') || "ios";
    return path.join(
        __dirname, "platforms",
        target, "cordova", cmd);
  }
```

Now we can use the `cordova_cmd()` function to find these local Cordova commands. With these local commands we can modify our shell tasks from above to include these custom tasks:

```
shell: {
  build: {
    command: 'cordova build && ' +
      cordova_cmd('emulate')
  },
  run: {
    command: 'cordova build &&' +
      cordova_cmd("run")
  }
}
```

We can use these commands simply by running them directly in the shell to test them out:

```
$ grunt shell:build
```

 Depending upon the platform we're developing with, we may need to install dependencies. For instance, with `ios`, we need to make sure we have `ios-sim` installed. Check the official Cordova docs[120] for information on dependencies for your platform.

---

[120]http://docs.phonegap.com/en/3.1.0/index.html

These commands are semi-useless without being wrapped into another command that *actually* builds the app from our app/ directory into the www/ directory.

Grunt makes this process easy: We can simply register a new task that runs of multiple Grunt tasks. In this case, we can simply wrap our build and run commands into a new task that calls build first:

```
    // task configuration above here
  }
});
// ...
grunt.registerTask('devemulate', [
  'build',
  'shell:build',
]);

grunt.registerTask('devrun', [
  'build',
  'shell:run'
]);

grunt.registerTask('server', function (target) {
  // ...
```

This code makes the devemulate command available to us: We can use it to run our app in a simulator environment and on our device.

```
$ grunt devemulate
```

 Note, if the command is not working as expected, using the --verbose flag with grunt will often reveal issues, such as missing dependencies.

We can also use the devrun task to run the application on a mobile device that is set up to accept development applications:

```
$ grunt devrun
```

Handling the Navigator

Lastly, the Cordova platform uses the deviceready event, fired on the DOM, to indicate that the device itself is ready for action. We run into a timing issue between the time that the Cordova app is ready to go and before our Angular app has bootstrapped. We can get around this issue by creating a service that captures the deviceready event and resolves to a variable on the outset with which we can work. The service is very simple:

```
angular.module('gapappApp.services')
.factory('Cordova', function($q) {
  var d = $q.defer();
  if (window.navigator) {
    d.resolve(window.navigator);
  } else {
    document
      .addEventListener('deviceready', function(evt) {
        d.resolve(navigator);
      });
  }
  return {
    navigator: function() {
      return d.promise;
    }
  }
})
```

Now, when we want to use Cordova's navigator, we just use the following syntax, which will resolve once the device is ready:

```
angular.module('gapappApp')
  .controller('MainController',
  function($scope, Cordova) {
    Cordova.navigator().then(function(navigator) {
      navigator.notification.vibrate();
    });
  });
```

Localization

As worldwide access to the web increases, we as developers are constantly pressed to make our apps internationally and locally accessible. When a user visits our apps, he or she should be able to switch languages on the fly at run time.

Given that we are building AngularJS client-side apps, we don't particularly want the user to have to refresh the page or visit an entirely different URL. Of course, AngularJS could easily accommodate your international audience natively, perhaps by generating different templates for different languages and serving those within the app.

This process can become cumbersome, however, and what happens when you want to change the layout of the app? Every single template needs to be rebuilt and redeployed. This process should just be *easy*.

angular-translate

Instead of creating new templates, we can use `angular-translate`, an AngularJS module that brings i18n (internationalization) to your Angular app. `angularjs-translate` requires us to create a JSON file that represents translation data per language. It lazy loads the language-specific translation data from the server only when necessary.

The `angular-translate` library comes with built-in directives and filters that make it simple to internationalize our apps. Let's get started.

Installation

To use angular-translate, we need to load the library. We can install it in several different ways, but we prefer using Bower.

Bower is a front-end package manager. It handles not only JavaScript libraries, but also HTML, CSS, and image packages. A package is simply encapsulated, third-party code that is typically publicly accessible in a repository.

- Using Bower

We install angular-translate using the normal Bower process:

```
$ bower install angular-translate
```

Alternatively, we can download the minified version of angular-translate from GitHub.

Once we've installed the latest stable version of angular-translate, we can simply embed it in our HTML document. Just make sure it's embedded after Angular itself, as it depends on the core `angular` library.

```
<script src="path/to/angular.js"></script>
<script src="path/to/angular-translate.js"></script>
```

Last but not least, our app has to declare angular-translate as a load dependency:

```
var app = angular.module('myApp', ['pascalprecht.translate']);
```

Great! Now we're ready to use angular-translate's components to translate our app.

Teaching Your App a New Language

Our app depends upon angular-translate as installed, and our app declares it as a dependency, so we can use it to translate our app's contents.

First, we need to provide translation material so our app can actually *speak* a new language. This step entails configuring the $translate service through our fresh $translateProvider service.

Training our app to use a new language is simple. Using the `config` function on our app, we provide the different language translations for our app (i.e., English, German, Hebrew, etc.). First, we inject our $translateProvider in the config function, like so:

```
angular.module('angularTranslateApp', ['pascalprecht.translate'])
  .config(['$translateProvider', function($translateProvider) {
    // Our translations will go in here
}]);
```

To add a language, we have to make $translateProvider aware of a **translation table**, which is a JSON object containing our messages (keys) that we will translate into values. Using a **translation table** enables us to write our translations as simple JSON for loading remotely or setting at compile time, such as:

```
{
  'MESSAGE': 'Hello world',
}
```

In a translation table, the key represents a translation ID, whereas the value represents the concrete translation for a certain language. Now we add a translation table to your app. `$translateProvider` provides a method called `translations()` to take care of that.

```
app.config(function ['$translateProvider', ($translateProvider) {
  $translateProvider.translations({
    HEADLINE: 'Hello there, This is my awesome app!',
    INTRO_TEXT: 'And it has i18n support!'
  });
}]);
```

With this translation table in place, our app is set to use angular-translate. Since we're adding the translation table at configuration time, angular-translate's components are able to access it as soon as they are instantiated.

Let's switch over to our app template. Adding translations in the view layer is as simple as binding our *key* to the view. Using the `translate` filter, we don't even have to engage our controller or services or worry about the view layer: We're able to decouple the translate logic from any controller or service and make our view replaceable without touching business logic code.

Basically, the `translate` filter works like so:

```
<h2>{{ 'TRANSLATION_ID' | translate }}</h2>
```

To update our example app, we make use of the `translate` filter:

```
<h2>{{ 'HEADLINE' | translate }}</h2>
<p>{{ 'INTRO_TEXT' | translate }}</p>
```

Great! We're now able to translate our content within the view layer without polluting our controllers' logic with translation logic; however, we could achieve the same result without using angular-translate at all, since our app only knows about one language.

Let's see angular-translate's real power and learn how to teach our app more than one language.

Multi-language Support

We've already added a translation table to the app via the `translations()` method.

The `$translateProvider` knows one language, as we set it with the `translations()` method. Now, we can add an additional language in the same way by providing a second **translation table**.

When we set our first translation table, we can provide it a key (a language key) that specifies the language we're translating. We can simply add another translation key with another language key.

Let's update our app to include a second language:

```
app.config(function ['$translateProvider', ($translateProvider) {
  $translateProvider.translations('en_US', {
    HEADLINE: 'Hello there, This is my awesome app!',
    INTRO_TEXT: 'And it has i18n support!'
  });
}]);
```

To add a second translation table for another language, let's say German, we want to just do the same with a different language key:

```
app.config(function ['$translateProvider', ($translateProvider) {
  $translateProvider.translations('en', {
    HEADLINE: 'Hello there, This is my awesome app!',
    INTRO_TEXT: 'And it has i18n support!'
  })
  .translations('de', {
    HEADLINE: 'Hey, das ist meine großartige App!',
    INTRO_TEXT: 'Und sie untersützt mehrere Sprachen!'
  });
}]);
```

Now our app knows about two different languages. We can add as many languages as needed – there's no limit; however, since there are now two languages available, how does our app know which language to use? `angular-translate` doesn't prefer any language until you tell it to do so.

To set a *preferred* language, we can use the method `$translateProvider.preferredLanguage()`. This method tells angular-translate which of the registered languages is the one that our app should use by default. It expects an argument with the value of the language key, which points to a certain translation table.

Now, let's tell our app that it should use English as its default language:

```
app.config(function ['$translateProvider', ($translateProvider) {
  $translateProvider.translations('en', {
    HEADLINE: 'Hello there, This is my awesome app!',
    INTRO_TEXT: 'And it has i18n support!'
  })
  .translations('de', {
    HEADLINE: 'Hey, das ist meine großartige App!',
    INTRO_TEXT: 'Und sie untersützt mehrere Sprachen!'
  });
  $translateProvider.preferredLanguage('en');
}]);
```

Switching the Language at Run Time

To switch to a new language at run time, we have to use angular-translate's $translate service. It has a method, uses(), that either returns the language key of the currently used language, or, when passing a language key as argument, tells angular-translate to use the corresponding language.

To get a feeling for how this capability works in a real app, we can add two new translation IDs that represent translations for buttons we'll add later in our HTML template:

```
app.config(function ['$translateProvider', ($translateProvider) {
  $translateProvider.translations('en', {
    HEADLINE: 'Hello there, This is my awesome app!',
    INTRO_TEXT: 'And it has i18n support!',
    BUTTON_TEXT_EN: 'english',
    BUTTON_TEXT_DE: 'german'
  })
  .translations('de', {
    HEADLINE: 'Hey, das ist meine großartige App!',
    INTRO_TEXT: 'Und sie untersützt mehrere Sprachen!'
    BUTTON_TEXT_EN: 'englisch',
    BUTTON_TEXT_DE: 'deutsch'
  });
  $translateProvider.preferredLanguage('en');
}]);
```

Next, we implement a function on a controller that uses the $translate service and its uses() method to change the language at run time. To do that, we inject the $translate service in our app's controller and add a function on its $scope:

```
app.controller('TranslateController', function($translate, $scope) {
  $scope.changeLanguage = function (langKey) {
    $translate.uses(langKey);
  };
});
```

Now, let's reflect this change in the HTML template by adding a button for each language. We also have to set up an ng-click directive on each button to call the function that changes the language at run time:

```
<div ng-controller="TranslateController">
  <button ng-click="changeLanguage('de')" translate="BUTTON_TEXT_DE"></button>
  <button ng-click="changeLanguage('en')" translate="BUTTON_TEXT_EN"></button>
</div>
```

Et voilà! We now have an app with multi-language support!

Loading Languages

What fun would it be if we were going to set the languages statically? We can dynamically load languages thanks to Angular's $http service, through the $translateProvider's registerLoader function.

First, we need to install the angular-translate-loader-url extension by setting the loader-url service, which expects that there is a back-end server to send back JSON by handling the lang parameter. If you do have a back end that handles the route with the lang parameter, install the loader-url service with Bower like so:

```
bower install angular-translate-loader-url
```

If you prefer to have a service that loads static files, we can use the static-files loader that loads JSON files from a path with language files. Since this router is simpler, we'll go ahead and install this service through Bower:

```
bower install angular-translate-loader-static-files
```

Now, let's make sure this file is loaded in our view through a script tag:

```
<script src="/js/angular-translate-loader-url.min.js"></script>
```

To configure our service to use the `static-files` loader, we need to tell our `$translateProvider` to use the loader with a configuration object. The configuration object takes two parameters:

- **prefix** - specifies the file prefix (including file paths)
- **suffix** - specifies the file suffix (usually the extension)

The file loader attempts to fetch files at the following URL path: `[prefix]/[langKey]/[suffix]`. For instance, if we set our config object as:

```
$translateProvider.useStaticFilesLoader({
  prefix: '/languages/',
  suffix: '.json'
});
```

`angular-translate` attempts to load the en_US language from `/languages/en_US.json`. Using the `StaticFilesLoader` like so gives us the additional benefit of **lazy loading**. `$translate` will only pull down the language files it needs at run time.

Of course, using asynchronous loading will cause a flash of untranslated content as the app loads. We can circumvent this side effect by setting a default language that is packaged with the app.

One last cool feature: We can use local storage to store our language files. `angular-translate` provides us the ability to use local storage; we can enable this capability with one function:

```
$translateProvider.useLocalStorage();
```

We've covered how to use `angular-translate` to bring i18n support to your Angular app using `$translateProvider.translations()` and the `translate` filter. We've also shown how to change the language at run time using `$translate` service and its `uses()` method.

Try out `angular-translate`. It comes with a lot of really nice built-in features, such as handling pluralization, using custom loaders, and setting translations through a service. The docs are fantastic; we suggest you check them out here[121].

There are a lot of examples that you can play with directly on the site! There's also an API Reference[122] that shows all available components and the interfaces you can use to build awesome apps with internationalization support.

---

[121]http://pascalprecht.github.io/angular-translate

[122]http://pascalprecht.github.io/angular-translate/#/api

angular-gettext

Similar to `angular-translate`, `angular-gettext` also provides translation in a completely different method. Rather than relying on us to embed the strings we want to translate into the app, we abstract out the specific strings and let our library handle them.

`Gettext` is an internationalization and localization system that is sponsored by the GNU Project and was first released in 1995. It's a popular system for wrapping new language support because it wraps strings that can later be translated to support new languages.

The `angular-gettext` library works in the same way, by providing string wrapping for strings we want to translate later.

Installation

To use `angular-gettext`, we need to load the angular-gettext library. We can install it in several different ways, but we prefer using Bower.

- Using Bower

We can install `angular-gettext` with Bower like so:

```
$ bower install --save angular-gettext
```

Alternatively, we can download the minified version of `angular-gettext` from GitHub.

Once we've installed the latest stable version of `angular-gettext`, we can simply embed it in our HTML document. We just need to make sure it's embedded after Angular itself, as it depends on the core `angular` library as well as `jquery` (as it's a dependency of `angular-gettext`)

```html
<script src="path/to/jquery.js"></script>
<script src="path/to/angular.js"></script>
<script src="path/to/angular-gettext.js"></script>
```

Last but not least, our app has to declare `angular-gettext` as a load dependency:

```javascript
var app = angular.module('myApp', ['gettext']);
```

Now we're ready to use `angular-gettext`'s components to translate our app!

Usage

The `angular-gettext` library includes the `translate` directive, which is simply a directive that we place on any of the DOM elements where we want strings to be replaced by their translated counterparts.

```
<h1 translate>Hello!</h1>
```

Our `<h1>` contents will *automatically* be translated using the translated strings we'll define in a few minutes.

The strings to be translated don't need to be handled differently than regular strings, giving us the power to have full interpolation support from within inside our app.

```
<h1 translate>Hello {{ name }}</h1>
```

We can support translating plural notation as well. For instance, let's say we want to translate apple into it's plural form of apples.

```
<h1 translate>One apple</h1>
```

We can add two more directives to our `<h1>` element that signify the current count and the eventual string to translate.

```
<h1 translate
  translate-n="count"
  translate-plural="{{ count }} apples">
  One apple
</h1>
```

If the string `translate-n` expression results in more than 1, then `gettext` uses the `translate-plural` string; otherwise, it uses the value of the `<h1>` DOM element.

The extra `translate-n` directive accepts any Angular expression, including functions. For more information on expressions, check out the expressions chapter.

The `translate-plural` is simply a string that replaces the inner value of the DOM element upon which the directive is called.

Lastly, we can also use the `translate` filter inside of our app. Sometimes we can't use a directive, for instance:

```
<input type="text" placeholder="Username" />
```

We *can* use the `translate` filter to substitute the Username value in the placeholder:

```
<input type="text"
       placeholder="{{'Username'|translate}}" />
```

String Extraction

Now, instead of providing the strings upfront that we'll need to translate, we *extract* the strings from our templates to build translations. We'll be generating a .pot file, the standard gettext template.

The *easiest* method for extracting these strings to be translated is to use the grunt-angular-gettext utility.

 For more information about Grunt, check out the Grunt section in the next steps chapter.

In order to use the grunt-angular-gettext Grunt task, we need to install it with npm:

```
$ npm install grunt-angular-gettext --save-dev
```

Once our Grunt task is installed, we need to load it in our Gruntfile. Using the standard Grunt method for referencing Grunt tasks, we enable it like so inside of our Gruntfile:

```
grunt.loadNpmTasks('grunt-angular-gettext');
```

Once that's set, we need to extract the strings to be translated from our app. We can do this using the nggettext_extract task.

To set up this task, we need to provide our configuration.

Effectively, the most important key that matters in our nggettext_extract task is the files key:

```
grunt.initConfig({
  nggettext_extract: {
    pot: {
      files: {
        'po/template.pot': ['src/views/*.html']
      }
    },
  },
});
```

We can also include a few options in our task that set the start and end delimiters. If we've configured Angular to use different delimiters, we can set those in our task as options:

```
grunt.initConfig({
  nggettext_extract: {
    pot: {
      options: {
        startDelim: '//',
        endDelim: '//'
      },
      files: {
        'po/template.pot': ['src/views/*.html']
      }
    },
  },
})
```

Now, we can run this task using the Grunt, like so:

```
$ grunt nggettext_extract
```

Once we're done running this task, we will have a `po/template.pot` file. For instance, for the template:

```html
<div ng-controller="HomeController">
  <h1 translate>Hello {{ user.name }}</h1>
  <h2 translate translate-n="count"
      translate-plural="{{ count }} books">
      {{ count }} books
  </h2>
</div>
```

We get a `po/template.pot` file that looks like:

```
msgid ""
msgstr ""
"Content-Type: text/plain; charset=UTF-8\n"
"Content-Transfer-Encoding: 8bit\n"

#: app/index.html
msgid "Hello {{ user.name }}"
msgstr ""

#: app/index.html
```

```
msgid "{{ count }} books"
msgid_plural "{{ count }} books"
msgstr[0] ""
msgstr[1] ""
```

Translating Our Strings

Now that we have our .pot file ready to go, we can start translating it. One of the great reasons to use open-source software is that there are many tools available for us to create translations.

We're going to focus on using the Poedit tool, which is an open-source tool that enables us to edit our .pot file.

First, we need to download the tool. We can get it from the Poedit site at www.poedit.net[123].

Once we have this tool installed, we can open the application and select File -> New Catalog from POT File...:

New Catalog from Pot File...

From here, we find our file and select it. We need to make sure that we include the plural form exactly as follows:

---

[123]http://www.poedit.net/

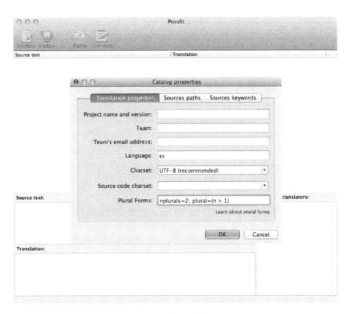

Setting plural forms

Select "OK", and we should be brought to a screen that shows the strings to be translated. We should fill these strings out for a specific language.

For instance, if we want to translate our app into Spanish, we should use the es language. We'll save our file as es.po in the same directory as our templates.pot file as is conventional for gettext.

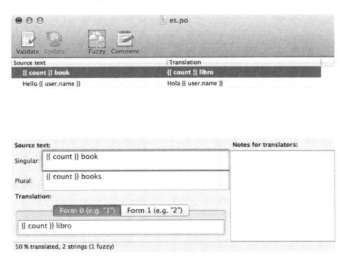

Translating our app

Once we're done editing, we can save this file and continue on our way.

 If we make changes to our app, we can simply re-run Grunt and select "Update from POT File..." in Poedit. This step updates our new strings, removes old ones, and makes suggestions for those that have changed.

Translating our app

Compiling Our New Language

Finally, we can use our new compiled language formats to generate our new `translation.js` file.

We'll use Grunt one more time to compile our new `.po` files into the `translations.js` file that we'll use at run time.

We need to add a new task: the `nggettext_compile` task, which takes our `.po` files and wraps them into the language that we can use in our app.

The basic configuration task looks like:

```
grunt.initConfig({
  nggettext_compile: {
    all: {
      files: {
        'app/scripts/translations.js': ['po/*.po']
      }
    },
  },
})
```

This configuration generates the `app/scripts/translations.js` file out of all of the `po/*.po` files.

We can also specify a specific module that we want to our translations to be defined within, such as:

```
grunt.initConfig({
  nggettext_compile: {
    all: {
      options: {
        module: 'myApp.translations'
      },
      files: {
        'app/scripts/translations.js': ['po/*.po']
      }
    },
  },
})
```

We suggest setting a Gruntfile task to call both of the nggettext_* functions, such as grunt.registerTask('default', ['nggettext_extract', 'nggettext_compile']);.

Now, when we run our Grunt task, it generates our translations.js file for us. We only need to include this file in our run-time .html file, and our app will be ready for translation.

Changing Languages

We're ready to set our language and use our translations to support different languages.

The gettext module includes a service called gettextCatalog that we can inject into our app to set the current language. To set the language, we can simply call:

```
angular.module('myApp')
.run(function (gettextCatalog) {
    gettextCatalog.currentLanguage = 'es';
});
```

The code above loads the application's current language as our Spanish language translations.

Note that we can the same thing on the fly, as we only need to *inject* the gettextCatalog into our Angular object, like so:

```
.controller('HomeController',
function($scope, gettextCatalog) {
  $scope.user = { name: "Ari" }
  $scope.count = 1;
  $scope.changeLanguage = function() {
    gettextCatalog.currentLanguage = 'es';
  }
})
```

In English:

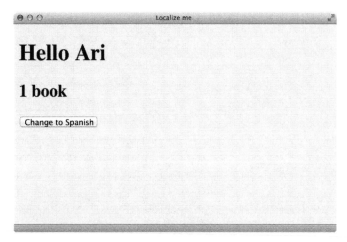

English

In Spanish, after we change the language:

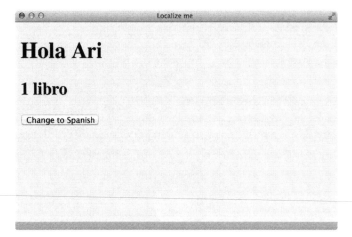

Spanish

Caching

In large, internet-scale web apps, the ability to limit API calls from the client side enables us to create scalable web apps.

Not only does it make the front end appear quicker and more responsive, but it also protects our back end by reducing the amount of work that our back end needs to perform. That way, our back end can serve more client consumers on the front end.

What Is a Cache?

A **Cache** is a component that transparently stores data so that future requests can be served more quickly. It is safe to cache data that doesn't need to be recomputed often, whereas fetching new data would result in duplicated data.

The more requests we can serve from cache, the more our overall system performance increases.

Traditionally, caching servers, such as Memcache, can be served on the same system that's serving the content to clients or on remote systems. Choosing between options comes down to server size and traffic.

Depending upon the volatility of the content, we can focus our efforts on storing cached content in long-term storage (e.g., storing it on disk or for the short term and only keeping it in memory).

Caching works like a big key-value store. There's a *key* that points to a cached piece of content. When the content is requested, if the key is found in the cache and is available (i.e., we get a cache hit), then the related content will be served.

If the key is not (i.e., we get a cache miss), then the caching server will need to know how to fetch the data, store it, and return it back to the original requester of the data.

In this section, we'll discuss caching strategies within Angular, from how to set up memcache (lightly) for server-side content to using Angular's built-in caching mechanisms. There are good libraries that will handle it for us.

Angular Caching

Angular offers caching as a feature out of the box for built-in services and gives us the ability to use the same mechanisms to cache our own custom content.

Introducing the $cacheFactory

The $cacheFactory is the service that generates cache objects for all Angular services. Internally, the $cacheFactory creates a default cache object, even if we don't create one explicitly.

To create a cache object, we use the $cacheFactory and create a cache by ID:

```
var cache = $cacheFactory.
  create('myCache');
```

Here, we've defined a cache with the *ID* myCache. The $cacheFactory function can take up to two arguments:

cacheId (string)   The cacheId is the name of ID of the cache that we're creating. It can be referenced by the get() method by the name of the cache.

options (object)   The options specify how the cache will behave. Currently, the options object can take a key:

- capacity (number)

The capacity describes the maximum number of cache key-value pairs the cache will store and keep at any given time.

The $cacheFactory() method returns a cache object.

Cache Object

The cache object itself has the following methods that we can use to interact with the cache.

info()   The info() method returns the ID, size, and options of the cache object.

put()   The put() method allows us to put a key (string) of any JavaScript object value into the cache.

```
cache.put("hello", "world");
```

The put() method returns the value of the cache that we put in.

get()   The get() method gives us access to the cache value for a *key*. If the key is found, it returns the value, whereas if it is not found, it returns *undefined*.

```
cache.get("hello");
```

remove() The `remove()` function removes a key-value pair from the cache, if it's found. If it's not found, then it just returns `undefined`.

```
cache.remove("hello");
```

removeAll() The `removeAll()` function resets the cache and removes **all** cached values.

destroy() The `destroy()` method removes all references of this cache from the `$cacheFactory` cache registry.

Caching through $http

Angular's `$http` service creates a cache with the ID $http (surprise, right?). Enabling the $http request to use this default cache object is simple: The $http method(s) allow us to pass a `cache` parameter.

Default $http Cache

The default `$http` cache can be particularly useful when our data doesn't change very often. We can set it like so:

```
$http({
  method: 'GET',
  url: '/api/users.json',
  cache: true
});
// Or, using the .get helper
$http.get('/api/users.json', {
  cache: true
});
```

Now, every request that is made through $http to the URL `/api/users.json` will be stored in the default $http cache. The *key* for this request in the $http cache is the full-path URL.

By passing the `true` parameter in the $http options, we're telling the $http service to use the default cache. It's useful to use the default cache if we don't want to mess with the cache all that often.

We can, however, manipulate the default $http cache if we need to (e.g., if another request we make without caching notifies us of a delta change, we can clear the request in the default $http request).

To reference the $http default request, we simply fetch the cache through the $cacheFactory by ID:

```
var cache = $cacheFactory.get('$http');
```

With the cache in hand, we can do all the normal operations we need and want to do on it, such as retrieve the cached responses, clear items from the cache, or blow away all cached references:

```
// Fetch the cache for the previous request
var usersCache =
  cache.get('http://example.com/api/users.json');
// Delete the cache entry for the
// previous request
cache.remove('http://example.com/api/users.json');
// Start over and remove the entire cache
cache.removeAll();
```

Although we can reference the default cache, it is sometimes more useful to have more control over the cache and create rules around how the cache behaves. We'll need to create a new cache to use with our requests.

Custom Cache

Telling our $http requests to make requests through our own custom cache is simple. Instead of passing a boolean true with the request, we can pass the instance of the cache.

```
var myCache = $cacheFactory.get('myCache');
$http({
  method: 'GET',
  url: '/api/users.json',
  cache: myCache
});
// Or, using the .get helper
$http.get('/api/users.json', {
  cache: myCache
});
```

Now, instead of using the default cache, $http will use our custom cache.

Setting Default Cache for $http

Although it is easy, it's not convenient to need to pass an instance of the cache every time we want to make an $http request, especially if we're using the same cache for every request.

We can set the cache object that $http uses by default through the $httpProvider in a .config() method on our module.

```
angular.module('myApp')
.config(function($httpProvider) {
    $httpProvider.defaults.cache =
      $cacheFactory('myCache', {capacity: 20});
});
```

The $http service will no longer use the default cache it creates for us; it will use our own cache, which is effectively now a Least Recently Used (LRU) cache.

> An LRU cache keeps only the latest number of caches based upon the capacity of the cache. That is, in our cache that has a capacity of 20, the first 20 requests will be cached, but when the 21st comes in, the least recently requested item will be deleted from the cache. The cache itself takes care of maintaining the details about what to maintain and what to remove.

Security

With any client-side app, it's always a good idea to think about security at build time. Additionally, it's relatively tough to deliver 100% protection in any situation, and even more difficult to do it when the client can see the entire code.

In this chapter, we're going to take a look at some techniques for keeping our application secure. We'll look at how to master the $sce service to secure our text input through wrapping authorized requests with tokens (when talking to a protected back end).

Strict Contextual Escaping: the $sce Service

The strict contextual escaping mode (available by default in Angular version 1.2 and higher) tells our app that it *requires* bindings in certain contexts to result in a value that is marked as safe for use inside the context.

For instance, when we want to bind raw HTML to an element using `ng-bind-html`, we want Angular to render the element with HTML, rather than escaped text.

```
<textarea ng-model="htmlBody"></textarea>
<div ng-bind-html="{{htmlBody}}"></div>
```

$sce is a fantastic service that allows us to write whitelisted, secure code by default and goes a long way toward helping us prevent XSS and other vulnerabilities. Given this power, it's important to understand what it is that we're doing so we can use it wisely.

In the above example, the `<textarea>` is bound to the `htmlBody` model. In this textarea, the user can input whatever arbitrary code they would like to see rendered in the div. For instance, it might be a live preview for writing a blog post or comments, etc.

If the user can input any arbitrary text into the text field, we have essentially opened ourselves up to a giant security hole.

In order to protect ourselves against malicious users, it's a good idea to run our unsafe text through a sanitizer.

The $sce service does that for us, by default, on all interpolated expressions. No constant literals are ever untrusted. For instance, this value is always a trusted one, as the value is a string.

```
<div ng-html-bind-unsafe="'<h1>Trusted</h1>'"></div>
```

Basically, at the root of embedded directives starting in version 1.2 and on, $scope values are not bound directly to the value of the binding, but to the result of the $sce.getTrusted() method.

Directives use the new $sce.parseAs() method instead of the $parse service to watch attribute bindings. The $sce.parseAs() method calls $sce.getTrusted() on all non-constant literals.

In effect, the ng-bind-html directive calls $sce.parseAsHtml() behind the scenes and binds the value to the DOM element. The ng-include directive runs this same behavior and any templateUrl defined on a directive.

When enabled, all built-in directives call out to $sce automatically. We can use this same behavior in our own directives and other custom components.

To set up $sce protection, we need to *inject* the $sce service.

```
angular.module('myApp', [])
  .directive('myDirective', ['$sce',
    function($sce) {
      // We have access to the $sce service
  }])
  .controller('MyController', [
    '$scope', '$sce',
    function($scope, $sce) {
      // We have access to the $sce service
  }]);
```

Inside of our directive and our controller, we want to give Angular the ability to both allow *trusted* content back into the view and take trusted interpolated input.

The $sce service has a simple API that gives us the ability to both set and get trusted content of explicitly specific types.

For instance, let's build an email previewer. This email client will allow users to write HTML in their email; we want to give them a live preview of their text.

The HTML we can use might look something like:

```
<div ng-app="myApp">
  <div ng-controller="MyController">
    <textarea ng-model="email.rawHtml"></textarea>
    <pre ng-bind-html="email.htmlBody"></pre>
```

Now, notice that we are taking a body of text in a <textarea></textarea> on a different property of email: email.rawHtml vs. email.htmlBody. Inside of our controller, we *parse* this email.rawHtml as HTML and output it to the browser.

Inside our controller, we can set up a $watch to monitor changes on the email.rawHtml and run a trusted parser on the HTML content any time it changes.

```
.controller('MyController', [
  '$scope', '$sce',
    function($scope, $sce) {
      // set up a watch on the email.rawHtml
      $scope.$watch('email.rawHtml', function(v) {
        // so long as we are not in the
        // $compile phase
        if (v) {
          // Render the htmlBody as trusted HTML
          $scope.email.htmlBody =
            $sce.trustAsHtml($scope.email.rawHtml);
        }
      })
  }]);
```

Now, whenever the content of email.rawHtml changes, we'll run a parser on the content and get back suitable HTML contents. Note that the content will be rendered as sanitized HTML that's safe to source in the application.

Now, what if we want to support the user to write custom JavaScript to execute on the page? For instance, if we want to enable the user to write an ecard that includes custom JavaScript, we'll want to enable specify they can run this custom JavaScript on the page.

The HTML invocation for this might look like:

```
<textarea ng-model="email.rawJs"></textarea>
<pre ng-bind="email.jsBody"></pre>
<button ng-click="runJs()">Run</button>
```

With this snippet, we're running the same mechanism for parsing our raw text into *safe* text. This time, we also add a third element, a button that calls runJs() on our scope.

As we saw with our HTML bindings, we'll watch the JavaScript snippet:

```
.controller('MyController', [
  '$scope', '$sce',
    function($scope, $sce) {
      // set up a watch on email.rawJs
      $scope.$watch('email.rawJs', function(v) {
        if (v) {
          $scope.email.jsBody =
            $sce.trustAsJs($scope.email.rawJs);
        }
      });
    }]);
```

Notice that this time we did not use trustAsHtml(), but used the trustAsJs() method. This method tells Angular to parse the text as executable JavaScript code. At the end of this call, we'll have a safe, parsed JavaScript snippet we can eval() in the context of the application.

We can now enable the runJs() method to be set by the user and run the JavaScript snippet supplied by email.rawJs.

```
// ...
$scope.runJs = function() {
  eval($scope.email.jsBody.toString());
}
```

> There are more intelligent methods of running *eval* on JavaScript snippets. For production use, we recommend against using *eval*.

We get built-in protection in Angular: It will only load templates from the same domain and protocol as those within which the app is loaded. Angular enforces this protection by calling the $sce.getTrustedResourceUrl on the templateUrl.

This protocol does not replace the browser's Same Origin policies and Cross-Origin Resource Sharing, or CORS. These policies will still be in effect to protect the browser.

We can override this value by whitelisting or blacklisting domains with the $sceDelegateProvider.

Whitelisting URLs

In the module's config() function, we can set new whitelist and blacklists.

```
angular.module('myApp', [])
  .config(['$sceDelegateProvider',
    function($sceDelegateProvider) {
      // Set a new whitelist
      $sceDelegateProvider.resourceUrlWhitelist(['self']);
  }]);
```

To set a new whitelist, we use the resourceUrlWhitelist() method. The function takes one optional parameter.

- whitelist (array)

If a parameter is **not** passed, then this function serves as a getter and returns the currently set whitelist array.

If the whitelist parameter is passed in, the array of replaces the resourceUrlWhitelist with the new array.

Each element of the array must either be a regex or the string 'self'. When set to 'self', Angular ensures that all URLs match only URLs of the same domain as the app. When a regex is used, Angular matches it against the absolute URL of the resource we're testing.

If the array is empty, $sce blocks ALL URLs.

> Using 'self' enables sourcing https resources from HTML documents.

To enable the every single URL, we whitelist every domain:

```
angular.module('myApp', [])
  .config(['$sceDelegateProvider',
    function($sceDelegateProvider) {
      // Set a new whitelist
      $sceDelegateProvider.resourceUrlWhitelist(['.*']);
  }]);
```

By default, the whitelist is set to ['self'].

Blacklisting URLs

It's also possible to blacklist URLs instead of whitelisting. It's often much safer to depend on whitelisting, but we can use them in combination. It's useful to whitelist a trusted domain and blacklist open redirects served by our domains.

To set a new blacklist, we use the resourceUrlBlacklist() method. This method takes one optional parameter.

- blacklist (array)

If a parameter is **not** passed in, the function returns the currently set blacklist array.

If the blacklist parameter is passed in, the new array replaces the blacklist.

Each element of the array must be either a regex or the string 'self', although in the case of the blacklist, it's not useful. When a regex is used, it is matched against the absolute URL of the resource being tested.

The blacklist always has the *final say* in what is acceptable and what is not acceptable for trusted content.

By default, the blacklist is set to an empty array, [].

$sce API

The $sce library holds two *main* functions that we'll use, as well as several helper functions.

getTrusted

To get the trusted version of a value of a specific type, we can call the getTrusted() method.

The getTrusted() method takes two arguments:

- type (string)

This string is the type of context where the value will be used. See sce types for available types.

- maybeTrusted

This value is the return value from $sce.trustAs. If it is invalid, then it will throw an exception.

The $sce library has a few helper methods for the getTrusted() method.

The following method calls are functionally equivalent:

```
getTrustedCss(value)             getTrusted($sce.CSS, value)
getTrustedHtml(value)            getTrusted($sce.HTML, value)
getTrustedJs(value)              getTrusted($sce.JS, value)
getTrustedResourceUrl(value)     getTrusted($sce.RESOURCE_URL, value)
getTrustedUrl(value)             getTrusted($sce.URL, value)
```

parse

Similar to the $parse service, the parse method converts an Angular expression into a function. If the expression is a literal constant, it calls the $parse service; otherwise, it calls the $sce.getTrusted() service.

The parse() method takes two arguments:

- type (string)

The type of $sce context where we're going to use the value. See sce types for available types.

- expression (string)

The Angular expression to compile

The parse() method returns a function of the form: function(context, locals) where:

- context (object)

The object where the expression should be evaluated against. Typically, this will be a $scope object.

- locals (object)

These are local variables, mostly useful for overriding values in the context.

The $sce library has a few helper methods for the parse() method.

The following method calls are functionally equivalent:

parseAsCss(expr)	parseAs($sce.CSS, expr)
parseAsHtml(expr)	parseAs($sce.HTML, expr)
parseAsJs(expr)	parseAs($sce.JS, expr)
parseAsResourceUrl(expr)	parseAs($sce.RESOURCE_URL, expr)
parseAsUrl(expr)	parseAs($sce.URL, expr)

trustAs

The trustAs() method returns an object that Angular trusts for use in a specific strict contextual escaping context. Bindings, such as ng-bind-html and ng-include, use the provided value.

The trustAs() method takes two arguments:

- type (string)

The type of $sce context where the value is safe for us. See sce types for available types.

- value

The value that we can use to stand in for the provided value.

The trustAs() method returns a value that can be used where Angular expects a $sce.trustAs() return value.

The $sce library has a few helper methods for the trustAs() method.

The following method calls are functionally equivalent:

trustAsHtml(value)	trustAs($sce.HTML, value)
trustAsJs(value)	trustAs($sce.JS, value)
trustAsResourceUrl(value)	trustAs($sce.RESOURCE_URL, value)
trustAsUrl(value)	trustAs($sce.URL, value)

isEnabled()

The isEnabled() method takes no parameters and returns a boolean that tells us if the sce environment is enabled. If it is, then it returns true; otherwise, it returns false.

Configuring $sce

If we want to completely disable the sce subsystem from running our app (although we discourage this move, as it provides security by default), we can disable it in the config() function of our app like so:

```
angular.module('myApp', [])
  .config(['$sceProvider',
    function($sceProvider) {
      // Turn off SCE
      $sceProvider.enabled(false);
}]);
```

Trusted Context Types

The $sce library has five built-in context types that are supported by default. These context types are what Angular uses to parse and determine what is *safe* in one context vs. another.

Context	Description
$sce.HTML	Tells Angular this is safe HTML to source in the app
$sce.CSS	Tells Angular that it's safe to source this as CSS in the app
$sce.URL	Tells Angular that the URL is safe to follow as a link
$sce.RESOURCE_URL	Tells Angular that the URL is safe to follow as a link and that the contents are safe to include in the app
$sce.JS	Tells Angular that the contents are safe to execute in the application

AngularJS and Internet Explorer

AngularJS works seamlessly with most modern browsers. Safari, Google Chrome, Google Chrome Canary, and Firefox work great. The notorious Internet Explorer version 8 and earlier can cause us problems.

 For more information, read the AngularJS docs guide on IE[124].

If we are planning release our applications for Internet Explorer v8.0 or earlier, we need to pay some extra attention to help support it.

Internet Explorer does not like element names that start with a prefix ng: because it considers the prefix to be an XML namespace. IE will ignore these elements unless the elements have a corresponding namespace declaration:

```
<html xmlns:my="ignored">
```

 This xmlns:ng="http://angularjs.org" makes IE feel more comfortable.

If we use non-standard HTML tags, we need to create the tags in the head of the document if we want IE to recognize them. We can do so simply in the head element.

```
<!doctype html>
<html xmlns:ng="http://angularjs.org">
  <head>
    <!--[if lte IE 8]
      <script>
        document.createElement('ng-view');
        // Other custom elements
      </script>
    <![endif]-->
  </head>
  <body>
    <!-- ... -->
```

It is recommended that we use the attribute directive form, as we don't need to create custom elements to support IE:

---

[124]http://docs.angularjs.org/guide/ie

```
<div data-ng-view></div>
```

To make AngularJS work with IE7 and earlier, we need to polyfill JSON.stringify. We can use the JSON3[125] or JSON2[126] implementations.

In our browser, we need to conditionally include this file in the head. We must download the file, store it in a location relative to the root of our application, and reference it in the head, like so:

```
<!doctype html>
<html xmlns:ng="http://angularjs.org">
  <head>
    <!--[if lte IE 8]
    <script src="lib/json2.js"></script>
    <![endif]-->
  </head>
  <body>
  <!-- ... -->
```

To use the ng-app directive with IE support, we set the element id to ng-app, as well.

```
<body id="ng-app" ng-app="myApp">
<!-- ... -->
```

We can take advantage of the angular-ui-utils library's ie-shiv module to help give us custom elements in our DOM.

In order to use the ui-utils ie-shiv library, we need to ensure that we have the angular-ui library installed. Installation is easy if we download the ui-utils library and include the module. We can find the ui-utils library on GitHub here: https://github.com/angular-ui/ui-utils[127].

Let's ensure that we've included the ui-utils module in an accessible location to your app and include the file just like this:

---

[125]http://bestiejs.github.io/json3/

[126]https://github.com/douglascrockford/JSON-js

[127]https://github.com/angular-ui/ui-utils

```
<!--[if lte IE 8]>
<script type="text/javascript">
  // define our custom directives here
</script>
<script src="lib/angular-ui-ieshiv.js"></script>
<![endif]-->
```

With that in place, we only activate the ie-shiv on Internet Explorer versions 8 and earlier. The shiv enables us to add our custom directives onto its global object, which, in turn, creates the proper declarations for IE.

The shiv library looks for the window.myCustomTags object. If the window.myCustomTags is defined, the library will include these tags at load time along with the rest of the Angular library directives:

```
<!--[if lte IE 8]>
<script type="text/javascript">
  // define our custom directives here
  window.myCustomTags = ['myDirective'];
</script>
<script src="lib/angular-ui-ieshiv.js"></script>
<![endif]-->
```

Ajax Caching

IE is the only major browser that caches XHR requests. An efficient way to avoid this poor behavior is to set an HTTP response header of Cache-Control to be no-cache for every request.

This behavior is the default behavior for modern browsers and helps to provide a better experience for IE users.

We can change the default headers for every single request like so:

```
.config(function($httpProvider) {
  $httpProvider.defaults
    .headers.common['Cache-Control'] = 'no-cache';
});
```

SEO with AngularJS

Search engines, such as Google and Bing, are engineered to crawl static web pages, not JavaScript-heavy, client-side apps. Search engine robots are typically designed to be quick and efficient, so most do not render JavaScript when crawling over a page.

That's because our JavaScript-heavy apps need a JavaScript engine to run, like PhantomJS or v8, for instance. Web crawlers typically load a web page without using a JavaScript interpreter.

It is for good reason that search engines do not include JS interpreters in their crawlers: They don't need to, and doing so slows them down and makes them more inefficient for crawling the web.

Getting Angular Apps Indexed

There are several different ways that we can tell Google to handle indexing our app. The first, more common approach is to use a back end to serve our Angular app. This method has the advantage of being simple to implement without much duplication of code.

The second approach is to render all of the content delivered by our Angular app inside a `<noscript>` tag in our JavaScript. We'll cover this topic lightly, as implementing the `<noscript>` approach depends heavily upon how we deliver our apps. For instance, we can use a `<noscript>` tag when we're rendering our pages on the server-side.

Server Side

Google and other advanced search engines support the hashbang URL format, which we use to identify the current page that's being accessed at a given URL. These search engines transform this URL into a custom URL format that makes them accessible to the server.

The search engine visits the URL and expects to get the HTML (with the fully rendered HTML content) that our browsers will receive. For instance, Google will turn the hashbang URL from:

```
http://www.ng-newsletter.com/#!/signup/page
```

into the URL:

```
http://www.ng-newsletter.com/?_escaped_fragment_=/signup/page
```

Within our Angular app, we need to tell Google to handle our site slightly differently depending upon which style we handle.

Hashbang Syntax

Google's Ajax crawling specification was written and originally intended for delivering URLs with the hashbang syntax, which was an original method of creating permalinks for JS applications.

We need to configure our app to use the `hashPrefix` (default) in our routing:

```
angular.module('myApp', [])
.configure(['$location', function($location) {
  $location.hashPrefix('!');
}]);
```

HTML5 Routing Mode

The new HTML5 pushState doesn't work the same way: It modifies the browser's URL and history. To get Angular apps to "fool" the search bot, we can add a simple element to the header:

```
<meta name="fragment" content="!">
```

This element tells the Google spider to use the new crawling spec to crawl our site. When it encounters this tag, instead of crawling our site like *normal*, it will revisit the site using the ?_escaped_fragment_= tag.

Assuming we're using HTML5 mode with the $location service, we can set our page to use html5Mode like so:

```
angular.module('myApp', [])
.configure(['$routeProvider',
function($routeProvider) {
  $routeProvider.html5Mode(true);
}]);
```

With the _escaped_fragment_ in our query string, we can use our back-end server to serve static HTML instead of our client-side app.

Now, our back end can detect if the request has the _escaped_fragment_ in the request, and, if so, we can serve static HTML back instead of our pure Angular app.

 We can achieve this result using a proxy, like Apache or Nginx, or our back-end service. Setting these up is out of scope of this book; however, we'll discuss how to set them up with a NodeJS app.

Options for Handling SEO from the Server Side

We have a number of options available to us to make our site SEO-friendly. We'll walk through three different ways to deliver our apps from the server side:

- Using Node/Express middleware
- Using Apache to rewrite URLs
- Using Nginx to proxy URLs

Using Node/Express Middleware

 Although we are using NodeJS in this example, this implementation is simply one way to serve static HTML snapshots to our back end. This technique works regardless of the back end you're using to deliver your HTML.

To deliver static HTML using NodeJS and Express (the web application framework for NodeJS), we must add some middleware that looks for the _escaped_fragment_ in our query parameters:

```
// ideas shared by
// In our app.js configuration
app.use(function(req, res, next) {
  var fragment = req.query._escaped_fragment_;

  if (!fragment) return next();

  // If the fragment is empty, serve the
  // index page
  if (fragment === "" || fragment === "/")
    fragment = "/index.html";

  // If fragment does not start with '/'
  // prepend it to our fragment
  if (fragment.charAt(0) !== "/")
    fragment = '/' + fragment;

  // If fragment does not end with '.html'
  // append it to the fragment
  if (fragment.indexOf('.html') == -1)
    fragment += ".html";

  // Serve the static html snapshot
  try {
    var file = __dirname + "/snapshots" + fragment;
    res.sendfile(file);
  } catch (err) {
    res.send(404);
  }
});
```

This middleware expects our snapshots to exist in a top-level directory called '/snapshots' and serve files based upon the request path.

For instance, it will serve a request to / as index.html, while it will serve a request to /about as about.html in the snapshots directory.

Use Apache to Rewrite URLs

If we're using the Apache server[128] to deliver our Angular app, we can add a few lines to our configuration that will serve snapshots instead of our JavaScript app.

We can use the mod_rewrite mod to detect if the route requested includes the _escaped_fragment_- query parameter or not. If it **does** include it, then we'll rewrite the request to point to the static version in the /snapshots directory.

In order to set the rewrite in motion, we need to enable the appropriate modules:

```
$ a2enmod proxy
$ a2enmod proxy_http
```

Then we need to reload the Apache config:

```
$ sudo /etc/init.d/apache2 reload
```

We can set the rewrite rules either in the virtual host configuration for the site or the .htaccess file that sits at the root of the server directory.

```
RewriteEngine On
Options +FollowSymLinks
RewriteCond %{REQUEST_URI}  ^/$
RewriteCond %{QUERY_STRING} ^_escaped_fragment_=/?(.*)$
RewriteRule ^(.*)$ /snapshots/%1? [NC,L]
```

Use Nginx to Proxy URLs

If we're using Nginx[129] to serve our Angular app, we can add some configuration to serve snapshots of our app if there is an _escaped_fragment_ parameter in the query strings.

Unlike Apache, Nginx does not require us to enable a module, so we can simply update our configuration to replace the path with the question file instead.

In our Nginx configuration file (e.g., /etc/nginx/nginx.conf), we need to ensure our configuration looks like:

---

[128]http://httpd.apache.org/
[129]http://wiki.nginx.org/Main

```
server {
  listen 80;
  server_name example;

  if ($args ~ "_escaped_fragment_=/?(.+)") {
    set $path $1;
    rewrite ^ /snapshots/$path last;
  }

  location / {
    root /web/example/current/;
    # Comment out if using hash urls
    if (!-e $request_filename) {
      rewrite ^(.*)$ /index.html break;
    }
    index index.html;
  }
}
```

Once this step is complete, we're good to reload our configuration:

```
sudo /etc/init.d/nginx reload
```

Taking Snapshots

We can take snapshots of our HTML app to deliver our back-end app, using a tool like PhantomJS[130] or zombie.js[131] to render our pages. When Google requests a page using the `_escaped_fragment_` query parameter, we can simply return and render this page.

We'll discuss two methods to take snapshots: using Zombie.js and using a Grunt tool. We're not going to cover using the fantastic PhantomJS[132] tool, as there are plenty of great resources that demonstrate it.

Using Zombie.js to Grab HTML Snapshots

To set up Zombie.js[133], we need to install the `npm` package `zombie`:

---

[130]http://phantomjs.org/

[131]http://zombie.labnotes.org/

[132]http://phantomjs.org/

[133]http://zombie.labnotes.org/

```
$ npm install zombie
```

Now, we can save our file with NodeJS by using `zombie`. First, a few helper methods we'll use in the process:

```javascript
var Browser = require('zombie'),
    url     = require('url'),
    fs      = require('fs'),
    saveDir = __dirname + '/snapshots';

var scriptTagRegex = /<script\b[^<]*(?:(?!<\/script>)<[^<]*)*<\/script>/gi;

var stripScriptTags = function(html) {
  return html.replace(scriptTagRegex, '');
}

var browserOpts = {
  waitFor: 2000,
  loadCSS: false,
  runScripts: true
}

var saveSnapshot = function(uri, body) {
  var lastIdx = uri.lastIndexOf('#/');

  if (lastIdx < 0) {
    // If we're using html5mode
    path = url.parse(uri).pathname;
  } else {
    // If we're using hashbang mode
    path =
      uri.substring(lastIdx + 1, uri.length);
  }

  if (path === '/') path = "/index.html";

  if (path.indexOf('.html') == -1)
    path += ".html";

  var filename = saveDir + path;
  fs.open(filename, 'w', function(e, fd) {
    if (e) return;
```

```
    fs.write(fd, body);
  });
};
```

Now all we need to do is run through our pages, turn every link from a relative link into an absolute link (so the crawler can follow them), and save the resulting HTML.

We're setting a relatively high `waitFor` in the browser options above. This option will cover 90% of the cases we care about. If we want to get more precise on how and when we take a snapshot, instead of waiting the two seconds, we need to modify our Angular app to fire an event and listen for the event in our Zombie browser.

Since we like to automate as much as possible and prefer not to muck with our Angular code, we prefer to set our timeout relatively high to attempt to let the code settle down.

Our `crawlPage()` function:

```
var crawlPage = function(idx, arr) {
  // location = window.location
  if (idx < arr.length) {
    var uri = arr[idx];
    var browser = new Browser(browserOpts);
    var promise = browser.visit(uri)
    .then(function() {

      // Turn links into absolute links
      // and save them, if we need to
      // and we haven't already crawled them
      var links = browser.queryAll('a');
      links.forEach(function(link) {
        var href = link.getAttribute('href');
        var absUrl = url.resolve(uri, href);
        link.setAttribute('href', absUrl);
        if (arr.indexOf(absUrl) < 0) {
          arr.push(absUrl);
        }
      });

      // Save
      saveSnapshot(uri, browser.html());
      // Call again on the next iteration
      crawlPage(idx+1, arr);
    });
  }
}
```

Now we can simply call the method on our first page:

```
crawlPage(0, ["http://localhost:9000"]);
```

Using grunt-html-snapshot

Our preferred method of taking snapshots is by using the Grunt tool `grunt-html-snapshot`. Since we use Yeoman[134], and Grunt is already in our build process, we set up this task to run after we make a release of our apps.

To install `grunt-html-snapshot`, we can use npm like so:

```
npm install grunt-html-snapshot --save-dev
```

If we're not using Yeoman[135], we need to include this task as a Grunt task in our `Gruntfile.js`:

```
grunt.loadNpmTasks('grunt-html-snapshot');
```

Once this task is set, we'll set some configuration about our site. To set up configuration, we create a new config block in our `Gruntfile.js` that looks like:

```
htmlSnapshot: {
  debug: {
    options: {}
  },
  prod: {
    options: {}
  }
}
```

Now we get to add our preferred options for the different stages:

[134]http://yeoman.io
[135]http://yeoman.io

```
htmlSnapshot: {
  debug: {
    options: {
      snapshotPath: 'snapshots/',
      sitePath: 'http://127.0.0.1:9000/',
      msWaitForPages: 1000,
      urls: [
        '/',
        '/about'
      ]
    }
  },
  prod: {
    options: {}
  }
}
```

To see a list of all of the available configuration options, check out the documentation page at https://github.com/cburgdorf/grunt-html-snapshot[136].

Prerender.io

Alternatively, we can use an open-source tool, such as Prerender.io[137], which includes a Node server that renders our site on the fly, and an Express middleware that communicates with the back end to prerender HTML on the fly.

Essentially, prerender.io takes a URL and returns the rendered HTML (with no script tags). Essentially, the prerender server we deploy is called from our app like so:

```
GET http://our-prerenderserver.com/http://localhost:9000/#/about
```

This GET returns the rendered content of our #/about page.

Setting up a prerender cluster is actually pretty easy to do. We'll show you how to integrate your own prerender server into your Node app, as well. Prerender.io is also available for Ruby on Rails through a gem called prerender_rails, but we won't cover how to set it up.

Setting up our own server to run it is pretty easy. We simply run npm install to install the dependencies and run the command through either Foreman or Node:

---

[136]https://github.com/cburgdorf/grunt-html-snapshot
[137]http://prerender.io/

```
$ npm install
$ node index.js
# Or through foreman
$ foreman start
```

The prerender library is also convenient to run on heroku:

```
$ git clone https://github.com/collectiveip/prerender.git
$ heroku create
$ git push heroku master
```

We store our rendered HTML in S3, so we recommend you use the built-in s3 cache. Read the docs how to set up this cache here[138].

After our server is running, we just need to integrate the fetching through our app. In Express, this integration is very easy using the Node library prerender-node.

To install prerender-node, we use npm again:

```
$ npm install --save prerender-node
```

After we've installed this library, we can tell our Express app to use this middleware:

```
var prerender =
  require('prerender-node')
  .set('prerenderServiceUrl', 'http://our-prerenderserver.com/');
app.use(prerender);
```

And that is it! This last bit tells our Express app that if we see a crawler request (defined by having the _escaped_fragment_ or the user agent string), it should make a GET request to our prerender service at the appropriate URL and get the prerendered HTML for the page.

<noscript> Approach

We can also use the <noscript> tag to render our pages without needing to resort to using a server back end. Unfortunately, this method is complex in that for all of our pages, we'd need to copy all of the elements of the page from outside of the <noscript> tag into such a tag.

Doing so can become cumbersome and take a lot of work to keep the two in sync, so we don't recommend this approach without a build tool to assist.

---

[138]https://github.com/collectiveip/prerender#s3-html-cache

Building Angular Chrome Apps

The Chrome[139] web browser is Google's custom browser. Not only is it incredibly speedy and on the bleeding edge of web development, it is at the forefront of delivering web experiences both on and off the web.

Chrome Apps are embedded applications that run within the web browser, but are intended to deliver a native app feel. Since they run within Chrome itself, they are written in HTML5, JavaScript, and CSS3, and they have access to native-like capabilities that true web applications do not.

Chrome apps have access to the Chrome API and services and can provide an integrated desktop-like experience to the user.

One more interesting difference between Chrome apps and web apps is that they always load locally, so they show up immediately, rather than waiting for the network to fully download the components. This feature greatly improves the apps' performance and our user's experience with running our apps.

Understanding Chrome Apps

Let's dive into looking at how Chrome apps actually work and how we can start building our own.

Every Chrome application has three core files:

manifest.json

This `manifest.json` file describes metadata about the application, such as the name, description, version, and how to launch our application.

A Background Script

This background script sets up how our application responds to system-level events, such as a user installing our app or launching it, etc.

A View

Most Chrome applications have a view. This component is optional, but is most generally used for our applications.

---

[139]https://www.google.com/intl/en/chrome/browser/

Building our Chrome App

In this section, we'll walk through creating an advanced Chrome application using Angular. We're going to create a clone of the *fantastic* Chrome web app *Currently* by the team at Rainfall[140].

Currently

We'll be building a clone that we'll call *Presently*.

Architecting Presently

When we're building Presently, we'll need to take into account the application architecture. Doing so will give us insight into how we'll build the app when we get to code.

Like *Currently*, *Presently* will be a "newtab" app, meaning that it will launch every time we open a new tab.

Presently has two main screens:

- The home screen

This screen features the current time and the current weather. It also features several weather icons beside the weather.

- The settings screen

This screen allows our users to change their location within the app.

In order to support the home screen, we need to be able to show a properly formatted date and time as well as fetch weather from a remote API service.

To support the settings screen, we must integrate with a remote API service to auto-suggest potential locations for an input box.

Finally, we'll use the basic local storage (session storage) to persist our settings across the app.

---

[140]http://blog.rainfalldesign.com/

Building the Skeleton

Building our app, we'll set up a file structure like this one:

```
● ● ●              📁 presently — zsh — Solarized Dark xterm-256color — 71×21
$ tree
.
├── css
│   └── main.css
├── fonts
├── js
│   ├── app.js
│   └── vendor
│       └── angular.min.js
├── manifest.json
├── tab.html
└── templates

5 directories, 5 files
$
```

File structure

We'll place our CSS files in `css/`, our custom fonts in `fonts/`, and our JavaScript files in `js/`. We'll set the main JavaScript file in the `js/app.js` file and the HTML for our app in `tab.html` at the root.

 There are great tools to help bootstrap Chrome app extensions, such as Yeoman[141].

Before we can start up our Chrome extension, we'll need to grab a few dependencies.

We'll grab the *latest* version of angular.min.js[142] (1.2.6), as well as angular-route.min.js[143], from angularjs.org[144] and save them to the `js/vendor/` directory.

Lastly, we'll use Twitter's Bootstrap 3 framework to style our app, so we'll need to get the `bootstrap.min.css` and save it to `css/` from getbootstrap.com[145].

 In production, when working with multiple developers, it's often more efficient to use a tool like Bower[146] to manage dependencies. Since we're building a newtab app, however, it's important that we keep our app lightweight so it launches quickly.

---

[141]http://yeoman.io

[142]http://code.angularjs.org/1.2.6/angular.min.js

[143]http://code.angularjs.org/1.2.6/angular-route.min.js

[144]http://angularjs.org/

[145]http://getbootstrap.com/

[146]http://bower.io/

manifest.json

With every Chrome app we write, we need to set up a manifest.json. This manifest tells Chrome how the application should run, what files it should use, what permissions it has, etc.

Our manifest.json needs to describe our app as a *newtab* app and describe the content_security_policy (the policies that describe what our application can and cannot do) and the background script that Chrome needs.

```json
{
  "manifest_version": 2,
  "name": "Presently",
  "description": "A currently clone",
  "version": "0.1",
  "permissions": [],
  "background": {
    "scripts": ["js/vendor/angular.min.js"]
  },
  "content_security_policy": "script-src 'self'; object-src 'self'",
  "chrome_url_overrides" : {
    "newtab": "tab.html"
  }
}
```

The keys in the manifest.json are relatively straightforward and allows us to set the name, the manifest_version, the version, etc. In order to tell Chrome to launch our app as a newtab app, we set the app to *override* the newtab page.

tab.html

The main HTML file for our application is the tab.html file. This file loads when we open a new tab in Chrome.

We'll set up the basic Angular app inside of the tab.html file:

```
<!doctype html>
<html data-ng-app="myApp" data-ng-csp="">
  <head>
    <meta charset="UTF-8">
    <title>Presently</title>
    <link rel="stylesheet" href="css/bootstrap.min.css">
    <link rel="stylesheet" href="css/main.css">
  </head>
  <body>
    <div class="container">
    </div>
    <script src="./js/vendor/angular.min.js"></script>
    <script src="./js/vendor/angular-route.min.js"></script>
    <script src="./js/app.js"></script>
  </body>
</html>
```

This very basic structure of an Angular application looks almost identical to any Angular app, with one exception: `data-ng-csp=""`.

The `ngCsp` directive enables Content Security Policy (or CSP) support for our Angular app. Since Chrome apps prevent the browser from using `eval` or `function(string)` generated functions, and Angular uses the `function(string)` generated function for speed, `ngCsp` causes Angular to evaluate all expressions.

This compatibility mode comes as a cost of performance, however, as it executes operations much more slowly, but it won't throw any security violations in the process.

CSP also forbids JavaScript files from inlining stylesheet rules, so we need to include `angular-csp.css` manually.

We can find the `angular-csp.css` file at http://code.angularjs.org/snapshot/angular-csp.css[147].

Lastly, we must place `ngCsp` alongside the root of our Angular apps:

```
<html ng-app ng-csp>
```

> Without the `ng-csp` directive, our Chrome app will **not** run; it will throw a security exception. If you see a security exception thrown, make sure you check the root element for the directive.

---

[147]http://code.angularjs.org/snapshot/angular-csp.css

Loading the App in Chrome

With our app in progress, let's load it into Chrome so we can follow our progress in the browser. To load our app in Chrome, we should navigate to the URL `chrome://extensions/`.

Once there, we can click on the button "Load unpackged extension..." and find the root directory (the directory that contains our `manifest.json` file from above).

Load unpacked extension

Once the application has been *loaded* into the Chrome browser, we open a new tab and should see our empty app with one error (don't worry, we'll fix it shortly):

Load unpacked extension in browser

 Whenever we update or modify our `manifest.json` file, we need to click on the `Reload` link underneath our Chrome app in `chrome://extensions`.

The Main Module

We'll build our entire Angular application in the `js/app.js` file. For production versions of our app, we may want to split this functionality into multiple files or use a tool like Grunt[148] to compress and concatenate them for us.

Our app is called `myApp`, so let's create an Angular module with the same name:

---

[148]http://gruntjs.com/

```
angular.module('myApp', [])
```

With this step, our app runs in the browser without any issues.

Building the Home Page

We'll start by building the home section in our app. In this section, we'll work on putting together components of our app that will make the application run. In the next section, we'll set up the multi-route application.

Building the Clock

The main feature of *Presently* is the large clock that sits right at the top of the application and updates every second. In Angular, we can set up this clock pretty simply.

We start by building a `MainController` that is responsible for managing the home screen. Inside this `MainController` controller, we set up a timeout that ticks every second and updates a local scope variable.

```
angular.module('myApp', [])
.controller('MainController', function($scope, $timeout) {
  // Build the date object
  $scope.date = {};

  // Update function
  var updateTime = function() {
    $scope.date.raw = new Date();
    $timeout(updateTime, 1000);
  }

  // Kick off the update function
  updateTime();
});
```

Every second that our `MainController` is visible, the `updateTime()` function runs to update the `$scope.date.raw` timestamp, and our view updates.

In order for us to see anything in the view load in our Chrome app, we need to bind this data to the document. We can set up this binding using the normal {{ }} template syntax:

```
<div class="container">
  <div ng-controller="MainController">
    {{ date.raw }}
  </div>
</div>
```

When we go back to the browser and refresh, we should see an unformatted date object ticking in the view.

As it currently stands, the date is very ugly in the browser. We can utilize Angular's built-in filters to format our date in a much more elegant manner.

Let's format our date similarly to how *Currently* formats the date on its home screen. Updating the view, we need to move our date into its own nested div and add formatting to display the date:

```
<div class="container">
  <div ng-controller="MainController">
    <div id="datetime">
      <h1>{{ date.raw | date:'hh mm ss' }}</h1>
    </div>
  </div>
</div>
```

With a little CSS and help from Bootstrap, our dates will appear on the screen in a much more human-friendly format.

First screen

We're using CSS rules to align the date and times to the center of the screen and increasing the font-size to be prominently displayed on screen.

```
#datetime {
  text-align: center;
}
#datetime h1 {
  font-size: 6.1em;
}
```

We can add a second date in our view that simply shows our date with a human-friendly display. Doing so is simply a matter of adding a second formatted date:

```
<!-- ... -->
<div id="datetime">
  <h1>{{ date.raw | date:'hh mm ss' }}</h1>
  <h2>{{ date.raw | date:'EEEE, MMMM yyyy' }}</h2>
</div>
<!-- ... -->
```

Our CSS for the #datetime h2 tag simply increases the size of the <h2> tag:

```
#datetime h2 {
  font-size: 1.0em;
}
```

Full dates

Sign Up for Wunderground's Weather API

Our app needs to reach out to foreign sources to fetch the current weather for the location in which we're interested. In this application, we're using the Wunderground[149] API.

---

[149]http://www.wunderground.com/

In order to use the Wunderground APi, we need to get an access API key.

To get an access API key, we first need to sign up. Let's head to the weather API Wunderground page at http://www.wunderground.com/weather/api/[150] and click "Sign Up for Free!".

Once we fill out the relevant details on the following page, we can click through until we reach the detail page that shows our API key.

Once we're set, we can locate the Wunderground API key and save it. We'll be using it shortly.

Building the Angular Service

We won't place our logic into the Controller to fetch the weather, as it is both inefficient (the controller will be blown away when we navigate to another page, and we'll need to re-call the API every time the controller is loaded) and poor design to mix in business logic details with implementation details.

Instead, we'll use a service. A service persists across controllers for the duration of the application's lifetime and is the appropriate place for us to hide business logic away from the controller.

We need to *configure* our app when it boots up, so we need to create our service using the .provider() method. This method is the **only** service creation method that we can inject into .config() functions.

To build the service, we'll use the .provider() API method that takes both a name of the service as well as a function that defines the actual provider.

```
angular.module('myApp', [])
.provider('Weather', function() {
})
```

Inside of this method, we need to define a $get() function that returns the methods available to the service. To configure this service, we need to allow a method for the API key to be set on configuration. These methods live outside of the scope of the $get() function.

```
.provider('Weather', function() {
  var apiKey = "";

  this.setApiKey = function(key) {
    if (key) this.apiKey = key;
  };

  this.$get = function($http) {
    return {
      // Service object
    }
  }
})
```

With this minimal amount of code, we can now *inject* the Weather service into our .config() function and configure the service with our Wunderground API key.

When Angular encounters a provider created with the .provider() API method, it creates a [Name]Provider injectable object. This object is what we'll inject into our config function:

```
// .provider('Weather', function() {
//   ...
// })
.config(function(WeatherProvider) {
  WeatherProvider.setApiKey('YOUR_API_KEY');
})
// .controller('MainController', function($scope, $timeout) {
//   ...
```

The Wunderground API requires that we pass the API key with our request in the URL. In order to pass our API key in with every request, we need to create a function that will generate the URL.

```
var apiKey = "";
// ...
this.getUrl = function(type, ext) {
  return "http://api.wunderground.com/api/" +
    this.apiKey + "/" + type + "/q/" +
    ext + '.json';
};
```

Now, we can create our API call for the Weather service to get us the latest forecast data from the Wunderground API.

We'll create our own promises that we can use to resolve in the view, because we'll want to return only the relevant results from our API call:

```
this.$get = function($q, $http) {
  var self = this;
  return {
    getWeatherForecast: function(city) {
      var d = $q.defer();
      $http({
        method: 'GET',
        url: self.getUrl("forecast", city),
        cache: true
      }).success(function(data) {
        // The wunderground API returns the
        // object that nests the forecasts inside
        // the forecast.simpleforecast key
        d.resolve(data.forecast.simpleforecast);
      }).error(function(err) {
        d.reject(err);
      });
      return d.promise;
    }
  }
}
```

Now, we can inject the `Weather` service into our controller and call the `getWeatherForecast()` method and respond to the promise instead of dealing with the complexity of the API in our controller.

Back to our `MainController`: We can now inject the `Weather` service and set the result on our scope:

```
.controller('MainController',
  function($scope, $timeout, Weather) {
    // ...
    $scope.weather = {}
    // Hardcode San_Francisco for now
    Weather.getWeatherForecast("CA/San_Francisco")
    .then(function(data) {
      $scope.weather.forecast = data;
    });
    // ...
```

To view the result of the API call in our view, we need to update our `tab.html`. For debugging purposes, we like to use the `json` filter inside a `<pre>` tag:

```
<div id="forecast">
  <pre>{{ weather.forecast | json }}</pre>
</div>
```

Weather API debugging call

We can see that the view is updated with the latest weather, and now we're good to go to create a more polished view.

The view itself iterates over the forecast.forecastday collection. For each element, we're creating a view that displays the weather icon given to us by the Wunderground API as well as the human-readable date and high temperature.

```
<div id="forecast">
  <ul class="row list-unstyled">
    <li ng-repeat="day in weather.forecast.forecastday" class="col-md-3">
      <div ng-class="{today: $index == 0}">
        <img class="{{ day.icon }}" ng-src="{{ day.icon_url }}" />
        <h3>{{ day.high.fahrenheit }}</h3>
        <h4 ng-if="$index == 0">Now</h4>
        <h4 ng-if="$index != 0">{{ day.date.weekday }}</h4>
      </div>
    </li>
  </ul>
</div>
```

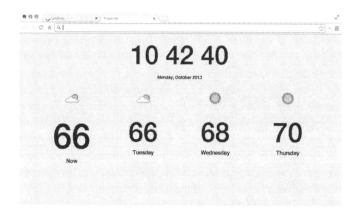

Clean HTML weather view

The style we've set in the view is:

```
#forecast ul li {
  font-size: 4.5em;
  text-align: center;
}
#forecast ul li h3 {
  font-size: 1.4em;
}
#forecast ul li .today h3 {
  font-size: 1.8em;
}
```

A Settings Screen

Currently, our app only has one view, with a hard-coded city that we fetch for every browser. Although this setup works for all of us here in San Francisco, it does **not** work for anyone elsewhere.

In order to allow our users the ability to customize their experience with *Presently*, we need to add a second screen: a setting screen.

To introduce a second screen (and multiple views), we need to add the `ngRoute` module as a dependency of our app module.

```
angular.module('myApp', ['ngRoute'])
```

Now we can define our separate views and routes and pull our home screen view out of the main `tab.html` view.

In defining our routes, note that we'll need two: one for each of the two different screens of our app.

```
// angular.module(...)
// ...
.config(function($routeProvider) {
  $routeProvider
    .when('/', {
      templateUrl: 'templates/home.html',
      controller: 'MainController'
    })
    .when('/settings', {
      templateUrl: 'templates/settings.html',
      controller: 'SettingsController'
    })
    .otherwise({redirectTo: '/'});
})
```

We can now take our entire tab.html HTML between the .container div, move it into the file templates/home.html, and replace it with <div ng-view></div>.

```
<div class="container">
  <div ng-view></div>
</div>
```

When we refresh the page, we can see that nothing appears to have *changed*, but our HTML is loaded from the templates/home.html template instead of inside the tab.html.

Currently, we have no way of navigating between our two screens. We can add some footer-based navigation that allows our users to navigate between the pages. We simply need to add two links at the bottom of the page to navigate between pages, like so:

```
<div id="actionbar">
  <ul class="list-inline">
    <li><a class="glyphicon glyphicon-home" href="#/"></a></li>
    <li><a class="glyphicon glyphicon-cog" href="#/settings"></a></li>
  </ul>
</div>
```

In order to add them to the the bottom right-hand corner of the screen, we must apply a bit of CSS to absolutely position them:

```css
#actionbar {
  position: absolute;
  bottom: 0.5em;
  right: 1.0em;
}
#actionbar a {
  font-size: 2.2rem;
  color: #000;
}
```

Now, if we navigate to our settings page by clicking on the cog button, we see that nothing is rendered. We need to define our `SettingsController` so we can start manipulating the view and working with our user.

```javascript
// ...
.controller('SettingsController',
  function($scope) {
    // Our controller will go here
})
```

The settings screen itself features a single form that will be responsible for allowing the user to change the cities in which they are interested. The HTML itself will look similar to this block (with a few features we have yet to implement):

```html
<h2>Settings</h2>
<form ng-submit="save()">
  <input type="text"
         ng-model="user.location"
         placeholder="Enter a location" />
  <input class="btn btn-primary"
       type="submit" value="Save" />
</form>
```

Implementing a User Service

For the same reasons that we are hiding away the complexity of the Wunderground API, we also want to hide away our user API. Doing so enables us to use local storage as well as communicate across our controllers about the user settings at any part of the app.

The `UserService` itself is straightforward and does not need to be configured in our app. Without the use of local storage, our `UserService` will simply be:

```
// ...
.factory('UserService', function() {
  var defaults = {
    location: 'autoip'
  };
  var service = {
    user: defaults
  };

  return service;
})
```

This service holds onto our user object for the lifetime of the application. That is to say that while the browser window is open, the settings of the application will remain constant to the user's settings; however, if our user opens a new tab in Chrome, these settings disappear, which is not ideal.

We can persist our settings across our app by using Chrome's sessionStorage capabilities. Luckily, this API is straightforward and simple.

We just add two functions to the UserService:

- save
- restore

Even with these capabilities, the UserService has not grown:

```
// ...
.factory('UserService', function() {
  var defaults = {
    location: 'autoip'
  };

  var service = {
    user: {},
    save: function() {
      sessionStorage.presently =
        angular.toJson(service.user);
    },
    restore: function() {
      // Pull from sessionStorage
      service.user =
        angular.fromJson(sessionStorage.presently) || defaults
```

```
      return service.user;
    }
  };
  // Immediately call restore from the session storage
  // so we have our user data available immediately
  service.restore();
  return service;
})
// ...
```

We can inject this `UserService` across our Chrome app and have access to the same user data. Heading back to our `SettingsController`, we can now set up a user object to define settings with the new service:

```
.controller('SettingsController',
  function($scope, UserService) {
    $scope.user = UserService.user;
});
```

If we refresh the browser, we can see that we have a default set for the user as `'autoip'`, which is the default we set up in the `UserService` definition.

We only need a way for our user to save their data into their session storage so we can use it across the app. In our `templates/settings.html`, we defined the form as having a `ng-submit="save()"` action; thus, when our user submits the form, the `save()` function is called.

Inside our `SettingsController`, we need to implement the `save()` function that will call save on the `UserService` and persist the user's data into their sessionStorage.

```
.controller('SettingsController',
  function($scope, UserService) {
    $scope.user = UserService.user;

    $scope.save = function() {
      UserService.save();
    }
});
```

With the single input field bound to `user.location`, if we change the value and press save, our user's `sessionStorage` will update:

sessionStorage

By using the `UserService` in our `HomeController`, we can now remove the hardcoded value of "'CA/San_Francisco'" and replace it with our new `UserService` object's location.

```
// ...
.controller('MainController',
  function($scope, $timeout, Weather, UserService) {
    // ...
    $scope.user = UserService.user;
    Weather.getWeatherForecast($scope.user.location)
    .then(function(data) {
      $scope.weather.forecast = data;
    });
    // ...
})
```

As we can see, if we flip back and forth from the settings view and input "NY/New_York", for instance, we can see the weather changing based upon the location we place in the settings page.

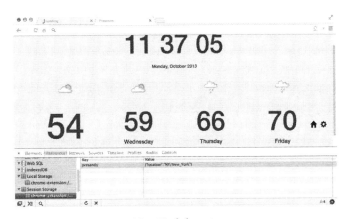

New York location

City Autofill/Autocomplete

It's pretty inconvenient to need to type a city that conforms to the Wunderground API formats (lat/long, city and state, country codes, etc.). Luckily, the Wunderground APi also provides us an autocomplete API[151].

Instead of requiring our users to *know* the specific city format, we can provide a list of them for our users to select.

 For the sake of simplicity and flexibility, we're only going to create a raw JavaScript-based autocomplete rather than use plugin libraries, such as the typeahead.js or jQuery plugin libraries.

To do that, we create a directive on the `<input>` element that will append a `<ul>` element with a list of suggested places.

```
.directive('autoFill', function($timeout) {
  return {
    restrict: 'EA',
    scope: {
      autoFill: '&',
      ngModel: '='
    },
    compile: function(tEle, tAttrs) {
      // Our compile function
      return function(scope, ele, attrs, ctrl) {
        // Our link function
      }
    }
  }
})
```

As we are creating a new element, we need to use the `compile` function rather than just the link function and a template, since our `<ul>` element cannot be nested underneath an `<input>` element.

Without diving too deeply into how the `compile` function works, we're going to create a new element, and we'll set up the bindings on it:

---

[151]http://www.wunderground.com/weather/api/d/docs?d=autocomplete-api

```
// ...
compile: function(tEle, tAttrs) {
  var tplEl = angular.element('<div class="typeahead">' +
  '<input type="text" autocomplete="off" />' +
  '<ul id="autolist" ng-show="reslist">' +
    '<li ng-repeat="res in reslist" ' +
      '>{{res.name}}</li>' +
  '</ul>' +
  '</div>');
  var input = tplEl.find('input');
  input.attr('type', tAttrs.type);
  input.attr('ng-model', tAttrs.ngModel);
  tEle.replaceWith(tplEl);

  return function(scope, ele, attrs, ctrl) {
    // ...
```

Inside of our link function, we need to bind a function to the keyup event and check that we have at least a minimum number of characters in our input field. Once we hit the minimum number of characters, we run a function set by the use of the directive to fetch the auto-suggested values.

Autocomplete API

Let's examine how we invoke this directive: We call it by passing a function to the auto-fill directive call and bind the location to the user.location value:

```
<input type="text"
  ng-model="user.location"
  auto-fill="fetchCities"
  autocomplete="off"
  placeholder="Location" />
```

In our Weather service, we'll create another function that specifically calls the autocomplete API and resolves a promise with a list of suggested completions for a query term.

```
getWeatherForecast: function(city) {
  // ...
},
getCityDetails: function(query) {
  var d = $q.defer();
  $http({
    method: 'GET',
    url: "http://autocomplete.wunderground.com/' +
          'aq?query=" +
          query
  }).success(function(data) {
    d.resolve(data.RESULTS);
  }).error(function(err) {
    d.reject(err);
  });
  return d.promise;
}
```

Back in our SettingsController, we can simply reference this function as the one that retrieves the list of suggested values. Remember, we need to inject the Weather service in the controller to reference it.

```
.controller('SettingsController',
  function($scope, UserService, Weather) {
    // ...
    $scope.fetchCities = Weather.getCityDetails;
});
```

In the directive, we can now call the function that references the action we want to fire upon modification.

```
// ...
tEle.replaceWith(tplEl);
return function(scope, ele, attrs, ctrl) {
  var minKeyCount = attrs.minKeyCount || 3,
      timer,
      input = ele.find('input');

  input.bind('keyup', function(e) {
    val = ele.val();
    if (val.length < minKeyCount) {
      if (timer) $timeout.cancel(timer);
```

```
    scope.reslist = null;
    return;
  } else {
    if (timer) $timeout.cancel(timer);
    timer = $timeout(function() {
      scope.autoFill()(val)
      .then(function(data) {
        if (data && data.length > 0) {
          scope.reslist = data;
          scope.ngModel = data[0].zmw;
        }
      });
    }, 300);
  }
});
// Hide the reslist on blur
input.bind('blur', function(e) {
  scope.reslist = null;
  scope.$digest();
});
}
```

We're using a *timeout* so that we only call the function once we are done typing. Using timeouts is a simple way to prevent the function from being called repeatedly while we're really only interested in the first call to the suggestion API.

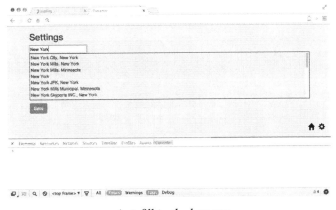

Autofill in the browser

Sprinkling in Time Zone Support

Finally, we also want our clock to update and reflect the new location that the user has chosen in his or her settings. Updating the clock to include time zone support is easy: We've implemented the most difficult part already through the autocomplete API.

First, we must add one more attribute to our directive usage as `timezone`:

```
<input type="text"
    ng-model="user.location"
    timezone="user.timezone"
    auto-fill="fetchCities"
    autocomplete="off"
    placeholder="Location" />
```

Next, we need to add the `timezone` attribute to our generated `<input>` field in our directive's compile function:

```
// ...
input.attr('type', tAttrs.type);
input.attr('ng-model', tAttrs.ngModel);
input.attr('timezone', tAttrs.timezone);
tEle.replaceWith(tplEl);
// ...
```

Last, but not least, we simply save the user's time zone when we save the topmost value for the user's location in the autocomplete link function:

```
// ...
scope.reslist = data;
scope.ngModel = data[0].zmw;
scope.timezone = data[0].tz;
// ...
```

Back in the browser, when we type our city, we also save the time zone alongside the new value of the city:

Time zone support

We now need to update the time and date in our `MainController` to take into account the new time zone.

Previously, matching time zone names to their GMT offsets was a difficult task. The Mozilla and Chrome teams have implemented the toLocaleString with the new `timeZone` argument that enables us to remap a date according to its timezone. Since we are writing a Chrome app, this function is available for our use in our app.

Back in our `MainController`, we simply create a new date based on the saved time zone:

```
.controller('MainController',
  function($scope, $timeout, Weather, UserService) {
    $scope.date = {};

    var updateTime = function() {
      $scope.date.tz = new Date(new Date().toLocaleString(
          "en-US", {timeZone: $scope.user.timezone}
        ));
      $timeout(updateTime, 1000);
    }
    // ...
```

Now, instead of using the `$scope.date.raw` in our view, we switch over to using the `$scope.date.tz`. The time changes with modifications to the time zone.

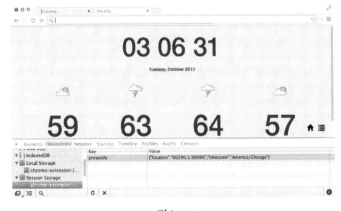

Chicago

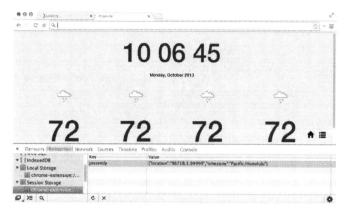

Hawaii

Optimizing Angular Apps

Angular is clearly great for optimizing development time, but how does it stack up in terms of performance, and what can we do to get it to be as fast as possible?

For most web applications, the native speed of Angular is fast enough, and don't need to pay any special attention to optimizing its performance. When our applications get slow or show poor performance, we can then attack optimizing our Angular apps.

What to Optimize

In order to know where to focus on the optimizing our app, we need to understand what's happening under the Angular hood. As with any applications, we start by focusing on the cause of our issues.

Optimizing the $digest Loop

The obvious place to start looking for performance issues is in the $digest loop. In short, Angular runs through a watch list that is responsible for keeping track of the live data bindings. Every single piece of *live* data that can possibly change on the page has a *watch* applied to it.

> The Under the Hood chapter discusses the $watch list and the $digest loop in detail.

Each of these watches causes the $digest loop to take more time to finish rendering, as Angular needs to keep track of the the value and check if it's changed on each loop.

Focusing on limiting the number of unnecessary watches will gain us the biggest performance boosts. Additionally, keeping the bi-directional data comparisons simple will give us even more performance boosts, because the browser can check these quickly.

In our apps, we should be mindful that the number of bi-directional data bindings should not exceed more than 2000 data bindings on the page for each $digest loop.

Sometimes we don't even want the full $digest loop to run on our app. For instance, imagine we have a polling loop that checks our server several times a second. If we receive a websocket event that fires a full digest loop with every message, we'll have a pretty slow application.

> We recommend using websockets, as they are more production-friendly and less prone to errors.

```
app.factory('poller', function($rootScope, $http) {
  var pollForEvent = function(timeout) {
    $http.get('/events')
    .success(function(data) {
      var events = data.events;
      for (var i = 0; i < events.length; i++) {
        var event = events[i];
        if (service.handlers[event])
          for (handler in service.handlers[event])
            $rootScope.$apply(function() {
              handler.apply(event);
            });
      }
      // Set the next timeout
      setTimeout(pollForEvent, timeout);
    });
  };
  // poll every half-second
  setTimeout(function() { pollForEvents(500); });
  var service = {
    handlers: {},
    on: function(evt, callback) {
      if (!service.handlers[evt])
        service.handlers[evt] = [];

      service.handlers[evt].push(callback);
    }
  }
  return service;
});
```

The major issue with this code is that we'll end up running the $rootScope.$apply() method for every single event that gets fired, which can add up to many $digest loops per second.

Limiting the number of $digest loops per second is a great way to start *upgrading* the performance of our app. We can throttle the events to happen only at a maximum of times we want per second.

```
// throttle function
var throttle = function(fn, atMost, ctx) {
  var ctx    = ctx || this;
  var atMost = atMost || 250; // milliseconds
  var last, defer, result;
  return function() {
    var now = new Date(),
        args = arguments;
    if (last && now < last + atMost) {
      // Execute this later
      clearTimeout(defer);
      defer = setTimeout(function() {
        last = now;
        fn.apply(ctx, args);
      }, atMost);
    } else {
      result = fn.apply(ctx, args);
    }
    return result;
  }
}
```

This *relatively* ugly `throttle()` function only triggers the function once, at most, per `atMost` cycle.

 The Underscore.js[152] library has a much better production-ready, battle-tested version of this code.

To set our `$digest` loop to throttle using our `throttle` function, we can simply invoke it in the event loop:

```
// ...
for (var i = 0; i < events.length; i++) {
  var event = events[i];
  if (service.handlers[event])
    for (handler in service.handlers[event])
      throttle(function() {
        $rootScope.$apply(function() {
          handler.apply(event);
        });
      }, 500);
}
```

---

[152]http://underscorejs.org/

Optimizing ng-repeat

One of the biggest sources of delay in Angular is the ng-repeat directive. For every single element that ng-repeat places, there will be at *least* one data binding per entry in the list, and this fact does not even count any of the bindings that we create inside of the list elements.

Let's take a look at the performance of the following repeating list generated by ng-repeat:

```
<ul>
  <li ng-repeat="email in emails">
    <a ng-href="#/from/{{ email.sender }}">
      {{ email.sender }}
    </a>
    <a ng-href="#/email/{{ email.id }}">
      {{ email.subject }}
    </a>
  </li>
</ul>
```

For every single email in our list, we're going to have, at minimum, one watch generated by the ngRepeat directive (this watch monitors the list for changes). Since Angular creates a $watch for every single ng directive, the above list has 4 + 1 watches per email. For a list of 100 emails, the usages above already creates 500 watches, and the above example list is not even a complex one for the entire page.

With this relatively short list, it's obvious to see how the performance of the app can be greatly reduced with any significantly sized app. There are some relatively simple ways that we can speed up our application.

Optimizing the $digest Call

We can often determine when and to which scope(s) running the $digest loop will affect when we change a variable. When this is the case, we don't need to invoke the entire $digest loop on the $rootScope using $scope.$apply() (which causes every child $scope to run in the $digest loop). Instead, we can directly call $scope.$digest().

Calling $scope.$digest() only runs the digest loop on the specific scope that called $digest() and all of its children.

Optimizing $watch Functions

Since the $watch list expressions are executed every $digest loop, it's important that we keep the functionality tiny. The smaller and more focused the $watch expression, the more performant our application will be.

Avoiding deep comparisons, complex logic, and any loops in our $watch() functions will help speed up our applications.

For instance, we could set up a watch that watches an object. Imagine we have an Account object:

```
$scope.account = {
  active: true,
  userId: 123,
  balance: 1000 // in cents
}
```

Presumably, we'd want to watch for any time the balance changes and set the account to not active if the balance reaches zero. We can set up a $watch function that watches the account object and updates the account whenever the balance object changes:

```
$scope.$watch('user', function(newAccount) {
  if (newAccount.balance <= 0) {
    $scope.account.active = false
  }
}, true);
```

The third argument in the $watch() function tells Angular to watch the object using deep comparison, checking every property with the angular.equals() function.

This choice will cause **terrible** performance. Not only is Angular making a copy of the object, but it stores and saves it while it needs to walk through every property to check if any of them have changed it.

A tip for building our $watch functions: Use them to keep track of variables that clearly affect the view. Anything that does not affect the view does not need a $watch function.

Sometimes it makes sense for us to remove watchers, specifically when a $watch function becomes irrelevant because the data is static and we just want to expose it in our view the first time.

We can easily remove custom watchers from our view: The $watch function itself returns a function that enables us to remove the $watch function.

For instance, say we have a custom directive that is waiting for the resolution of a variable name:

```
<div data-my-directive name="customerName"></div>
```

Since the customerName isn't likely to change once it's set, we see we can optimize the use of this directive by removing the $watch function we've set up:

```
.directive('myDirective', function($q) {
  return {
    // ...
    scope: {
      name: '='
    },
    link: function(scope, ele, attrs, ctrl) {
      var unWatch =
        scope.$watch(attrs.name, function(n, o) {
          if (n != o) {
            // Do something with the resolution of
            // name and remove the watch
            unWatch();
          }
        });
    }
  };
});
```

We can gain in performance by removing any and all of the unnecessary watches in our application. This process can be particularly cumbersome when trying to remove every watch from our application, especially when we're trying to remove the default watchers that Angular sets up.

We can write our own directives to manage watchers instead of working with the built-in directives that Angular provides. Luckily, we don't have to write these directives for ourselves as they've already been written for us in a library called *bindonce*.

Bindonce

Bindonce is a drop-in module we can use in our apps that contain directives that hang on to a watch once and only once; it gives us the ability to pass in asynchronous data.

The library works by creating new directives that we attach to DOM elements where we don't require live updating. These directives watch for the value to be filled and validated. Once the data is available, it renders its contents, as well as its children's contents, and promptly removes the watcher.

Using the *bindonce* directive creates a single *temporary* watcher that is is removed after the data becomes available. If the data is already available on the scope, then the watcher is not created and the children are rendered.

Recall our previous example. We'll create the same example with **zero** permanent watchers, using *bindonce*:

```
<ul>
  <li bindonce="email" ng-repeat="email in emails">
    <a bo-href-i="#/from/{{ email.sender }}"
       bo-text="email.sender"></a>
    <a bo-href-i="#/email/{{ email.id }}"
       bo-text="email.subject"></a>
  </li>
</ul>
```

To use *bindonce*, we first need to grab the source. We can either get it directly from GitHub at the project page (https://github.com/pasvaz/bindonce[153]) or through Bower by installing it like so:

```
bower install angular-bindonce
```

Once we have the source, we need to reference it in our main view:

```
<script src="scripts/vendor/bindonce.js"></script>
```

Lastly, we need to set it as a dependency for our application module:

```
angular.module('myApp', ['pasvaz.bindonce']);
```

Now, when we're dealing with static data, we can be sure, with the help of the bo-* tags, that we're not using unnecessary watchers.

The *bindonce* library gives us many directives. As we can see above, we're using two custom directives.

 Every time we use any bo-* tag, we need to ensure a part of it contains the bindonce directive. All of the children bo-* directives will watch for the data in this directive to resolve.

bo-if="condition"

This directive is the same as calling ng-if, but without using extra watchers.

bo-show="condition" / bo-hide="condition"

This directive is the same as calling ng-show or ng-hide, but without using any extra watchers.

---

[153]https://github.com/pasvaz/bindonce

bo-text="text"

This directive evaluates the text and places it inside of the element. It's similar to `ng-bind`.

bo-href="url" / bo-href-i="url"

Using `bo-href` does not allow the "url" to require interpolation, while `bo-href-i` enables the URL to contain interpolation. These two calls are functionally equivalent:

```
// bo-href does not allow for any interpolation
<a bo-href="'/users/' + User.id">√</a>
// bo-href-i does allow interpolation
<a bo-href-i="'/users/{{ User.id }}'">√</a>
```

bo-src="url" / bo-src-i="url"

The `bo-src` doesn't allow for interpolation inside the URL, while `bo-src-i` does.

These two calls are functionally equivalent:

```
// bo-href does not allow for any interpolation
<img bo-src="'/users/'+User.gravatar" />
// bo-href-i does allow interpolation
<img bo-src-i="/users/{{ User.gravatar }}"/>
```

bo-alt="text"

Similar to the `bo-text`, this directive renders text inside a DOM element and sets the text as the `alt` attribute on the element.

bo-title="title"

The `bo-title` directive renders text inside a DOM element and sets the text as the `title` attribute on the element.

bo-id="id"

This directive renders the "id" and sets it as the `id` attribute on the element.

bo-style="style"

This directive renders the style as an expression with the same syntax as `ng-style` without using a watcher.

bo-value="value"

This directive renders the value and sets it as the value attribute of the element.

bo-attr bo-attr-foo="hello"

This directive renders the text 'foo' as a custom attribute in the DOM.

Bindonce is a great place to start optimizing any pages that use ng-repeat for mostly static data.

Auto-optimization of $watch Functions

The latest version of Angular **automatically** removes $watch functions that it finds to be of a constant value (e.g., if the expression resolves to a boolean or a static integer).

```
// These watchers will be automatically removed
// as $watches as Angular detects these as
// constant values
$scope.$watch('true', function() {});
$scope.$watch('2 + 2', function() {});
```

Optimizing Filters

Every filter that is placed in the view will be called a minimum of two times due to the nature of filters. The more we can keep these functions lightweight and optimized, the faster our applications will be.

Unchanging Data

For this reason, it's often a good idea to analyze where and why we are using a filter in our view. Generally, a good rule of thumb is that any filter that needs to be *transformed* for the view once can be moved out of the view.

That is to say that, rather than using the currency filter in the view, we can transform the model when we retrieve the data. That way, we don't display it in the view where it will be run twice.

That is to say instead of using the filter in the view, like so:

```
<!-- Using a filter -->
<div>{{ receipt.total_cost | currency }}</div>
```

We can transform the receipt.total_cost in our controller (or service) instead by using the $filter service:

```
.controller('ReceiptController', function($scope, $filter) {
  $scope.receipt.total_sum = 12345;
  $scope.receipt.total_cost =
    $filter('currency')($scope.receipt.total_sum);
});
```

Filtered Data

We have other filters, such as live-search filters, that limit the data in collections that are repeated using ng-repeat and through sorted orderBy filter uses. In these cases, the data doesn't change, but how they are presented on screen does.

Rather than calling these filters every single $digest loop, we can *cache* the sorted/filtered results so that we only calculate the sort and order when necessary. This variable caching is called *memoizing*.

 Memoization is an optimization technique used to speed up applications for function calls that have been previously called and whose results are not expected to changed for a given input.

In order to use memoization instead of a filter, we need to either implement our own memoize() function or use one from a library, such as Underscore.js[154] or Lo-Dash[155], that includes its own. Since the function itself is tiny, we've included the basic function definition from inside the Lo-Dash library:

```
function memoize(fn, resolver) {
  var memoized = {
    var cache = memoized.cache,
        key = resolver ? resolver.apply(this, arguments) :
              +new Date() + '' + arguments[0];
    return hasOwnProperty.call(cache, key) ?
            cache[key] :
            (cache[key] = fn.apply(this, arguments));
  }
  memoized.cache = {};
  return memoized;
}
```

Essentially, the function itself takes two arguments: a function to cache and, optionally, a resolver function that is called to determine the cache key for storing the result. The function returns a memoized version of the function.

---

[154]http://underscorejs.org/

[155]http://lodash.com/

When we use it, we set the memoize function to be a function call on our scope object so we can call it from the view.

```
angular.module('myApp', [])
.controller('MainController', function($scope, $filter) {
  $scope.getNames = memoize(function() {
    return $filter('orderBy')(
      $scope.names,
      $scope.orderBy, $scope.reverseList
    );
  },
  function() {
    // Resolver function returns a string that
    // represents the cache key
    return $scope.orderBy + '-' + $scope.reverseList;
  });
});
```

When we call getNames() in the view, the orderBy $filter runs for the first time. The second time the filter is called, it will not run as the cache will contain the sort key.

Sometimes, we may want to manually clear the cache (e.g.: adding or removing an update). Since the cache itself is held on the function object, we can clear the cache simply by setting its value to a new {} object.

```
$scope.getNames.cache = {};
```

Tips for Optimizing Page Load

We can also optimize the amount of time it takes the client-side browser to render our page. Of course, there is no silver bullet for determining the best mechanisms to best load our pages for clients, as a large portion of it depends upon server-side components, location, and hosting issues.

Minification

Minifying our code is the easiest method for optimizing perceived page load time.

Minification is the process of removing all unnecessary characters from the source code, reducing the size of variables to as small as we can get them, stripping away comments and block delimiters, and more.

This reduces the time it takes for our files to be transferred over the network, because it reduces the size of the complete file.

We can minify our HTML, JavaScript, CSS, and even our images. The more compression we can get without sacrificing functionality, the better experience our users will have.

There are many free tools available to help us with minification. We recommend using the `uglify` tool, available through Grunt. For more information about Grunt, see the Grunt chapter.

Utilizing the $templateCache

When we deploy our app in production, we'll want our app to load as quickly as possible and be as responsive as possible. Requiring templates to load over XHR can lead to slow or sluggish-feeling web apps. Instead of requiring our templates to be fetched via XHR, we can *fake* the template cache loading by wrapping it into a JavaScript file and simply shipping our JavaScript file along with the rest of the application.

For more information on how to efficiently wrap our templates, see the $templateCache tool grunt-angular-templates.

Debugging AngularJS

When we're building large Angular apps, it's not uncommon to run into head-scratching issues that are seemingly difficult to uncover and resolve.

Debugging from the DOM

Although not always necessary nor a first step, we can get access to the Angular properties that are attached to any DOM element. We can use these properties to peek into how the data is flowing in our application.

 We should never rely on fetching element properties from a DOM element during the lifecycle of an application. The techniques are presented as techniques for debugging purposes.

To fetch these properties from the DOM, we need to find the DOM element in which we're interested. If we have the full jQuery library available, we can use the jQuery selector syntax: $("selector").

We don't need to rely on jQuery, however, to target and fetch elements from the DOM. Instead, we can use the document.querySelector() method.

 Note that the document.querySelector() is not available on all browsers and is *generally* good for non-complex element selections, whereas Sizzle[156] (the library jQuery uses) or jQuery[157] support more complex selections.

We can retrieve the $rootScope from the DOM by selecting the element where the ngApp directive is placed and wrapping it in an Angular element (using the angular.element() method).

With an Angular element, we can call various methods to inspect our Angular app from inside the DOM. To do so, we need to select the element from the DOM. Using only JavaScript and Angular, we can do so in this way:

```
var rootEle = document.querySelector("html");
var ele = angular.element(rootEle);
```

With this element, we can fetch various parts of our application.

---

[156]http://sizzlejs.com/

[157]http://jquery.com/

scope()

We can fetch the $scope from the element (or its parent) by using the scope() method on the element:

```
var scope = ele.scope();
```

Using the element's scope, we can inspect any scope properties, such as custom variables that we set on the scope in our controllers. We can peek into the elements looking into its $id, its $parent object, the $$watchers that are set on it and even manually walk up the scope chain.

controller()

We can fetch the current element's controller (or its parent) by using the controller() method:

```
var ctrl = ele.controller();
// or
var ctrl = ele.controller('ngModel');
```

injector()

We can fetch the injector of the current element (or the containing element) by using the injector() method on the selected element.

```
var injector = ele.injector();
```

With this injector, we can then then instantiate any Angular object inside of our app, such as services, other controllers, or any other object.

inheritedData()

We can fetch the data associated with an element's $scope simply by using the inheritedData() method on the element:

```
ele.inheritedData();
```

This inheritedData() method is how Angular finds data up the scope chain as it walks up the DOM until it's found a particular value or until the top-most parent has been reached.

> If you're using Chrome, we can use a shortcut with the developer tools. Simply find the element you're interested in, right click on it in the browser, and select *inspect element*. The element itself is stored as the $0 variable, and we can fetch the Angular-ized element by calling: angular.element($0).

Debugger

Google's Chrome[158] has its own debugger tool to create a breakpoint in our code. The `debugger` statement will cause the browser to *freeze* during execution, allowing us to examine the running code from inside the actual application and at the point of execution inside the browser.

To use the `debugger`, we can simply add it inside the context of our application code:

```
angular.module('myApp')
.factory('SessionService', function($q, $http) {
  var service = {
    user_id: null,
    getCurrentUser: function() {
      debugger; // Set the debugger inside
                // this function
      return service.user_id;
    }
  }

  return service;
});
```

Inside this service, we'll call the `debugger;` method that effectively *freezes* our application.

As long as the Chrome development tools are open in our browser, we can use `console.log()` and other JavaScript commands at the point where this application code executes.

When we're done debugging the application code, we need to make sure we **remove this line**, because it will freeze the browser, even in production.

Angular Batarang

Angular Batarang is a Chrome extension developed by the Angular team at Google that integrates very nicely as a debugging tool for Angular apps.

---

[158]https://www.google.com/chrome

Batarang chrome extension

Installing Batarang

To install Batarang, we simply need to download the application from the web store or from the GitHub repo: https://github.com/angular/angularjs-batarang[159].

Once our installation is set, we can start up the extension by navigating to our developer tools and clicking *enable* to enable Batarang to start collecting debugging information about our page.

Batarang allows us to look at scopes, performance, dependencies, and other key metrics in Angular apps.

Inspecting the Models

After we've started up Batarang, the page will reload, and we'll notice that we have a panel that enables us to select different scopes in our page.

We can select a scope by clicking on the + button, finding the element we're interested in and clicking on it.

Once we select a scope using the inspector, we can look at all the different properties on our scope element and their current values.

---

[159]https://github.com/angular/angularjs-batarang

Model inspector

Inspecting Performance

We can also peek into the performance of our application by using the performance section of Batarang.

In this panel, we get a peek into the watch list of the application at the different scopes as well as the amount of time that each expression takes, both in absolute time and percentage of the overall application time.

Performance inspector

Inspecting the Dependency Graph

One very nice feature of the Batarang tool is its ability to visualize the dependency graph inline. We can look at the dependencies of our application and view the different libraries of our application to see what they depend upon and track libraries that aren't dependencies of the application at all.

Dependency graph

Visualizing the App

Batarang allows us to look deep into the application on the page itself. Using the Options panel, we can look at:

Applications   The different applications that are on a single page (the ngApp directive uses)

Bindings   The bindings that are set in the view, where we use either ng-bind or {{ }} elements

Scopes   The scopes in the view that we can target and inspect more deeply

The options panel also allows us view the Angular version of the app and what we're using or not using from a CDN.

Options

All in all, the Batarang tools gives us a lot of power when diving into how our Angular apps work in real time.

Next Steps

Now that we're familiar with AngularJS, let's take a deep-dive into the professional tools available to allows us to develop in a production environment.

jqLite and jQuery

Although Angular encourages breaking away from reliance on the jQuery[160] library, we can use it if we need to within our app by ensuring that we load it *before* the DOMContentLoaded event has been fired or we manually bootstrap our app.

Angular itself includes a compatible library called jqLite.

The angular.element() method that we've been using throughout this book returns a jqLite object, which is a *subset of the jQuery library that allows Angular to manipulate the DOM in a cross-browser compatible way.*

The jqLite library does not attempt to cover all of methods in the entire jQuery library, as it is meant to be light and cover only those methods that Angular needs.

The library itself covers the following jQuery methods:

addClass()   Adds the specified class(es) to the element

after()   Inserts content after the element

append()   Inserts content to the end of the element

attr()   Gets or sets the value of the attribute for the element

bind() / on()   Attaches an event handler function for one or more events of the selected element

children()   Gets the children of the element

clone()   Creates a deep copy of element

---

[160]http://jquery.com/

contents()   Gets the children of each element in the set including text and comment nodes

css()   Gets or sets the value of a style property for the element

data()   Stores or returns the value of arbitrary data associated with the element

eq()   Gets the element at the specified index

find()   Gets the descendants of the element filtered by tagname only

hasClass()   Determines if the element itself is assigned a given class

html()   Gets or sets the HTML contents of the element

next()   Gets the immediately following sibling of the element

off() / unbind()   Removes an event handler by name

parent()   Gets the parent of the element

prepend()   Inserts content to the beginning of the element

prop()   Gets or sets the value of a property for the element

ready()   Specifies a function to execute when the DOM is fully loaded

remove()   Removes the element from the DOM

removeAttr()   Removes an attribute from the element

removeClass()   Removes a single, multiple, or all classes from the element

removeData()   Removes the previously stored data from the element

replaceWith()   Replaces the element with the provided new content

text() Gets or sets the combined text contents of the element

toggleClass() Adds or removes one or multiple classes from the element

triggerHandler() Executes all handlers attached to an element for an event

val() Gets or sets the current value of the element

wrap() Wraps an HTML structure around the element

Essential Tools to Know About

The AngularJS community is fantastic and has written some great tools to support AngularJS development. We'll range from discussing build tools and frameworks to live interaction tools.

Grunt

Grunt[161] is a pure JavaScript task runner. It will save you tons of time in developing JavaScript applications, both server side and client side. It makes repetitive tasks disappear and handles running them for you automatically.

The JavaScript community has jumped all over the Grunt tool and created hundreds of plugins. If a plugin you need or want has not been developed, the Grunt tool makes it very easy to create your own.

Installation

First, we have to make sure you have NodeJS[162] installed. NodeJS is a *platform built on Chrome's JavaScript run time*; it allows you to write JavaScript as a server-side language.

To install Grunt, we can use the built-in *npm* tool that comes with NodeJS:

```
$ npm install -g grunt-cli
```

 Passing the -g flag makes the grunt command available in any directory on your computer.

---

[161]http://gruntjs.com/
[162]http://nodejs.org/

With Grunt installed, we also need to have a *Gruntfile* alongside our app to configure how and what Grunt runs. In order to do anything useful with Grunt, let's create a `Gruntfile.js` in our project.

First things first, we have to create a `package.json` file that tells Node what to install as dependencies.

 Just as AngularJS handles dependencies, NodeJS has a clever method of dependency management. The `package.json` file will be your friend as you write more NodeJS apps.

To make the default `package.json` file, you can either run a generator or copy and paste from the default `package.json`. Since the `npm init` command is built in, let's use that:

```
$ npm init
```

This command asks us a series of questions, such as what is the *name* of our new app, what *version*, and a few more. You can use all of the defaults it sets for you, but it's probably a good idea to set the name of our app.

Once this command completes, it'll create a `package.json` file that looks something like:

```
{
  "name": "myapp",
  "version": "0.0.0",
  "description": "Your myapp description",
  "main": "index.js",
  "scripts": {
    "test": "echo \"Error: no test specified\" && exit 1"
  },
  "author": "Your name",
  "license": "MIT"
}
```

We can install the basic `grunt` command in our `package.json` file by using the `npm` command again:

```
$ npm install grunt --save-dev
```

 The `--save-dev` flag saves the `grunt` as a dependency for development. If you want to save a dependency for run time, you can use the `--save` flag.

A common use of Grunt is to minify our JavaScript files so that we can send the smallest file possible to the browser. This process is particularly useful so that our app will load as quickly as possible, especially on mobile devices.

We want install the Uglify plugin to handle this process for us.

```
$ npm install grunt-contrib-uglify --save-dev
```

Great! Now we can configure Grunt using the Gruntfile. To configure Grunt, we load our `Gruntfile.js` in our text editor and add the following:

```
module.exports = function(grunt) {
  // Configuration
  grunt.initConfig({
    pkg: grunt.file.readJSON('package.json')
  });
  // Load plugins
  // Default task(s).

};
```

To set up a configuration, we need to tell Grunt to load the npm tasks of all the plugins we want to use. Since we're loading the `uglify` tasks, we need to tell Grunt to load our `grunt-contrib-uglify` plugin tasks:

```
grunt.loadNpmTasks('grunt-contrib-uglify');
```

To configure Uglify, we can place a configure block inside of the `initConfig` object with the key of `uglify`. In this case, we can make a minimal update to the configuration where we only set the `src` and the `dest` locations.

```
grunt.initConfig({
  pkg: grunt.file.readJSON('package.json'),
  uglify: {
    build: {
      src: 'src/<%= pkg.name %>.js',
      dest: 'build/<%= pkg.name %>.min.js'
    }
  }
});
```

All of the available options for the block of configuration code for the `grunt-contrib-uglify` module can be found in the README for the project (available here[163]).

 Note that when using Grunt modules, the configuration documentation is most often available in the project's README file, or the README might otherwise point to the available configuration options.

---

[163]https://github.com/gruntjs/grunt-contrib-uglify

With that set, Grunt looks for the JavaScript file by whatever name we gave our `package.json` in the `src/` directory. It then runs the Uglify task on this file.

To actually tell Grunt to run the task, we can simply run the task `uglify`:

```
$ grunt uglify
```

We can also configure Grunt to run multiple tasks in one go by declaring a task with multiple subtasks:

```
grunt.initConfig({
  // config
});
grunt.registerTask('default', ['uglify']);
```

Now you can run `grunt default`, and all of the tasks we've defined in the array will run. The `default` task has special meaning in `Grunt`. With the `default` task configured like so, we can just run the `grunt` command, and all of those tasks will run.

You might be wondering why this functionality even matters. In this example, we've only set one task to run, but if we're using CoffeeScript, want to package all of our Angular templates into a single file, package our `less` CSS files, etc., Grunt can handle it all for you.

Finally, one of the most useful features of Grunt is its ability to *watch* the filesystem for file changes and execute commands on the file changes.

To set up a watch, we follow the same two steps as we did above.

First, we install the `grunt-contrib-watch` npm package:

```
$ npm install grunt-contrib-watch --save-dev
```

Next, we set up a config block in the `initConfig` object:

```
grunt.initConfig({
  pkg: grunt.file.readJSON('package.json'),
  //
  watch: {
    js: {
      files: 'src/**/*.js',
      tasks: ['uglify']
    }
  }
});
```

Now we can run `grunt watch`, and Grunt will start watching all of the JavaScript files in our `src/` directory. When any of them change, it runs the `uglify` task.

grunt-angular-templates

By default, Angular fetches templates over XHR when it cannot find them locally in its $templateCache. When the XHR request is slow or our template is large, it can seriously negatively impact our users' experience of our app.

One way we can avoid this delay is by "faking" the $templateCache into thinking that it has already been filled up, so Angular doesn't have to load the templates from afar. We can do this trick manually in JavaScript like so:

```
angular.module('myApp', [])
.run(function($templateCache) {
  $templateCache.put('home.html',
    'This is the home template');
});
```

Now, when Angular needs to fetch the template named 'home.html', it will find it in the $templateCache and not need to fetch it from the server.

This step is quite cumbersome to do manually if we want to package our app for our servers. Luckily, the grunt-angular-templates Grunt task does it for us.

Installation

First, we need to install the Grunt task. We can install it with npm as follows:

```
$ npm install --save-dev grunt-angular-templates
```

 We use the --save-dev task to store the Grunt task in our package.json file, and it's good practice to do so. Saving the dependencies and their versions allows for easily creating new development environments for our application. If we're not using a package.json file, then we can ignore this flag, but it won't do any harm to keep it in. npm will simply output a message warning us that we're not using a package.json.

Next, we need to reference this new task in our Gruntfile.js file, like so:

```
grunt.loadTasks('grunt-angular-templates');
```

Now, we can safely use this task in our Grunt tasks.

Usage

The task itself compiles a JavaScript file that we need to load inside of our index.html. For instance, if we tell the task to generate the templates.js file, we need to load it inside of our index.html:

```
<script src="template.js"></script>
```

First off, like any other Grunt task, we need to configure it. The configuration template key is `ngtemplates`. Inside of this `ngtemplates` configuration block, we set a subtask that will become the name of the Angular module we're loading.

For example:

```
ngtemplates: {
  myApp: {}
}
```

This code generates the output of our `template.js` file as:

```
angular.module('myApp')
  .run(['$templateCache', function($templateCache) {
    $templateCache.put('home.html', ...);
  }])
```

The name of the subtask `myApp` is the same as the Angular module which is where the `$templateCache` will place it's templates.

We'll set our options inside of this subtask.

Available Options

bootstrap

By default, `angular-grunt-templates` wraps the `function($templateCache) {}` inside of the `angular.module('myApp').run(['$templateCache', ___]);` We can change this configuration if we're using CommonJS or RequireJS with the bootstrap option:

```
// ...
bootstrap: function(module, script) {
  return 'module.exports[module]= ' + script + ';';
}
```

concat

`concat` is the name of the target in the `concat` definitions where we want to append our compiled template path.

htmlmin

Just as we can minimize our CSS and JavaScript files, we can also minimize our HTML using a tool called (unsurprisingly) htmlmin. grunt-angular-templates plays nicely with htmlmin and even allows us to minimize the HTML inside of our templates, as well.

We can set options for htmlmin inside of our configuration, like so:

```
ngtemplates: {
  myApp: {
    options: {
      htmlmin: {
        collapseBooleanAttributes:      true,
        collapseWhitespace:             true,
        removeAttributeQuotes:          true,
        removeEmptyAttributes:          true,
        removeRedundantAttributes:      true
        removeScriptTypeAttributes:     true,
        removeStyleLinkTypeAttributes:  true
      }
    }
  }
}
```

module

The name of the angular.module with which the template cache will be registered is the name of the module where the templates will be cached.

```
ngtemplates: {
  myApp: {
    options: {
      module: 'myBestApp'
    }
  }
}
```

We will therefore see our templates set in the following way:

```
angular.module('myBestApp')
  .run(['$templateCache',
  function($templateCache) {
    // ...
  }
```

prefix

We can set a prefix for all of our template URLS. For instance, if we want to use absolute URLs where our templates are accessed from an absolute location in a different directory, we'd set our prefix to look like:

```
ngtemplates: {
  app: {
    options: {
      prefix: '/public'
    }
  }
}
```

source

We can set the source option to a function to be called before the rest of the templates are compiled and after the source has been minified so that we can customize the template source output. For instance, we can add a standard header to our source files.

The function is called with these options:

- source - the minified template source
- path - the path to the template file
- options - the task options object

standalone

This boolean options flag tells the Grunt task whether the templates are part of an existing module, such as myApp, or if they stand alone. Mostly, this option should be set to false (as it is by default).

url

Setting the url option overrides the template's $templateCache URL. Mostly, this option is here for special circumstances; we set the cwd and the src to make the templates available both through XHR and through the $templateCache.

Usage

The authors of `grunt-angular-templates` have given us a lot of options for how we can use this task.

concat

The *easiest* way to use the task is inside of the `concat` task. It places the responsibility of the location of the task into the minified `concat` task.

```
concat: {
  app: {
    src:  ['*.js','<%= ngtemplates.app.dest %>'],
    dest: [ 'app.js' ]
  }
}
```

Now our templates will be attached at the end of our `app.js` file.

usemin

Using `grunt-usemin`, which is a task that minifies and combines JavaScript inline request files, we get the ability to compress and concatenate our source files in production and list our non-compressed dependencies in development. For instance:

```
<!-- build:js module.js -->
<script src="scripts/app.js"></script>
<script src="scripts/controllers.js"></script>
<!-- endbuild -->
```

The file to be minified is `module.js`. We can use this file as a target to attach our templates.

```
ngtemplates: {
  app: {
    src: 'templates/*.html',
    dest: 'template.js',
    options: {
      concat: 'module.js'
    }
  }
}
```

dest

Lastly, we can normally generate the `templates.js` file by specifying a destination, rather than appending it to another file by simply assigning a `dest:` key as a filepath.

```
ngtemplates: {
  app: {
    src: 'templates/*.html',
    dest: 'template.js'
  }
}
```

Lineman

The Lineman tool is a a build tool that allows us to focus on building fat-client (or client-side) web apps. It mixes an incredible amount of functionality to make client-side webapp development fun and easy.

Lineman is built and maintained by the community to keep front-end webapp development *productive* in a maintainable, manageable manner.

We've been developing our client-side application in a single index.html file that we've been loading through our browser for most of this book. Lineman takes a different approach and serves the application through a local server.

By serving files through a local server, Lineman can offer unique functionality we can't get with static files. It:

- Compiles and serves CoffeeScript[164] files as JavaScript upon saving a file
- Runs Less[165] and Sass[166] preprocessors and serves the generated CSS
- Provides back-end stubbing tools so we can develop *with or without* a back-end server
- Pre-compiles our JavaScript templates
- Proxies XHR requests to our back-end server
- Makes testing incredibly easy and fun

Lineman explicitly does not deal with any back-end web server (although it does provide a way for us to stub back-end calls, as we'll see). Its focus is on building AngularJS apps that can be compiled, minified, and deployed as a static web app.

To use Lineman, we need to make sure we have NodeJS[167] installed; it comes prepackaged with the npm tool. To install *lineman* itself, we can install it with npm and install it globally.

```
$ npm install -g lineman
```

Although we'll be using Lineman itself to run our project, we won't use the packaged generator. Instead, we'll use the AngularJS template created by David Mosher.

---

[164]http://coffeescript.org/

[165]http://lesscss.org/

[166]http://sass-lang.com/

[167]http://nodejs.org

```
$ git clone https://github.com/davemo/lineman-angular-template my-app
```

Once we've cloned this template (using Git), we can use npm again to install the dependencies that Lineman needs in order to operate:

```
$ cd my-app && npm install -d
```

After the dependencies have been installed, we can start working on our app. We'll edit our app while running the tests as well as the server.

To run the app, we need to start the Lineman tool in the my-app directory.

```
$ lineman run
```

Now, we have our app running in the browser at http://localhost:8000.

Running Lineman

As we can see, the Angular template has a few templates generated with by our app. We can also see that the directory structure contains a bunch of directories:

- **app** - contains the app files
    - **css** - our CSS files (Less or CSS files)
    - **img** - our img files
    - **js** - our Angular app
    - **pages** - the HTML templates to be compiled
    - **templates** - the Angular templates
- **config** - the Lineman-specific configuration files
- **doc** - a directory for documentation for the app
- **dist** - a generated directory where we build our production app
- **generated** - a generated directory for the lineman run app
- **spec** - all specs that are not end-to-end specs

- **spec-e2e** - our *protractor* specs live here
- **tasks** - any custom Lineman tasks should go here
- **vendor** - contains any vendor CSS, JavaScript, and image files
- **Gruntfile.js** - the Gruntfile that powers `lineman`
- **package.json** - the app customization, which defines dependencies and other metadata

Lineman provides an efficient structure for editing web apps quickly and confidently.

Bower

Bower is a package manager for front-end files on the web. Similar to how `npm` is a package manager for Node modules, allowing developers to write *shareable* modules for the server, `bower` offers similar functionality for web components.

It offers a solution to the dependency problem through a generic, unopinionated and easy-to-use interface. It runs over Git and is package agnostic. It also supports any type of transport, like `requireJS`, `AMD`, and others.

Installation

Installation is simple: we just use the `npm` package manager to install `bower`:

```
$ npm install -g bower
```

 `bower` depends upon Git, Node, and npm.

From here, we can verify that it's working by typing the `help` command:

```
$ bower help
```

If output is displayed to the screen, then we are good to go.

Bower help screen

Bower Overview

 Although we'll only cover a brief overview, we encourage more exploration at the Bower homepage: bower.io[168].

With our web app, we're likely going to want to share the source with other developers or deploy to other development machines. Similar to the `package.json` file for npm, we can use a `bower.json` file to store our front-end dependencies.

To get started with a `bower.json`, we can use the `init` command that Bower provides. We should execute it in the root of our project directory:

```
$ bower init
```

This command launches a setup wizard that asks us a few questions about our new package. When it's done, it generates a new `bower.json` file in our current directory.

Configuring Bower

Bower comes with sane defaults, but it is highly configurable. We can configure what directory packages are installed and which registry to use to install components.

Bower has great configuration documentation available here[169]. We recommend you check it out for more detailed configuration.

---

[168]http://bower.io/

[169]https://docs.google.com/document/d/1APq7oA9tNao1UYWyOm8dKqlRP2blVkROYLZ2fLIjtWc/edit#heading=h.4pzytc1f9j8k

Although in-depth bower configuration is outside of the scope of this chapter, we'll look at the two most commonly modified configuration items (based upon our own experience).

To configure Bower, we can edit the .bowerrc file, pass config arguments, or set environment variables. We can place the .bowerrc file in several places:

- the current working directory of the project
- in any subfolder in the directory tree
- in the current user's home folder
- in the global Bower folder

The .bowerrc file contains a JSON object for configuration. For example, to change the color configuration, the .bowerrc file would contain:

```
{
  "color": false
}
```

For the sake of simplicity, we like to keep the .bowerrc file in the root of the project directory. If it doesn't already exist, we recommend creating it in the root of the project directory:

```
$ echo "{}" > .bowerrc
```

cwd   The cwd configuration variable is the directory from which Bower should run. All other paths should relate directly to this directory.

```
{
  "cwd": "app"
}
```

directory   The directory configuration variable is the path in which installed components should be saved. It defaults to bower_components. Depending on how we are creating an app, we can change this to suit a different directory structure:

```
{
  "directory": "app/components"
}
```

Searching for Packages

To find a package for installation, Bower includes a search command to search through the index of its registry:

```
## Searching for bootstrap-sass
$ bower search bootstrap-sass
```

Installing Packages

Installing packages is equally easy. If we have an existing bower.json file, we can simply run the install command. It pulls down and installs the front-end dependencies in the Bower directory.

```
$ bower install
```

We can install a package locally by explicitly calling install on the file. It's possible to install a specific version of the package and even set an *alias* for the package install.

```
# Install a local or
# default remote version of a package
$ bower install <package>
# Install a specific version of a package
$ bower install <package>#<version>
# Alias install a package
$ bower install name=<package>#<version>
# For instance
$ bower install bootstrap=bootstrap-sass
```

The bower.json file stores several types of dependencies: either dependencies needed by the run time (such as Angular or jQuery) or dependencies needed in the development process (like Karma or Bootstrap-sass).

```
# Install a run-time dependency
$ bower install angular-route --save
# Install a dev dependency
$ bower install bootstrap-sass --save-dev
```

If we dump out the contents of our bower.json, we'll see that it is updated with our new dependencies:

```
$ cat bower.json
{
  "name": "myApp",
  "version": "0.0.1",
  "authors": [
    "Ari Lerner <ari@fullstack.io>"
  ],
  "license": "MIT",
  "dependencies": {
    "angular-route": "~1.2.6"
  },
  "devDependencies": {
    "bootstrap-sass": "~3.0.0"
  }
}
```

Using Packages

Now that our packages are installed, we can include the packages just like any other script in our local directory, by using a script tag in the HTML source.

```
<script
  src="/bower_components/angular/angular.js">
</script>
```

Removing Packages

It's also possible to remove packages through Bower. We can either manually delete the files in our Bower directory, or we can run the uninstall command.

The uninstall command allows us to use the --save and --save-dev flags to reflect the changes in the bower.json file.

```
# Remove a dependency
$ bower uninstall --save-dev angular-route
# Remove a devDependency
$ bower uninstall --save-dev bootstrap-sass
```

Yeoman

Yeoman[170] is a collection of the previous tools we've been discussing in this chapter:

---

[170]http://yeoman.io/

- Yeoman
- Grunt
- Bower

Yeoman itself is a scaffolding tool that helps us build new applications by setting up our Grunt configuration, building our application workspace, and managing our workflow, regardless of the type of application we are building.

There are just under 300 community-written generators available, as of the time of this writing, that set up many projects of all sorts of different types from Angular[171] sites, to Backbone.js[172], and even Python flask[173] projects.

Grunt is set up as the build tool; Bower is set up for handling dependency management.

Installation

Installation for Yeoman is simple. First, we need to make sure we have Node.js[174] and Git[175] installed. Some generators require Ruby[176] and Compass[177] to be installed, as well.

Once we have the dependencies, we can install Yeoman itself using npm:

```
$ npm install -g yo
```

Installing Yeoman installs *Grunt* and *Bower* automatically.

Next, in order to use it, we need to install a generator (Yeoman is useless without a generator).

Let's install the Angular generator:

```
$ npm install -g generator-angular
```

 To search all of the available community generators, we can check out the web interface at http://yeoman.io/community-generators.html[178].

Usage

Using the Yeoman workflow is also easy. First and foremost, we'll want to create a directory in which we can work. Yeoman does not create a working directory for us; rather, it assumes the directory we're working in is the directory that will house our app.

---

[171]https://github.com/yeoman/generator-angular

[172]https://github.com/yeoman/generator-backbone

[173]https://github.com/romainberger/yeoman-flask

[174]http://nodejs.org

[175]http://git-scm.com/

[176]https://www.ruby-lang.org/

[177]http://compass-style.org/

[178]http://yeoman.io/community-generators.html

```
$ mkdir myapp && cd $_
```

Inside of this directory, we'll run the Yeoman generator, which scaffolds our project. In this example, we're using the Angular generator `generator-angular`:

```
$ yo angular
```

Yeoman install

Yeoman will ask us a few questions, then create our application. In these steps, it will call `npm install` and `bower install` for us to ensure we have all the dependencies we expect so we can get developing immediately.

We'll use the `grunt` command to kick off our development process.

```
$ grunt server
```

The `grunt server` command starts a local server that serves our app locally. It uses livereload[179] to automatically reload the browser when we save a file in our workspace.

The directory built for us has an opinionated structure that enforces an easily extensible design for our Angular apps.

---

[179]http://livereload.com/

Yeoman-generated structure

Yeoman creates a directory structure that builds both `app/` and `test/` directories. Inside the app, we'll build our Angular app and house our views, our styles, and other various parts of our application.

When we want to create a controller, we need to add a file to the controllers directory with a descriptive name. Then we need to ensure that we include it in our `index.html` as a file to load.

For instance, adding a dashboard controller, we'll create `app/scripts/controllers/dashboard.js` and our `DashboardController` definition:

```
'use strict';

// in app/scripts/controllers/dashboard.js
angular.module('myappApp')
  .controller('DashboardController', function($scope) {
  });
```

To include this controller we need to tell our application to load this file in our `index.html`. We want to make sure we include it inside the build comments in our app so that our `htmlmin` task includes it when it's minifying our HTML.

```
<!-- build:js({.tmp,app}) scripts/scripts.js -->
<script src="scripts/app.js"></script>
<script src="scripts/controllers/main.js">
</script>
<script src="scripts/controllers/dashboard.js">
</script>
<!-- endbuild -->
```

Now we can use the controller in our app. This same process will work for any type of Angular component that we'll use in our app (e.g., services, filters, directives).

If we break our app into multiple components (highly recommended) as dependencies of our app, we need to ensure we include those before our `app.js` file above. For instance, if we follow the multiple-module pattern where we generate a new module for each component:

```
// in app/scripts/services/api.js
angular.module('myApp.services', [])
.factory('ApiService', function() {
  return {};
});
```

and set these modules as dependencies for our app:

```
// in app.js
angular.module('myApp', ['myApp.services']);
```

we need to include these services *before* we include app.js in our HTML.

Alternatively, the Angular generator itself comes with a bunch of helpful generators that make the process of building an Angular app a cinch.

Create a Route

To create a route that includes a controller and the corresponding test for the controller, includes the <script> tag in the HTML, and creates a view for the route, we need to run the following in our terminal:

```
$ yo angular:route home
```

Create a new route

Create a Controller

To create a simple controller and the corresponding test, we can use the generator in the terminal:

```
$ yo angular:controller user
```

Create a Custom Directive

To create a directive and the corresponding test, we can create a directive using the following command:

```
$ yo angular:directive tabPanel
```

Create a Custom Filter

We can also create a custom filter in our app and the corresponding test. To do that, we can use the following generator:

```
$ yo angular:filter capitalize
```

Create a View

To generate a simple view, we can use the Angular generator command:

```
$ yo angular:view dashboard
```

Create a Service

It's possible to use the generator to create a service, as well. The following creates a service as well as the corresponding tests in the different formats in which we are able to create a service.

```
$ yo angular:service api
$ yo angular:factory api
$ yo angular:provider api
$ yo angular:value api
$ yo angular:constant api
```

Create a Decorator

The Angular generator also gives us the ability to create a decorator over other services. We just need to run this command in our terminal:

```
$ yo angular:decorator api
```

Configuring the Angular Generator

With any of the previous generators (including the main generator), we can pass options to configure our scripts in a custom manner.

CoffeeScript

If we want to generate CoffeeScript files instead of JavaScript files, we can easily do so by passing the --coffee option:

```
$ yo angular:controller user --coffee
```

Minification Safe

Although it is not strictly necessary (our Yeoman generator includes ngMin), we can tell the generator to add dependency injection annotations in our generated file using the --minsafe flag:

```
$ yo angular:controller user --minsafe
```

Skipping Index

By default, all of the previous generators add the appropriate files to be loaded in the index.html. We can tell the generator **not** to include the scripts in the index.html.

 We may want to skip adding a file to the index page, as we may be building a third-party plugin.

```
$ yo angular:factory session --skip-add
```

Testing Our App

One of the nicest features of the Yeoman Angular generator is its ability to allow us to seamlessly test our application as we are developing it.

The generator comes packaged with a test command that runs whenever we save a file in our app. This packaging makes the process of testing easily translatable into our workflow.

To run our tests without watching our files (i.e., to run it once), we can use the command:

```
$ grunt test
```

This command runs once and quits. We recommend making two changes to the workflow to introduce automated testing in the app.

First, we open the Gruntfile.js at the root of the application and we find the Karma task. Then, we want to change the option from singleRun: true to false:

```
    // ...
  ]
},
karma: {
  unit: {
    configFile: 'karma.conf.js',
    singleRun: false // CHANGE THIS TO FALSE
  }
},
cdnify: {
// ...
```

Second, we open the karma.conf.js file and change the autoWatch option from false to true.

Now, when we run grunt test, rather than running once and quitting, the task will stay open and *watch* our files. Once we change a file and save it, then the tests will re-run.

Packaging Our App

After we are done building our application, we'll want to set up a distribution for our app. Creating a distribution of our app includes minifying all of the JavaScripts and HTML, packaging the views, preprocessing the CSS, etc.

To run the build task, we can simply run the Grunt build command:

```
$ grunt build
```

It will take a few minutes to run the entire generator. When it has completed, we'll have a dist/ folder in the root of our app. The folder will contain all of the files suitable for production deployment.

We can upload this folder to our server as is or include it in deployment with our server and let our application run to the masses.

Packaging Our Templates

One method that we can use to make our apps appear incredibly fast and not depend upon servers to deliver our templates is to turn our template files into a JavaScript file.

Using the Angular templateCache, we'll include our templates in a JavaScript file. For instance, instead of telling Angular to fetch the HTML using XHR as HTML:

```html
<div class="hero-unit">
  <h1>'Allo, 'Allo!</h1>
  <p>You now have</p>
  <ul>
      <li ng-repeat="thing in awesomeThings">{{thing}}</li>
  </ul>
  <p>installed.</p>
  <h3>Enjoy coding! - Yeoman</h3>
</div>
```

We can package them up into a JavaScript file and let the JavaScript stand alone, like so:

```javascript
angular.module('myApp')
.run(['$templateCache', function($templateCache) {
  $templateCache.put('views/main.html',
    "<div class=\"hero-unit\">\n" +
    "  <h1>'Allo, 'Allo!</h1>\n" +
    "  <p>You now have</p>\n" +
    "  <ul>\n" +
    "      <li ng-repeat=\"thing in awesomeThings\">{{thing}}</li>\n" +
    "  </ul>\n" +
    "  <p>installed.</p>\n" +
    "  <h3>Enjoy coding! - Yeoman</h3>\n" +
    "</div>\n"
  );
}]);
```

To set that up, we need to modify our Gruntfile.js to include a new task definition using a new npm package grunt-angular-templates.

First, we install the package:

```
$ npm install --save-dev grunt-angular-templates
```

Next, we modify our Gruntfile.js to include the ngtemplates task.

```
// ...
  }
},
ngtemplates: {
  myappApp: {
    cwd: '<%= yeoman.app %>',
    src: 'views/**/*.html',
    dest: '<%= yeoman.app %>/scripts/templates.js'
  }
},
// Put files not handled in other tasks here
copy: {
// ...
```

This modification simply creates a new file in our app directory that will contain the template files loaded as JavaScript.

We need to make sure that this task runs in the build process. Luckily, it's easy to append tasks to the build process. We simply find the line: grunt.registerTask('build', [and make sure we've added ngTemplates into the array of tasks **after** the concat task:

```
grunt.registerTask('build', [
  // ...
  'concat',
  // ...
  'cssmin',
  'ngtemplates',
  'uglify',
  'rev',
  'usemin'
]);
```

Lastly, we need to ensure that we include the templates.js file in our app/index.html file **after** we've included the scripts/app.js file:

```
<!-- build:js({.tmp,app}) scripts/scripts.js -->
<script src="scripts/app.js"></script>
<script src="scripts/controllers/main.js"></script>
<script src="scripts/templates.js"></script>
<!-- endbuild -->
```

Now, when we build our app, our templates will come packaged along with the rest of the application.

Note that when we're developing our application, if the template isn't found in the cache, it loads from the server automatically, so we can safely delete the `app/scripts/template.js` file if we need to at some point during our development process.

If this file exists, then the views that it caches won't be reloaded; it will *think* it has the template available.

Summary

You now have the knowledge and practice you need to take on masterfully building powerful apps using Angular. Thanks for exploring the framework with us. The community is large and constantly growing – let's keep it going! We look forward to seeing your applications out in the wild.

29526789R00347

Made in the USA
Middletown, DE
22 February 2016